I0004692

DADDY'S
LITTLE
FELONS

Also by Rick Bennett:

DESTROYING ANGEL

DADDY'S LITTLE FELONS

A Novel by Rick Bennett

Excerpt

I launched a pre-emptive peer-to-peer command that sent an email in perfect Arabic to his entire address book using quotes from Surahs number 4 and 7 in the Koran as proof that Mohammed was a Satan worshiper and romantically inclined toward swine…My software then erased any trace of itself on his system, after first verifying that the mail had been sent, spectacularly destroying his operating system, and finally displaying the image of a pig on his screen.

This trick really upped my game, even exceeding the nasty I unleashed on an Internet scammer who was using a burner cell phone to swindle an elderly friend of mine. Rather than go to the trouble of tracking down the scammer, I just sent him a text message from my own untraceable burner. It read: "The Revolutionary Council has approved your excellent plan to kill POTUS. Radio silence from now on. God be with you." Within twenty-four hours—thanks to the NSA snooping apparatus—the Secret Service descended on the poor devil who, as it turned out, lived just two doors down from my dear friend. Our last vision of him was his being perp-walked in shackles to a SWAT van, followed by agents hauling his computers and file cabinets. Naturally, I immediately disposed of my burner. Chances are, my Internet scammer had a much easier time explaining the text message about assassinating the president (POTUS) to the Secret Service than my Saudi hacker would have justifying his rash email.

Now, should I cause my Chinese and Russian friends the same level of discomfort? I could bring down all their servers, along with every other server that they touched in a self-propagating feral bloodbath…Sure, I knew all about the laws of unintended consequences. But if things got too dicey, I could always call back the hounds. I'd created The Perfect Virus against a template of twenty-two principles, the first of which was the principle of Oversight…In hindsight, my adventure might more closely demonstrate mathematically improbable degrees of separation, or coincidences and convergences so outrageous that they cannot be explained by anything other than Douglas Adams' infinite improbability drive. How could I have known that my computer virus would smoke out a serial killer? Or bring down an alien space ship (another story altogether)? Whatever the case, I let Judge O'Shea's request make my decision for me. Just one keystroke unleashed the Hounds of Hell.

Published by Rick Bennett himself.
2203 Fair Winns Lane
Draper, UT 84020

ISBN: 978-0-9701026-5-2
Library of Congress Control Number: 2014906625
eBook ISBN: 978-0-9701026-4-5

Cover Designed by Rick Bennett

Note: The electronic version of *Daddy's Little Felons* contains active hyperlinks to relevant information on the Internet.

2014.05.05

Dedication

This book is dedicated to my friend Judge Pat Brian, after whom Judge O'Shea is modeled. Judge Brian copied the quote at the beginning of Chapter 1 from the original ruling in the Ft. Smith, Arkansas courthouse presided over by the original Judge Roy Bean. And Pat subsequently used it as a model for some "creative sentencing rhetoric" in his own courtroom. Pat died of pancreatic cancer on June 28, 2010. Three months earlier, I delivered an early draft of *Daddy's Little Felons* to him. His wife Sherry reported that he laughed out loud many times over the few days it took him to read it. Here's to you, Your Honor.

Table of Contents

1

A Good Day to Leave Town

Jose Manuel Miguel Xaviar Gonzales, in a few short weeks it will be spring. The snows of winter will flow away, the ice will vanish, the air will become soft and balmy. In short, Jose Manuel Miguel Xaviar Gonzales, the annual miracle of the years will awaken and come to pass. But you won't be here. The rivulet will run its soaring course to the sea. The timid desert flowers will put forth their tender shoots. The glorious valleys of this imperial domain will blossom as the rose. Still, you will not be here to see. From every treetop, some wild woods songster will carol his mating song. Butterflies will sport in the sunshine. The gentle breeze will tease the tassels of the wild grasses, and all nature, Jose Manuel Miguel Xaviar Gonzales, will be glad. But you will not be here to enjoy it.

Because I command the sheriff of the county to lead you away to some remote spot, swing you by the neck from a knotting bough of some sturdy oak, and let you hang until dead. And then, Jose Manuel Miguel Xaviar Gonzales, I further command that such officer retire quickly from your dangling corpse, that the vultures may descend from the heavens upon your filthy body until nothing shall remain but bare, bleached bones of a cold blooded, bloodthirsty, throat-cutting, murdering son of a bitch.

Judge Roy Bean, Fort Smith, Arkansas, 1881.

The crime occurred on a Saturday night. The trial finished by Sunday noon, and the sentence was executed before 1:00 PM the same day.

s I sat in my San Francisco apartment, musing about declaring cyber war on Russia and China, the shrill ring of my telephone saved me from wrestling with that moral dilemma. Caller ID said an old Salt Lake City friend must be bored. It *should* have told me to let voice mail take the call so I could properly assess the trouble my cyber war would cause the world. Heck, the trouble it would wreak in the whole galaxy.

"Dirk Gently's Holistic Detective Agency," I answered, my private joke with Judge Patrick O'Shea acknowledging our mutual admiration of the late Douglas Adams' vision of a private eye who solved crimes before they happened.

"Still trying to get paid for losses you *say* you prevented for people?" shouted the voice I hadn't heard in three years.

"Yeah," I answered. "People don't believe me when I claim to have saved them a fortune."

"Tough sell!" I had to hold the phone away from my ear as he used exactly the same tone and volume with which he passed judgment in his live courtroom.

"What's up, Your Honor?"

"Got a murder on my hands," said Judge O'Shea.

Pat O'Shea presided over just about every conceivable criminal offense, including murder trials, so it wasn't hard to connect the dots.

"Let me guess: a murder but no murderer to try?" I said. "You don't trust the police in Salt Lake City?"

"Nothing like that, Morgan. This one is a little close to home. A friend of Sherry's." I could hear the sigh in his voice at the mention of his wife's name. "Any chance you could come out for a visit?"

"Funny you mention my leaving town," I said. Downright providential, my wondering if I should launch my attack on the Sino-Russian front and then getting this call from Pat. Maybe his call solved my moral dilemma for me. "I might see you as early as tomorrow."

"As much as I dare not ask why you're getting out of Dodge, I sure would appreciate it," he said. But he couldn't withhold his curiosity. "You're not…"

"Your Honor," I quickly filled in when he paused, "Since you're an officer of the court, let me assure you I have done nothing illegal."

Naturally, I didn't end my statement with "yet." Technically, my friend was off the hook, and I vowed to keep him safe from whatever consequences might follow after I most certainly *did* do something illegal. Illegal on so many levels that the jurisdiction of a district court judge would be immediately superseded by U.S. Marshals and federal warrants. Unfortunately for me, Judge Patrick O'Shea's finely tuned baloney detector saw right through me.

"But you're about to?" He didn't miss a thing, having spent his Gladwellian ten-thousand hours listening to much better liars than me.

"Depends what your definition of 'is' is," I shot back, a shorthand we'd worked out courtesy of a former president, designed to end discussion that might step over the bounds of friendship and compromise the reputation of a judge renowned for both integrity and virtually no appeals court reversals. Then I added, "But it's nothing that would ever come before your court."

His silence worried me that I might have said too much. So I continued, "Tell Sherry we're going out to dinner tomorrow night."

"Thanks, Morgan," he finally said. "You'll stay with us?"

"Not necessary to burden Sherry with a houseguest. My condo at Snowbird is vacant," I said. "Maid service will have it ship shape by the time I get there."

After the call, I looked up from a large-screen computer monitor to marvel at fog enveloping the Golden Gate Bridge, and wondered whether or not I really truly should declare war on China, Russia and maybe even Saudi Arabia. Nah, skip Saudi Arabia. Jihadists had yet to produce a decent hacker. But as my security violation logs showed, Russia and China did a world-class job of breaking into my Linux servers. Virtually every credible attack on my systems came from IP addresses in either China or the former USSR. The culprits could bounce around the world using proxy servers, but my pattern-based analytics software could back-track the attack vectors faster than the bad guys could cover their trail.

For months I'd resisted cataloging and blocking every IP address that made so much as a single probing attempt at my systems. Sure, I piped the offending addresses from my error logs into a retribution file I named payback-is-a-bitch, and maybe today would be D-Day. Heaven knows I'd spent enough time building *weapons of retribution*, and then covering my tracks.

My "honey pot" servers, the ones being attacked daily, would not be the instruments of my revenge. They just let me collect attacking server IP locations for transfer to warfare servers conveniently and quite covertly located across the street in the basement of the Church of Scientology. Close enough for my laser link to control them, but far enough so I'd be outside the security perimeter set up by any Homeland Security team descending on the site to find out who the hell had decided to create an international incident. Only the U. S. Congress may declare war, right? Well, the operative word is "may" as in "may declare war" on another country. "Can" though, that's something else entirely.

Of course, declaring today to be D-Day could cause the Scientology folk some grief, especially since two levels of anonymous cutouts meant they had no idea about my real identity. Besides, they hadn't balked at charging my pseudonym entity exorbitant rent on a windowless basement *storage room*, and I hadn't balked letting them siphon off additional air conditioning and power for their own uses. If they'd had *any* idea just how many BTUs it took to keep my server farm from melting down, and how much I paid for electricity invoices they never saw, they might start wondering about what lay beyond the steel fire door and biometric security system. I hadn't had to visit the farm after the first month, because I could manage it remotely from the next block thanks to a SFTP-encrypted line-of-sight link. I guess Homeland Security or the FBI or the NSA would have to fill them in during their not-so-social call.

O'Shea and I had some history together. A lot of history, since we'd grown up together in Wyoming. A good Catholic, the only reason he even associated with an Episcopalian like me owed to my dad, Morgan Rapier, Sr., having done a short stint at Notre Dame. That gave me my so-called *moral dispensation*.

As kids, we used to play characters from the movies. He played Harrison Ford's character Han Solo. I became Sylvester Stallone's Rocky Balboa. Later on, when we hit high school, our alter egos morphed. Patrick became Paul Newman's Judge Roy Bean. I became a hybrid Sylvester Stallone and Harrison Ford. More prep school than Rocky, tougher than Harrison Ford's subsequent Tom Clancy characters. Patrick went to law school and started a family. I became an electrical engineer after a tour with the U.S. Navy SEALs. We both set out to change the world, continually playing to our respective invisible audiences.

I vaguely remember some psychologist once writing that most human beings live life as if they are acting on a stage, performing for a current or future audience. Once upon a time, my guess had been that we'd all be playing to the audience convening on Judgment Day. Given the current ubiquity of high-bandwidth cell phones and free social networks, we could be living in a literal Judgment Day of real-life voyeurs with time on their hands.

My own metaphysical stage actor tried to fix things. Broken things, usually. But not always. Some genetic mutations enter civilized society incapable of functioning constructively. Not so much broken as just unworthy to exist in their current state of perfection. So they must either be re-engineered to cause no harm, or they must be eliminated from the planet. Tough assignment for anyone who has ever heard of The Sermon on the Mount. The part about "judge not lest ye be judged" severely proscribes certain rules of engagement. To put it unambiguously, I can't go around indiscriminately killing bad guys. At least I can't do so and expect to be greeted in the hereafter with enthusiasm. That is, enthusiasm from on high. Because the first words in eternity I do not want to hear are, "Hi, Morgan; welcome to Hell."

Morgan. That's me. Morgan Rapier. Morgan Rapier, Jr., to be precise. Morgan Senior, my dad, is also a U.S. Navy SEAL and owns a fairly exclusive bar in San Francisco called The Fist. But that's a whole different story. This story begins in the Salt Lake City domain of Judge Patrick O'Shea. True to our roots, neither one of us smokes or drinks, not so much out of religious conviction but because those vices are just not part of *The Program*. And we both take marital fidelity seriously, notwithstanding that I'm a widower who can't quite bring myself to consider getting back into the social scene.

"Hizonor" and I kind of chose similar paths of public service. He wore a black robe; I opted for black face paint and to follow my dad's footsteps in the U.S. Navy SEALs, after which I parlayed a couple of social networking computer patents to seed my career in electronic counter warfare. It's amazing how much money a dot-com megaprise will pay for a patent that puts their competition out of business. So now I have the freedom to fund a throw-away server farm that probably can't be traced to me and which I designed to bring down most of Eastern Europe's and China's illicit Internet business.

A beep from the computer alerted me to yet another attempt by someone to log in as system manager, and my security daemon identified the exception. Evidently someone from Saudi Arabia hadn't spent as much time as he should have on the *Koran*, and his persistent attacks seemed a good deal more creative. I'd previously let him into a sterile system long enough to poke around and download some interestingly named files, one of which gave me access to his email system and address book.

"Allah akbar!" I muttered, not that he could hear me clear over in Ar Riyad, listed as Riyadh on maps produced by *The Great Satan*, America. "You should never hack from your personal laptop."

I launched a pre-emptive peer-to-peer command that sent an email in perfect Arabic to his entire address book using quotes from Surahs number 4 and 7 in the *Koran* as proof that Mohammed was a Satan worshiper and romantically inclined toward swine. I came up with this thesis in my formative years at Andover and had the message ready to go from my what-if bag of tricks. My software then erased any trace of itself on his system, after first verifying that the mail had been sent, spectacularly destroying his operating system, and finally displaying the image of a pig on his screen.

This trick really upped my game, even exceeding the nasty I unleashed on an Internet scammer who was using a burner cell phone to swindle an elderly friend of mine. Rather than go to the trouble of tracking down the scammer, I just sent him a text message from my own untraceable burner. It read: "The Revolutionary Council has approved your excellent plan to kill POTUS. Radio silence from now on. God be with you." Within twenty-four hours—thanks to the NSA snooping apparatus—the Secret Service descended on the poor devil who lived just two doors down from my dear friend. Our last vision of him was being perp-walked in shackles to a SWAT van, followed by agents hauling his computers and file cabinets. Naturally, I immediately disposed of my burner. Chances are, my Internet scammer had a much easier time explaining the text message about assassinating the president (POTUS) to the Secret Service than my Saudi hacker would have justifying his rash email.

Should I cause my Chinese and Russian friends the same level of discomfort? I could bring down all their servers, along with every other server that they touched in a self-propagating feral bloodbath. Too bad I couldn't profit from it, like the Revolutionary War privateers who had *Letters of Marque* to raid British shipping and sell their loot around Europe. Privateering financed most of the American Revolution, and I could never understand why the U. S. Congress didn't just deputize a bunch of hackers to raise hell with the sneaks who attacked our Internet infrastructures every minute of every hour of every day. Or why those same deputized "bounty hunters" couldn't loot the bank accounts of porn operations and share the proceeds to reduce the national debt.

Closing up the apartment required no more thought than emptying my refrigerator into the grateful hands of my neighbors, one of whom promised to keep an eye on the place. Unbeknownst to him, my network of pinhole cameras continuously streamed encrypted signals of every room at every angle in my abode to redundant security services on both coasts. Encryption protected my privacy, and I'm pretty sure even the NSA didn't have the technology to spy on me, since I invented something sufficiently advanced to make current 128-bit encryption appear to be little more than the daily newspaper cryptoquip puzzle.

Now, should I or shouldn't I let loose the cyberhounds of hell? Sure, I knew all about the laws of unintended consequences. But if things got too dicey, I could always call back the hounds. I'd created The Perfect Virus against a template of twenty-two principles, the first of which was the principle of Oversight. After all, you can't have a virus running amok.

In hindsight, my adventure might more closely demonstrate mathematically improbable degrees of separation, or coincidences and convergences so outrageous that they cannot be explained by anything other than Douglas Adams' infinite improbability drive. How could I have known that my computer virus would smoke out a serial killer? Or bring down an alien space ship (another story altogether)? Whatever the case, I let Judge O'Shea's request make my decision for me. Just one keystroke unleashed the Hounds of Hell.

I called my dad at The Fist and told him I'd be out of town for a few days. I had lunch there a couple of times a week with Senior and a few of his SEAL buddies. Yeah, like father like son: U.S. Navy SEALs. Most of our conversations could be started and ended with a nod or gesture, except of course on the phone. I suggested he *not* check out my apartment in my absence. No need to spell things out for him. He knew all he needed to know and asked me to call him if I needed some muscle. His Fist associates knew how to keep order in the bar, and sometimes helped him project power beyond his neighborhood. Nobody had a criminal record from their activities, which couldn't have happened had they not had a close relationship with the SFPD.

My last official acts before leaving town for the 12-hour drive from San Francisco to Salt Lake City were to launch the "attack" command to my trusty cyber-army across the street, and then to disassemble and pack away the directional laser on my balcony. I'd do the same for the receiver below as I left the underground garage. The Church of Scientology security cameras would merely record, thanks to a 90-second loop I'd dropped into their system, the subtle disappearance of a miniature laser receiver hidden behind a drain spout. Inside my server farm, the retraction of the antenna would cause a take-up reel to spool into a fire safe, where an acid bath obliterated its existence. The retraction also issued the final "Go" to my attack servers.

"Yippie ki yay!" I said in my best Bruce *Die Hard* Willis imitation, powering my Mercedes S550 past the soon-to-be-scrutinized Church of Scientology. Minutes later, the Bay Bridge welcomed me as I headed toward Utah.

2

"Guy Movie" vs. "Chick Flick"

 parked the S550 in the underground garage of my Snowbird condo around noon on a Thursday, having made the expected twelve-hour drive in less than ten hours. Flying into the Salt Lake City airport might have been faster, but leaving an easily searchable record of my trip didn't seem wise. Nor did coming on this errand of mercy unarmed, due to the constraints of airport security. I really should have driven more slowly, as a speeding ticket would have created the very record my non-airline itinerary aimed to avoid. Luckily though, clear roads and light traffic left me alone to surf the news stations and telephone my property management people with a request to open up the condo. No news from Russia or China interrupted the drive.

Little Cottonwood Canyon exploded in May greenery, and snow melting from Alta and Snowbird ski resorts roared down the mountain toward reservoirs and the Great Salt Lake, not nearly so great a lake due to years of drought-induced shrinkage. A terrific winter snowfall kept the ski area open weekends through the end of May, and then again on July 4th for those who wanted bragging rights. I figured I should plan for a Saturday morning ski run, since I could ski right off my patio to a Snowbird lift. But at the moment, a shower and a nap before dinner with Pat and Sherry O'Shea took precedence.

The money I paid for weekly maid service appeared quite well spent, and the $20 bill still visible under a coffee table coaster testified to the honesty of the staff. Hard to believe I hadn't been here in over three ski seasons. Talk about my priorities being totally out of whack! How could I have resisted ski-on/ski-off access to Utah powder?

The smell of cedar permeated the 5200-square-foot aerie, from my study/library on the left of my slate entryway to a great room on the right. I deactivated the security system from the panel inside an enormous pine support pillar at the base of the stairs before coming up to the main floor. The magnificent southwest view down the mountain and into the Salt Lake valley reminded me that few other places on the planet could accommodate skiing, a long bike ride, and sail boating all on the same day. Although riding my bicycle the 10 miles and 3500 feet *down* Little Cottonwood Canyon took a darn sight less time than the one-hour return trip, I'd see soon enough if my racing bicycle messengers up and down the hills of San Francisco had kept me in good enough shape, or if the ride home took more like two hours. Big difference between sea level and 8,000 feet of altitude.

The main-floor bedroom sat just behind my library and opposite the great room/kitchen complex. I threw my duffel bag beside the man's chest that held the 60-inch plasma TV, outrageously expensive three years ago, set my mental alarm for 5:00 PM, and then wrapped myself in the comforter housekeeping had neatly folded at the foot of the bed. Kudos again for housekeeping. No dust, freshly laundered pillow cases (and sheets, I assumed). A dreamless sleep lasted exactly as long as I'd intended.

Even though granite mountains towered around Snowbird, long days of the approaching Summer Solstice guaranteed sunlight for another three hours. Birds nesting in the tree next to my slightly opened screen infected me with their melody of optimism. I kicked off the quilt, followed by my clothes, and headed toward a welcome shower. Since I am just a bit of an information junkie, the shower also offered a head-high LCD-TV monitor—I didn't let my hiatus keep me from ordering electronics upgrades to my eagle's nest in the Rocky Mountains—which came on automatically when I started the water. Facing away from the showerhead and a water stream that could peel the skin off an armadillo, I touch-screen channel surfed the news for anything interesting. Glad to see the waterproof glass still allowed my touch to activate the controls. After almost twenty-four hours of unprecedented cyber war, something, *anything,* ought to be hitting the news feeds. Either that, or I'm just not as smart as I thought, and my mountain of worthless servers had turned out to be nothing more than silicon bricks in a giant wall of stupidity.

So far, nothing on Bloomberg, MSNBC, CNN, Fox, or even my virus command and control system, which I had issuing status reports to an anonymous Twitter account. After lathering up and rinsing, and then letting the pulsating stream pound the long-drive kinks out of my neck and back, I cycled the monitor from HDTV to Internet browser mode and checked technology news feeds. Again nothing, even from my "Black Hat" cyber-underground RSS feed, although ZDNet of all places had a note about a sudden reduction in both spam email and random DNS probes. I didn't fathom how my attack had anything to do with spam reduction, but putting a check in the swing of address/port probers was indeed my baby. Cool. Very cool!

My turning off the shower also turned off my news monitor. Less than twenty minutes later, after securing the weapons from the trunk of my car into a hidden-access weapons safe in the garage floor, the big S550 engine braked in a low gear as I wound down Little Cottonwood Canyon toward the O'Sheas' gated community. Thanks to cell phone towers located on the mountain, I let Hizonor know my ETA and dinner plans.

"I'm ten minutes away," I told Pat, "And took the liberty of making dinner reservations at Tiburon for 7 PM, assuming Sherry is up to going out."

"We were *hoping* for Tiburon," he said. "Your coming to town has done something I couldn't do. Sherry has pretty much refused to leave her room since …"

He paused, obviously because his wife could hear his end of the conversation and words like "murder" and "death" tended to put a damper on an evening. I jumped in to let him off the hook.

"Tell Sherry I've reserved the end room, so we can chat freely without trying to talk over a lot of noise. See you in a bit," I said.

The O'Sheas lived in Pepperwood, located on what Salt Lake City locals called The Bench. Millennia ago, the valley was home to a massive glacier that pushed in from the north and plowed gravel, rock and sand against the Wasatch mountains. The glacier then melted, creating the Great Salt Lake, and leaving a rather nice plateau for real estate development. A revolutionary thinker named Sid Horman—also creator of Utah's first indoor shopping mall, the Cottonwood Mall—snapped up a bunch land and built a gated community called Pepperwood. Judge Patrick O'Shea naturally gravitated to its security, given the large numbers of murderers, molesters and polygamists he'd ushered off the streets and into the Draper prison.

Having previously lived in the same neighborhood, I'd kept my guard-gate remote unit and reprogrammed the automatic garage door opener on each subsequent new car. Good move. My S550 had no trouble at all activating the automatic gate, and I entered Pepperwood from the east gate, making my way down to Apple Hill Circle with the windows rolled down so I could smell and listen to my old stomping grounds. The pool hadn't opened yet, but the Pepperwood athletic field had a rousing soccer game in process, the tennis courts also fully occupied, and four pickup basketball games raged, all oblivious to the fact I may have just started the cyber equivalent of World War III.

Apple Hill Circle doesn't have any hills to speak of, but it boasts apple trees in front of every house. The quarter-mile dogleg barely qualifies as a street, more a cul-de-sac with a name. O'Sheas lived near the end of the street on a ledge overlooking the high-rent section of newly built Pepperwood homes, a twenty-five year old chalet with an end-to-end deck perfect for holding court over the *new-money* folk.

Their two-story home bespoke craftsmanship, much of it the handiwork of this civil servant who lived within his means and never *ever* demonstrated even the appearance of impropriety. When I'd moved into the neighborhood fifteen years ago, Pat helped me lay down the floor in my computer room and, looking out my living room window, laughed and said, "Don't worry, Morgan. In twenty years, those trees will be quite large." Heck, they dwarfed my lot in ten years, and I had to start thinning them out. Tonight, standing at the front door he'd bought from a soon-to-be razed church and installed himself, I didn't even have a chance to ring the chime before Sherry swung it open and grabbed me in a death hug.

"Morgan!" she half sobbed, half screamed.

I'm glad we weren't swimming, because she would have drowned both of us. At five feet six inches, Sherry O'Shea stood tall for a woman but still a head shorter than me. Petite and striking, her family literally owned the dinner-theater market in Utah, Idaho, Arizona and Wyoming. Her poise and regal bearing couldn't have hurt Pat's chances for judicial appointment, a fact he often affirmed when just the two of us philosophized about our respective paths in life. Now, seeing the extent of her emotional distress rather shocked me, as I'd never seen her vulnerable side. Pat stood in the slate foyer behind his bride, looking a bit helpless himself, and nodded to me.

She must have sensed my surprise, and I could feel as she steeled herself and stepped back.

"Sherry," I said. "The Marines have landed."

"And here I thought you were a Navy SEAL," she said, almost pulling off an air of strength and wit.

"I stand corrected, madam. The United States Navy SEAL Special Operations Command is at your service." I gave her a casual salute that would have made John Wayne proud, although it would have gotten me disciplined if tendered to an admiral.

"Let's talk about this SOCOM operation over dinner," she said, turning to have Judge O'Shea help her into a coat. He definitely had it ready, probably fearing any delay might scrub her first steps out of their home since the terrible news.

I ushered them to the back door of my car and grabbed the SEAL baseball cap from behind the headrest.

"At your service," I said. I didn't keep the cap so I could play chauffeur. I made it visible from the rear window so that fellow veterans might cut me some slack, and also that some more aggressive drivers might think twice before testing my patience.

Pat broke his uncharacteristic silence after he joined his wife in the back seat and I fired up the Mercedes. "This doesn't sound like your standard stock engine."

"Oh, you mean the throaty roar of a fully supercharged AMG power plant?" I answered.

"I didn't think Mercedes-Benz offered that in a 4Matic," he said. "I do remember seeing the 4Matic logo on your trunk, don't I?"

"Correct, Your Honor," I said, pulling away from his house. "There's some question about the transmission being able to handle the extra power. Took some re-engineering."

"I'll bet it did," he said. From my rearview mirror I could see him patting Sherry on the hand.

We turned left on Pepperwood Drive. "You two care if I take a quick gander at the old house on our way out?"

"Of course we don't care," said Sherry. "A lovely family lives there, now."

I could sense a change, maybe from her voice, maybe from the way she shifted position, a transfer from her personal feelings of grief for her murdered friend to a feminine empathy for my own past. I emphasize *feminine* because, in my opinion, we men tend to submerge our feelings. Show me a guy who goes around wining about the past, and I'll show you a guy people just hate being around. But if my wanting to drive by my old house could snap Sherry out of her own misery, then all the better.

About half-a-mile away from the O'Sheas', my former home—still my home, actually, as I rented it through a property management firm to the new tenants—sat on another cul-de-sac called Gatehouse Circle. Three years evaporated into a mere yesterday. The replica of the Eiffel Tower sat in my former front yard, with a miniature bicycle perched atop that had survived 10 years of Utah winters. A young mother knelt at the base of the tower, long red hair obscuring an obviously freckled face. The woman busily trimmed the base of my clematis vine that now completely covered the metal structure with purple blooms, and her toddler bobbled along beside her, trying to decide whether to eat a piece of grass or thread it up its nose.

"I *never* thought my clematis would get that tall," I said. And never thought I'd casually watch a stranger working in *Annie's* flowers, either.

"Didn't Annie do the flowerbeds?" asked Sherry with almost a quiver in her voice. Tenderly, afraid to open an old wound, yet courageous enough to put the so-called skunk on the table. Annie died in an auto-bicycle hit-and-run four years previous. She'd insisted on riding alone after three other women cancelled that day's ride for a variety of reasons. Gutsy move, Sherry's bringing my dead wife into the conversation.

"She owned all the flowerbeds except where it came to my Eiffel Tower," I said, trying to sound chipper. "She insisted my monument to the Tour de France belonged solely to me. The clematis, too."

As my monster white Mercedes rolled by at five miles per hour, the red headed mother weeding the base of the tower looked up and recognized the O'Sheas. Her smile radiated a simple innocence that thawed the ice castle I'd so carefully erected around my memories of Annie.

"Morgan," said Sherry. "You okay?"

Without consciously thinking of it, I'd put my hand over my heart. Somehow she'd noticed the movement, maybe through the rearview mirror where her eyes met mine.

"Just remembering an idyllic past," I answered. "You amaze me though, that you can worry about someone else after what you've been through."

I made a U-turn at the end of the cul-de-sac and drove back past the house. Sherry waved tentatively through the window, carefully walking again down her own memory lane. I felt rather obligated to walk it with her.

"One of Annie's friends came to me a few years ago," I began. "She said, 'Morgan, I have a problem.' A few days prior, Annie and I had been talking about differences between male and female thinking, so I decided to put my newfound knowledge to work. I told her friend, 'Let me get this straight. You have a problem, but do you want to *talk it through* or do you want me to help you solve it?'"

I looked in to rearview mirror to see if she'd re-engaged with me. Probably, as her eyes met mine.

"Anyhow, Annie's friend paused, laughed a little, and said she supposed she just wanted to talk it through."

Judge O'Shea snickered, and Sherry playfully elbowed him. I continued: "To get the ground rules straight, with your permission of course, I came out here to find a murderer if at all possible."

"That's kind of what I'd anticipated." His Honor put in his two cents.

Nobody spoke for a few blocks as we drove toward the restaurant. Then Sherry quite surprised me with a bit of insight that extended well beyond my previous education in feminine thinking styles.

"Then you'd classify your trip as a man's movie and not a ladies' movie?" she asked.

"Never quite thought of it in those terms," I paused, more than slightly oblivious to her intent.

"According to some talk-show comedian, I can't quite remember who," she said, "In a ladies' movie someone dies at the end. A man's movie has people dying throughout."

"Ah," I said.

"I didn't bring Morgan out here to start playing Destroying Angel, sweetheart" the judge piped in. "Even if he does catch the murderer, I couldn't be the judge at the trial, either. I'd have to recuse myself."

"Besides," I added, "Someone died at the *beginning* of our movie."

But Sherry didn't let us off the hook. "If he *does* catch the murderer, and if Morgan has to defend himself …"

"Objection, Your Honor," I interrupted. "Speculation."

"Sustained," said the judge. "The witness will not answer that question."

"Morgan," Sherry sighed as the judge got another elbow.

"Since someone died at the beginning of this movie, murdered actually," I said, and then rather prophetically added, "Looks like we've started a guy flick. We'll have to see how it plays out.

"Now," before she could derail my train of thought, "Please tell me about your poor friend."

"Little Olive," said Sherry, softly.

When the silence lingered, Pat put his arm around his wife and leaned toward the front seat. "Olive Curtis Jenkins. The nicest, most humble lady you'd ever want to meet."

Stifling my desire to get the questions of when, where and how answered, I said nothing, pretending instead to concentrate on the route toward our restaurant. The story would unfold on its own. Pat finally filled the vacuum of silence.

"Olive had been a widow for fifty years, and friends with Sherry for the last ten. Sherry helped Olive when she had computer problems, or when she needed a ride downtown to the family history library."

"Most men give their wives the same wedding gift," Sherry sighed. "At least two decades as a widow. Olive's husband almost tripled that."

"We don't do it on purpose, Sher." The judge's voice almost pleaded with her to change the subject, but she'd have none of it.

"Oh come on Pat. He became rich enough to have anything he wanted," she continued. "He proved it every meal, pushing 325 pounds the day his heart stopped."

Time for the cavalry to rescue Hizonor. "She never remarried?" I asked.

"A couple of close calls," said Sherry. "But no. Most unmarried older men are barely employed and tend to get a job only long enough to find a meal ticket. Pickings are lean."

"Present company excluded," I said.

"Oh Morgan, I absolutely didn't mean you," she gasped, my current marital status suddenly dawning on her.

"Remember, this is a guy movie," I said as lightly as possible. "We don't do introspection. Please continue about Olive."

Sherry fumbled in her purse for a handkerchief, so Pat resumed. "Tuesday, two days ago, Sherry stopped by Olive's apartment to see why the phone went unanswered. She found Olive dead, apparently strangled and definitely mutilated."

Restraining my curiosity took considerable discipline. I waited for an answer to the obvious question, and Pat didn't disappoint me.

"Her little fingers had been cut off and nailed to the ceiling." He then quickly added for his suffering wife's benefit, "According to the medical examiner, there is no evidence of sexual assault or other pre-mortem trauma."

I wanted to ask a whole bunch of questions about the finger amputations, but that could wait for another time.

"Motives?" I asked. "Anything missing?"

"The murderer took her computer," said the judge. "But just the computer. Not the display or keyboard. And both her desk and purse had been thoroughly rifled, yet her pocketbook and money remained intact."

Missing computer, but robbery not the motive. Even the most callous thief would *not* take the time to cut off and then nail fingers to the ceiling. But the computer. Somebody definitely wanted whatever the computer contained. As well as something in the purse besides money. And they got a little emotional about it. Food for thought.

Now ready for regular food, too, we arrived at Tiburon, my favorite restaurant on the planet. I furiously prayed I wouldn't regret taking Sherry out to dinner just a few days after her friend's murder.

3
"My concealed weapon permit still valid?"

iburon opened just before the turn of the century. That's 1999, not 1899. Claude Indjic, the owner/chef, bolted from a five-star European resort to do his own thing in the Utah mountains. My first and all subsequent food experiences had rendered his pedigree irrelevant. Meritocracy pure and simple.

The staff greeted me like a returning hero and quickly ushered us past a large Saudi family gathering, seating us at the far end of the room behind a privacy partition near the fireplace. Across the room I could see through a serving shelf into the kitchen, where a television set displayed some muted talking heads. Probably CNN, if I didn't miss my guess that Claude still liked to keep up on world events.

The Tiburon menu came from afar—New Zealand, Moscow and Australia—and nearby—beef, tuna and halibut. The chef himself came out to greet us and take our order.

"Morgan Rapier!" gushed Claude Indjic, pronouncing my name 'Rah-pi-*yay*' as he would in Paris. "It's been such a long time."

"Good to be back, Claude," I said, shaking his hand. "And you know the O'Sheas."

"But of course. Your Honor, Madam O'Shea, welcome."

"Claude," smiled the judge. Sherry nodded.

"Would the O'Sheas be interested in hearing today's specials?" asked Claude, raising one eyebrow in my direction. "If I am not mistaken, Monsieur Rapier will be having the Australian lamb?"

Sherry appeared confused, between listening to the specials or outright laughing at Claude's prodigious memory after my long absence. She did both, and eventually Patrick and Sherry each selected the Alaskan halibut over pineapple fried rice. And I confirmed my Australian lamb.

The O'Sheas had virgin daiquiris with umbrellas in them, and I stayed with ice water. Over our salads of pan-seared scallops on a bed of brown rice and lightly steamed asparagus, Sherry finally got down to business.

"Morgan, where do you start looking for Olive's murderer?"

"Oh," I began, since the thought had occurred to me once or twice since I planned this trip. "My first stop, with your husband's help, is to chat with the detectives assigned to the case."

"That can be arranged," said Patrick.

"Sherry, I call it a reconnaissance in force. This carry permit still valid in Salt Lake County?" I said, passing my concealed weapons permit under the table to O'Shea.

"I'd say so," answered the judge, pocketing the laminated card. "But let me call Sheriff Running to make sure. I'll give this back to you, tomorrow."

"Tomorrow is Friday," I said. "That's still your show-cause hearing day?"

"Yes it is," he said. "Want to come to the freak show?"

"Figured I hang around your courtroom, waiting for you to grease the skids with Sheriff Running." Fridays in Judge O'Shea's courtroom had always been one of my favorite diversions. Unlike trials, which can last for weeks or months, show-cause hearings usually dealt with revocation of bail, violations of probation, or sentencing. Each case completely encapsulated a life, few had witnesses, and virtually all saw complete closure in the space of half an hour. Hence the name 'Show Cause' hearings. The bail jumper, parole violator, etc. must show cause why he or she shouldn't be put in jail forthwith, which makes for some wonderful drama.

"So you'll spend tomorrow with Daddy's little felons?" Sherry piped in.

"Daddy's little what?" I asked.

"That's what Sherry calls the denizens of my domain: 'Daddy's little felons.' Most are literally childlike, lacking some degree of impulse control. Very few are the personification of evil as you and I would define it. Just emotional pygmies or intelligence-challenged little felons dealing with the cascading consequences of one or two bad decisions. In other words…"

"In other words," Sherry added, "Daddy's little felons. Maybe you'll keep

Daddy Himself out of trouble tomorrow?"

"Daddy Himself," sputtered the judge. "Daddy Himself has the lowest recidivism rate of any court in the history of Utah. And in a world full of emotional pygmies, the patient man is king."

"Speaking of emotional pygmies, would the powers that be grant me access to the crime scene?" I continued.

"Let me ask the county attorney," said Patrick. "He'll generally want to keep his district court judges happy, as a professional courtesy, if you get my drift."

Later, while I finished my rack of lamb and as the O'Sheas enjoyed their halibut, Sherry told me more about her friend, Olive Curtis Jenkins. For the life of me, I couldn't figure out why anyone would harm a widow who sang in the Mormon Tabernacle Choir and who anonymously donated most of her substantial inheritance income to neighbors in need. She lived simply, and her only vice seemed to be buying the latest, greatest computer equipment on which to do genealogy and family history work. Looking around the crime scene became more and more important, as something on her missing computer had to be the motive for the crime. Judge O'Shea reiterated his commitment to legitimizing my access to case evidence.

The Saudi Arabian skyline displayed on Claude's kitchen television caught my eye. I couldn't read the scrolling banner beneath the picture, but a large crowd of people seemed to be quite agitated.

"I'll leave you two to the news and Hizonor's sentencing recommendations, and plan to be at the Matheson Court House at 9:00 AM sharp, tomorrow."

"Sustained," said the judge. "Hold off on your personal artillery until I clear your carry permit with the Sheriff."

"Yes sir."

"That would be yes, Your Honor," he said. But I could hear the smile in his voice. Already getting *in character* for his morning duties as judge, jury and… executioner.

"Yes, *Your Honor*," I said.

4
Sorry, Benny!

hat are the odds that my response to one Arabian hacker attack would start a holy war? What bookie *wouldn't* take that kind of a bet until the cows come home? Such a hypothetical bookie would have taken it in the shorts spectacularly, as it now appeared. I didn't have the local news stations programmed into my radio, nor even into my satellite channels, so rather than try to drive up a winding mountain road and fiddle with the tuner, I paid attention to driving as fast as humanly possible.

After parking in my ski lodge's underground garage, I hotfooted it upstairs and set my living room flat-screen to one main channel and not one but two picture-in-picture channels—a little hardware trick any OCD-type with EPROM burner and a thorough familiarity with Fry's Electronics could manage—through which I could rotate to my little heart's content. CNN, MSNBC and Fox News had gone into relatively commercial-free breaking-news mode in the Middle East, with Fox appearing to have feet on the ground actually reporting from Riyadh, with cameras smack dab in the middle of a riot in Riyadh, outside the royal palace. The other two channels had talking heads, so I stayed with Fox.

Interesting how worked up people can get protecting God, or Allah in this case. To be fair, though, just try telling a "good Christian" that he's not really a Christian and then watch the fireworks. His rather uncharitable reaction almost proves your point. The people on the Fox News screen appeared to be anything but pious.

Unlike the anti-American demonstrations where flags burned and placards were conveniently written in English for easy dissemination by the media throughout the English-speaking world, this ugly crowd showed nothing but fists and teeth. The Fox reporter recapped events leading up to the demonstration.

"Again, this spontaneous scene is apparently reaction to Mohammed bin

Faisal Al Saud's massive email to press, friends and associates claiming the Prophet Mohammed worshiped Satan. Mohammed, not the prophet but the son of former Saudi ambassador to the United States Turki bin Faisal Al Saud, is said to have made a compelling case using the *Koran* as his proof."

Yeah, and the crowd is doubly worked up, I thought, *because they can't yell "Death to Mohammed" without appearing to further slander the Prophet Mohammed and not his namesake.*

"The ambassador and his extended family," continued the reporter, "including his son, the target of this angry demonstration, have been moved to the royal palace for their own protection. This might not have been the wisest move, since the entire Saudi monarchy seems to have been put at risk. The royal family has made no official statement, nor has the Saudi foreign minister."

"No," I opined, mimicking the live news reporter, "King Abdullah has hauled his massive carcass off the throne and is probably whacking his nephew—his former ambassador to Britain and the U.S.—along with the ambassador's son Mohammed—in the head with a riding crop and screaming 'What *were* you thinking?'"

Oh to be an aphid on a palm frond in that room about now, although I'm not sure an aphid would have anything to do with a palm frond. I surely wouldn't want to be a lap dog and risk being crushed by shaking royal stubby fingers connected to a distraught chubby wrist and controlled by a bile-filled brain. If Mohammed, the hacker and not the prophet, had any brains, he'd admit he'd been hacked and disavow the worthless screed being spewed by his computer. The computer that he'd hopefully brought with him for forensic analysis, since my virus would have double and triple-erased everything in memory, on the hard disk, and even in the BIOS EPROMs. The absence of anything, anywhere on his computer should be proof enough that something bad, very bad indeed, had befallen the system. And an analysis of ISP traffic preceding the offensive-in-the-extreme email broadcast would point to a last incoming series of packets from…oops…China and Russia.

I dashed into the bedroom and retrieved my laptop, returning to my living room sofa and linking wirelessly to my custom-encrypted server. A slight diversion here: I wrote my own wireless encryption system because anybody can hack commercially available systems in less than half an hour. All you need is your own wireless computer, proximity to the target router, and the smarts to log onto YouTube and follow along with one of the many hacking video tutorials available to the public. Most of the aforementioned tutorials are narrated by the cracking voices of sixteen-year-old social misfits who can show off to millions without being embarrassed by acne-scarred faces and skinny pale arms that haven't been in contact with the sun for months. Publicly available security is a myth, second in popularity only to the belief that (a) privacy is a constitutionally protected right, and (b) privacy is even possible in today's globalized, interdependent world order.

Since I'd left for dinner, the news feeds to which I subscribed had exploded with stories and blogs about the complete shutdown of any communication with Eastern Europe or China. Conspiracy theorists speculated that this "profound silence" might be the precursor to a massive cyber attack. Wishful thinkers opined that Russia and China currently engaged in an all-out cyber war with each other. And U.S.-based security entrepreneurs couldn't resist taking the opportunity to cajole their customers into buying or upgrading to their latest anti-virus products, before the war came ashore and into their homes and businesses. At that moment, I noticed that CNN had switched to a feed from Pat Robertson's "700 Club" set. I cycled my screen-in-screen to enlarge the scene, sound and all. Good old Pat. I always figured he'd misnamed his 700 Club, and that poor arithmetic had caused him to err by 34. Should have been the 666 Club. Pat immediately made the connection. He seemed animated, excited.

"…the Book of Revelation," he said. "Chapter 13 talks about a beast, and the name of the beast is a number. Six hundred three score and six. Six-six-six. And I quote: 'And that no man might buy or sell, save he that had the mark, or the name of the beast, or the number of his name. Here is wisdom. Let him that hath understanding count the number of the beast: for it is the number of a man; and his number is Six hundred threescore and six.'"

Yes, my day started weird and it just kept getting weirder. Pat got more and more excited and continued. "The number six-hundred-sixty-six can be represented in Hebrew as Vav-Vav-Vav, or as double-you-double-you-double-you (www). The beast is on the attack, just as Saint John the Apostle of Jesus Christ predicted in his revelation from the isle of Patmos. The bear and the dragon are locked in battle. Soon, they will turn on the Eagle, the United States of America."

"Why is CNN carrying this crap?" Wow. Talking to myself. Yesterday, I sat in San Francisco not yet an international felon. Then Sherry O'Shea's friend Olive Curtis Jenkins has the bad manners to get herself murdered, Sherry's husband calls me, thereby motivating me to launch my cyber retaliation much sooner than I'd planned and then leave town. Heaven help the Church of Scientology if they trace my virus incubator to their basement. The blowback will be way worse than putting a rattlesnake into someone's mailbox.

What did my Rabbi friend Ken Cohen say at the turn of the century? "How about you choose another 'chosen people' for the next millennium, because your Christian charity has just about wiped us out over the last two millennia." Celebrity endorsements aside, the Saudi and Sino-Russian fiascos get laid at the feet of Scientology, they may transcend the Jews as the new chosen people, bull's eye and all.

I had a decision to make. Should I try to stop the mushrooming insanity and fess up to my shenanigans, or should I hunker down and focus on the reason for my trip, finding the killer of Sherry's friend? After about a microsecond of reflection, I concluded that no one would believe me if I did confess to the world. Well, my Department of Defense contacts would probably believe me, but no experienced bureaucrat would dare run my confession up the chain of command. Or would they? And did I owe it to the innocent people who might soon be dying to at least try and undo the mess I'd started? One thing became clear: such a confession would end my life as I know it.

Then my self-preservation rationalization engine kicked on, that metaphorical devil on my left shoulder. These guys attacked me. The Chinese hackers. The Russian Hackers. Mohammed bin Faisal Al Saud—bless his Koran-slacking soul—attacked me. I simply gave as good as I got, to quote a Rudyard Kipling line.

Aw, who the hell did I think I was kidding? I didn't merely give as good as I got. I launched a massively disproportionate response which, at the very least, would severely inconvenience my San Francisco Scientology landlords. And at worst? Great jumping Jehoshaphat, at worst thousands, maybe millions of innocent people could die. Clearly, my OCD-induced passion for "getting even" with people attacking me ignored my conscience. But my life-long overwhelming desire to *Never Shed Innocent Blood* appeared to be in serious jeopardy. And along with it, my soul. I believe in an eventual Judgment Day, and that those who shed innocent blood, those who destroy innocence through either commission or omission, and those who rationalize doing so for the greater good, are doomed.

I had acted without imagining the tremendous domino effectiveness of my creation, numbing my conscience with a here's-an-interesting-problem-to-solve! anesthetic. That had to stop, and it had to stop now. Before I went to bed. And to insure that the DOD didn't sit on my confession, I decided to send a copy of my DOD disclosure to editors of both *The New York Times* and to *The Washington Post*. My decision made, I muted the television sound and began typing my email, sentence by prison sentence, addressing my DOD contact and visibly CC-ing the two newspaper editors.

Poised to click my mouse on the SEND icon, I noticed the Fox News picture-in-picture interior of the Saudi royal palace and several regally attired gentlemen behind a podium. I turned up the sound and slid the mouse off the trigger that would end my happy days on earth.

The speaker obviously spoke to his countrymen in Arabic, and a translator followed with the English-language version. I listened to both. And I recognized the speaker, an Andover classmate of mine we called Benny. We graduated together in 1988. Had I just royally screwed my buddy Benny?

"My name is Mohammed bin Faisal Al Saud. My father, Turki bin Faisal Al Saud, is the former ambassador to both Great Britain and to the United States, and the nephew to King Abdullah. Both sit behind me.

"Early yesterday, a message was sent from my computer to my entire mailing list. It accused the Prophet Mohammed of being deceived by Satan who spoke as Allah. The *Holy Qur'an* provided a case-by-case proof."

Benny, you poor wretch, forgive me! I would have added his name to the CC list on my confession, but I'd fried his computer along with his email server. If I'd had his cell phone number, I'd have text messaged him immediately. But since I didn't, all I could do was watch him deal with my treachery. His next statement, though, nearly stopped my heart.

"My computer did indeed send this message. For many years, I have had great concerns as to the validity of the *Holy Qur'an* and of Mohammed's pronouncements. Either he'd been deceived, or the *Holy Qur'an* is a fraud. But in either case, I belive the *Qur'an* is not consistent with God's—that's God and not Allah—with God's rules of engagement with man. I can no longer sit idly and watch our religion, Islam, used to destroy peace. I cannot sit idly and see Islam used as the basis for murder and cruelty among the faithful."

The picture temporarily lost stability amid shouts and the firing of a single shot somewhere in the palace. Black-clad guards with drawn weapons quickly stood between the camera and King Abdullah. After a momentary scuffle and receding screams, the camera settled down and the palace guards stepped out of the frame.

Benny continued: "I would prefer not to live a lie, a fabrication. Yet I do not wish to subject my family, nor my country, to bloodshed over my views. The letter is in many hands and is now posted on the Al Jazeera Web site. I intend to go into exile immediately, and seek the truth I feel has eluded our wonderful people. I shall try to go in secret, and to renounce this world for a better next one.

"The letter represents my opinion and mine alone. My family was not aware of my views, nor do they agree with them. They are with me, here today, this morning, because I asked them to witness my public statement. I wish you the blessings of The One True God, and admonish all to renounce killing and death. To those who follow this path, I promise we shall meet again, in this life or in the next. And to those of you who reject my plea, then I bid you an everlasting farewell, as we are not headed in the same direction. Ma' Alsalam."

During his speech, all the talking-head channels had cut to the Fox feed. The imaginary angel and devil on each shoulder debated editing and/or even deleting my email confession. I opted to sleep on it. We had a ten-hour time difference between Utah and Riyadh. Ten P.M. my time equated to 7:00 A.M. there, since they don't observe daylight savings time. Which meant that by midnight tomorrow, my time, good old Benny, a.k.a. Mohammed bin Faisal Al Saud, should have made good on his escape. Not exactly bosom buddies, Benny and I had shared some soccer and chess time together. As tonight's speech demonstrated, and borrowing one of my favorite analogies from Henry Kissinger, Benny had done a far better job than I had in *rescuing the element of choice from the pressure of circumstance.* Benny's a better man than I am.

Could I sleep on it? Not very soundly, it turned out.

5
Dominos Start to Fall

awoke at 5:15 AM after a somewhat on-again/off-again sleep, plagued by dreams of fratricide in the Arab world. My virus trip-wire notification system, indeed my primary command and control mechanism, used innocuous Twitter accounts which I aggregated with anonymized queries and then sent to my cell phone. The Russian and Chinese penetration statistics seemed staggering. Too staggering, given the lack of headline news they should have generated.

I quickly scanned the Internet news feeds, figuring that Benny had punched a lot of Imam meal tickets and probably got murdered for his efforts. Murdered and burned. Or burned *then* murdered. But no, quite to the contrary, the news reported an absolute calm throughout the Arab world. Russia and China hadn't nuked each other in the night—*my* night, *their* daytime. In fact, media silence seemed uncharacteristic based on the geometric expansion of my virus in Eastern Europe and Asia. Nor did it appear that the Church of Scientology in San Francisco had been raided overnight by FBI SWAT teams.

My shower behind-the-glass TV only allowed one channel at a time, and I settled on CNN coverage of a quiet evening in Riyadh. The reporter had done some homework, and talked about King Abdullah's 2008 call for a dialogue between 'believers' and all other religions. And then he reported the king's February 2009 firing of his hard-line/let's-murder-immoral-TV-station-managers chief of religious police and replacing him with a Saudi *woman*. Clearly, something *had* been going on that saved Benny from summary beheading, and that *something* rolled down hill from the king himself. Especially since King Abdullah did not have absolute power, for him to be leading this charge meant he'd rather skillfully assembled support from the Sunni religious elite as well as the royal family. The closest music metaphor to my current situation might be a country song along the lines, "How could something so bad feel so good?"

Quite a few people milled about the palace grounds, but they had either run out of steam or had become truly introspective. The Arabian Sunni Muslims, by far the largest Islamic sect, seemed to be quiet. Islam's second largest sect, the

Shias, had several Irani imams issue fatwas demanding Benny be put to death. But these seemed half-hearted and hadn't evoked anything approaching massive public demonstrations. Academics, talking heads, pundits, and governments around the world seemed almost awestruck, as nothing like this had happened in modern history.

The *whole earth* hadn't been holding its collective breath for six hours. News channels seemed intent on quickly reporting the speech, and then spending all their air time wondering where exactly Benny had gone off into exile. Of course, every Shia or Sunni in the world *could* have been busying themselves sharpening knives or placing bets in the Jihad mosque pool on the time and place of Benny's execution. Had that been the case, though, it seemed to me the crowds around the palace should have been a little more energized. Or the Shia crowds in Iran.

I changed my in-shower terminal to Internet mode and pulled up my newsbot screen. Other than a low-key report of Russian and Chinese hackers going at each other, nothing. Again, cooler heads seemed to prevail at the highest levels, and rather than making the Russo-Chinese server meltdown a nationalistic issue, the news feeds categorized the phenomenon as a war between the Russian Mafia and Chinese tong societies. What a bunch of garbage! Both the Russian and Chinese governments were into hacking and Web penetration in BIG ways, especially the Chinese. But at least I didn't have governments going to war over my retaliation to their hacking. Now, we'll see how truly smart they are as they "de-louse" all those servers. Without plugging an ICE unit (Inline Circuit Emulator) to each processor and painstakingly looking at the executing code, instruction by instruction, they simply didn't have a chance of discovering my elusive and self-aware viral components, which could hide themselves in EPROMs located in peripherals and just go to sleep at randomly long intervals.

Dried off and dressed in black slacks and shirt—my one and only ensemble since Annie's death—I deleted my draft email confession. Although I was not yet completely off *The Scroll of the Damned*, Benny had let me off one hook, and the Russo-Chinese hacker story had at least been put into context as a hacker war. Of course, that could change, once the forensic gurus traced the source of the initial virus attack, but for now I could breathe a little easier.

I made it down the mountain and to the Grand America coffee shop about a block from the court house by 6:30 AM. On my way through the lobby, I stopped at the hotel news stand and picked up the local newspapers, plus copies of *The New York Times*, *The Wall Street Journal* and *USA Today*. Both the local and the national papers had Benny's picture on the front page, but the papers must have gone to press before much else had happened. And the Russian-Chinese hacker war didn't rate a mention anywhere. Ready for some *displacement activity*, I finished the *USA Today* crossword puzzle over bacon, eggs, toast, hash browns and orange juice. Three glasses of orange juice. I'd save the Friday *New York Times* slugfest for hours of courtroom diversion, given the usually diabolic nature of Friday's and Saturday's puzzles. I guess *every* Friday is Friday the Thirteenth for *Times'* editor Will Shortz.

The Grand America Hotel is one of the crown jewels in the late billionaire entrepreneur Earl Holding's oil and recreational empire. Sinclair Oil seeded his acquisition of the Sun Valley and Snowbasin ski resorts along with the Westgate Hotel in San Diego and Little America properties in Arizona and Wyoming. I'd seen them all, but Salt Lake's Grand America topped the chart for elegance and service. A coffee shop off the main lobby reminded me of a ballroom in Saddam Hussein's Tikrit palace, or at least what I thought might be the Saddam's ball room, since I saw the palace through a night-vision scope from the middle of a lake as my Special Operations Command SEAL platoon did laser spotting for the pre-invasion force. My knack for language and my electronics countermeasures skills got me a front-row seat to some spectacular fireworks on my last tour of duty before coming back home to Annie and my computer business. So here I sat, now 7:30AM, contemplating opulence, Benny, Russia, China, and the late Olive Jenkins.

I arrived in Judge O'Shea's courtroom about ten minutes until eight, and sat thumbing through the local papers for news of Olive Jenkins' murder three days before. Buried inside both papers, the investigation into her death rated about three paragraphs each. The front pages concerned Utah Jazz basketball rumors and the political fallout from a former governor, former ambassador to China and former candidate for President of the United States who took a decidedly un-Utahish stand on same-sex marriage. No details on the murder, and it didn't appear anybody built up much anxiety over it, ranking it in the same bucket as West Valley gang-related shootings, of which there appeared to be one or two a week. Just as I thought about getting out my *New York Times* crossword, a Marine-sized court bailiff with a crew cut leaned over the railing separating the spectator gallery from the attorney tables and asked me to follow him to the judge's chamber. He stood almost as tall as I did but outweighed me by at least 50 pounds. All muscle, too. I followed him through the gate and then right, past the jury box and into a conference room where three men sat around a utilitarian conference table.

"Your Honor," I said.

"You've met Stan," said Judge O'Shea, standing to shake my hand and signaling a formal-pecking-order meeting. "Morgan Rapier, I'd like you to meet Sheriff Running and Detective Sergeant Hank Davidson."

"Sheriff Running," I said as I shook his hand. Sheriff Running offered a firm grip, no-nonsense eye contact and a what-you-see-is-all-there-is straightforwardness common to Utah. I liked him immediately, and my opinion didn't change when I shook hands with his detective. "Sergeant Davidson, a pleasure."

"Call me Hank, Mister Rapier," said the detective. While the sheriff stood almost tall enough to make level eye contact with me, the detective would have had to stand on a chair. Lean, ramrod straight, the little guy definitely topped the scale at one-fifty max and probably had a pet German Shepherd who could bring down a bull elephant.

"And Hank, please call me Morgan," I said. Another firm handshake. Playing a hunch, I added, "You know, Hank, it's a sin against humanity if you haven't named one of your children Harley."

The sheriff immediately laughed. "Harley Y. Davidson is one spitfire of a seventeen year old girl."

Judge O'Shea couldn't resist adding, "When I asked what the 'Y' stood for, she said 'My name is Harley You-Bet-Your-Ass Davidson.'"

Good for the judge. He not only established a pecking order for the meeting but he set the ground rules that we should trust each other as friends. And since neither Sheriff Running nor Detective Davidson asked me about my family, obviously Hizonor had told them of Annie's death and our lack of children.

"This looks good to me, Morgan," said the sheriff as he handed me my concealed weapon carry permit. Then, nodding toward Detective Davidson, "But just to be clear, we're not expecting to behave like a vigilante, are we?"

"No sir!" I said. "And I'm not here to do Detective Davidson's job for him, either. Treat me the same as any other citizen who wants to help out, and lower the boom on me if it needs lowering."

Davidson looked almost relieved. Almost. His trust was mine to lose, but at least I didn't have to win it. My friendship with the judge cleared that hurdle. He took out his spiral notepad and then craned his neck to make eye contact: "Judge O'Shea said you wanted to see the crime scene?"

"Yes, if that would be at all possible?"

"I've got to do a couple of interviews from people that turned up during our canvassing," said Davidson. "After that though, perhaps around three o'clock this afternoon, I could meet you at the scene. I'd like another set of eyes out there, and I understand from the judge that you are somewhat of a computer wizard."

"I'll be there at three," I said.

"One more thing," said Sheriff Running as he handed me a thick leather case the size of a wallet. "I hope I don't regret this, but raise your right hand and repeat Judge O'Shea's words."

My thumb flipped open the case to reveal a badge, a deputy's badge, and Patrick O'Shea said, "Repeat after me."

I don't remember what he said, but I managed to repeat the oath. Deputy Morgan Rapier didn't think anybody had done such a thing since Wyatt Earp in Tombstone. Or more precisely, since Patrick O'Shea's alter ego Judge Roy Bean in Fort Smith Arkansas circa 1881. So here I stood, a newly deputized gunslinger in the Wild West, holding a badge and, unknown to my new friends, holding the potential of dramatically embarrassing them. Having committed numerous felonies on multiple continents, having singlehandedly set in motion massive international forces, and having done so illegally, my next few days could likely destroy three careers if I weren't absolutely careful.

The sheriff and the detective excused themselves after Davidson gave me Olive Jenkins' address, and Judge O'Shea yelled out the door for his bailiff to find me a seat in the gallery. He couldn't do it himself, as judges always need to make a grand entrance through another door.

"You're looking a little pale, Morgan."

Given the weight of my duty to our friendship, it's a miracle I could still stand. All I could say was, "This, uh, deputy thing is a big responsibility."

"Yes it is, Morgan You-Bet-Your-Ass Rapier."

6

A Day in the Court of Judge Roy Bean

Bailiff Stan Fawcett unceremoniously reseated someone from the front row so I could have the spot by the wall that offered easy eye contact with the judge. A fairly big guy with prison tattoos up and down each neck glared at me from his new seat one row back. He glared until I gave him my full six-foot-five-inch make-my-day-you-dirtbag look, whereupon he jerked his head to smirk to someone on his left. An imaginary someone, since the vacant bench remained his only audience.

The prosecution table sat directly in front of me, to the left of which was a lectern and then the defense table. At least six feet higher on the other side of the room stood the massive structure from which O'Shea presided over his kingdom. I knew from my previous visits to the courtroom that Judge Patrick O'Shea kept a loaded Colt Python revolver with a six-inch barrel beneath the lip of his desk. Given the size of the room and our shared expertise at drawing and shooting moving objects in the desert, I also knew the judge could plug anyone in the courtroom without risking collateral damage, thanks to the particular hollow-head .357 shell and special load. To my knowledge, he'd never even had to brandish the weapon, but something about his absolute confidence on the bench undoubtedly let even the most serious felon know the judge shouldn't be trifled with.

I'd taken many a Boy Scout group, at least the older boys, to his Friday show-cause hearings. More times than not, O'Shea's booming voice would echo throughout the cavernous chamber and dash the hopes of some miscreant who hadn't taken the terms of his probation quite seriously enough: "I can see that this court has not gotten your attention; maybe a weekend in jail will."

As opposed to long trials and civil motions, Fridays seemed the epitome of law and judgment. The time for argument and legal games had passed. In the case of sentencing, the jury had rendered a verdict, and the prosecutors had made their written recommendations for sentencing. In other instances, where the terms of probation had either been violated or were up for review in a show-cause hearing, the judge had identical prerogatives. Quite simply, O'Shea and God had a lot in common. He applied the law as he and he alone saw fit. To be sure, the door of appeal always lay open. But the small community of criminal defense attorneys, both court-appointed and for hire in Salt Lake City, didn't lightly knock on *that* door. Because they'd have to face the same judge another day, on another case. Besides, Judge Patrick O'Shea had not only the lowest reversal record of any judge in history, but he had the lowest recidivism rate, too. Which meant that a public defender could actually be doing his guilty client a favor by *losing* the case! How? Simply because O'Shea's creative sentencing achieved a result revered by liberal academics world-wide: reformation.

Odd though, that while reformation occurred, his methods had the ACLU apoplectic, ranting their cruel-and-unusual talking points, especially about Judge O'Shea's phenomenally successful I-am-a-drunk-driver T-shirts. First offenders are given the choice of serving thirty days in the spacious new county jail, or wearing a set of identical T-shirts twenty-four hours a day for the same thirty days. The T-shirts have the same message, front and back. Large letters proclaim, "I Am A Drunk Driver." Naturally, the judge has a standing arrangement with a T-shirt silk screener down the block from the courthouse, lest one of his defendants opt for his own supplier and fudge the type size or color to make the message less legible. And spot-checks by deputized M.A.D.D. (Mothers Against Drunk Driving) volunteers guaranteed not only quantitative compliance—nobody dared even sleep naked—but qualitative compliance. The T-shirts must be worn as the outer layer of clothing at all times. Even in winter, over jackets. Heaven forbid a deputy should find a non-compliant offender. "MADD Mother" sometimes modified an appropriately vitriolic verb as said offender found himself cuffed and in the back of a squad car.

After thirty days in their new ensembles, formerly drunk drivers experienced a remarkable awakening, often commenting in court that they never realized how much people hated drunk drivers. Extremely low recidivism and ACLU chagrin formed the liberal paradox of Judge O'Shea's evermore-famous reputation.

So there I sat this first Friday in three years, killing time awaiting my crime scene appointment, now a sworn-in Salt Lake County Deputy Sheriff. What an act of genius, Sherry O'Shea's coining the term "Daddy's little felons." Victims viewed life as a nightmare. Many religionists viewed life as a trial, or a veil of tears. But Sherry always harped that the words with which we describe events often dictate the outcome. She talked about life's *adventures* and refused to call them trials, and that the word "*adventure*" implied optimism. Ditto for her newest metaphor, *Daddy's little felons*, a term that implied hope amid the confines of jail, and which almost made the reclamation of innocence a foregone conclusion.

The bailiff's "All rise!" interrupted my reflections as Hizonor mounted the steps to his castle-within-a-castle. The announcement caused a general shuffling of people from the corridors, and the gallery quickly filled. The prison-tattooed guy behind me finally had someone to whom he could turn and smirk, should the occasion arise.

"Thank you," said the judge. "Please be seated."

We obeyed. A gaggle of defense attorneys crowded the gate, not as bold as the prosecutors who quickly took their places at the desk in front of me. But even *they* didn't speak until invited.

"We have a full calendar," said Judge O'Shea. "Are there urgencies that need to be considered out of order?"

"If it please the court, Your Honor," said an attorney near the front of the line.

"Yes?" said the judge.

"Your Honor, Sheridan Burgess representing Lyle Kendrick. I have another trial in the building, and wonder if we might consider case 33659433 and the matter of the State of Utah vs. Lyle Kendrick?"

O'Shea shuffled through the file folders on his desk until he found the right one. Looking toward the bailiff he asked, "Has Mister Kendrick been brought over from the county jail?"

"Yes sir," said the bailiff.

"Do any of the other members of the court have an objection to my considering this mater out of sequence?" O'Shea looked for input from the conga line behind the gate, all of whom apparently found something interesting about the tile on the courtroom floor. Upon seeing no objection, he looked toward the prosecution table. "Is the state ready to proceed?"

"Jeff Levy for the prosecution, Your Honor. Yes, we are ready."

"Very well, then," said O'Shea. "Bailiff, please bring Mister Kendrick from lockup."

Minutes later, a cuffed and shackled Lyle Kendrick shuffled into the room. Lyle might well have been the twin brother of the fellow sitting behind me, complete with prison tattoos. Their only major distinguishing difference involved Lyle's short-sleeved orange jump suit. His legs made a swishing sound as he rounded the defense table and took his seat next to his attorney, who remained standing. He leaned behind his attorney so he could covertly make eye contact with the kindred spirit sitting behind me without the judge seeing it, and gave the family smirk. Definitely a brother, maybe even an identical twin.

"Mister Levy, does the state have a recommendation?" asked O'Shea.

"Your Honor, Mister Kendrick is on parole for gang-related violence, grand theft auto, and assault," said the prosecutor. Kendrick looked at the prosecutor in disbelief, as if Levy *must* have been talking about someone else. "He's here today for violating a no-contact order issued by this court, and for not only visiting his former wife but damaging her property and resisting arrest when neighbors called the police."

"Mister Burgess, would your client care to explain himself?"

"Your Honor," said the defense attorney, "My client believes this to be a complete misunderstanding …"

"Mister Burgess, this is a show-cause hearing. I believe I asked if *your client* cared to explain himself, which I suggest he do forthwith," said O'Shea. "Bailiff, would you please swear in Mister Kendrick?"

The bailiff complied, and Kendrick swore to tell the whole truth and nothing but the truth. Amazingly, he yes-I-do'd with a completely straight face.

"Thank you Mister Kendrick," said the judge. "Now please explain the *complete misunderstanding* to this court."

Kendrick stood Boy Scout straight and looked as wronged as possible, notwithstanding his orange jump suit, shaved head and prison tattoos. "Your Honor, I just wanted to drive by the house and see my daughter. As I drove by, she waived at me from the flower bed, and it broke my heart. I hadn't seen her for three years and couldn't resist stopping to give her a little hug. Her mother was nowhere in sight."

"It says here in the arrest report," interrupted O'Shea, "that your wife came out and witnessed you trying to put your daughter into your car."

"That's not true, Your Honor. I just hugged her and said goodbye. When I went back to my car, she followed me. My little girl didn't want to see me leave again."

"I see," said O'Shea. "I can see how that might engender a misunderstanding on the part of your wife."

"Yes, Your Honor. When my wife saw our daughter by the car, she just snapped and started throwing rocks and buckets at me."

I even started feeling sympathy for the poor, misunderstood father, notwithstanding his no-contact order. But then the judge closed the trap.

"So the witnesses who say you slugged your ex-wife, snatched up the little girl from the flower bed, and ran with her to the car as her mother fought to get her back, those witnesses lied?"

"Your Honor," said Kendrick as if reciting the Scout Oath, "That just didn't happen."

"And when one of those lying witnesses called the police, you did not subsequently attack the responding officers with a baseball bat that magically materialized from the back seat of your car?"

"Your Honor, my wife…"

"…that would be ex-wife," corrected the judge.

"Okay, my ex-wife hit me with a bucket, knocking me to the ground. I didn't see the officers at all, and the bucket stunned me. I was just trying to get up when someone grabbed me. I thought the neighbors were attacking me, and I defended myself."

"Mister Levy?" said the judge to the prosecuting attorney.

"According to the arresting officer, Your Honor," said Levy, "Mister Kendrick saw the police car and immediately went to his automobile for the purpose of retrieving his baseball bat, whereupon he rushed the cruiser and began smashing headlights and the windshield."

"Mister Kendrick, does this bring back any kind of memory?" asked the judge.

"Your Honor, that police report is a lie!" spat the suddenly less-than-Boy-Scout-calm Kendrick.

"And I suppose the paramedic's report on your ex-wife's injuries is a lie, too?"

Kendrick's attorney Sheridan Burgess tried to jump in and do damage control: "We request the court's permission to cross examine the arresting officers and the attending EMT."

"Objection," shouted the prosecutor. "This is…"

"I'll take it from here," interjected the judge. "Mister Burgess, this is a show-cause hearing, not a trial. Mister Kendrick has already had several of those. One more question for Mister Kendrick."

Kendrick seemed undecided whether to look at his defense attorney or the judge or the gallery, perhaps wondering if his ex-wife wanted to display her bruised face or if the neighbor he'd cold-cocked whilst retrieving his baseball bat might want to add further damning testimony. Beyond the beginning of a sputter, Lyle Kendrick evidently spent a few introspective seconds willing his complexion to match the orange of his jump suit, a job at which he succeeded admirably. So the judge asked his question.

"Mister Kendrick?" whispered the judge, all the while smiling serenely. "Are there butterflies around that garden in front of your ex-wife's house?"

Oh no! I knew what came next: the *Judge Roy Bean* speech, modified from the original 1881 Fort Smith, Arkansas declaration that Patrick O'Shea had framed in his office. The prosecutors seemed to know it, too, judging by their now-relaxed posture and foreknowledge that Kendrick wouldn't be seeing freedom anytime soon. The original defendant was hung the same day, so Hizonor would have to creatively modify the sentencing. The defendant, Lyle Kendrick, sensing a change in the aura of those around him, spat a frustrated, "Whaaaaaat?"

"That would be 'Whaaaaat, *Your Honor*,'" corrected the judge.

"I'm sorry, Your Honor?" said Kendrick.

"I asked a simple question. Are there butterflies in that garden, your ex-wife's garden?"

"I dunno," said Kendrick, quickly adding, "Your Honor." Confused, Kendrick quickly glanced around at the man behind me, who sat in silence, obviously as mystified as his orange-clad clone.

The judge quickly cleared up the confusion. "Lyle Wilbur Kendrick," he began, this time in no whisper but in a voice the timbre of The Lord God Almighty talking from the mountain. "It's been spring for a few short weeks. The snows of winter are flowing wildly down Cottonwood Canyon, the ice is vanishing and the air is about to become soft and balmy. In short, Lyle Wilbur Kendrick, the annual miracle of the years will awaken and come to pass. But you won't be around to see it. The rivulet will run its serpentine course into the Great Salt Lake. The glorious valleys of this imperial domain will blossom as the rose. Still, you will not be here to see. From every treetop, some wild woods songster will carol his mating song. Butterflies will sport in the sunshine. The gentle breeze will tease the tassels of the wild grasses, and all nature, Lyle Wilbur Kendrick, will be glad. But you will not be here to see whether or not your ex-wife's garden does indeed have butterflies.

"Because I command the sheriff of the county to lead you away to a god-forsaken cell at the state prison in Draper, where you will rot out the remainder of the sentence from which you were shown such lenience by this state, without the possibility of another parole. And I further command that such officer of the law retire completely from your rotting carcass, even though you might well die in prison. And if such should be the case, then I sincerely hope you will be left in your cell, that the vultures may descend from the heavens upon your filthy body until nothing shall remain but bare, bleached bones of a cold blooded, child stealing, wife beating son of a bitch."

Silence filled the courtroom until the judge commanded, "Bailiff, get this man out of my sight!"

The slam of Judge O'Shea's gavel sounded like a gunshot and set off murmurs throughout the gallery. Bailiff Stan Fawcett guided Lyle Kendrick toward the prisoners' exit, and Kendrick stared so intently at Judge O'Shea that he walked right into a post. I couldn't help but snicker, and hoped the general din of the gallery didn't allow the sound to reach Hizonor. If the judge did hear me, he showed now sign of it. The fellow behind me just growled and stood to glare down Kendrick's defense attorney, just coming through the gate. Burgess, the defense attorney, cowered under his gaze. The walking mountain obviously intended to step into Burgess's path, so I quickly snaked my hand over the bench and yanked. The effect exceeded my original goal, since it not only stopped the menacing cretin from blocking Burgess, but caused said cretin's low-slung/loose-fitting pants to drop past his knees. As did he, his menacing concentration directed now to quickly protecting his dignity. And while his pants hung loose enough on his hips to easily drop, they proved tight enough to require considerable effort in bringing them back up, his attention to the task made more difficult by the muted laughter from the rest of the gallery. By the time he completed the task and turned to glare at me, Burgess had made it past him and out the door. He glared, and I just sat there batting my eyelashes at him. Not smart on my part, but I figured even this cretin wouldn't risk starting a fistfight in a courtroom.

He finally broke eye contact and left the room, this time not even contemplating a smirk to the rest of the gallery, and the judge's gavel quickly commanded silence. I turned my attention back to the judge and noticed Hizonor barely suppressing his own smile.

"Next case," said O'Shea.

"Stephanie Steel versus the State of Utah and the United States of America," announced the court clerk.

"Jeff Levy for the State of Utah, Your Honor."

"Ronald St. Clair for the United States, Your Honor."

A middle-aged lady stood in the gallery about half way back and to my left. She scooted toward the aisle, balancing an armload of paper and a briefcase. The bailiff opened the gate for her and she took her place to the left of the prosecutor's table.

"Ms. Steele, I understand you are here representing yourself?" asked the judge.

"Yes, Your Honor," she said somewhat breathlessly.

"And you understand the seriousness of the penalties for refusing to file state and federal income tax returns?"

"Your Honor, since there is no constitutional basis for imposing a federal income tax, then any penalties you might impose are also unconstitutional?" Stephanie Steele looked over her left shoulder, as did the entire gallery. A tall man wearing a nattily striped suit nodded approvingly at her.

"You sir, at the door!" said Judge O'Shea. "Are you a member of the Utah bar?"

Stephanie Steele's head snapped back around, wide eyed as she stared at the judge.

"No, Your Honor," said the man.

"Are you giving this defendant legal advice?" asked the judge.

"No, Your Honor," he replied.

"Ms. Steele, is this man giving you legal advice?" asked O'Shea, a few decibels louder.

Two things happened simultaneously. First, Stephanie Steele snatched a hard-cover book from her pile of legal ammunition, on the back of which was a photograph of what appeared to be the man standing by the door, clad in a different but similarly jaunty suit. The second event concerned the abrupt exit into the hallway of the self-help author, who beat a retreat rather than stick around to help one of his customers truly beat the IRS. The defendant must have heard the swish of her tax guru's exit, because she turned again to blink repeatedly at the place once occupied by, if you could believe the book jacket, the smartest man in the world. Given that Utah is the pyramid-scheme marketing capital of the world—called "network marketing" or MLM in an attempt to become more politically correct—good old Joe Striped-suit must have been there to see *someone else* risk life and freedom following his advice, to see if his bilious screed stuck to the wall. Apparently not, based upon Hizonor's next pronouncement.

"Ms. Steele, I asked you a question. Has that man, who has now seen fit to remove himself from my court room, been giving you legal advice?"

Torn between perjuring herself or further enraging the bad-humored judge who just threw Lyle Wilbur Kendrick into jail until his bleached bones got picked clean by buzzards, she just held up the book and let her mouth hang open in growing horror. On a roll, Judge Patrick O'Shea took her off the hook.

"Maybe this court should take that as a no. Would you like the bailiff to dispose of that worthless piece of trash for you?" asked the judge, pointing to the book. "Or would you like to tell me why I shouldn't throw you into jail for violation of a court order to file your income tax returns?"

"Your Honor," began the ashen Ms. Steele, down but not yet out. "According to the 2002 case *United States v. Craft*, Chief Justice Rhenquist admitted there is not statute that makes it a crime for failure to file an income tax return. Furthermore…"

O'Shea didn't let her continue. "Well then, Ms. Steele, you'll have to take this up with the United States Supreme Court yourself. Because I am issuing a court order giving you one week to file your back tax returns or go directly to jail for contempt of court. Do you understand?"

Not being an attorney myself, I didn't know whether or not the judge could do that. But neither did Stephanie Steele. She just couldn't resist turning around for some kind of nod from the gallery, and the absence of her tax guru made a red-faced, bald man in an open-collar white shirt her next choice. He just sat there, looking like Wile E. Coyote sitting atop an Acme rocket sled after discovering he'd run out of gas in thin air. And good old Wile E. Coyote let slip a grimace and quick side-to-side shake of his head.

"Who are you sir?" said the judge, slamming his gavel hard enough to shatter granite. "And are *you* providing legal representation for this woman?"

"N-no," sputtered Wile E. "I-I'm her husband."

"Ms. Steele," said the judge, redirecting his attention to a visibly shaking defendant. "Do you understand what I just said? The federal statutes provide for a maximum penalty of two years imprisonment without parole, a fifty-thousand dollar fine, two years of supervised release, an order of restitution, and last but not least, a fifty dollar mandatory special assessment."

She nodded in the affirmative.

"I didn't hear you! Please state for the court that you understand."

"I understand, Your Honor."

"Very good, Ms. Steele. Now, what is your decision? Are you and your *husband* going to be working on income tax returns after dinner tonight, or would you prefer that I remand you immediately to lockup?"

This surely didn't turn out the way The Book must have said it would turn out. Slowly, softly, the anything-but-iron Ms. Steele said, "I'll file my taxes."

"I'll file my taxes *Your Honor*!" said O'Shea.

"I'm sorry, Your Honor. I will file my taxes Your Honor," said the humiliated woman, but not adding an emotional *right after I beat the author of that book to death with the arms I've ripped off his worthless body.*

"This is the first smart thing you've done, today. Bailiff, please make sure

Ms. Steele pays $250 in court costs before she leaves the building."

"Yes, Your Honor," said Bailiff Stan Fawcett.

As the clerk called up the next cases, I definitely got the impression that my old friend was performing for me. As if we sat in that bygone Wyoming fantasy world—Han Solo piloting the Millennium Falcon and Rocky Balboa duking it out against overwhelming odds—solving the world's problems with flair and unbreakable resolve.

O'Shea and I laughed over lunch in his chambers.

"Man," I said. "Two years in prison, a fifty grand fine *and* a fifty dollar mandatory special assessment!"

"I get about one of those a month," said Patrick, wiping a daub of mustard from the corner of his mouth with a governor's office linen napkin embroidered with the State of Utah seal. "The part about a fifty dollar mandatory special assessment is like salt in the wound."

"Nice napkin," I noticed.

"Evidence from a catering heist," he said. "Culprit pled and the court never got around to returning several complete place settings."

Only then did the silver, the china plates, the crystal *and* the linen register.

"*That* must be why the corned beef on rye and Coke taste so good," I said. And they honestly did taste better than any lunch in memory.

"By the way," he said. "You shouldn't have pulled that guy's pants down. He's going to be looking for you."

"He's just a brawler. Any one of my SOCOM team could take five of him."

"Not if they're armed. Maybe you should borrow my Colt until you can get to your own gun safe at Snowbird?"

"Even armed, Goofy and his friends won't be a problem. Besides, that would leave you defenseless."

"Au contraire, mon petit chu chu," said the judge as he opened his robe to reveal not one but two .45 automatics, one holstered beneath each arm.

"Whoa!" I gasped. "You're going to hurt somebody if you're not careful."

"Ten bucks says I can outshoot *you*, Rambo."

"Maybe we should take a little trip to the West Desert tomorrow after the funeral," said O'Shea.

"Funeral?"

"I forgot to tell you? Olive's funeral is tomorrow morning at 10:00 A.M. Figured you'd want to be there to see if any likely suspects show up."

"There goes my bike ride, huh?"

"Not to change the subject, but you want the Colt before you leave the courthouse, today?"

"Nope," I said. "Even if Kendrick's offended relative jumps me, I don't want to kill him. If I had the Colt, I might inadvertently make it my first defensive option."

"What if he has a weapon?" Judge O'Shea leaned close to emphasize his point.

"I disrespected him big time. He'll want to get close and personal," I said. "When he does, it'll be too close for his continued health."

"Fair enough," said O'Shea. "Time to get back to work."

His chambers clock read just about 1:00 PM, so I made my way back to the courtroom. My front-row seat against the wall hadn't been taken by anyone else, so I eased myself in for the afternoon show, or at least the show until about 2:15 when I figured I should leave to make it to meet with Detective Davidson at the murder scene.

The first defendant planned to represent himself. The judge put a stop to the proceeding until he could reschedule and come back dressed like an attorney. "If you're going to behave like an attorney, then you will darn well dress like one!"

The next case involved a drunk driver who was caught *not* wearing his 'I am a DRUNK DRIVER' T-shirt on a construction job. I mused how the judge's low recidivism rate probably correlated with creative sentencing. The defendant thought his transparent rain gear made the T-shirt beneath it quite visible, and O'Shea cut him some slack.

I noticed that the public defender did not interject, object or otherwise insert herself into the proceedings. Given that O'Shea had the lowest recidivism rate of any court in the United States, let alone Utah, she definitely didn't want to rock the boat. As I remembered it, the ACLU seemed to shriek about Judge O'Shea's violation of civil liberties, combined with cruel and unusual punishment at every election. But O'Shea kept getting elected, largely because his most ardent supporters happened to be former defendants and families of those defendants.

O'Shea mellowed during the remainder of my stay in his court, and I excused myself around 2:15 PM to meet Detective Davidson out in Sandy.

7

U.S. Navy SEAL Recruitment Ad

 hopped down the courthouse steps two at a time and made the pedestrian light on 500 South perfectly, on my way to the Grand America underground parking garage. I'd programmed the crime site into my cell phone so I could get voice-activated Bluetooth driving directions from my car's speaker system. As I turned right, I caught some movement inside a flower shop on my left. Sure, it could have been anybody, but the hairs on the back of my neck sent a different signal. It made sense to pick up the pace a bit, since someone with a handgun would have to be close in to stand any chance at all of popping me in the back, and at six-five my stride would cause most other men to make a spectacle of themselves if they intended to overtake me.

I turned left in front of the Grand America hotel and spotted two men about fifty yards behind, one of whom I recognized from the Kendrick hearing. I wondered if he'd gotten a belt since our last encounter. It wouldn't be at all cool if his pants fell down during our next conversation. His companion looked about the same size, which meant they thought the two of them could handle me. Deciding not to risk involving bystanders in the hotel elevator lobby, I walked down the underground parking ramp from the outside. Once out of their line of sight, I hurried even faster toward my car. Luckily, less than a dozen cars occupied the space near the elevator, which meant we'd have the garage to ourselves. It also meant that the inevitable security cameras near the elevators would put any physical activities in context. But to be sure, I hung my cell phone from a lanyard around my neck and connect through the hotel's Wi-Fi system to a streaming video. Both sound and video would instantly stream to the Internet, creating a record of the encounter. If I played this fair and square, notwithstanding greater risk to myself, Lyle Kendrick might have some friends and family with whom to while away the hours behind bars in Draper. Greater risk to myself, because I'd have to let them make the first solid move, as opposed to my OPA philosophy—that's Overwhelming Preemptive Assault philosophy— intercepting the first incoming fist and pulverizing everything in sight with overwhelming retaliation.

The two guys following me didn't take any great pains to do it stealthily. Interesting. Maybe they hoped I'd run from them. Or die of fright. Or let me get my car door half open before rushing and pinning me half way into the seat. Upon reaching the car I examined their reflection behind me from my tinted glass windows, and they didn't appear to come armed, walking with their arms loosely hanging away from their bodies the way weight lifters strut around the gym—or the prison yard—after getting pumped up.

"Hi, guys," I said, turning slowly to size up the visiting team. Then, to Lyle's look-alike, "You must be a Kendrick?"

"You owe me an apology," he replied.

"They don't teach manners in the trailer park, huh?" I said. "My name is Morgan. And you are?"

"I'm Lavar. Lavar Kendrick," he said. He didn't seem to take my trailer park comment as an insult, possibly wondering instead how I knew where he lived. Gesturing to his companion, "This is Lamar Kendrick."

"Lyle's brothers?" I asked.

"Yep," said Lavar.

"Cousin," said Lamar.

"Like I said, you owe me an apology," restated Lavar.

And at that moment, I realized I probably did owe the poor blighted soul an apology. Sure, he'd been about to vent his frustration on a poor defense attorney, but I'd humiliated him in public just after his brother had been thrown into the slammer. Maybe the two of them had endured quite a few beatings in their respective lives. Maybe the abused hadn't yet become the abuser, and Lavar's problem solving skills had evolved past physical confrontation. I decided to cut him some slack.

"You're right, Lavar. I guess I do owe you an apology," I began. Neither one of them could make eye contact without looking up at me, and I hoped they'd use my apology as an face-saving excuse to back off. "I was just trying to stop you from giving that poor attorney a heart attack. The pants thing just happened."

Alas, Lavar didn't take my apology in the spirit I'd intended. Instead, he did his smirk toward Lamar, incorrectly assessing my honest apology as cowardice. Then back to me, "Too little. Too late, Morgan."

"So I don't suppose you'll let me buy you guys a beer and call it even?" I asked.

"You'd probably get arrested for walking into a bar without your pants on," smirked Lavar.

"Ah, quid pro quo," I said.

"What'd you call me?" said Lavar, flexing to keep his pump-up going. Lamar looked equally confused and flexed, too.

"Boys, that means eye for an eye. Pants for pants."

"Yes it do," said Lamar, wanting to keep up his end of the conversation.

"Too bad you feel that way, Lamar, Lavar," I sighed. "Let me therefore apologize in advance."

"In advance of what," said Lamar.

"I truly didn't want to hurt you guys, but you're not leaving me much choice."

The faintest shadow of concern registered as Lamar's eyebrows seemed to grow together. He looked about to step back, but Cousin Lavar seemed to miss the implication of my pre-pology. He snickered and said, "We've taken down big guys before."

"In a bar fight, maybe," I said. "Fair warning. I'm a U.S. Navy SEAL. Team Three if you know anything about SEALs. I've seen a lot of combat, and I could whip ten of you. So, last chance Lamar and Lavar Kendrick."

I repeated their last name, for my streaming video record.

"Don't forget Cousin Laverl," said a voice behind me. Obviously, he couldn't get to me with the car to my back, but perhaps he wanted me to turn so the other two could sucker punch me. My only risk in not assessing the threat might be a baseball bat to the head, but I mitigated against that threat by stepping away from the car and toward the two guys in front of me. Laverl would have to throw his bat, if he had one.

My forward motion threw off the timing of Lavar's round house punch, which glanced off my shoulder, instead of my jaw. Lamar also stepped forward, which accelerated his throat into my two right knuckles headed for his larynx. Luckily, I pulled the thrust at the last instant, thereby saving Lamar's life. But even the pulled punch put him out of the fight, which I knew it would. Lavar had quickly followed his right-hand round house with a left jab to my solar plexus, and it might have hurt me if I didn't have the reach advantage. A split second after I'd slugged Lamar in the throat, the heel of my left hand slammed into Lavar's unprotected chin. Combined with his forward momentum, the force snapped his head back and into a garage supporting post. He bounced rather nicely with eyes rolled back before he hit the ground. Now, where was that little scamp, Cousin Laverl?

I turned to see a wide-eyed statue on the other side of my car. He hadn't moved since his opening line of the scene. A quick glance behind me at Lamar on his hands and knees and breathing, albeit with difficulty, reassured me that I hadn't killed the poor devil. Maybe time for an olive branch?

"Laverl is it?" I said. "You want to take a crack at me, that's fine. Or you can give me a hand with your cousins to make sure I haven't hurt them too badly. Your call."

He came around the car, both hands with palms raised and facing me. "Okay, mister. Whoever you are, we don't want any more whup-ass."

"Good call." I knelt by Lamar and massaged his throat. "Relax man, you're panicking and that'll just make it harder to breathe. I'm not going to hurt you unless you give me a reason to."

Laverl was shaking his unconscious cousin. "Lavar?"

"Is he breathing?" I asked.

"Y-yeah, he is," stuttered Laverl.

"Good," I said. "I've got a bottle of water in my car."

I opened the car door, the remote-proximity feature of the key in my pocket unlocking it, and grabbed a bottle of water from the door pocket. After squirting a little into Lavar's face and seeing a quick shudder, I handed it to the now sitting Lamar. "Take a very small sip of this water."

He accepted the water tentatively, as if expecting the bottle to get jammed down his throat or into an eyeball.

"Okay, Mom, I'll go feed the chickens," came Lavar's voice to my left.

"He's probably got a concussion," I said. "Would you guys like a ride into emergency? Lamar ought to have his throat looked at. If his larynx is bleeding, he could drown in his sleep."

Both Lamar and Laverl stared at me in disbelief. Lamar croaked something unintelligible and then shook his head to decline the offer. Laverl got the gist of the message and said, "Lamar's truck is on the corner. We can take it."

I helped Lamar to his feet. Laverl grabbed the semi conscious Lavar and walked between them toward the parking lot ramp. Lavar looked up and around, probably wondering how he got here, and Lamar carried my water bottle in his free right hand, using the left to steady himself against his cousin.

"I'm serious, Laverl," I said. "I know your name, and if you don't go to emergency and something bad happens to either one of these guys, me and a bunch of SEAL buddies are going to pay you a midnight visit."

"Yes sir," said Laverl. I watched them disappear up the ramp, and turned off my telephone streaming video. My one or two video followers would probably have some fun passing around the link.

"You were kinder to those creeps than they deserved," came a voice from the shadows near the elevator. She stepped into the light, toward my car.

I vaguely remembered the waitress. "From the coffee shop upstairs."

"Taking out the trash, I see," she said.

"Just holding a class in manners."

"Think it'll take?"

"Probably not," I concluded. "The abused have evidently become the abusers. Introspection isn't high on their list of things to do."

"Ya never know."

"Glad one of us is an optimist. Well, have a nice afternoon."

"Thanks," she smiled with a weariness born of ten hours on her feet in a coffee shop. "Try not to be a magnet for any more trouble, today."

Too late, I thought as I got into my car and drove away.

8
Hacking the Crime Scene

etective Davidson stood in front of the house looking at his watch, obviously irritated by my fifteen-minute tardiness. Evidently, he hadn't yet received my email link to the Kendrick streaming video from the garage. The detective's salary must not cover a phone with video-reception capability. Some people get pretty anal about punctuality, and since I really did feel bad about being late I decided not to make any excuses.

"Detective Davidson, I should have allowed myself more time today," I said. "Please accept my apologies."

Detective Sergeant Henry Davidson just stood there giving me "the eye." Without a word, he turned and walked toward the yellow crime scene tape. I caught up quite easily and followed him into the townhouse complex. He ducked under the tape and then held it for me. Olive's automatic watering system kept the hanging baskets of flowers well cared for, vibrant, beautiful, and oblivious to the fact the gardener would never be back. Her first-floor door had "OCJ" engraved on a gold knocker, which hung just above a similarly engraved gold plate proclaiming "Your name is safe in this house."

"Too bad the sentiment didn't apply to the owner" said Davidson, pointing to the gold plate. His first words spoke volumes about his focus, his head thoroughly in the game, gathering evidence and sniffing for motive. We stood on a doormat that matched the hanging flowers, and he opened the deadbolt with a key he retrieved from a Ziploc bag in his jacket pocket.

"Nor should it apply to her murderer," I added, stepping with him into the airy room. The metallic smell of spilled blood snapped me back to a war half-a-world away. The house had been closed up, the air conditioning turned off. Finger printing dust evidenced a thorough crime scene effort by the Sandy police department, with yellow evidence markers still denoting where photographers had collected mega-pixels worth of data.

"I'm curious why Judge O'Shea thought you could help, here," said Davidson, talking directly to me for the first time since I'd arrived.

"Probably the missing computer," I surmised. "I'm pretty good at sniffing out computer trails."

Davidson pursed his lips, about to say something, then thinking better of it reversing himself with a what-the-hell shrug.

"If you're a fraction as good with computers as you were half-an-hour ago with the Kendrick boys, I guess that says something."

Ah, you did get my video link on your cell phone, I thought.

"I shouldn't have provoked Lavar in court," I said. "I knew better, damn it."

"Yeah, I talked with Judge O'Shea when I got your video link. He called me actually, right after I sent it to him."

"My apology didn't go over as I'd hoped."

"You're lucky they didn't bring guns," he said, again looking carefully at my reaction. "Awh, you're packing, already? We don't need a damned vigilante on this case!"

"Nope, I'm unarmed," I responded. "Wouldn't have mattered, though."

"You scare the living hell out of me."

"Detective, I'm a deputy sheriff, reporting to you."

"Call me Henry," he said. "And you'd damned well better remember you're reporting to me, deputy."

"You're the boss. And I promise not to pull anyone else's pants down, today at least."

"That puts me *so much* more at ease."

"Glad I could help," I smiled. "Now, Henry, could you walk me through the crime, as best as you've been able to put it together?"

I liked Henry Davidson. Not full of himself. No hidden agendas. No guile. And he seemed to be a good judge of character, at least as far as his attitude toward me. In his position, I might slap myself in cuffs and haul my felon-baiting carcass off to jail. Yeah, Henry had definitely been around the block, yet he cut me a lot more slack than I felt I would have had our positions been reversed. Of course, Henry didn't know about my cyber war against Russia and China. Nor did he connect me to the storm brewing in Saudi Arabia. Come to think of it, maybe he truly sucked as a judge of character. Which meant I'd better keep an eye on him.

"No sign of forced entry," began Davidson.

"How much force would it take, though, for someone to make it past an old lady who answered her front door?"

"A lot less than it took you to slug Lamar Kendrick in the throat," he said.

"Point taken."

He walked from the entryway and through the kitchen, to a nook surrounded by bookshelves.

"Nothing disturbed in the kitchen," Davidson said. "So he didn't appear to drag her from the doorway to the living room, where we found the body."

"Either he cold cocked her at the door, or she had a reason to let him through the kitchen and into the living room."

"Or to the computer. Could have been a customer service rep."

"Then what?" I asked, anxious to get to the meat of the matter. He did get to the "meat" issue.

"At some point late Monday night, the UnSub strangled Olive and," Davidson pointed to two blood-smeared holes in the kitchen beam, "he severed both her little fingers and nailed them to that wooden crossbeam."

"Woof! That's an odd one," I said. "Have you run this against the FBI's databases?" The FBI's National Crime Information Center, called NCIC, as well as their National Center for the Analysis of Violent Crime or VICAP systems allowed law enforcement organizations to instantly spot trends nationwide.

Davidson paused a little too long before offering an answer he knew to be lacking. "We've got a relatively new police department, and I haven't stayed on top of this one."

"No problem." I brushed past Davidson and went to the computer desk to see if the murderer had taken OliveW Jenkins' wireless Internet router along with the computer. He hadn't, and it sat there on the floor, green connection light still on. I pulled out my "seriously modified" Android phone and brought up my CiscoCracker WiFi application. "While I'm cracking her router's encryption, let me run out to the car and get my laptop so we can log into NCIC and VICAP."

Moments later, I'd returned and saw Olive's encryption key on my phone's screen. I opened my laptop and joined the network.

"Tell me you're not breaking a bunch of laws, Morgan."

"Not if I'm a deputy sheriff solving a murder."

"You just hacked the security on a wireless modem?"

"Yep," I said as I typed the encryption key into my laptop. "Log into YouTube and have a fifteen year old kid show you how to do it from a car parked within 100 feet of any Cisco wireless router."

"You're kidding me!"

"Oh no. And if the kid in front of your house wants to, he can drop a keystroke-capture utility into every one of your computers and come back in a week to clean out your online bank account or buy cool stuff with your credit cards."

"What about accessing NCIC and VICAP?" Davidson added. "You're not law enforcement, and the last time I checked, only law enforcement had access to those systems."

"But I do have access to those systems," I said. "My status as a defense contractor and NSA cybercrime consultant has me cleared onto those systems. Now, let's see what they can tell us."

Davidson looked over my shoulder as I logged onto VICAP and entered the search parameters. All four of our eyes got pretty big, pretty fast.

"Morgan, what's going on here?"

"The little fingers are the signature of a serial killer who appears to roam the country, killing at will. This is news?"

"Yes, this is news!" gasped Davidson. He instantly had his cell phone speed dialing somebody pretty important. I could only hear his side of the conversation. "Detective Davidson here with a priority call…I don't give a damn if the Utah State employees *are* off on Friday; you get the former ambassador to China on the phone and tell him that his wife's great aunt was murdered by a serial killer!" He ended the call without waiting for a response.

"Even though the murderer stole Olive's computer, cracking her router encryption gave me everything I needed to know. While I download her incoming and outgoing email logs for last seven days, maybe you could check around for Olive's credit card bills."

"Why the credit card bills and why only seven days of email?" Davidson asked.

"Just a long shot. Maybe we can see some pattern if she made any online purchases. As for the seven days, most ISPs only log sending and receiving addresses for seven days. We won't know what they contained, but we'll have a complete list of email addresses with which she has had electronic contact."

"Uh, doesn't getting those email logs require some kind of court order?" Davidson asked.

"Yes it does," I answered. "You should probably have someone get a court order today, so the fruits of any search will be admissible in court. Might I suggest the order come from Judge O'Shea and that you timestamp it for one hour ago?"

"Got 'cha!"

Before I'd finished downloading the email logs, Davidson held out a hanging file folder he'd retrieved from the desk drawer.

"A very organized lady," he said. "Here's all her bills, stapled by category and sorted by month. What's with the computer?"

Davidson's phone rang, and he answered after checking his caller ID. "Sheriff Running…Yes, I *did* call the former ambassador's office with the news… No, sir, NCIC and VICAP confirm it, thanks to Morgan's accessing them, which we should have done instantly…Okay, I'll be right there."

"The sheriff bent about your message to the ambassador?" I asked.

Davidson flipped his phone shut and looked to be winding up for a high-speed pitch.

"You probably can't expense that," I said. His confused look deserved a more clear explanation. "The phone. You probably can't expense it if you smash it against the wall."

"Might get me abandoned, too. My daughter gave me the phone for Christmas."

"I take it the victim is not only a friend to Sherry O'Shea but she's also the Utah former First Lady's great aunt?"

"Was."

"Right. *Was* her great aunt."

"And she's no longer the Utah First Lady. But still, until now, we thought politics might be the motive," said Davidson.

"Yup. Serial killer puts a whole other light on it, now." I didn't ask the obvious question of *what the hell happened with NCIC/VICAP!* If he wanted to vent about it, he would.

Which did. "We're a relatively new police department, and sometimes that gets in our way, like linking with NCIC and VICAP." He paused before asking *his* obvious question. "You sure you've never been in law enforcement? You nailed this thing pretty fast."

"Let me tell you a story," I said. "I went to Andover with a kid who took the college board exam in chemistry, yet he'd never taken a chem class in his life. Later in the term, we had a school assembly announcing the National Merit Scholars. Not only did he make the list, but he ranked number one. On the way back to the dorm, I asked him how he did it, and why he took the risk of screwing up his college chances taking a test for which he had no training. His answer changed my whole outlook on life. He told me he just used common sense. The test had pictures of tubes and beakers, and the questions asked how they functioned together in various systems. So Henry, in answer to your question, I just use common sense."

"Just common sense?" Davidson said.

"And the Internet makes us all geniuses."

"What's your *common sense* telling you about this crime?" he asked.

"Right this moment, it's telling me we should take a close look at the killer's other victims to see what they have in common. Oh, and it also says your police chief should call in the FBI's behavioral analysis unit as fast as his dimpled little fingers can dial them."

Davidson noticed my laptop screen scrolling rapidly. "You breaking the law again?"

Olive Jenkins' email log displayed on my screen. "Absolutely not. I'm a deputy sheriff investigating a murder." I pulled a 16GB thumb drive out of my jacket pocket and plugged it into the computer's USB port. I drug the file folder I'd created for Olive's email onto the external drive icon. "I'll give you a copy of all Olive's incoming and outgoing email contacts, as well as my NCIC/VICAP download. Let's spend the evening with them and compare records in the morning. I take it the sheriff wants you somewhere?"

"The serial killer thing needs an immediate press conference," Davidson said. "I need to get right down to the office.

"Uh, I don't suppose the sheriff asked you to bring a spare sphincter?"

"Not at all. I don't know what kind of politics you're used to, but Sheriff

Running is an up-front guy who only wants me to do my job and who lets the consequences be damned."

What a novel idea, I thought. And I wondered if Sheriff Running belonged to the same club as Phoenix's Sheriff Joe Arpaio. That would sure make my task easier.

We arranged to meet for breakfast at eight o'clock A.M. and then hit Olive's ten o'clock funeral with the O'Sheas. I then handed him the USB drive and, after he locked up the crime scene and walked me past the yellow tape, watched him walk to his car as he muttered something about "common sense."

9
Digging Into a Murder

checked the time. Four o'clock, and I didn't have to be at the O'Sheas' until six. That gave me two hours to check Olive Jenkins' email traffic, which could be done just as easily sitting in my car by her house as my going back up to Snowbird. But before I so much as opened my car door, my Android text message tone started chiming, and the messages made my decision for me. My news-gathering agents started firing high-priority alerts like a Mexican drug lord whose finger locked on the trigger of an Uzi. The gist of the messages: Sino-Russian cyber war seemed to be a growing black hole that threatened to suck the rest of the world into its vortex. My white Mercedes made it up the mountain in record time, where I might visualize far more of the unfolding events than my laptop could display.

By 4:30 the LCD screen in my condo split itself between network news and three computer feeds. Virtually all server traffic in Eastern Europe and Asia had screeched to a blinding halt. The talking heads on FOX, CNN and MSNBC had finally found a breaking news story they could sink their perfectly capped and bright-white teeth into.

"The Secretary General of the United Nations has just issued a statement reiterating his previously stated position that the prospects for an all-out cyber attack and their associated cyber weapons should fall under the UN Advisory Board on Disarmament," said one reporter.

"Good stinking luck," I shot back at the screen. What could possibly make that power-mad little moron believe the UN or anybody else could control cyber weapons? WMDs and nuclear weapons required resources on a government scale. But an all-out cyber attack? That could be launched by a single student from his dorm or from his college library computers. Or from the basement of the Church of Scientology in San Francisco.

"...the UN Secretary General said recent breaches of critical government and industrial computer systems represent, and I quote, 'a clear and present threat to international security' unquote," continued the anchorman, now built up to a full head of steam. "Despite this threat, it is the consensus of senior White House officials who asked to remain anonymous, that current NATO war games tend to treat cyber-attack simulations as an afterthought.

"We are told that the Defense Advanced Research Projects Agency, or DARPA, is plowing roughly $30 million into developing its testing range for cyber-warfare countermeasures ...."

"Wow," I shouted to no one. "$30 million!" Thirty million dollars in the hands of government agencies might buy the equivalent of my San Francisco based server farm, for which I had spent less than a hundred thousand.

"Estonia Internet infrastructures were completely shut down by a sustained Russian denial of service attack in 2007," said the reporter. "Heli Tirmaa-Klaar, an advisor to the Estonian ministry of defense, said that because a cyber-attack can destabilize a country without sending forces across a border, it is a likely first-strike tactic."

Woah fat hippo! A first-strike tactic? First strike! Please don't let these morons start nuking each other because of me. Someone appeared to be feeding the press hogwash to further their own agenda. Obviously, the politicians started their scramble for power and taxpayer dollars, more out of habit to deflect public attention from their own incompetence than because they had the faintest idea how to do their jobs.

I doubted the poor devils in Russia or China could mount a coherent trip to the bathroom, let alone launch nukes. Anybody with a USB memory device plugged into an infected computer or who had a cell phone or iPod synched to that computer would spread my virus until the cows came home. All they had to do was reconnect their device into a new, virgin just-out-of-the-box computer, and the first time they accessed a static IP address registered in Russia or Asia, my mutating virus would wake up and beat them like a Persian rug on cleaning day in Mecca. And ironically, the news turned toward the Holy Land.

"In yet another growing controversy," said the breathless reporter, "Saudi news sources cannot shed light on the whereabouts of Mohammed Al Saud, who we reported last night had renounced Islam and its prophet Mohammed. King Abdullah has placed the entire country of Saudi Arabia on full military alert after demands by Iranian clerics for, and I quote, 'Al Saud's head' unquote."

This guy should get over his quote 'propensity for verbal punctuation' unquote. I sincerely hoped my old buddy Benny could keep his head. Andover tended not to countenance dummies, notwithstanding the public impression of George W. Bush, and I believed Benny must have a well-thought-out plan of action. Too bad I couldn't help solve the problem I'd created for him, but more time zones than I had on the fingers of one hand separated us. In the meantime, urgent problems demanded my attention: Olive Curtis Jenkins' email files.

I queued up a Webcam I'd installed on the ledge of my San Francisco apartment, so I could see any unusual activity in front of the Scientology building. No news. Things seemed calm. That would be my first signal that somebody, somewhere, knew diddly squat about cyber forensics. Olive's email beckoned me, though. Pat and Sherry would want a report, beyond the serial-killer aspect of the case.

Switching my brain off Saudi, Russian and Chinese demons in order to focus on the email involved the same kind of *displacement mentality* as doing the *New York Times* crossword puzzles. To be sure, my subconscious churned all the chess pieces of those battles, coming up with scenarios twenty and thirty moves toward end game, but Olive's emails gave my conscious self something on which to fixate, and allowed me to release the other problems for solution by my inner battle management system. And with that release came an emotional peace I in no way deserved, given the crap storm I'd projected all over the world. Ah the wonders of compartmentalization.

I copied the email logs from Olive's ISP onto a spare USB thumb drive and then slid it into a protected server located under a desk but within view of my four-in-one LCD big screen TV. I didn't dare open any of the files on my laptop, just for security reasons. My server didn't run a Macintosh or PC-based operating system, so virus infections built into Olive's incoming email wouldn't know what to do on my server. Sure, I ran a variant of Linux, but I'd created a closed virtual system that simply couldn't access any of the files or resources on the computer. And if such a virus tried to do something, my system would go into ICE mode and let my in-circuit emulator (or ICE system) watch the offending commands instruction by instruction. Since I'd written virus routines that could tell if they were being watched by a debugger running on the same processor and then go into hiding for another day, my ICE system just looked over the shoulder of the executing processor clock-tick by clock-tick. As far as the program knew, it ran without hindrance from a debugger. But my ICE system slowed down the system clock so I could watch the magic happen in minutes that would have normally taken mere microseconds. That's why Russian and Chinese systems without an ICE debugging technology would never *ever* find my attacking viri.

To add insult to the Sino-Soviet injuries, if they'd ripped off the Intel ICE system, I'd provided some microcode under contract to the NSA that would throw the Intel ICE processors into an unsecure acquisition mode for long enough that my virus would infect *them*. Which means that in less than a second after trying to de-ICE a server carrying my virus, an Intel ICE system would magically transform into a terrific boat anchor or super-size paper weight. But it would no longer be a workable ICE unit.

So with the protection of my system pretty well insured, I sat down to look through a dead woman's email, starting with the most recent correspondence and working backward. Over the next half hour, I drew some conclusions.

Most interesting, Olive sent and received *a lot* of email. In just seven days, a good three of which she'd been dead, she'd corresponded with over a hundred people. Equally interesting, Olive appeared quite computer savvy. Most neophytes used their broadband carrier's services or one of the free email services from MSN, AOL or Yahoo. Olive's email came to olive@ouroots.com. I did a "whois" search and discovered that she'd registered and hosted her own domain, *www.ouroots.com*. Interesting. The site appeared to be a genealogy database of her ancestors.

Since I'd captured her outgoing email server password earlier in the day, I used it to access her ISP's statistics for visitors to her site. Again, very impressive. This little lady's site garnered thousands of hits a week. Not big time for the likes of Amazon or Google, but certainly respectable for a niche genealogy researcher. What little I knew about genealogy could be etched on the head of a pin. Most of her email probably dealt with genealogy correspondence, so the best hope for finding my serial killer would be to see if the NCIC and VICAP databases showed any genealogy interest on the part of the other victims.

Half an hour later, I'd found no correlation with the other victims. Besides being mid-to-older women, no other common socio-psycho-economic trends matched up. The clock next to my webcam shot of San Francisco and the Church of Scientology showed 5:30 PM, which meant I needed to hustle down the mountain for a 6:00 PM dinner at the O'Sheas'. And as a dinner guest, I needed to make a stop on the way to pick up a gift for my hostess. Maybe some flowers, or chocolates. No unusual activity outside the Scientology building and no newsflashes of Sino-Soviet nuke activity meant I could take a couple of hours for dinner with my friends.

After changing into slacks and a blue blazer, I drove down the mountain and detoured into a shopping center to pick up a box of See's chocolates. Then to O'Sheas', arriving exactly at six.

10
Guess Who's Coming to Dinner?

herry O'Shea met me at the door with the same kind of enthusiasm she might have bestowed on visiting royalty, and treated my box of See's chocolate as if each morsel contained a priceless gem. Her surprisingly chipper mood caught me unprepared, until she announced, "We have other guests for dinner, tonight."

My first reaction verged on exasperation that Sherry's own form of displacement activity might have devolved into matchmaking. Again. Why is it that women simply don't believe that a man can be truly happy without a soul mate? And why can't Sherry just have one person over for dinner, without rounding up the most recent stray woman to come into her acquaintance? Not to paint Sherry in a poor light, the women to whom she continuously tried to introduce me sparkled rather nicely. Educated, athletic and even good looking, sometimes drop-dead gorgeous. The problem had to do with my emotional fragility. Simply, I couldn't open up the part of my heart that had been exclusively reserved for Annie.

She must have seen every one of those thoughts, because she poked me in the stomach with the box of chocolates while grabbing my arm with her free hand. "Come and meet a couple of men you might have heard about."

Men? Men I might have heard about? I must have breathed a sigh of relief, because she chuckled as we entered the O'Sheas' "great" room. In front of the fireplace with Hizonor stood two men I'd definitely heard about, both of whom served as United States Senators from Utah: Gordon Kimball and Robert Hyde.

I felt like looking around to see if they had U.S. Marshals with them to facilitate my arrest for declaring war on Russia and China. Judge O'Shea posed as if for a photo. His antennae had evidently retracted, because he didn't immediately start cross-examining me.

"Morgan," O'Shea bellowed. "I'd like you to meet a couple of old friends."

"Senator Hyde," I said, shaking his hand first. And then, "Senator Kimball. A pleasure to finally meet you." Senator Kimball took my hand while giving me an oddly familiar look. Before I could ask Kimball if we somehow *had* met in the past, Senator Hyde piped in.

"How's Tommy Trout?" asked Senator Hyde.

"You have a remarkable memory, Senator," I said.

"Who's Tommy Trout?" Hizonor asked, still in his courtroom bellow.

"Trouts lived across the street from us down on Gatehouse," I said. "Years ago, just after Watergate, the Trouts lived in California down the street from the Hydes. Their son Tommy had the school assignment to do a paper on Nixon and the Watergate scandal, so Tom Trout had his son walk down the street and ask Bob Hyde to give him a summary."

Senator Kimball jumped in. "If you'll remember, my esteemed colleague's law firm swam in the vortex of that storm. In fact, Bob Hyde received a good deal of publicity speculating that he fed reporter Bob Woodward information under the pseudonym of 'Deep Throat.'"

"Of course, in 2005 Woodward identified former assistant FBI director Mark Felt as 'deep throat,'" said Hyde.

"Unbeknownst to his teacher," I continued, "Tommy Trout got help on his high school paper from one of the principal figures in Watergate."

Senator Hyde drolly added, "And he got a 'C' on the paper!"

Everyone's laughter thoroughly broke the ice for the evening. I'd previously shared my friendship with the Trouts and my knowledge of the Watergate story with Senator Hyde during one of his Middle East fact-finding tours. Since I was a Navy SEAL, they made me wear a suit and head the Senator's security detail. It quite surprised me that he remembered me *and* the story. Annie and I lived across the street from the Trouts, and Tom had told me about Tommy's paper, which I had the unusual opportunity to confirm when I met the Senator.

"Morgan," said Senator Hyde. "I understand you've given up risking your life around the world in favor of waging cyber-warfare from the comfort of your living room."

Again, I felt like looking around for U.S. Marshals who'd accompanied two United States senators to make a very public arrest. But no, not even a seasoned politician could be that good an actor. Nevertheless, I knew my answer had better be convincing or Judge O'Shea's built-in lie detector would fire all kinds of alarms. Truth turned out to be my best defense.

"Absolutely, Senator," I replied. "A lot less wear and tear on my carcass."

And more wear and tear on multiple carcasses in China, Russia and Saudi Arabia.

Sherry O'Shea jumped in to rescue me from further discussion. "Morgan has taken a break from his business to help us find out what happened to dear Olive."

"I guess that's why we're all here," said Senator Kimball. "At least to some extent."

"Morgan," said Judge O'Shea, "Both of these men have tender feelings about Olive Jenkins, and have come out to say their farewells at her funeral tomorrow. I knew you wouldn't object if Sherry and I shared dinner tonight with three of our dearest friends."

Object? I thought. *Other than briefly thinking my life and freedom might be coming to an end, no problem!*

"I'm honored to be on your A-list tonight," I said.

Sherry then busied herself shooing us into the dining room, adjacent to the O'Sheas' great room and past an authentic Remington bronze of the *Bronco Buster*. While tens of thousands of Frederick Remington's first and most famous sculpture decorated homes and businesses around the country, I knew for a fact that this particular piece came from the first batch produced in 1895. One of its companion pieces, a gift to president Teddy Roosevelt, decorated the Oval Office. As we passed the piece, Senator Kimball did a double take. He must have seen the White House version.

Judge O'Shea seated Sherry at one end of the gigantic oak table and then took his position at the other end. The senators sat opposite each other, and I took the spot just to the right of Senator Hyde. Symbolically, that was…just about right. The China place settings carried an Americana motif and featured none other than a Frederick Remington scene. While no place setting occupied the table opposite me, Sherry had left the chair as a conspicuous reminder that she *could* have filled it with a female dinner companion for me. Bless you, Sherry O'Shea, for never giving up. Just as I started to wonder who might be serving us, the double-swinging door to the kitchen opened and a woman dressed in white brought our salads.

"Thank you, Marta," Sherry said. "Senators Hyde and Kimball, and Morgan, I'd like to introduce Marta Molina, who lives with us and gives me a hand around the house."

Marta nodded ever so politely and served Sherry first.

"Molina means windmill, in Spanish," I offered. "Pleased to meet you, Marta."

"She's certainly a whirling dervish around here," Patrick said. "You speak Spanish as well as Arabic, Morgan?"

"Just a smattering," I said. Marta nodded shyly as she served the rest of us, and departed silently.

"Marta's husband is one of Daddy's little felons," said Sherry after Marta had gone back into the kitchen. "We're sponsoring her for U.S. citizenship, but she's here so she can visit her husband in Draper."

"Daddy's little felons?" queried Senator Kimball.

"I sent him to prison," said Judge O'Shea. "Wrong place, wrong time, wrong crowd for a nice kid who got in way over his head. In return for his testimony against a very not-so-nice drug importer who threatened to enslave Marta in a Nevada bordello if her husband didn't stay quiet, I promised him we'd look after his wife until he could support her."

"No wonder you have such low recidivism numbers," said Senator Hyde.

"So Daddy's little felons refers to…?" began Kimball.

"That just refers to the people in whose lives I spend my days doing interventions," said the judge.

"They're just Daddy's little felons," smiled Sherry. Then she asked, "Morgan, how did you enjoy *your* day with them?" She seemed to notice nobody had taken a bite of their salad, so she made a point of spearing a kiwi slice and eating it.

"I'd forgotten how terribly entertaining Hizonor could be," I answered. "He even got in a Judge Roy Bean sentencing for a wife-beater who tried to kidnap one of his ex-wife's children."

Both senators nodded knowingly as they ate their salads. Senator Kimball had more than once read of Judge O'Shea's colorful diatribes to a nominee appearing before the judicial committee, asking said nominee to comment on the O'Shea/Bean doctrine. The questions turned out to be more rhetorical and designed to lighten up the proceedings, although one Supreme Court nominee opined that such a pronouncement might be grounds for an appeal. But that particular nomination didn't make it out of committee for a Senate vote.

"Morgan?" said Senator Hyde, between bites. "Did I understand Patrick correctly that you speak Arabic?"

"Yes I do, Senator." *Brain like a trap,* I thought. And I correctly sensed the direction of the Senator's question. Damned if I knew how to derail him, though. But I had to give it the best shot. "A lot of misspent time in Iraq and Saudi Arabia I'd like to forget."

"What do you think of the Mohammed Al Saud fracas?" he asked.

Well let's see, Senator. I planted a virus in his computer and composed the letter allegedly sent under his name, and the poor devil got a lemon…and decided to leave the keys in it. The jury is still out whether or not the Middle East will go up in smoke. Whatever I *did* answer, it had better not get Judge O'Shea's antennae quivering. Once again, the whole truth and nothing but the truth.

"I went to Andover with Benny," I began. "That's what we called Mohammed bin Faisal Al Saud back in 1984 at Andover."

"Really!" exclaimed Sherry. "You know him?"

"Not well, but I remember him as a very sharp kid out to make a difference." The "I'd like to forget" line would let any modestly sensitive person know I didn't want to do a travelogue on clandestine warfare. Unfortunately, Senator Hyde didn't want to hear any war stories.

"Senator Kimball and I both know his father," said Hyde. "Turki bin Faisal Al Saud served as the ambassador to the United States until December of 2006, and he got wide accolades as ambassador to Britain."

"I can see some very positive signs in Saudi Arabia," added Kimball. "In June 2008, King Abdullah called for a dialogue between all religions. I think Benny, as you called him, has some fine tutoring from the royal family."

"Unless his last little escapade pushes the whole region over the edge," said Hyde.

I started to choke on a piece of salad, likely a guilty reaction to my culpability at inciting an Islamic civil war. "Sorry," I wheezed and took a sip of water.

Ever the conscientious hostess, Sherry took turns letting the alpha males around the table perform. Jokes, anecdotes, family stories and assorted other small talk took us through the salad, shrimp cocktail, gazpacho soup, and the finest beef tenderloin I can ever remember eating. Each time we saw her, Marta warmed up a little more. Clearly, she took pride in the gazpacho and beef, prepared as only someone who grew up in Argentina could manage it. Dessert proved to be her crowning glory as she set Dulce de Leche before each of us. Out of courtesy to the two Mormon senators, the O'Sheas didn't even offer coffee or wine, but the Dulce de Leche should have been against everyone's religion. The caramel-like syrup, prepared from sweetened milk, covered a pastry topped with fresh strawberries. Don't cry for me Argentina, because my arteries happily clogged away like they didn't care whether or not I saw tomorrow.

Always the consummate stage director, Sherry waited until dessert before bringing the conversation around to Olive.

"Any news on poor Olive?" she asked.

Indeed, the reason for our dinner together, the reason both senators came to town, boiled down to Olive Jenkins and her funeral tomorrow. Sherry O'Shea dared not risk spoiling everyone's dinner with a discussion that might lead to crime forensics. But now, on the downhill side of dessert, it came time for me to earn my supper.

"I think Sheriff Running is about to hold a press conference," I began. "Olive appears to be the victim of a serial killer."

"We don't generally have any kind of killings not related to drugs or gang activity," said the judge.

"The sheriff evidently hadn't done a VICAP/NCIC search of similar crimes," I said. "I have access to the system because of my NSA contract work, and ran a query based upon one unique crime detail. This particular serial killer has been quite active across the country for several years." *Please don't ask that detail, Sherry.* But she did.

"What detail?" Sherry O'Shea chirped.

"A particular mutilation," I said, and then quickly added, "of a non-sexual nature. This wasn't a sex crime Sherry, and the particular *signature* used by the killer uniquely distinguished this crime and identified it with others."

"How come this just came to light?" asked Senator Kimball.

"I don't know for sure. The Salt Lake County Sheriff's Department could have moved a little faster connecting the dots. Given Olive's relationship to the former ambassador's wife, the two most likely motives appeared to be either robbery or politics."

"Couldn't that still be the case?" pressed Kimball.

"Anything's possible, but the peculiar circumstances of this crime make those less probable scenarios," I said. "I recommended that Sheriff Running make a formal request to have the FBI's Behavioral Analysis Unit get involved right away. In the meantime, the local detective in charge of the case is following up on other leads."

"Do we have anything to go on?" asked Kimball, obviously running point on the legal issues.

"The computer theft has me quite curious," I answered. "I've downloaded Olive's email log files from her Internet service provider, in the hope that some pattern of activity might shed some light on things."

"That's quick work," said Kimball.

Judge O'Shea jumped in: "I signed that court order *before* Morgan accessed the log files."

Thank you, Your Honor. And thank you for not winking at me in front of the senator. Since Sheriff Running had deputized me earlier in the day, my accessing the ISP's email log files without a court order could have jeopardized the evidence value any subsequent discoveries. It looked like Detective Davidson hadn't wasted any time getting a court order in front of Judge O'Shea.

"To keep things totally honest here, Senator Kimball, we did not take the time to serve the ISP with a search warrant. I used some clandestine expertise to immediately get that email log file."

"Actually Morgan," said Kimball, smiling and giving me that same wry look I noticed the when we shook hands, "I am familiar with some of your clandestine expertise. I serve on the Senate intelligence committee and recall an interesting briefing on some of your cyber-warfare exploits in Iraq and... *elsewhere.*"

"But we can't talk about that here, can we." My turn to smile. Bringing down Iraq, Afghanistan and even Indian and Pakistan command and control systems from virus kernels launched from memory devices in peripheral printers and disk array flash memory generated some notoriety for me in certain small circles. Of course Senator Kimball would have been thoroughly briefed.

"No, I suppose we can't talk about some of your more entertaining adventures," said the senator. Then that smile, again. "Unless we want to chat about a certain video you put online this afternoon, after you left Judge O'Shea's courtroom."

The senators and both O'Sheas smiled hard enough to blind me with light reflected from their teeth. I really should have taken a look at my video encounter before coming to dinner. Detective Davidson had indeed mentioned sending the video to Judge O'Shea, even chatting with him about it.

"So my little leprechaun friend had a little pre-function screening before dinner?" I rhetorically asked.

"More of a premier, actually," smirked Sherry. "Great sound quality and production values, too."

"And good enough to prove self defense," O'Shea mirrored his wife's grin. "Not to mention restraint on your part."

"No matter how hard I tried *not* to escalate the situation," I shrugged, "I didn't try hard enough."

"Morgan," injected Senator Kimball, holding up his own Android. "You seem to have coaxed some stuff from *your* Android I can't even begin to get mine to do. But all that aside, from what I saw, you could just as easily have badly injured or even killed those two men."

"It's amazing what you can do with a decent operating system," I noted, holding up my own cell phone. "This isn't your ordinary Android."

"Those *three* men," added Senator Hyde, correcting Kimball's number. "Remember the guy sneaking up from the back?"

"I wonder how many other people are seeing Lavar's and Lamar's little tactical miscalculation?" I said, resisting the urge to thumb my cell phone's power switch and check out my video-streaming website site.

"As of two hours ago, just before dinner, a couple hundred or so," began the perpetual bean-counting Senator Hyde.

"Two hundred isn't too embarrassing for them," I jumped in.

"Excuse me," said Senator Hyde. "That's two-hundred thousand views. I think you're a best-seller for streaming cell phone videos."

"Ooh, did I say their names?"

"Worse," said Hizonor. "They said their own names. Clearly. First and last."

"Two-hundred thousand, huh?" I said, stunned.

"Probably double that by now," said Sherry O'Shea. "Maybe you can make a similar recording of Olive's murderer's confession."

"Ooh," said Senator Kimball. "Diabolical."

"Not to mention a severe pollution of the jury pool," said Judge O'Shea.

"Well, at least I'm not on camera," I said in a frivolous flight of wishful thinking.

"True," began the judge. "But your Twitter page not only has your picture, but the background photo has all six-foot-plus of you in your BDUs. Nice photo, Morgan!"

Suddenly, the dynamics of this whole evening changed. My dinner companions knew I'd had a busy day, yet they'd waited. For what, though? To see if I'd bring it up, myself? Perhaps do a little alpha-male chest thumping, or shameless self promotion? Or did my hosts want to give the senators a chance to take stock on their own of a relative stranger? Maybe they needed to know whether or not they could trust me. As if sensing my social computations, Senator Kimball laid out his own agenda.

"Morgan, sorry to turn you into the evening's entertainment," Kimball said. "When we're done here, could you possibly give me a ride back to my house. I need to get your opinion on some classified data that I believe you're cleared to discuss."

Since no U.S. Marshalls appeared yet to cuff me, it couldn't be the Russians or the Chinese. Or Benny, for that matter. Had the senator premeditated this encounter? If not, then my *gift and/or calling* that continually put me in the vortex of any given storm still functioned perfectly.

"Sure, Senator," I said. "You didn't bring a car here, yourself?"

"I'll call my driver and tell him a United States Navy SEAL will be seeing me safely home," he said and then winked.

So probably not premeditated, then, if his driver planned to pick him up. I didn't get any particular vibes of premeditation from the O'Sheas *or* from Senator Hyde. If they *had* pre-planned this, then I certainly wouldn't want to play poker with any of them.

Sherry O'Shea herded us into the great room and served herbal tea herself, evidently having given Marta the rest of the evening off. Again no coffee, in deference to the two Mormon senators. She also herded the conversation back to Olive, and the funeral tomorrow.

"What can you learn from Olive's email?" asked Sherry.

"Actually, it's just her email log file, and they only keep them for one week," I said. "But we can learn the senders and the recipients, as well as their frequency of communication."

"But if the murderer is a serial killer…" began Judge O'Shea, hanging with the implication.

"We don't know how the serial killer selects victims," I answered. "That's why the NCIC/VICAP database could give us some clues. Sure, it's a long shot, but every avenue should be pursued. That's why I felt we needed the FBI's behavior analysis help right away."

"Gordon," said Senator Hyde, "I think a request from both Utah members of the Senate could move the FBI to expedite Sheriff Running's request."

"I'm texting my chief of staff as we speak," said Kimball, who had been two-thumbing a message below our line of sight.

It briefly occurred to me to sneak out my own cell phone and surreptitiously suck the address book out of the senator's. Very briefly, since who knows what his buddies in the intelligence community had given him in the way of countermeasures? Besides, sneaking Senator Kimball's phone data would be wrong. I'd stepped so far over that line as to make the question moot. Best though, not to make an enemy out of someone through whom I might need to approach the president for a pardon. Or pass a retroactive law exonerating me from major felonies.

"We greased the skids for Morgan to work with Sheriff Running and Detective Davidson," said the judge. "Senator Kimball, maybe you could let the FBI BAU know he's on the team, too."

"My guess is, they already do." The senator couldn't restrain a snort and continued to compose a text message. "But I'll add that note."

At the moment Lavar and Lamar accosted me in the Grand America parking garage, it seemed like a really good idea to protect myself with a video record of the event. In retrospect, maybe I should have used some ruse to take a policeman to my car with me. Nobody, not even jailhouse denizens like the Kendricks, would risk assaulting someone in front of a cop. Too late, now. That particular cow had roared out of the barn and jumped over the moon. While

Senator Kimball finished texting, I did take the time to log onto my streaming account and see how many people found Lavar and Lamar entertaining.

"Four-hundred-thirty-seven thousand!" I gasped.

"Morgan?" asked Sherry.

"Sorry. Nothing." I put the phone back into my jacket pocket.

Of course, she got it. Sherry turned her face away from me, but not before I saw the difficulty she had to keep from laughing out loud. Poor Lavar and Lamar probably couldn't show their faces in the local bars, motorcycle shops or even Seven-Elevens. The least I could have done would have been to put them in the hospital. It would have kept them out of the public eye until the snickering had died down.

My larger problem, notwithstanding ending life as they'd know it for Lavar and Lamar, dealt with the FBI and my now-close association with Senators Hyde and Kimball. These guys had just come to town for a funeral. And now, by association, their reputations would be tainted not *if* but *when* my responsibility for the first world cyber war came out. Why did I ever think I could launch such an attack and escape detection? Yes, the day of reckoning would certainly come, and it would take all my intellect not to splash disgrace all over my friends and *their* friends. Worse yet, I dared not tell them now, lest they become, like Richard Nixon and immediate staff, accessories *after the fact*. Sure, they could immediately turn me in, but without free access to my computer, nobody could possibly launch a massive virus inoculation to bring the world back to normal. Because if they had their man behind bars, me being *their man*, no law enforcement agency in the world would let me anywhere near a computer.

Sorry, Henry Kissinger. My trying to 'rescue the element of choice from the pressure of circumstance' ended up in the crapper, I thought to myself. I had no choices here. We chatted for a few more minutes about next steps in the investigation. Everyone agreed with my assessment that the killer, serial or not, might well be at or near tomorrow's funeral. Given the prominent funeral attendees, Senator Hyde offered to get his chief of staff to arrange an unofficial pool of television news footage for use by the police and the FBI. Each senator gave me his super-secret text message number, in case something broke in the case that needed their muscle. Judge O'Shea asked Senator Kimball—a member of the judiciary committee and a likely nominee to the U. S. Supreme Court if ever a Republican found his way into the White House again—whether or not he could preside at the trial of Olive's murderer, should there ever be an arrest. To his credit, the senator didn't blow smoke, and told Hizonor he'd most definitely have to recuse himself from the case. O'Shea already knew this, but he exaggerated bitter disappointment at *not* being able to pronounce a Judge Roy Bean-type of death sentence.

Sherry thanked such distinguished guests profusely for honoring her home. I knew she meant the senators. My slot on the distinguished-guest pecking order sat closer to the O'Sheas' gardener than to the halls of Congress. That the senators would show up at all tonight testified of the genuine regard in which they held Patrick and Sherry. I needed to find a way to tactfully get my friends and former neighbors to explain their relationship with Hyde and Kimball. Sure, the senators came to town for a funeral certain to be attended by the former ambassador, who'd been in Utah anyway and couldn't quite manage to get reliable air traffic vectors for a personal trip back into China. And while Patrick cut a wide swath locally, it made no sense at all that they would *both* spend an evening in the O'Shea home unless they had a close personal bond.

With that question still ricocheting around my skull, we excused ourselves, Senator Hyde to his car and Senator Kimball and me to my car.

11
Letters of Marque

 waited to start the car until the senator had buckled himself in. As we pulled around the cul-de-sac and passed in front of their house, both Sherry and Patrick waived to us from the front porch.

"Where to, Senator?" I asked.

"If we were in a handcart instead of your Mercedes, then I'd say we're going to hell," muttered Senator Kimball. He then, however, gave me his address. And due to the Salt Lake City street numbering convention based on compass directions from Temple Square, I knew exactly how to get him there. Our conversation then turned to his anxiety over the Russia-China cyber war.

"Hell in a handcart?" I asked.

"Morgan, I don't think anybody in our government knows what's going on over there. When Patrick and Sherry said you'd be coming to dinner tonight, given what I know you've done for the NSA, it occurred to me you might have some insights."

Well yeah, Senator, as a matter of fact… almost slid to my tongue. *Of course I had some sinking insights!* But I made the decision right there, whatever the consequences, that I would not lie to the senator. If he came right out and asked the right question, like did I write and deploy the virus currently attacking everything in Asia, then I'd own up to it. Even by the strictest definition of a lie, which made headlines back when Annie and I lived in Utah and heard the Mormon prophet define a lie as *any communication the intent of which is to deceive*, I slowly began the discussion to ascertain at what level the senator had most concern.

"Senator Kimball, you know of course that we've been in a full-scale cyber war with both China and Russia for at least fifteen years?"

"And I'm also aware of your adventures in the basements of the NSA when you dropped your magic box behind the fire wall and showed the director his systems had already been breached by the Chinese," said Kimball. "It's a small circle, but you're still famous in it."

"Could I speak frankly, Senator?"

"Wouldn't have it any other way."

"The current cyber crime act has completely tied American businesses' hands and made it impossible for us to fight these attacks," I said.

"Tell me something I don't know." The senator didn't seem surprised by my statement. Given his participation in drafting the legislation, my assessment of *his baby* might well have been a slap in his face. I decided to be deliberate, nonthreatening in tone and content.

"My computer servers are attacked hundreds of times a day, attempts to take them over with dozens of passwords used by lazy systems administrators. When I look at the system error logs, fully ninety-five percent of the attacks come from either China or Eastern Europe."

"So you build a good firewall to keep them from getting into your systems."

"Suppose Senator, that you and your wife are awakened in the middle of the night by someone trying to pick your door locks, or raise your windows. What do you do? Do you say, 'Awh honey, go back to sleep. Our locks and windows are impenetrable.' Or do you make sure the intruder hears a double-ought shell being chambered into your twelve-gauge shotgun?"

"I'd call the police," said the senator too quickly, before the logical implication hit him.

"Okay, you call the police. So who am I going to call to report attempted computer break-ins? Or more precisely, thousands of break-ins? Thousands *per day*?"

"There are some practicalities involved here," he said. "But what is the alternative?"

"I'm glad you didn't tell me to call the FBI. But what is the cyber-equivalent of chambering a round into my shot gun?"

"You're saying there is no credible threat of retaliation available to you."

"Correct, Senator." My answer mixed exasperation with sarcasm. "Your cyber-crime bill calls any threatened retaliation a restraint of interstate commerce, punishable by a stiff fine and years in prison. And international law makes the declaration of war an exclusive prerogative of the government."

"Again, Morgan, what is the alternative? Should we turn every computer user into the equivalent of a vigilante? Because unlike someone breaking into your house, who you have every right to shoot dead while the intruder is on your property, with cyber crime, he can break into your house while he's still in his house. For you to attack him, you'd have to go to his house, possibly through a number of homes occupied by innocent and unsuspecting people. And that's where your analogy fails."

"So we use another analogy, Senator. Have you considered *privateers*?"

"Like in the Revolutionary War?" he asked.

"Exactly. We almost completely financed our side of the Revolutionary War from privateering proceeds. Letters of Marque were issued, allowing men like John Paul Jones and Jean Lafitte to attack British shipping and either arm the Continental Army or sell their booty at French auctions and contribute financially to the war. In fact, privateering won the war for us."

"I wouldn't go that far…" began the senator. I had to interrupt.

"You're a numbers man. Consider that the Continental Navy had only 64 ships. Compare this to 1,697 privateers. The Continental Navy captured 196 enemy ships, compared to 2283 captured by privateers. In a survey by George Washington, in 1776 he had 9 rounds of ammunition per man to fight his war. By 1777, privateers had secured over two million pounds of gunpowder and saltpeter. You don't believe me, google the American Merchant Marine at War Web site."

"So you're saying…?" The senator raised his eyebrows. Somehow, he'd found a scrap of paper in his jacket pocket and repeated the privateering numbers to me to make sure he had them right. After confirming them, I continued.

"Why not issue Letters of Marque that, under certain circumstances and with appropriate oversight and performance bonds, legalize some cyber privateering?"

"What would constitute an attack?"

"How about five attempts to take over a server from one IP address, for starters?"

"That could start a full-scale cyber war," Kimball said.

"With all due respect, we're already *in* a full-scale cyber war senator." I paused, considering my own attack. I didn't have a Letter of Marque. But another analogy came to the fore. "This afternoon, Sheriff Running deputized me. Rather than calling them privateers, why not deputize some U. S. Marshalls?"

"But U. S. Marshalls cannot operate outside the borders of our country. Otherwise, they'd be violating the sovereignty of those countries."

"But if they're in hot pursuit and stay within our borders, they could engage in a cross-border firefight, couldn't they?"

"That is a political hot potato all by itself." The senator paused, clearly thinking of legal issues beyond my education or experience. "International laws governing hot pursuit concern the law of the sea and are addressed by UN convention."

"And the United States pursued Pancho Villa into Mexico," I added.

"Yes, that and the capture of Adolf Eichman by the Israelis in Argentina is still widely held to be a violation of international law," added Kimball. "Not to mention how the world is dealing with Somali pirates, or our finally nailing bin Laden."

"That's easy. We need a new law, or at least an unambiguously stated reality."

"Ah, the equivalent of the Monroe Doctrine?" Then the senator shook his head. "I don't think the United States can lead that charge. Our actions in the Middle East have given us a tremendous international PR problem."

"And your cyber-crime statute has made all those arguments moot. Like I said, we are under serious attack, yet our hands are tied."

Senator Kimball spoke after several seconds of contemplation, attempting to offer *some* hope. "One initiative put forth by the secretary-general of the United Nations is to put cyber warfare and cyber weapons to the list of arms falling under disarmament matters."

"That's not only dumb, but plays right into the hands of conspiracy theorists who would correctly claim this infringes on American sovereignty."

"I agree with the sovereignty argument, but dumb?"

"You ever hear of a guy named Larry Ellison?" I asked.

"Hear of him!" Senator Kimball laughed out loud. "He once said the only way he'd see the Oracle database system delivered to the Soviet Union would be if it functioned in the head of an Uncle Sam ICBM."

"That's the guy." I couldn't help but laugh, too. "Since we're talking metaphors, let me give you an Ellison analogy that applies to disarmament philosophy and cyber weapons."

"Something tells me this is going to be a pip," said Kimball.

"Good guess!" I said. "It has to do with economies of scale. If you had a modern jet fighter, it might take you the better part of a year to learn to fly it, but you could kill everyone in your neighborhood in one pass. On the other hand, you could learn to use a machine gun in a few minutes, but it would take you the better part of a week to eliminate all your neighbors. It takes the resources of a government to produce jet fighters and weapons of mass destruction, and that's why those things easily fall under the realm of disarmament and the United Nations. But anybody with a machine shop can build an assault rifle, and no serious United Nations effort can or ever will be mounted to include such weapons in under the disarmament umbrella. You with me so far?"

"That Ellison is a piece of work," said Kimball. "You're saying that cyber warfare can't possibly fall under the realm of the United Nations and disarmament because …?"

I quickly completed the thought: "…because anybody with a laptop and an Internet connection could create and launch weapons of mass-cyber-disruption."

"You paint a bleak picture, Morgan."

"It shouldn't be a surprise to anybody. The late science fiction author Frank Herbert told us all about this landscape back in the early seventies. In his novel *Dune*, and even before that, he pointed out that society will dramatically change when advanced technology at the disposal of any given individual can be used by that individual to destroy an entire city or even a planet."

Kimball audibly sighed. "Back to the cyber war between Russia and China."

Careful, Morgan, I thought to myself. *Say too much and the senator could ask the question to which you have chosen not lie.*

"Senator, I contend that an individual started that war," I said, committing myself to a forthright position, black-or-white, no shades of uncertainty. If he could read between the lines and pin me down, so be it. "That individual most certainly reacted to being attacked by servers in that part of the world."

Silence from my passenger seat. We drove to within a block of the senator's home before he spoke again.

"How do we find this individual?" he finally asked.

"I don't want him found, senator." Boy, now there sat a statement that lent itself to multiple parsings.

"Why on earth not!"

"What are you going to do to him?" I couldn't help but laugh. "Shoot him? Give him a medal? Or both?"

"But what if Beijing and Moscow start dropping nukes on each other over this? Maybe identifying the source could calm them all down."

We pulled up in front of the address he'd given me, and I put the car in park. From my pocket, I retrieved my phone and tapped my text message icon. The large, high-resolution screen immediately filled with news feed headlines.

"I've been following this story since last night, Senator." I held the screen so we could both see it. "Right now, those poor devils can't complete a cell phone call, let alone access their command-and-control systems to launch ICBMs. About all they can do is yell at each other and the rest of the world over analog phone lines."

"A better question, then Morgan," he said. "What can or should the United States of America do about this?"

"In a perfect world, Senator, the president would address the United Nations General Assembly and acknowledge the reality of the current cyber war. I'd say Russia and China have been on the attack for over a decade, and that somebody, somewhere, has had enough. The president should suggest that if an individual within the United States had launched this attack, that in exchange for a neutralizing virus the culprit would earn a full presidential pardon. And if the individual happened to live or work outside the United States, that we would guarantee his safety and future prosperity within this country."

"This is way, way off the charts," said Kimball. "How would the culprit even respond? To whom would he respond? And how would the people to whom he responded even know to take him seriously? You know we'd be deluged with people taking credit."

"I'm sure some smart guys could figure that out."

"How about you?" he said. "Could you figure it out?"

"Yep," I quickly answered. "But I won't."

"You won't?" The senator's startled look appeared on the verge of revelation. Had I gone too far? Did I fit the profile of a serial killer who really wanted to get caught? I could see the right question formulating, quickly followed by the realization that a wrong answer from me could destroy his political career. His brilliant tutor in such things might well have been Bill don't-ask-don't-tell Clinton. No dummy, Senator Kimball asked again, "Why not?"

"Simple, Senator. I won't because there is no possibility in the world that our president would ever put such a scenario into play."

"But if he did? Would you help?"

"If you ever sit before the United States Senate in a confirmation hearing for the U.S. Supreme Court, at some point in time you'll have to brush off a question as being hypothetical. Senator Kimball, that is a hypothetical question with which I just don't care to deal." I extended my hand, and he shook it. "Good night, Senator. I'll see you tomorrow morning at Olive's funeral."

12
A Break in the Case

etective Davidson once again beat me to our scheduled appointment, this time for our 8:00 AM breakfast at Mimi's Cafe in Sandy. Luckily, my arrival at 7:55 AM spared me the glare he probably gave his teenage daughter, Harley "You Bet Your Ass" Davidson, when she got home five minutes after curfew. Then again, to thrive with a name like that, she probably had *him* on a curfew.

"Morning, Morgan," Davidson said. I sat down and grabbed a menu.

"Detective," I answered. The waitress appeared at the speed of light. "Orange juice and white toast, please."

"Not a big breakfast eater?" Davidson slapped a file folder on the table in front of me.

"Big dinner last night," I said, opening the folder. "Ah, a of copy Olive's bill folder."

"Figured that would be more valuable than her email logs." Davidson handed me a copy of a note he'd sent to every address on the log, requesting information that might be helpful in solving her murder.

"Nice initiative, Henry," I said. "On multiple levels, too. First, we can eliminate some people, and second, if she corresponded with her murderer, and the murderer stole her computer to cover up something, then the culprit will know he didn't completely erase the trail. Maybe he'll do something stupid."

"You catch Sheriff Running's press briefing last night?" asked Davidson.

"Caught the tail end of it on the ten o'clock news," I said. Truth be known, news feeds from Russia, China and the Middle East grabbed more of my attention. But I *had* seen the Sheriff notify the public that we may have a serial killer in our midst. "He didn't mention the severed little fingers, did he?"

"Unfortunately, I'm afraid he did." Davidson quickly added, "But he didn't say how we found them, nailed to the ceiling beam."

I slipped out my Android and added the terms "serial killer" and "little finger" to my news feed filters. "Given the prominence of the funeral guest list, today, I expect Olive's murder will make national headlines."

"And?" said Davidson.

"And since this particular serial killer has been active all over the country, something may shake loose somewhere." Then, as an afterthought, "By the way, did the sheriff contact the Quantico Behavioral Analysis People?"

"Funny, but they contacted him last night. Seems a couple of United States Senators wanted to make sure they acted with alacrity."

"Alacrity. Now that's a ten dollar word," I said.

"A senator-type word, wouldn't you agree?"

"Two of O'Shea's dinner guests last night happened to be our senators."

"You travel in higher circles than I do, Morgan."

Yeah Henry, and one of those senators probably awoke this morning with a strong desire to see my head on a stick, I thought. *With alacrity, too.* Davidson stared at me, possibly to gauge the size of my ego, and then again, possibly noticing the cloud of doom that swept through my brain. "Senator Hyde and I had met before, and Senator Kimball knew of some classified intelligence work I'd done. But the 'higher circles' are definitely orbiting around Judge O'Shea. I got included more as a remora on the back of a shark."

"More like riding on the back of a tiger, the way this investigation is going."

How about THREE tigers, if I included China/Russia *and* Saudi Arabia? I shuffled through Olive's credit card and bill files just as my orange juice and toast appeared. Henry Davidson didn't seem to have my aversion to calories, and dug into French toast and bacon and sausage *and* ham. He must have seen my double take on his breakfast.

"I had a bowl of cereal for dinner last night," he said sheepishly.

"Got home a little late?"

"The press conference and all," he said.

"Family eat earlier?" I just made small talk while looking through Olive's credit card billing statements.

"Just me and Harley," he said. "She grounded me for getting home late."

This got my full attention. "No Mrs. Davidson?"

"Now she's Mrs. Williams and lives in Chicago," said Davidson with a rueful look.

"Sorry about that?" But what else could I say. Obviously he'd gotten custody of his daughter.

"Life's full of woulda/shoulda/couldas. The judge told me you lost your wife about three years ago in a hit and run car/bicycle accident. No kids, huh?"

"Planned to have a family," I said. "But unlike the A-Team, our plan didn't quite come together."

"So you're out saving the world, now."

"Just like you, Henry. Only I get to pick my own hours."

"And kick some serious ass when the situation requires it?" Before I'd left for breakfast, I checked the viewer count for my Lavar/Lamar virtual circus. Viewings had climbed to over half-a-million eyeballs. The website had it on the home page as the number one video. Pages and pages of comments either excoriated me for not continuing the beating, or they called me the *senior statesman of whup-ass*, a term Laverl Kendrick used when he threw in the towel.

"Yeah, when the situation requires it," I said. Something in Olive's credit card statement from two months ago caught my eye. "Awh, this is just too easy!"

"What have you got?" asked Davidson.

"Looks like Olive not only hosted her own blog, but she signed up for one of those online file backup services." I handed Davidson the credit card statement and pointed out the expenditure.

"What's a file backup service," he asked.

"People who don't want to lose one-of-a-kind data can have their files automatically backed up over the Internet. Looks like Olive just started doing that."

"So anything on her computer would be on this site?" Davidson sounded as excited as I felt.

"Yesiree. Let's do *this* one right. We need a court order to get those files. ASAP."

Davidson quickly finished his three-meat French toast, plowing a last piece of sausage through a plateful of gravy. He quickly wiped his face and stood. "I'll have a court order for someone to sign at the funeral, if you can find someone to sign it."

"Breakfast is on me," I said and grabbed the check. "I'll get it signed all right."

"Thanks," he said, turning to leave. Then as an afterthought, "Do you think all her email files will be at the backup site?"

"I'm counting on it," I said. "Henry, if the murderer killed Olive because of something on her computer, we'll find it. Then, you can *bet your own ass* we'll find the murderer."

Davidson left the restaurant shaking his head and chuckling. I savored my toast and orange juice, and checked my news feeds. Based upon the quantity of activity around the world, today would be a busy one.

Between unconfirmed reports of Mohammed "Benny" bin Faisal Al Saud being seen in New York's JFK airport, and complaints of massive transportation disruptions in both Russia and China, I found it amazing that no SWAT units had descended on the Scientology building in San Francisco. And given my tacit revelations of last night to Senator Kimball, what seemed like a fool-proof plan to run a phantom server farm just across the street from my San Francisco apartment now seemed like sheer idiocy. Who'd seriously believe it a mere coincidence? Certainly not Senator Kimball. Certainly not a federal grand jury considering an indictment. And definitely not a jury of my peers, even ones located in Los Angeles with the O.J. trial under their belts.

So my last act as a free man could be, no, it *should*, be to help apprehend Olive Jenkins' murderer. Maybe such a victory could mitigate things, as the judge considers my sentence. And I wondered if Lavar and Lamar would be in the court gallery that day.

13
A Big Fat Mormon Funeral

 can't think of a more symbolic way of starting *Chapter Thirteen* of this or any story than with a funeral. Olive Curtis Jenkins certainly wouldn't disagree. Of course, she couldn't meaningfully express her disagreement with much of anything, being dead. The crowds at the Mormon Church building at 1700 East and 10945 South—Brigham Young's perfect compass mapping system extended from downtown Salt Lake City even to Sandy, 17 blocks east and 109.45 blocks south of the Salt Lake Temple—testified to the publicity as well as to the importance of the visiting dignitaries. Two United States senators, one mayor, one former ambassador to China, and none other than the president of the worldwide Church of Jesus Christ of Latter-day Saints all congregated with their respective security details and hoards of cameras, news vans, satellite feeds and talking heads.

Incredibly, traffic flowed smoothly, thanks to volunteers who directed every aspect of parking. News vans got a clear-sky shot for their transmitters, friends and family found themselves efficiently directed to ushers, and the rest of us slid quickly into wide parking spaces designed for mothers driving minivans and SUVs. My volunteer even got me a nose-out position in a new row of cars, so I could pull forward, and my exit wouldn't be complicated by backing into the traffic stream.

As I walked toward the chapel, a pack of bicycle riders out for their Saturday morning ride went screaming south. Gentle breeze, spring blossoms, and cavorting birds reminded me why I'd rather be outside on a bicycle than attending a funeral.

"Morgan," yelled Judge O'Shea from across sidewalk. "I think this is only the second time I've ever seen you in a suit."

"It's the same suit, Your Honor," I said. The one I bought for Annie's funeral, actually.

The judge caught up with me just as Davidson's unmarked car entered the drive, the magnetic roof-attached light flashing. He pulled even with us and held out a sheaf of papers. "Nice timing, Morgan. Here's that court order."

"Nice indeed." I took the papers and handed them to Judge O'Shea. "Your Honor, we've discovered that Olive backed up her computer files with an Internet service. Could you sign this court order allowing us access to those files?"

"You have two copies, I presume?"

I shuffled through the papers and found a second copy for the court. "One for you, Your Honor."

"Done," he said as he signed the execution copy. "This is quite a break, isn't it?"

"Damned right it is," I said. "If anything on that computer got Olive killed, we'll find it."

"Good. Then let's go find a seat."

I handed the signed court order through the driver's side window. He moved his car out of the way so additional mourners could file into the lot.

"Where's Sherry?" I asked.

"Already inside, sitting with the choir," said the judge. "We're on our own."

"A dangerous combination to unleash upon all these unsuspecting Mormons," I said.

As if on cue, two teenage boys passed me, did a double take and yelled, "Ooh-rah!" in unison. The taller one gave me a high five.

"You're famous, Morgan," said the judge.

Soon to be infamous, I thought. Signs on the windows as we entered the foyer "respectfully" cautioned against recording devices, and a few enormous Samoan gentlemen—quite a large Mormon community in Utah, due probably to the fact that almost a quarter of the population of Samoa is Mormon—seemed quite capable of enforcing the proscription. "Talofa," I said to the nearest Samoan.

"Talofa lava," he replied with a big smile.

"Is there a language you don't know?" O'Shea muttered. "What if he'd been a Tongan?"

"Then I would have said 'Mano-lay!'"

"But how did you know he *wasn't* Tongan?" said Hizonor.

"Must have been the Samoan flag pin on his lapel." I nudged the judge with my elbow, and could see him shaking his head out the corner of my eye.

We entered the jam-packed chapel. People overflowed from the pulpit clear back through two massive sliding partitions that opened up the rear of the room into a full basketball court. Chairs even filled the stage at the opposite end of the building. I could see Sherry in the choir, singing a soft prelude. Amazingly, the former ambassador/governor and both Utah senators sat in some solitude, *not* surrounded by throngs of hand shakers. Judge O'Shea craned his neck, looking toward the friends-and-family section and the soft seats. His head barely came to my shoulders, and I had to give him the no-go sign and nudge him toward the folding metal chairs in the gym. At that moment, a well-dressed young man approached Judge O'Shea and whispered to him. The judge nodded and guided me by the elbow as we followed the stranger toward the senators, who I could see had been saving places for us. Padded seats in the chapel. Ooh-rah. Both senators stood as we approached and shook our hands. Kimball held mine a little longer than necessary and pulled me to sit between him and Senator Hyde.

Swell, I thought. Not only am I trapped between two well-known Utah figures, but my nearly six-and-a-half foot tall figure could easily be observed by everyone in the room. Notwithstanding the uncommon reverence in the chapel, a good deal of twittering and pointing from the younger attendees confirmed that the Lavar/Lamar episode had now associated itself with the senators. And so will my eventual newsworthy arrest and conviction, unless I figure something out.

As the prelude choir music continued, Judge O'Shea handed his copy of the computer data recovery warrant to Senator Hyde, who read it carefully.

"Nice work, Morgan," whispered Hyde as he passed the document across me to Senator Kimball, who also read it and nodded. He returned the warrant to the judge just as the music went silent and the funeral program began.

Olive's Mormon bishop conducted the service, as is custom. He quickly acknowledged that the church's prophet and president presided at the meeting, and welcomed friends—the poor woman had no family left alive to attend her funeral—and visitors, mentioning the senators and ambassador by name. Great. So everybody can wonder about the giant sitting between Hyde and Kimball.

Given that Mormons do not have a paid clergy, this guy's poise and his general organization of the service impressed me greatly. He announced the program up to the point where he'd give a few remarks. After the congregation sang an opening hymn, the bishop had someone he called Olive Jenkins' *home teacher* offer an invocation.

A line from the opening hymn, *God Speed The Right*, caught my attention: "*And if we fail, we fail with glory, God speed the right, God speed the right.*" Maybe they'll put that on my tombstone: *Morgan Rapier failed with glory.* This thought took over throughout the prayer, so I don't remember a thing about the invocation, being too busy planning my own funeral at the moment. Neither senator would likely be inclined to attend my final rites, as some municipal employee would be bulldozing my body into a landfill, or someone else would be auctioning various body parts to Eastern European, Asian and Middle Eastern governments for display in museums of infamy. Kind of like John Dillinger's mythical male member that's supposedly in the Smithsonian. Mine would probably be diced and scattered around Mecca. With one testicle displayed in Beijing and the other in Moscow. And a nipple or two in Bangalore. How's *that* for failing with glory?

God speed the right. Had I done anything approaching God's will this week? A few little clicks of the keyboard had started dominos falling all over the world. That's speedy work in just three days' time. China, Russia, Saudi Arabia and, from my now-most-referred-by-Twitter view count, any positive future prospects for Lavar and Lamar Kendrick.

The magnitude of the mountain climb ahead of me monopolized my imagination. I came back to the here and now somewhere in the middle of Olive's friend Roses reading the obituary, when Senator Kimball nudged me. He tilted the screen of his Blackberry so I could read that the president had scheduled a national broadcast at 9:00 PM Eastern time, or 7:00 PM in Utah, to deal with the Russian-Chinese cyber war. I couldn't detect a single nuance or prediction from his expression, at least until he winked at me. I *think* he winked anyway, since I couldn't see both eyes. Either he had far better communication with the opposition party that I gave him credit for, or he'd deduced exactly what I'd done and when I'd done it. I fervently prayed for the first choice with a newfound piety that would have made the president of the Mormon Church proud, notwithstanding my Episcopalian heritage.

After the reading of the obituary, a distinguished gray-haired lady came to the podium and introduced herself as Gail Miller. I remembered that the bishop had announced her as the current owner of the Salt Lake Utah Jazz basketball team. Not your ordinary speaker for what turned out *not* to be your ordinary funeral. Gail, widow of business tycoon Larry Miller, spoke of Olive Jenkins' tireless and anonymous work with Miller Charities. Unlike the typical charity-as-a-business model followed by everyone from the MS Society to the March of Dimes to the United Way and especially to the Red Cross, one hundred percent of donations to Miller charities found their way to the recipients, without a nickel of management overhead being deducted. The Miller family paid all overhead, and Olive helped administer their Wounded Warriors' Children's Scholarship Fund. Personally close to Gail Miller, Olive Jenkins spent many hours over many weeks over several years helping her on their family history.

Senator Hyde leaned over and whispered, "Evidently Olive knew quite a bit about computers."

I nodded. Good thing she knew enough to do off-site file backups, anyway.

After Miller spoke, about thirty small children came forward and sang *I'm Trying to be Like Jesus*. After hearing Olive's obituary and tribute by her friend Gail Miller, I sincerely hoped I could facilitate her murderer's meeting Jesus Himself, himself. That is, meeting Jesus long enough to get his transfer pass properly punched to the darkest pit. Those little kids sounded like a choir of angels, and brought back ever so subtly a memory of undefiled innocence and optimism. We'd had no children, Annie and I. But those heavenly voices and cherubic faces suddenly took the weight of the world off my shoulders. I had no *material thing* on earth that really broke my heart to lose. To this point, I'd told no lies, nor had I defrauded anyone. And if attacking people who had attacked me, and done so repeatedly, if attacking those people worked against me legally, so be it. Then and there, I knew I could take anything they threw at me. Heck, what's the worst thing they could do? Kill me? No big deal, especially if I could see Annie again.

Thanks, kids. Nothing like a spiritual shot in the arm on a day with the world crushing down on my shoulders. I felt like nudging Senator Kimball and winking back at him. I didn't, but somebody once said it's the thought that counts.

The bishop then spoke of purity and redemption, and testified that whoever had taken Olive's life had shed innocent blood. This is evidently theologically serious enough amongst Mormons to earn the culprit redemption neither in this world nor in the next. He also talked about Olive's work as the children's chorister in something called Primary, and congratulated the children who had just sung. He also promised them that Olive had heard them sing her favorite Primary song just now. Strangely enough, I believed him. Pretty darned strange, as I had personally sent more than a handful of kidnappers, terrorists and jihadists into the next life, many of whom expected large numbers of virgins to be their reward. If Olive somehow attended her own funeral and interment, I wondered how a couple of Islamic terrorists had reacted to my burying them alone, in the desert, wrapped in the bloody carcass of a pig. Douglas McArthur had thwarted an Islamic uprising in the Philippines with such a ritual, since Muslims viewed pigs as unclean enough to keep them out of Heaven and would do anything to avoid such an end. In my opinion, though, a just and loving God wouldn't send someone to eternal misery for such a dumb-ass reason. Nor would he reward the murderer of innocent children, or of Olive Curtis Jenkins, with even one virgin. At least, a virgin of the human species. An amorous orangutan, now, that's quite another eternal reward. Seventy-two of them, half of which are male? If I happened to be God, maybe. Einstein once said that the more we understand how God created the mechanics of the Universe, that's how we would have done it ourselves. Smart man, that Einstein. But prophetic, too? Ooh-gah, ooh-gah!

Senator Hyde noticed my unconscious smile. He patted me on the knee and smiled back. Maybe he'd been thinking about orangutans, too.

The bishop turned the remainder of the meeting over to Thomas Monson, president of the Mormon Church. An imposing man in his 80s, Monson looked to be well over six feet tall. And whatever else gave him uniqueness in the hearts and lives of fourteen million followers, I'd have to say his affinity for the plight of widows and other women left alone in life certainly pulled on my heartstrings. He spoke of once being a bishop in a ward with large numbers of widows and, as they died and he rose in the church hierarchy, he attended and spoke at every single one of their funerals.

While Olive Curtis Jenkins hadn't been one of *those* widows, the Mormon prophet had done his homework on her lifelong service to those around her. To his knowledge, they'd never met. But he *had* known people whose lives she'd changed for the better. In fact, he named them, enumerating the ways Olive's life had brightened theirs.

He probably gave the local bishop momentary heart failure when he said, "It's an unwritten law of the church that the individual presiding at meetings be the last speaker, so as to set straight any incorrect doctrine taught by earlier speakers." I could see the bishop swallow hard as he sat behind his prophet, bracing himself for the gentle reprimand that never came. Monson continued, "The bishop spoke earlier that whoever had taken Olive's life had shed innocent blood.

"Bishop," continued Monson, turning momentarily to the slightly cowering man sitting behind him, "You spoke the truth. Yet the gentle, decent Olive Curtis Jenkins will probably be first in line to plead the cause of mercy for her slayer on judgment day. And I counsel all within the sound of my voice to carry on her spirit of love, and purge thoughts of hate and revenge. Love and hate cannot coexist. Let us make this a day of love and joy, happiness that dear Sister Jenkins is in a better place now, continuing her service to us all on the other side of the veil."

Okay, maybe he did ever so slightly reprimand the bishop. He reprimanded me too, because love and mercy toward Olive's murderer didn't exactly ooze from every pore of my body. Listening to this man's talk left me with the sinking feeling that God might be going *way* too easy on some malefactors who left a lot of death and misery in their wake. *A lot of grief, a lot of tears*, I thought. *So I'm no spiritual giant.* At least *I think* I thought it, as opposed to speaking it out loud. But Monson's next statement seemed as if he'd heard me thinking.

"Today we live in the world foretold by prophets of old," said the Mormon prophet as he looked right at me. "Wars and rumors of wars, secret murders, disease, natural disasters. Yet our *tears of grief* water the seeds of a brighter future."

He paused, not taking his eyes from mine. I sneaked a look at the senators on either side of me, and to my surprise they returned my stare. They recognized he directed the tears of grief remark to me, too. Quite eerie, to be perfectly honest. A lot of times, the eyes in a photograph appear to follow you, and I'd kind of hoped that everybody in our general area got the impression the church president focused directly on them. Fat chance! I sat tall enough that nobody in front or behind me could have mistaken his gaze, and the two men seated to either side of me hadn't drawn that conclusion, either.

I didn't hear much else of his sermon, pondering instead his contention that "...our tears of grief water the seeds of a brighter future." My tears over losing Annie should have grown a rain forest, but grief completely eclipsed anything I could possibly imagine in the future. Period. End of story. And *my* formula for dealing with grief and creating a brighter future involved blowing something up. In that sense, the flash of an explosion could qualify as a kind of brightness. Or maybe wiping away other people's tears in such a way as to brighten *their* future could compensate in some cosmic sense for my own grief. Okay, then. Maybe in that broad stroke, Thomas Monson had a point. At least he didn't parrot that self-absorbed lunatic Nietzsche who said, "What doesn't kill us makes us stronger." *That* would have sent me completely over the top, since VA hospitals are full of quadriplegics and semi-vegetables who couldn't be ranked as stronger by any twisted, creative or otherwise-spun definition of the term.

Before I knew it, the congregation had sung a moving rendition of *God Be With You Till We Meet Again*, and Olive's other home teacher—a fourteen-year-old boy—offered a benediction. We stood and Judge O'Shea excused himself to join his wife at a luncheon prepared by the local church women's organization prior to the interment. I respectfully declined the invitation to join them, figuring my time could be better spent tracking down Detective Davidson to see if any suspicious characters in the audience had caught his attention. Oftentimes, serial murderers show up to insert themselves into an investigation.

Both senators stuck close to me as we left the building, and I figured they used the implication of serious conversation with me to run interference for themselves and avoid turning a solemn occasion into a campaign rally. We made it into the parking lot when Senator Kimball finally got snagged into a conversation with a short man sporting a thin tuft of red hair. It took every bit of self-control I could muster to stifle a laugh at his resemblance to an orangutan, as I remembered my imagining non-human virgins rewarding Islamic martyrs with an eternity far beyond their expectations. A short, fleshy man, round Harry Potter-like eye glasses exaggerating the size of his eyes, elbowed his way past a large man in a suit to reach us. The big guy must have been one of the senators' security guys, because he never turned to look at us, but kept his eyes on the crowd. A dead giveaway was the flesh-colored cord that ran from the back of his collar to his earpiece. He even steadied the red-haired man who bumped him, whose combination of large eyes and slightly upturned nose completed the orangutan look.

"Morgan Rapier," said Senator Kimball. "This is Heber King, the ambassador's chief of staff. As you remember, Ambassador Young's wife Mary Kaye is Olive Jenkins' grand niece."

"Mr. King," I said and shook his hand, as did Senator Hyde.

"Sorry to bother you, Senators and, of course, Mr. Rapier," he said. "I understand that Judge O'Shea asked Mr. Rapier's help in finding this serial murderer, and wondered if I could report any progress to the ambassador and his wife?"

"Morgan?" said Kimball. "Do you have anything you think we should share with the *former* ambassador's wife about her great aunt?" The senator must have had the same thought I did, which caused him to emphasize the word "former." Why did a *former* ambassador have a chief of staff? Did this chief-without-portfolio aspire to maybe become a White House chief of staff at some point down the road?

My pity for this poor yutz replaced a first inclination to stonewall him. Guys like this progressed in life based solely upon their sheer competence and not due to anything approaching handsome charm. And yes, I felt ashamed of myself for finding humor in his orangutan-like demeanor. The *former* ambassador, also the *former* governor, sent him to do a job.

"It's still early in the investigation," I said. "Sheriff Running has requested help from the FBI, who should be sending in a team."

"I understand you identified the serial killer pattern," said King.

"The medical examiner would have eventually linked with the FBI database, Mr. King," I said. "I may have bought us a few days."

"Please don't take this question as rude, Mr. Rapier, because I'm just wondering is all," he said. "Are you in law enforcement?"

"Not at all. Initially, before we made the serial killer connection, Olive's missing computer led Judge O'Shea and his wife to speculate that her murderer's motive might have to do with something on the computer. That's kind of my specialty."

"But with no computer to analyze, how could you help?"

"Good question. Olive's ISP maintained email log files, to which we have access now," I said.

"Then you have the email she sent and received?" asked King.

"No, just the logs," I answered. "But we know the senders and the recipients, so we're tracking those people down to get some idea of their content."

"Thank you for your time," said King, handing me his business card and nodding as he backed away. "If you find out anything the ambassador should know, please give me a call. Senator Kimball, Senator Hyde, Mr. Rapier. I'd best rejoin the ambassador and his wife. We're having a little trouble getting them back into China, what with this computer fiasco and all."

Heaven help me! I thought. *Talk about a convergence of interests and events!*

"Heber," said Senator Hyde as he put his hand on King's forearm. "You can also tell Mary Kaye we're going to be able to recover everything that Olive had on her computer. If this killer somehow targeted her because any data she may have filed, we'll find it."

"Oh?" said Heber King, turning back to Hyde. "But without a computer to investigate…"

Hyde patted King's forearm. "Olive backed up everything over the Internet. Judge O'Shea just signed a court order to get that data."

"Interesting," said King, nodding again. "I'll be sure to let the ambassador and his wife know. Well, good luck and thank you."

"Odd duck," said Kimball after King had disappeared in the crowd.

"Smart as a whip, though," added Hyde. "If the former governor had successfully made it to the White House in 2012, Heber would have either managed the campaign or at least become his chief of staff."

Guy looks like that, he just has *to be good*, I thought, pocketing King's business card.

"Senator Hyde, Senator Kimball," I said. "I'd better track down Detective Davidson. We've got some digging to do in Olive's computer files."

"Morgan, please keep us posted on your progress," said Kimball. "We gave you our numbers last night, right?

"Correct, Senator."

"And feel free to call either of us, any time," added Hyde. "If you need help, we'll apply whatever pressure we can."

"Thank you," I said. Senator Kimball seemed insistent that he have my local number, so I gave them both my *Titanium Eagles* cyber security card after I'd written my private cell phone number on it. "I'll try not to abuse your offers of help."

"Morgan, be sure to watch the President's address to the nation, tonight," said Kimball. Hyde looked quizzically at his friend who took him by the arm and walked toward their waiting limo. "Morgan gave me an idea that I passed to the right people. Tonight could be interesting."

Now I can destroy two careers and not just one. The television camera trucks mingled with free-roaming still and video cameras, and no small number of them panned the senators, the ambassador's party, and of course the president of the Mormon church. Nice video record for a retrospective on The Man Who Declared War on Russia and China. And just what *idea* of mine had the senator run up the flagpole?

I had to start thinking of this as a computer program. One never sets out to create an application without building it around a debugging/testing technology. Something as simple as missing punctuation or misspelling a command can bring a computer system crashing to a stop. Or worse, a memory overflow can be exploited by an outside hacker to take over an otherwise secure system. Somehow, some way, I needed a process debugger that helped me shield those people who trusted me from the unintended consequences of my unrelated but grossly rash forays. And, I had to find a murderer before the hounds of hell brought me down.

But right now, I had to locate Detective Davidson.

14
Avoiding the Media,
Big-Dave Style

 ctually, Davidson found me. Or at least the Channel 2 News camera found me. Davidson waived from the door of the satellite upload van parked diagonally across the lot. I loped between cars and people walking to theirs.

"Morgan, I'd like you to meet a buddy of mine," said Davidson. "Dave Turner is the general manager of the CBS affiliate here in Salt Lake City."

Inside the news van, a large man wearing a Harley-Davidson bandanna and vest sat in a captain's chair overlooking his console operator. He extended a beefy hand. "Hi ya!"

The big guy smiled like he really meant it. I shook his hand. Utah *had* to be the handshaking capital of the world. "Mr. Turner."

"I'm Dave."

"And I'm just Morgan."

"I doubt you're *just* anything," he said. Those dimples of his continued as his smile deepened them. "Abandon hope all ye who enter here, especially Lavar and Lamar."

"Please don't tell me…" I sighed.

"Too late," said Davidson. He didn't have dimples.

"Video of a big guy trying to talk two morons off the ledge," continued Turner. "Juxtaposed on the screen to the same big guy chumming around with our two senators."

"I, uh, don't suppose I could talk you out of doing the story that way?"

"Problem is, I'd be the only station that *didn't* carry the story." But Turner still smiled, like he had something up his sleeve. Davidson's silence indicated they'd talked about effective ways to spike the story.

"However?" I said.

"When you step out of my mobile newsroom," said Turner, "you *could* tell every other cameraman and news anchor and reporter that you've agreed to give an exclusive story to KUTV Channel Two. Those swine would rather eat a shit sandwich than pimp my newscast." He then laughed like a madman. I couldn't help liking this guy. No guile. No pretense.

"Dave, you sure can cut to the chase," I said, almost relaxing. "And you think that might kill the story?"

"That, and *this*," he said as he handed me a new twenty-mega-pixel video camera/phone. "This is a much higher-quality streaming video than your quaint little Android. Go ahead and set it up for streaming to our website. All I want is the exclusive when you break the Olive Jenkins case."

"*If* I break case," I quickly qualified the agreement.

"Fair enough." Again, the dimples formed and his puffy little cheeks jiggled when he laughed.

"Okay," I said. Then turning to Davidson, "Detective, we have some work to do."

"Tut tut tut, not quite so fast," said Davidson. "Dave has also agreed to let me have all the raw footage KUTV shot of the funeral attendees, right Big Dog?"

"She just got done copying," said Turner as he looked at his control console, tapped an eject icon and then reached beneath the bench. He came up with a USB disk drive. "Here's about two-hundred gigabytes of rough footage."

Davidson took the drive and power adapter, nodded and started to open the mobile news studio door.

"Hold on, Hoss!" said Turner. "Let me change clothes."

Then, as if he'd had the wardrobe mechanics planned all along, he stripped off his vest and bandanna, squirmed out of his Sturgis—Black Hills, South Dakota—T-shirt and pulled on a white one with an enormous "CBS KUTV2 News" on the front and back. And given Dave's size, he became one giant walking KUTV billboard.

"Okay, Morgan. Now, how about I walk you to your car."

I wanted to tell him that he just might be doing his part to save the careers of two senators, but instead I followed Davidson out the door and into the parking lot. At least three other shoulder-mounted cameras caught us. We had a straight shot out the van, probably because the ABC, NBC and Fox affiliate stations didn't want the CBS truck in their frames. With Davidson in the lead and the KUTV2 News billboard walking beside me, the phalanx of reporters didn't converge on us until we veered toward my car and away from the news van. Then, we faced a wall of microphones. I raised my hands until the din of voices and shouted questions ceased.

"Ladies, gentlemen," I said. "If you have any questions, please address them to my good friend Dave Turner of Channel Two News."

I heard at least one "Awh shit!" as we left an open-mouthed gaggle of now-speechless egomaniacs and went to my car, where Dave the walking billboard opened the door for me and then waived goodbye when I pulled forward and out of the parking lot. Detective Davidson's own car caught up with me by the time I hit the first stop light. He came around me and motioned that I should follow him west. We passed a bunch of Boy Scouts who had set up a blue pyramid of fifty-gallon water storage barrels they sold for emergency preparedness. Be prepared. Words to live by. Tough words, when you find yourself ripped off a ski slope in an avalanche and remember you don't have a locator beacon for rescuers to track.

Davidson and I eventually went north on the freeway and arrived at the Salt Lake County Sheriff's office fifteen minutes later. Gosh I liked Brigham Young's street numbering system—900 West and 3365 South. A stranger comes to town and is an immediate expert finding his way around. Even when developers name their streets, like Pepperwood Drive or Gatehouse Lane, residents always give the geographically numbered coordinates in parentheses.

Though his office measured not much larger than my walk-in clothes closet at the condo, Davidson's workspace bespoke the compulsive neatness of a man forced by wifelessness to be self-sufficient. Socks left on the bathroom floor would still be there after a week. The detective's wall displayed the usual diplomas and certificates, but the only photograph anywhere in sight showed hm and his daughter astride heavily customized Harley-Davidson motorcycles.

"Harley *you bet your ass* Davidson and the old man?" I asked.

"The one and only," he said. "And just to make sure I wouldn't further pollute the gene pool, her mother tried to castrate me in the divorce."

"Her mother doesn't like Harley?"

"She went for custody and won," said Davidson.

"But she lives with you," I began.

"That's because Harley told the judge to shove it you know where and that she damned well intended to stay with her father and let her slut mother go wherever the hell nature called her."

"Wow. How'd the judge take it?"

"You tell me," he smiled. "Patrick O'Shea told her she be going where he told her to go, and she told him she'd run away, come back to Salt Lake, sneak into his bedroom late at night and beat him to death with a baseball bat."

"I can't believe she's not serving a life sentence!" I said.

"That started an interesting friendship, first between the judge and Harley and, eventually, between the judge and me."

"He didn't throw her into jail for contempt?" My friend Patrick O'Shea would have pounced on her like a lioness dropping a wildebeest in the Serengeti.

"No, quite the contrary. Judge O'Shea tried to explain to her that her mother's character or lack thereof had not been presented to the court, so he couldn't consider those factors in his decision."

"To which she…?" I let the question hang.

"To which she told him to blow it out his ass. She knew who she wanted to live with and to get ready for a midnight baseball bat to his ugly noggin, right after she took a bat to her sleeping slut of a mother along with whoever she chose for that weekend's slumber party." Davidson shrugged with a you-had-to-have-been-there expression.

"And he gave you immediately custody?"

"Oh, no! But when my ex-wife heard our daughter's outburst, she came completely unglued. Profanely so, to Harley, to the judge, to the bailiff, and to her own attorney. *Then* judge O'Shea gave me custody!" said Davidson. "*And* he threw her into jail overnight for contempt of court. We haven't seen her since."

"Unbelievable!" I laid my computer case on one corner of the detective's pristine desktop. "Someday I'd like to meet this spitfire daughter of yours."

"You telling stories about me again, Dad?" came the voice from behind me. Davidson hadn't seen his daughter come in, because I blocked his view of the door. I turned to see the girl from the photo in real life.

She stood about five nine, and jet black hair cascaded over the collar of her riding leathers. A matching black helmet hung from her left hand, and with her right she underhanded a digital camera to her dad. Clearly, she got her stunning Mediterranean looks from her mother.

"Harley, meet Morgan Rapier," Davidson said, hefting his daughter's camera.

"That's the idea, Henry," she said to her dad, taking my left elbow and turning so we both faced her father. "I saw you guys on TV today and wanted to get a picture of me with the famous Lavar-bashing Navy SEAL. The camera's all set; just aim it and push the button."

I did my best smile for the photo. Henry took the shot of me with his daughter. She took the camera from him and checked the digital image. "Great shot! Yep, that ought to keep the knuckle draggers off my bones."

Harley pocketed the camera and whisked out of the room as quickly as she'd entered. Over her shoulder she called, "Hamburgers at six. Bring Morgan."

"Pleased to meet you, Harley," I said to the empty space.

"Let me get this court order in process." Detective Davidson acted as if nothing unusual had happened, and stepped around me to his office door.

He didn't wait for my answer and went to a woman sitting in a corner desk, to whom he handed the court order he'd been carrying in his jacket pocket. I sat down and jacked my laptop into a free Ethernet wall plug. I also used an available AC power outlet. Never can tell when you'll need a fully charged battery. Be prepared, as the Boy Scouts would say. Davidson returned while I awakened my computer from sleep mode.

"She called you Henry? Not Dad or maybe even Father?" What a spitfire.

"Do you have dinner plans, tonight?" he asked, ignoring my question completely.

"I do now, huh?" I took a close look at his expression, just to see if his tornado of a daughter's brief appearance really didn't register as an unusual event. The little twitch at the corner of his mouth told me he'd lost the battle to blow it off as nothing at all. "I don't want a baseball bat nailing *me* in the middle of the night."

"Word to the wise for tonight," he said. "Remember, she's only seventeen."

"Henry, give me a bullet and I'll write my name on it for you." While Harley might be seventeen going on thirty, I'd put enough lives in jeopardy in the last week without resorting to the ultimate act of alpha-male selfishness.

"Forget the bullet. Just help me figure out how fast we can get Olive's backup data." Davidson sat down behind his desk and tapped the space bar on his own keyboard to bring his screen alive. "I haven't done this before. Who do we call to get the ball rolling?"

"Nobody," I said.

"Huh?" Davidson did a dead stop and just stared at me.

"Oh, have your secretary call the backup company and tell them we have a court order," I said. "But give me about two minutes and I'll create a disk partition on my system and begin restoring Olive's files to it."

"Don't you need some kind of a password or something?"

I just shook my head and gave him my this-is-child's-play smirk. I had Olive's static IP address from her home router, and her email username from when I snagged her ISP's email logs. So I just went into the backup Web site, entered Olive's email address in the username field and clicked on the 'Forgot Password' box. Within sixty seconds I had the password-reset instructions emailed to me via her account. A few more minutes setting up a virgin restore to my disk partition and then nothing to do but wait.

"Says here we're going to need about ten hours to do a full restore. Her email files will take about 25 minutes. I did those separately so we can look at email while the rest of the system rebuilds. In the meantime, shall we start looking at the video KUTV shot at the funeral?"

"Sparkling idea," said Davidson. His phone rang and he had a short conversation. He hung up and filled me in. "The FBI's behavioral analysis unit will be here first thing Monday morning. In my opinion we could have used their help today eyeballing funeral attendees."

"This isn't the *Criminal Minds* TV show, this is real life and your tax dollars at work," I muttered. The progress bar on the email file restore had moved noticeably already. "Without calls from two senators, they wouldn't be here for another week at best."

Davidson grimaced and said, "Let's take a look at some raw video."

15
A Little Solid Cyber Sleuthing

 showed Davidson how to plug the USB drive into his computer and queue up the video files. While he scoured the images, letting his detective's *sixth sense* loose on all those strangers, I finished downloading Olive's entire email file and started the much more lengthy file downloads. Then I started the long process of dissecting the late Olive Jenkins' life through her email correspondence. I also surreptitiously opened a separate window to check the flow of the Russia/China/Saudi news feeds I'd set up. From my brief appraisal, the world had taken the weekend off, at least until the president's address to the nation, scheduled for 7:00 PM Utah time.

At about 3:00 in the afternoon, two detectives came in. Both had attended Olive's interment as well as the earlier funeral. One of them had a USB thumb drive onto which they'd stored car license numbers and locations of the cars that attended both events. Davidson told them to run DMV checks and put the results—location, plate number, and registered owner—into a spreadsheet for him. He especially wanted to see owners of cars parked on the street and any rental cars.

"Smart, Henry," I said. "Parked on the street for quick getaway and rental cars because the serial killer probably came from out of state?"

"Good old-fashioned police work."

"One more correlation you might want to make, Henry."

"Which is?"

"Match with stolen cars. A *really* careful serial killer would steal a car with which to attend the funeral. Probably from the airport parking lot, especially the long-term parking lot. Rent a car so you could get an exit coupon, steal a car that you witness someone just park, then put the rental in the same space, go to the funeral and then return the stolen car before it's missed, and finally return the rental."

"Wow, you *are* devious," said Davidson.

"On a whim," I said, "why don't I see if any of the rental car companies had a quick-turnaround rental today?"

"Like I said, just good old-fashioned police work."

"Actually, I just got a better idea," I said. "I'll hack the airport security cameras and see if any rental car license plates have left the long-term parking lot between noon today and midnight."

"That's a lot of license plates to visually eyeball, Morgan."

"Too many for me, too," I said. "I'll write a license plate recognition and conversion program and capture the numbers to a database. Then another entry/exit timestamp routine to test for quick-turnaround customers. It's computationally intensive, so I'll have to offload the process to the Wolfram Alpha Grid. But if we find even one that fits the criteria, then he's our man. How's that for a little new-fashioned police work?"

Over the next hour I wrote and tested my license plate recognition program and then launched it, got a copy of the license plates of cars that attended the funeral, and then started reading Olive's email. In the background, my computer cranked away rebuilding Olive's other computer files. I finally came up for a breather.

"Yo, Henry?" I said.

"Yeah?" He paused the video replay and looked up.

"Most of these emails in Olive's directories are about genealogy. Dates. Legal certificates. Little histories. Vignettes. A few black sheep from a hundred years ago. But do you think hundred-year-old skeletons in somebody's closet justify murdering this lady?"

"Not likely," Davidson said after a moment of thinking. "We had a thing called *The Mountain Meadows Massacre* near Cedar City, but we figure most everybody in town had something to do with it. I'd say everyone around here is willing to let the cards fall where they may."

"Alright. I don't see any email smoking guns, then," I said. "One of her direct ancestors appears to have been murdered by a guy named George Wood. This seems to be the subject of quite a few recent emails. But he went to prison for the offense, according the attachments."

"While I wouldn't rule it out, unless direct descendants of George Wood are currently running for office—names like Leavitt, Young, Kimball, Matheson or Hyde—I'd say it's a long shot," said the detective. "Besides, the odds that *any* of these guys are serial murderers is just about zero."

"Just thought I'd ask," I said. "Any strange looking ducks at the funeral?"

"Just you," smirked Davidson. "You stand out like a big old sore thumb. Have any confessions to make?"

"The list is long and sordid," I said. Total truth. But something in my voice must have triggered Henry Davidson's radar, or at least his attempt at X-Ray vision into my soul. He just raised his eyebrows and stared at me. "A little too much feeling in that statement?"

He didn't say a word. Okay, the first guy that talks loses, so I put my laptop on the corner of his desk and peeled off the least incriminating layer of my guilt.

"Henry, I'm still feeling pretty bad about what I did to Lavar and Lamar Kendrick." I held up my Android and showed him that the video had topped the charts with over seven-hundred-thousand viewings. With pages and pages of comments.

"You're kidding!" he sputtered. "You don't know about Lavar Kendrick?"

"Should I?"

"When you sent me the video link, I ran Lavar's sheet while I chatted with Judge O'Shea about you." Davidson slid a quarter-inch thick printout toward me, stapled at the corner. "Lavar likes to beat on his wife and kids. Several domestic disturbances required police intervention, double that number of reports from the emergency room. Broken bones from pretty lame accidents. Wife wouldn't press charges. I personally think you let him off far too easy, but look this stuff over yourself and see if you agree."

I scanned through Lavar's history as an abuser, and agreed with Davidson that Lavar probably got off with far less of a thumping than he deserved. But if I had indeed erred, then I am more than happy to have made the mistake on the side of mercy.

Davidson took until 5:00 in the afternoon to finish looking at all the raw footage. After I set up the phone KUTV's Turner had given me so it would send videos to my streaming video account, I looked over the detective's shoulder at the video clips. He'd captured five screen shots of markedly non-Mormon-looking spectators at the funeral and printed them in color, one copy for each of us. The two detectives returned with a spreadsheet on their thumb drive, listing license plate numbers, parking locations and registered owners of all the cars at the funeral. As I'd expected, none of the 317 cars happened to be a rental.

"I don't suppose you captured the phone numbers on those car registrations?" asked Davidson. The scowl he got for an answer said enough.

"Not to worry, guys," I said. "I'll write a Perl script to do a lookup and fill out the spreadsheet. Which I did in about 3 minutes, and it took another two minutes to run the program. I printed the list on a network printer in the main bullpen.

"Here, guys," said Davidson. "Let's get some people on the phones and find out if any of these cars *shouldn't* have been at the funeral, today. Like maybe they'd been parked at the airport in the long-term lot."

In answer to their questioning looks, Davidson explained that a smart serial killer would have come back to town for the funeral and stolen a car from the airport long-term parking lot. They nodded appreciatively and went to work. Then he patted his stomach.

"Ready for hamburgers with Harley?"

"Lead the way!" We hadn't had lunch, and I really truly could use a home-cooked burger. Or two. "Let's leave my laptop computer here cranking on rebuilding Olive's files, and come back in the wee hours to see what we can see."

Whether in paranoia or compulsion, I gently took my laptop from the corner of his desk and laid it on the floor, sliding it just under the lip of his desk. Sensing exactly my point, Davidson wrote "Do not clean this office tonight" on a piece of masking tape and affixed it to his office door before locking the room on our way out.

(Sweet) 16
Hostess Harley
"You Bet Your Ass" Davidson

arley you-bet-your-ass Davidson had the barbecue going by the time her dad and I arrived at their White City home. A humble neighborhood with ranch-style single-level homes sat in the middle of Sandy. Some surrounded by white fences Tom Sawyer would have had a heyday painting, more with chain-link fences to corral dogs that would probably lick an intruder to death, White City seemed a throwback to an age of innocence. Mature trees framed the humble-but-immaculate houses with their manicured yards, and the curbs had the house street numbers painted on them by Boy Scouts out raising money for their summer campouts. I felt guilty pulling my suddenly ostentatious S550 into the driveway, following Henry, who drove his Crown Victoria squad car into the garage to make room for me. The two-car garage, neat as a pin, had room for one car, two Harley-Davidson motorcycles, and a life-size poster of Marlon Brando on *his* motorcycle. Red brick with recently painted white framing and window boxes filled with all kinds of flowers, the names of which had never graced my brain, almost sneered at a car that probably cost me more than this house would currently bring on the real estate market.

Detective Davidson came out of his garage and keyed the pad on the wall to close the garage. I followed him to the front of the house, where he unlocked the door. Good habits, even in Utah. We walked through an immaculate living room, through an equally tidy kitchen and onto a back porch where what had to be Harley's twin sister busied herself flipping enormous hamburgers on a gas grill. I said twin, because instead of the biking leathers this girl wore a flowery calf-length summer dress, which she protected from the grill with an equally feminine apron. Even though she had her back toward us, she had no doubt who and how many people had just stepped onto the deck.

"Glad you're not late Henry, Morgan," she said. Okay, same voice, same edge, same profound situational control. Clearly not a twin, not that there could be a chance in God's Universe that two identical girls might have made it off the cosmic drawing board. Henry had his hands full. Come to think of it, so did I. She turned and handed each of us a glass of what looked to be iced strawberry lemonade decorated with an umbrella spearing a slice of orange. "Let me take your suit coats and hang them up."

I quickly moved my lemonade glass from hand to hand as she quite expertly removed my suit coat and then her father's. Something told me she could just as easily have pulled the back of my jacket over my head, pinning both arms, and then beat me with the baseball bat with which she'd threatened Judge O'Shea at her parents' custody hearing.

While she took the coats inside the house, Henry guided me to a round oak table beneath a cloth umbrella, and we sat down in enormous Adirondack chairs made of cut-up skis. The deck overlooked a small yard populated with fruit trees—apple, cherry and plum—along with well-organized vegetable gardens planted in raised beds.

"Are these chair pads made of what I think they are?" I asked.

"Yep," Henry smiled. "Surplus Kevlar vests."

"You're quite the handyman," I commented.

"Hah!" came Harley's voice as she emerged back onto the deck. "Henry goes to the mechanic when he needs to change license plates on the Crown Vic."

"Harley, how many times have I asked you to call me Dad?"

"I did the chairs in metal shop at school, as a birthday present for *Henry*, and the garden grow boxes in wood shop," she said. An impish twinkle escaped when she raised her eyebrows.

"Oh, I suppose you made your baseball bat on the woodshop lathe?"

"My what?" she asked, confused.

Gotcha! I thought, and said, "You know, the baseball bat you threatened to club Judge O'Shea with in the middle of the night if he made you live with your mother."

Harley waggled a finger at her dad and shook her head. Then she turned serious and directed those magnificent brown eyes at me. "Morgan, I was wondering if you could show me that throat punch thing you did to take the fight out of Lavar, yesterday?"

No doubt at all that this young woman attracted all manner of advances, and she needed the very best advice I could muster. I put my lemonade glass on the oak table and eased myself off the Adirondack's Kevlar cushion. Even at five-nine, the top of her head barely came to my neck.

"Try to touch my throat," I said.

Her hand shot out more quickly than I'd expected, but not quickly enough. I swatted her hand away with my left forearm. She countered with her other hand, which I also swatted away with my right. I then placed my left hand just below her jaw and held her at arm's length. Now, she couldn't reach me with either hand, nor could she get any leverage to launch a kick.

"No matter how fast you are, no matter how much you practice Harley, you just can't take on a big guy." I released her throat and took a step back. "Even if you *did* land a punch to his throat, you don't have the power behind that punch to do what I did to Lavar."

"Oh," she said.

"But," I quickly added, seeing her look of disappointment, "after one of those wonderful hamburgers, I'll show you one high-risk move that could get you out of a very bad situation if all else fails."

"The burgers!" she exclaimed, remembering the task our entrance had interrupted. She quickly turned her attention to the smoking barbecue.

In no time at all, the three of us sat around the table eating the best hamburgers I've ever encountered. Walla Walla Sweet Onions, beefsteak tomatoes, sweet pickles and sesame seed buns contributed to the experience, but Harley had done *something* unusual with the meat that entirely escaped me.

"Now I know what Elvis thought heaven should be like," I said between bites. "This isn't ordinary hamburger meat."

"I kneaded Lipton onion soup mix into extra-lean ground beef," she confirmed. "But I've never seen anyone put away *two* of them!"

"We missed lunch, today," said Henry, who had still only managed one burger, himself.

"The Olive Jenkins investigation?" Harley asked.

"Yep," said her dad.

"I hope you get this guy."

"You and us both, unless I die of a coronary blockage first." The detective patted his stomach.

"Don't worry, Henry," she said. "You're going on a five mile run tomorrow morning."

Henry groaned and looked to me for some help. After my own overindulgence, I left him on his own and upped the ante: "Yeah, I think I'd better plan on rising early myself and climbing Little Cottonwood Canyon on my bicycle."

"You staying up at the Bird?" Harley asked.

"I've got a condo up there," I said.

"Cool. Did you know they open Snowbird for skiing on the fourth of July?" she said.

"So I hear." *Of course, by then I should be in a maximum-security federal prison,* I thought to myself. And speaking about prisons, I kind of wanted to hear the president's address. I looked at my watch, and Harley misinterpreted the action as boredom with her conversation.

"Gotta run, huh?" For the first time in our conversation, she didn't look me in the eye.

"Oh no!" I quickly answered. "At the funeral, Senator Kimball told me the president would be speaking at seven, and that I might want to see it. Any chance we could move indoors?"

"Sure." That perked her up. "We could have apple pie a la mode inside. But we have a few minutes, so could you show me that last-ditch self-defense move?"

I looked at Henry for the okay to proceed, and he nodded in the affirmative.

"Okay Harley you-bet-your-ass Davidson, here's the deal," I began. She rolled her eyes again toward her father and gave a boy-you-have-a-big-mouth sigh. "You're a beautiful young woman who's emotionally tough and mature beyond your years. But you're a woman and don't stand a chance in a physical contest with most any man. So if you're expecting a silver bullet that would let you pick fights in biker bars, forget it."

I had her undivided attention. Her father's, too. "I used to be a Navy SEAL, and they didn't teach us to fight for sport. They taught us to kill or cripple the enemy. That's why I called it a high-risk move, a last shot so to speak. You won't be doing this to send a signal to a high school date who may have *slightly* miscalculated your willingness to take the next step. I'm going to show you how to completely stop a bad man from doing something very bad to you. Understand?"

Harley looked at her father, and then and me. "I understand."

"In order of vulnerability, remember EKGT," I said. "Sounds like a medical term, and it really is. A man's most vulnerable areas, in order of your probability of success, are EKGT. Eyes, Knees, Groin and Throat. For the record, Lavar's Throat ranks number four on *your* list."

"What about *your* list?" Harley asked.

"At the time, I didn't want to maim him, kill him, or put him in a full-body cast," I said. "And if I'd miscalculated on the throat, I'd have had to perform an emergency tracheotomy with a ball point pen to save his life. Besides Harley, I outweigh you by at least 100 pounds, I've been trained in hand-to-hand combat, and most importantly I can take a much harder punch than you can."

"So what exactly do I do with EKGT?"

"First, the eyes," I began. "Assuming the guy doesn't beat you unconscious before he, uh, has his way with you…"

"Awh crap!" said Detective Davidson, mostly to himself.

"…or have a buddy hold your hands above your head…"

"Double crap!" said Henry, more loudly.

"I know, Henry," I said. "But I don't want this young lady getting over confident and walking into a situation she shouldn't have even considered in the first place. Ninety percent of the battle is *not* getting into a bad situation, and that's between you and your daughter. High-risk behavior eventually catches up with you."

Harley swallowed. I continued.

"Let me see your thumbs." She held out her hands. "I don't know why, but men like to see a woman's arms above her head. You do *not* want your arms pinned to your sides, so slick back your hair with your hands, or do something else to imply your willingness to play along. Okay so far."

She nodded. I looked around and found exactly what I needed in the centerpiece. I held two oranges against my collarbones as I stepped closer to her.

"Now, Harley, I want you to take your thumbs and pretend the oranges are the eyes of your attacker. Shove those thumbs right through these babies and pop them outward in one smooth movement."

She hesitated.

"Now!" I yelled.

To her credit, she punctured the oranges and darn near did the same to my chest, flipping the oranges to the sides just as I'd told her to. My white shirt looked like I'd forgotten to put the top on a blender. Whether or not the mess on my shirt or the vision of what she'd done to an imaginary attacker's eyes brought it on, the horrified look on her face almost broke my heart. One more nail in the coffin of innocence, courtesy of Lt. Commander RET Morgan Rapier, U. S. Navy SEAL Team Three.

After a wide-eyed moment, Harley whispered, "W-w-will he be permanently blinded?"

"He will," I said, wiping the orange pulp from my shirt with a paper napkin, "if you yank those eyeballs right out of his head and toss them to the side. That is, if he lives through the ordeal. Blood loss and shock may kill him."

"Judas Priest, Morgan!" said Henry Davidson. He stood and walked to his daughter's side, wrapping her in his arms. She buried her face in his chest and gently shook.

"Harley, Henry," I said as I gently put my hand on her quivering back. "I don't fight for sport or for ego gratification. This isn't television, and there is no Vulcan Sleeper Hold that'll take the bad guy out until the next episode. At least, there's no such Kung Fu move that suits your height, weight and gender."

I could tell she heard me, because I could feel her head nodding in the affirmative.

"Maybe another time," I said, stepping back, "I can show you some knee kicks that'll just put him in rehab for a few months."

That promise got paid in spades sooner than either of us thought.

17

That Senator Really is Connected

 organ, you sure know how to sweet talk a girl," Davidson said. We sat in his living room, waiting for the president to make his address to the nation.

"For which you should be eternally grateful," I said. Harley had quietly gone to her bedroom after my unambiguous demonstration of brutality in the cause of keeping her virtue intact. "Maybe she'll avoid some high-risk behavior."

"Yeah, like having some romantic notions about one U.S. Navy SEAL I know."

Actually, one bright spot in my otherwise accelerating spiral to doom, I thought. Henry's living room had one stuffed chair and a matching couch, separated by a wrought iron coffee table I'd bet my car that Harley had built in metal shop. Of course, the multiple crafting of the Harley-Davidson logo etched into the glass top and polished in three-dimensional chrome on the legs and sides made it a bet I wouldn't lose. The forty-two-inch LCD TV stared down at us from a wall mount. No power or speaker cords of any kind snaked down the wall, so I gave it a high degree of probability that Harley had done a job that would have made a professional installer green with envy.

"Henry, if I happened to be twenty-three years younger, you'd have a serious problem on your hands," I finally said. "Truly though, if we'd had a daughter, Annie and me, I'd be proud if she turned out exactly like Harley."

"Thanks, Morgan," said Harley. She'd quietly stolen down the hallway and probably heard our complete conversation.

I quickly stood from my reclined position on the couch. Not often at a loss for words, I couldn't think of a single thing to say except, "Forgive me for being such a poor guest in your home."

"Forgive you for what, Morgan?" She tried to put on the veneer of invincibility, and nearly succeeded.

"You threw a perfect dinner party, and I couldn't have done a better job of wiping the smile off your face if I'd slapped you." I stood there awkwardly, not wanting to send any *wrong* signals, but definitely praying I could mend a badly startled psyche. Harley you-bet-your-ass Davidson might come on tough and world-wise, but at the end of the day, when you're done play-acting cool roles, I now saw an innocent, beautiful, shell-shocked little girl who had her Wonderland Tea Party spoiled by someone who *thought* he'd spent his life protecting such pure innocence. "After everything that your dad and even Judge O'Shea told me about you, and then meeting you in real life, I'd never forgive myself if I hadn't offered my very best advice on self defense. And I wish I had a daughter just like you, to whom I'd have given the very same advice."

She lightly slugged me in the chest and said, "Here comes the president. You guys enjoy the show while I make dessert."

Harley brushed her hand across her dad's head as she left the room, and I did some quick, reconfirming arithmetic. If I happened to go insane and marry a woman twenty-three years my junior, and if I lived to be eighty-five—a stretch given my current situation— and if she lived to be ninety, then my wedding gift to her would be at least a quarter-century as a widow. Now *that* would be the epitome of selfishness. Shocking. Less than an hour with a seventeen year old had me thinking thoughts I didn't think I'd *ever* feel after Annie's death.

Thankfully, Henry hit the un-mute button just as the network news anchor cut over to President Medina in the Oval office. Now *there* sat a man with the weight of the world on his shoulders. Idealism had to be an early casualty in his quest to overcome economic turmoil, wind up a war or two, and now watch the Web infrastructure—upon which all commerce depended—bring two major powers to the brink of war. Of course, that last problem had been delivered to him on a silver platter by moi. The poor devil.

"My fellow Americans," began the president. "As most of you are aware by now, Chinese and Russian computer systems have been attacking each other for the past three days. Virtually all services in those countries that depend upon interconnected computers have failed. What little communication that *is* coming from those countries is over obsolete analog phone lines and human-assisted switches. Both China and Russia are blaming each other for the attacks, and the rhetoric is becoming quite heated. It is for that reason that I wanted to take some time tonight and tell you what we know about the situation, as well as how we are trying to help both parties step back from a dangerous precipice."

His *what we know about the situation* sent a cold chill up my spine. What indeed do *we* know about the situation? *Yes sir, I hang on your every word, maybe quite literally.*

"Both Russia and China have been waging an undeclared cyber war against both public and private institutions in the United States for years. Few of their attacks made headlines until early 2009. On April 8th, *The Wall Street Journal* broke the story detailing how our electricity grid had been penetrated by so-called spies. A little over two weeks later, on April 21st, they carried a front-page story of spies breaking into the Defense Department's Joint Strike Fighter project and siphoning off several terabytes of data related to design and electronics systems. Since then, the floodgates have opened and new incidents have been reported almost daily. But this is the least of what I am about to tell you, tonight." The president clicked a remote and the screen split, with him on the left and a computer presentation screen on the right.

"Jeeze, Morgan," said Henry for the second time…tonight. "You say Senator Kimball told you at the funeral that he wanted you to see this?"

I just nodded, not wanting to miss a single world from the president.

"According to the cyber war task force I formed in 2009, every single server located in the United States, public or private, however large or small, is attacked by hackers based in either China or Russia hundreds of times every day. There have been three-hundred-twenty-nine extortion attempts in the past two years from international criminals. However, those same attackers are using the identical systems our cyber war task force has identified to attack strategic defense installations and which search for specific technical information that only a well-organized and well-financed government could possibly know about."

Old news, I thought. *Now, tell us the rest of the story.*

"Until this week, our own cyber crime laws have made it impossible for individuals or corporations to do more than put up fences. Any attempt to retaliate, to disable the attacking computer systems, is not only illegal but carries stiff penalties. We call it restraint of trade if the counter attack crosses state or international boundaries. I call it stupid, antiquated, and wrong headed in today's globalized economy. Here, now, today, I refuse to continue penalizing people who play by the rules. Our law enforcement structures make it impossible to find and prosecute the cyber crime that dwarfs any attempt at reporting and identification."

"Last night, Republican Senator Gordon Kimball reached across the aisle with a proposal I find quite compelling. In addition, the Democratic leadership in the Senate also finds the argument persuasive. Because of current international volatility, I am sending a bill to Congress for immediate action. The sponsor, Senator Kimball, is ideally suited to shepherd the bill, since he sits on the Judiciary Committee, and since the mechanics of his elegant solution will be implemented by the United States Marshals' organization under the aegis of the Justice Department.

"First, some background. We do not, indeed we cannot, condone vigilantism in America. While the right to protect yourself from imminent death or injury is fundamental to our law, the minute you aggressively go out to retaliate against a threat or an attempted intrusion, you are breaking the law. Yet our law enforcement organizations are woefully unequipped to enforce the law on your behalf. This is reminiscent of the sorry state of our Continental Army in the Revolutionary War."

Wow, that Senator Kimball is one articulate, well-connected guy, I immediately thought. And since the senator didn't take notes during our conversation, he had to be off the charts smart with one fine memory. Henry must have seen me leaning forward, hanging on Medina's every word, because he could see out the corner of my eye when he turned and gave me a long, hard look. I ignored him, not wanting to start a conversation that caused me to miss anything the president said.

"Our country found itself outgunned, outnumbered, out financed and just about out of rope," continued the president. "Letters of Marque were issued to bonded and licensed *privateers* who attacked British shipping. Privateer-generated proceeds virtually financed the entire Revolutionary War. In fact, privateers captured ten times the number of enemy ships as the Continental Navy. The numbers may surprise you. The Continental Navy operated 64 ships, while the privateers had 1,607. The Continental Navy had 1,242 guns; the privateers had almost 15,000. The Continental Navy captured fewer than 200 enemy ships;

the privateers captured and, more importantly, monetized 2,283 ships. In my opinion, the profit motive can eclipse any forces this federal government could amass, and do so almost instantly."

Exactly the numbers I'd seen the senator write down during our conversation. Good thing I hadn't been standing, as I felt distinctly dizzy.

"Analogies aren't perfect, and precedents require modification. I am not proposing that modern-day privateers prey upon foreign interests for profit. But consider deputizing cyber-marshals to engage in electronic *hot pursuit* and destruction of hostile cyber-forces anywhere in the world. These United States Cyber Deputies would work under contract for the United States Marshal organization and under the supervision of the Department of Justice. They would be bonded but for the most part simply *turned loose* on our enemies. Their *rules of engagement* will be a work in progress, and I do *not* want the lack of specificity in these rules or their definition to delay this legislation. Indeed, time is of the essence."

The slightest glimmer of hope peeked into my consciousness. Could I get off the hook, legally speaking, for starting this firestorm? Such a thing had never occurred to me, and no legal defense remotely suggested itself. But maybe…

"The most relevant legal doctrine of national sovereignty is a 1823 statement called *The Monroe Doctrine*. It stated that, and I quote, *any attempt by European governments to colonize land or interfere with states in the Americas would be viewed by the United States of America as acts of aggression requiring U.S. intervention*, unquote. I will therefore explain a new doctrine of digital sovereignty appropriate for this day and age.

"Any attack or attempted attack by individuals or governments on American public or private computer systems will be viewed as acts of aggression requiring *immediate* intervention. Period. I am implementing this via executive order today.

"Are there legal ambiguities? Unfortunately, the answer is yes. Senator Kimball gave me an excellent tutorial, which I've validated with legal experts in my own party. International law governing hot pursuit generally deals with oceanic chase. The legality of the U.S. actually pursuing Pancho Villa across sovereign borders into Mexico and the Israeli capture of Adolf Eichman in Argentina is hotly debated. But notwithstanding these issues, technology and globalization of the world economy demand we take a firm stand. But our stand must be clearly articulated and based upon the rule of law."

The president paused for effect, then continued: "Therefore, any individuals or corporations who unilaterally take it upon themselves to retaliate against attacks on their computer infrastructures are in violation of law and will be prosecuted to the full extent of current cyber crime law. Thank you and goodnight."

So much for my grandfathering some kind of legal defense for my actions. Thoughts of arrest and doom so fully engulfed me that I didn't notice Harley standing by my side, holding a plate of apple pie a la mode. She got my attention by clearing her throat, and I took the dessert.

"Sorry, Harley," I said. "I didn't see you. Thanks for the pie."

"Henry, here's yours, too," she said, placing the plate on the arm of his easy chair. Henry muted the television, and we both waited to take our first bites until Harley retrieved her own dessert from the kitchen and sat on the floor between us.

"Why would Senator Kimball want you to hear the president's speech, tonight?" asked the detective.

Total truth, Morgan, I told myself. *This guy could arrest you just as easily as the FBI, and the president didn't sound like he wanted to cut you any slack.* "Last night, the senator wanted to talk about some classified adventures in which I'd played a part, computer stuff, so he asked me for a ride home. During the ride I gave him my thoughts on an effective cyber-war countermeasures. Tonight, the president announced pretty well what I told him should be done."

"That's impressive," said Harley.

"And completely, totally impossible to believe, speed and all, how a Republican senator could so quickly galvanize a Democratic president to take action," said Henry between bites of some pretty impressive cinnamon apple pie topped with French vanilla ice cream.

As if in answer to Henry's assessment, my cell phone rang. Though the caller had blocked his identity, I immediately recognized Senator Kimball's voice after I answered.

"Morgan," said the senator. "Did you hear the president?"

"Yes I did, Senator Kimball." Both Henry's and Harley's mouths slackened in identical expressions of incredulity that flatly guaranteed their genetic relationship, not that I'd ever questioned it. "No offense, but no government on earth could work that quickly, especially not mine."

"As you might guess," he said, "there's a story to be told, my boy."

"I'd love to hear it," I said.

"That's why I'm calling. You available to come over to the house about ten o'clock PM?" he asked.

"Tonight? You're in town? You did this all by phone with the president?" I thought about all the work I ought to be doing on Olive's computer files, but I couldn't realistically expect them to be rebuilt until after midnight.

"Sorry for the fire drill, but I have to head back to Washington, D.C. right after church in the morning," he said.

"Under the circumstances, how could I turn you down?" After his most amazing feat of political legerdemain, I truly couldn't blow him off, especially since his openness to me would likely be his ruin. "Your house, ten PM?"

After we hung up, I couldn't help but shiver at the direction my life had taken. Less than a week earlier, I'd been a hermit, killing my legs racing bicycle messengers up and down San Francisco hills, shooting a few hoops in pickup basketball games, and plotting revenge on all the people that had been attacking my servers. Henry saw my shiver.

"S'up?" He tried to sound casual.

"The senator is heading back to D.C. tomorrow, and wanted to chat about computer stuff later."

"You have to go soon?" asked the again-fragile Harley.

"Heck no!" I said. "And certainly not until I finish this dessert, lick the plate clean and then help with the dishes.

"No need," she said.

"Oh yes," I said then, actually licking my plate clean. "You've been a wonderful hostess, and I had the bad manners to not even bring a gift. No more bad manners. Henry, you done with that plate?"

I stood and snatched his plate from the armrest. Harley tried to get around me to block the kitchen entrance, but I took up far too much of the hallway. Especially when I leaned my shoulder into the route I heard her try to take. The three of us found ourselves in front of the sink, where I did the scrubbing/rinsing and Henry loaded the dishwasher. Harley figured out she wouldn't be winning this particular battle, so she perched atop a barstool, one of four identical wrought iron pieces she probably made in metal shop.

"Henry, I've got to meet with the senator at ten. How about we link up back at the station by midnight and see how Olive's computer backup is coming?"

"You found her computer?" asked Harley.

"Next best thing," said Henry. "Morgan spotted an Internet backup service in her credit card statements. Judge O'Shea signed a court order for us to get the data and rebuild Olive's files."

"And that's going to help you how?" she asked.

"We're hoping she had something on her computer that the murderer didn't want us to see," said the detective.

"Sounds like a needle in a haystack, Henry," she said.

"No, it sounds like a needle in a haystack *Dad*," he quickly responded.

"Right, Henry." Again, the twinkle.

We finished the dishes, Henry and Harley shooting across each other's bows, and then adjourned to sit on the deck in the cool evening air.

"Did you make the picnic table?" I asked Harley.

"Nope. Henry," she paused and winked at her dad. "*Father* bought it off the back of a truck from some traveling gypsies. Not bad wood, but they nail these things together in about twenty minutes. They look good, but fall to pieces in a season. I replaced all the nails with screws and then properly sealed and stained the wood."

"Nice job," I said. "That's how a beautiful young lady spends her Saturday nights in Salt Lake City? Building tables and chairs?"

"Pretty much," she almost sighed. "I scare the good Mormon boys and don't meet very many high-caliber of the other kind in wood shop, metal shop, or at picnics with Hen- er *Father's* work buddies and their families. So I figured I'd wait until after medical school before I get too serious about a social life."

Now it came my turn to go slack jawed. *Medical school!* All I could think of to continue my side of the conversation seemed lame. "Have you chosen a specialty, yet?"

"Orthopedic surgery," she answered. "I laid down my bike on a sandy turn, and a surgeon named Ed Weeks put my ankle back together rather nicely."

"Henry, your kid really does know what she wants," I said.

"Morgan," she started, after a pause. "You covered the *E* part of *EKGT*, earlier. How about a less-damaging *K* routine?"

"Well, Harley, given your future vocation maybe it *is* fitting that I show you the other side of the orthopedic equation."

For the next hour I showed her several varieties of side kicks that would take down the biggest of the big and which would definitely require thorough ACL surgery. I did *not* show her the follow-through killing blows, once she had disabled her attacker. Instead, we concentrated on escape moves in the event more than one attacker tried to help his now-crippled buddy by grabbing her from behind. Henry became quite agitated at the thought of two-on-one confrontations and called the session to an end around 9:15 PM.

"Okay guys, *daughter*. Morgan has an appointment, and you've thoroughly destroyed any possibility that I'm going to get a good night's sleep."

I picked up on the signal, more the desperate plea of a father petrified for his daughter's future, and made a big deal of looking at my wristwatch. "You're right, Henry. You've got almost three hours to lock down Castle Davidson with Princess Harley safely inside before we meet at the station."

"What about the *G*roin and the *T*hroat of *EKGT*?" said Harley.

"The *G* is a long shot. Too easy to block or deflect with a hip," I said. "And you don't have the innate power to go for the *T*, period. Honest Harley, stick with the first two. The rest only work in movies."

18

"Senator,
if you don't mind my asking…"

 enator Kimball met me at the key-card operated gate located on the long driveway leading to his house. He hopped into my passenger seat after locking down the entrance and we drove to his portico. Neither of us spoke until he'd given me a seat across from his in a book-lined study. Before he sat down, the senator seemed to get a wonderful idea.

"Care for a bowl of pistachio ice cream?"

"I'm not so sure ice cream at ten o'clock PM is a good idea," I said.

"It's a *wonderful* idea! Ben and Jerry's. And my wife, Elaine, is in D.C., so what do you say, Morgan?" Surrounded by photos of his six children and numerous grandchildren, he seemed like one of them, like a little boy plotting grand mischief. He couldn't have survived over thirty years in the senate without shielding himself from institutional cynicism somehow, and besides, I found myself quite intrigued by the man himself. How could he be a power player without guile?

"Well then, it's Ben and Jerry's," I conceded. "You're not bothered that they're off-the-charts liberal?"

The senator bade me follow him into the kitchen. "Morgan, if I made all my purchases based on political orientation, well, actually I don't have a good metaphor worked up for it. But it has never been my nature to keep any kind of enemies list."

"And here I thought you might deliver a canned one-liner penned by one of your speech writers," I said, quite surprised by his unassuming candor.

Kimball invited me to sit on a bar stool, nice but not nearly the quirky quality of Harley's handiwork. He went to a Sub-Zero and held up two individual containers. "You don't have to take *Pistachio Pistachio*, my favorite. Elaine likes *Cherry Garcia*, and the grandkids like *Chunky Monkey*, although I think it's the name rather than the flavor."

"You had me sold with pistachio," I said.

He underhanded a pint of *Pistachio Pistachio* to me and kept one for himself. Moments later we sat across from each other on the next-best thing to Harley-created bar stools. The senator dug into his like he hadn't eaten all week. I paced myself, knowing my own caloric intake had to be approaching three thousand in the last three hours.

"Your subpoena for Olive's computer backup files moving forward?"

"As we speak, my computer is recreating many gigabytes of data," I said. "I'll meet Detective Davidson about midnight to grab my laptop from his office. Then comes the fun stuff."

"Fun stuff?"

"Yeah. I'm never happier than when it's just me and the computer, solving the world's problems."

"Speaking about the world's problems," he paused, probably to let his tongue un-numb itself from the ice cream. "What did you think of the president's speech?"

I took a bite of ice cream so I could take some time to properly articulate my answer. If you've never had someone watch you completely dispose of a mouthful of food, holding his undivided attention, then you know how time seems to crawl as you suddenly need to consider every action of every muscle. Upon reflection, I don't recommend it. And I understand how women might develop eating disorders if they pay too much attention to how they look while eating. Luckily, boys learn early how to entertain friends of a certain class with belches and other bio-noises, so the experience didn't traumatize me. Rather, it provided me with just a little introspection about eating psychology. I finally got around to smacking my lips and tongue a couple of times, buying a last few moments to compose my answer.

"Senator Kimball, my net-net on tonight's presidential address?" I made one more lip smack for good measure. "There's a whole lot of something going on that I don't know about, because no government, nowhere, no how, can move that fast on a completely new policy initiative."

Now the senator took his turn rolling a big lump of pistachio ice cream around in his mouth, although he looked more to me like a cat gumming a canary. Big cat, very small canary, in order to make the metaphor work. He finally swallowed the canary and smacked *his* lips.

I smacked mine.

He smacked his, again.

He finally conceded defeat in the evening's lip smacking.

"Morgan, in one sense, your security clearance is about six levels too low for what I'm about to tell you. Can I trust that you are not streaming this conversation onto your *Beat Lamar like a Gong* show, and that you will *not* breathe a word of this to another living soul?"

"You may trust me," I answered. My thoughts churned on the concept of trust. *Yes, senator, you may also trust me to completely wreck your career if you ask me the wrong question, since I will not lie to you. Because I will not lie to you, I will in effect make you an accessory after the fact in numerous federal crimes.* Clearly, I had to set up some ground rules for our conversation, and hope this most astute politician could read between the lines. I had to tread carefully, yet make full disclosure of the senator's precarious position. "Senator, I know some things that you do not want to know. And I promise you, in the spirit of the trust you've placed in me, that I will not obfuscate or lie to you. But do *not* ask me any question the answer to which might place you in an untenable position."

He smiled ever so coyly. "Cuts to the chase, doesn't it?"

"Pretty much."

"Your caveat opens up a vast field of possibilities, Morgan." One smart guy, Gordon Kimball. A neuro-linguistic programming expert could have written a thesis on the eye movement, left-brain to right-brain to left-brain to right-brain deliberations as my host weighed the import of my disclosure. Should he have let this individual into his home, let alone share his precious store of Ben and Jerry's? What mine fields did he *not* want to know what I know? Well, as the English would say, in for a penny in for a pound. I could see he made his decision. I could almost relate to the serial bank robber who wanted to be caught. I didn't like the idea of being caught, but I didn't want to bring down any of these people with me.

"I take it this has nothing to do of any knowledge you might have of Olive's murder?" he cautiously asked.

"You are correct, Senator. Those aren't the mine fields."

"Ah," he said. Relieved, yet confused.

"Yep," I said. That would leave cyber warfare. The corners of his mouth almost ticked into a smile when his mental light finally clicked on. "You have a story for me about the president's quick action on my cyber war idea?"

"I do." He took a smaller bite of ice cream. "First, a little background. The president and I have had a lively ongoing conversation about the division of power between the defense department and intelligence gathering as related to cyber warfare. The door opened rather wide once I convinced the president that neither myself nor Senator Hyde had aspirations to run for president. The former governor of Massachusetts and the former ambassador are another story, but the president trusts the Utah Senators."

"Wait a minute!" His statement caught me completely by surprise. "Don't a significant number of senators seriously aspire to the presidency?"

"Boy do we!" he laughed. "As Senator Hyde has said on more than one occasion when asked whether senators think long and hard about a shot at the White House, *every damned one of them, every damned day.*"

"Then why…" I began.

"I personally didn't think a Mormon could be elected to the presidency," he cut in, "because I cannot survive the one hypothetical question. You refused to answer a hypothetical question for me last night, because you said the president would never put your concept of privateer or deputized marshals on the table. We'll get to that in a minute, now that your prediction has been proven dead wrong. Unfortunately for me at least, as well as for Senator Hyde, a devout Mormon candidate cannot duck *The Hypothetical Question*: *As president of the United States, if you get a call from your prophet who says that the Lord God Almighty commands you to do thus and so immediately, and that your refusal will condemn you for eternity, will you obey?*"

"Kennedy successfully deflected the same question concerning the pope," I said. "And both Mitt Romney and the president's former ambassador to China didn't let those thoughts put a check in their swing in 2012."

"The pope's different. Good Catholics have managed to disregard the pope's edicts for centuries. But I assure you, Morgan, that a truly devout Mormon would *not* go against his prophet. Sure, he could tell the press and the electorate that *I would have to pray about it and get the same answer directly from*

God Himself, but then the press would ask, *Okay, so what if God Himself told you to do thus and so, just like the prophet told you?* Either way he answers the question will alienate a large enough percentage of the conservative base. Either he'll be labeled an apostate or his enemies will ever so subtly hint at schizophrenia. Besides, most of the Protestant Christian world does not believe that God talks directly to man, anyhow. But the president believes my own position enough to trust me. Hence our close working relationship, at least on matters of national security."

"Hard to believe the evangelical resistance to a Mormon president," I said.

"You'd better believe it!" Kimball put the cardboard lid on his empty ice cream container and casually tossed it into a recycling container across the kitchen. "They'll use all kinds of religious dogma as arguments against supporting a Mormon candidate, but the overwhelming reason they'll fight us to the death is that our condemnation of a paid clergy effectively punches their meal ticket. We call it *priestcraft* and rather forcefully denounce the practice in *The Book of Mormon.*"

"Right. At the funeral your leader said you don't pay your priests, or whatever you call them?"

"Nope. We have a lay ministry that must work for a living. Our equivalent of priests and pastors are called bishops."

"And the president believes your assessment?"

"Absolutely," said Kimball, sighing. "He knew he'd never have to run against me. Which is why he didn't see much risk in reaching out to me for some advice on cyber defense. The president and I perfectly agree on the matter. He gets to increase the size of government, and I think defense is a legitimate responsibility of government. We just didn't have a handle on the mechanics. Not only did you provide those mechanics, but you gave me a stake to drive into the heart of the most popular competing idea."

"Which is?" I asked.

"Let's just say that some *very* liberal advisors to the president have been leaning toward some kind of international global arms mentality that would not only be impossible to enforce and manage, but which would cede some element of U.S. sovereignty. Your wooden stake in the heart of that argument had to do with economics of scale. Nuclear weapons take government-sized research and development budgets, but any smart yokel with a laptop and an Internet connection can single-handedly launch a global cyber war. Nobody but maybe a Rwandan considers machetes to be weapons of mass destruction, and now, thanks to your argument, nobody but a moron would consider applying WMD philosophies to cyber warfare."

"All good arguments, Senator," I said, failing to keep exasperation from my voice. "But the speed with which your communication of those arguments translated into presidential action is beyond comprehension."

"Now for the classified stuff." The senator took a deep breath. "Last night, you indicated that Russia and China couldn't complete a cell phone call, let alone access their command and control systems to launch ICBMs at each other. I shared this with the president, along with your recommendation that he announce a new cyber doctrine. Unbeknownst to me, after we completed our conversation, he had a conference call with both the Russian and the Chinese heads of government, trying to calm them down. As their rhetoric heated up, the president finally told them to shut the hell up and stop making threats they couldn't possibly deliver on. Further, he shared with them some specific cyber attack statistics provided by U.S. intelligence, told them, in your exact words, that they 'couldn't complete a cell phone call let alone access their command and control systems,' and finally that enough was enough and that he'd be announcing *your* cyber attack doctrine tonight on television."

"Their reaction?" I stammered.

"More yelling, at least until he offered our resources to help them inoculate their infrastructure and eradicate the virus that had crippled them."

"A big promise that I don't think he can keep."

"Which brings us to the hypothetical question you refused to answer last night. You said you could figure out a way to let an American-based creator of the virus properly communicate to the authorities in exchange for a pardon. But you wouldn't, you said, because the scenario couldn't come to pass. Since the issue is no longer hypothetical, I ask you again: Will you help us?"

Ooh Senator, you've inadvertently painted me into a nasty corner. I should have seen this question coming. But I didn't. The minute the president articulated his plan, I should have remembered my bravado of last night and planned accordingly. Now, either I come up with a fast, satisfactory answer, or I just spill the beans and watch this good man's career swirl counter-clockwise down the toilet. Of course, if he lived in South America it would swirl clockwise. In either case, though, swirl it would. Well, time for a senatorial IQ test.

"Senator Kimball, I will not help you."

"Why not, Morgan?" He couldn't help himself, so I had to remind him of the ground rules.

"Remember when I said there are some questions you do *not* want to know the answers to?" I paused and watched his eyes dart in and out of focus. "This is one of those questions."

"But..." he began.

I interrupted. "Be careful, here. If you insist on an answer, I will give you one. And when I answer you, you'll agree you didn't want to know it. But I cannot take it back once tendered."

Several times, his mouth almost formed a word. And several times, he stopped himself, mid-utterance. Eventually, he landed on a strategy: "Will there be a time where you *can* help us?"

"Yes sir, there is," I answered with relief. Smart guys, these senators.

"When might that be?" His words formed one question, and his eyes asked the real question: *Should I be asking this?*

"After I meet my commitment to Pat and Sherry O'Shea to solve Olive's murder, *then* I'll help you."

"So I should tell the president...?"

"You should tell the president that my sole focus in life at this moment is finding out who killed Olive Jenkins."

"You're serious," he said.

"Serious as cancer," I said. "The one thing that is accelerating the process is if your kicking the FBI in the ass, so they're getting their behavioral analysis unit out here *this* Monday and not a week later as was scheduled."

"What if the president won't accept your condition?"

"Assure him the Russians and the Chinese aren't going anywhere in the foreseeable future."

"Oh yes," said Kimball. "One more question the president himself wanted to ask. How did you know the virus had attacked their command and control systems? Neither the CIA nor the NSA had made that connection."

Well you see, Senator, I created the virus and know how it propagates and hides itself. And all someone connected to an infected server has to do is synch his cell phone, his PDA, or plug in a USB drive and then take it to work at a secure installation, and every computer in that secure installation will be infected. And every device connected to that computer that has RAM or EPROM memory associated with it will be infected. Luckily, the senator didn't come right out and ask me if I'd written the virus. Maybe I *could* give him a plausible answer without incriminating myself or making him an accessory after the fact to my crime.

"Senator, the speed with which the virus took over Chinese and Russian servers probably surprised even *this* programmer. Somebody learned a few things since I took down the Iraqi air defense system, so whatever I did *must* have been improved upon. Suppose you work in a Sino-Soviet defense industry. But you go home at night and play with your personal computer. Maybe you sync up the PDA that you painstakingly and lovingly procured from Google, Samsung or from Apple. And that device has a Bluetooth capability. Then you take it to work. But unbeknownst to you, the virus has surreptitiously changed the firmware in your precious little status symbol. You walk into your secure installation, and the little daemon program carefully finds a Wi-Fi or Bluetooth connection *behind* the firewall and ever so carefully and ever so stealthily probes and propagates itself. Pretty soon, the command and control system is compromised, and while it may not be connected to the Internet, it will find a military satellite on which to piggyback a sub-band encrypted control signal until it finds other friends in high places. In short, Senator Kimball, the speed of infection indicated that this virus didn't come from Ms. Nosky's how-to-write-a-virus class at the University of Calgary. This virus came from a serious developer who fully understands the twenty-two principles of creating a perfect virus, and the probability that he limited it to Internet-available servers approaches zero. In fact, the principle of black-box portability pretty well guarantees that the virus infected top-secret computer architectures that we haven't ever known about."

"But why wouldn't the president's intelligence cyber-experts have drawn this conclusion, too?"

"Because they're government employees, which means they couldn't get real jobs with real companies. And they're dealing with the old-boy network of beltway bandit contractors who have the fix in to get more business with the bureaucracy. You'll notice that neither the Russians nor the Chinese accused the president of launching the attack. That's because they face the same problem of competence. Only in their case, the supply chain is one step removed from ours. Since they steal most of their technology from us, our GS-whatever federal employees, why not get it from the liars and thieves who've figured out the federal procurement maze?"

"A profound indictment of our intelligence agencies," said Kimball. "So they know our government didn't launch the attack because…"

"…because they've thoroughly penetrated our government defense processes. After all, we provide *their* defense R&D." *And*, I thought to myself, *because nobody truly knows the twenty-two principles for creating the perfect virus but the person who coined them: me.*

Somehow, I'd managed to finish a whole vat of Ben and Jerry's pistachio ice cream. My host took the empty container and walked it over to the recycling bin, thinking hard as he walked. He seemed to step in cadence with each logical conclusion. I thought it would be prudent if I interrupted his convergence on *The Question* that could get him in some trouble.

"Senator, a slight change of subject?" I asked.

"What is it?" He blinked as if to clear out the cobwebs and give me full attention.

"What would bring two United States Senators back to the funeral of a very non-public, non-influential lady like Olive Jenkins? It's kind of been gnawing on me."

He chuckled, sounding relieved that I hadn't pressed him with a harder question. "We really have a small community, we Mormons. Bob Hyde and I have so many associations through marriage, friends, and various church assignments, that it's pretty easy to interact with the same person in many different roles. Not only has Olive sent many young people to college and even helped pay for their missions, but she's helped both Bob and me produce nice little family history booklets for visiting dignitaries from around the world. *Not* to take the time to attend her funeral would have been extremely ungrateful and rude."

"And in the midst of all this, you managed to take a scrap of information from our after-dinner conversation and make something happen pretty fast."

"I guess I did, didn't I?" he said. "Thanks to you and some actionable intelligence for the president."

Yeah well, don't be thanking me too soon. Instead, I tried to be gracious accepting the compliment. "Thanks, but I'll bet there's not another man in the country to whom I could have given that data and seen anything done with it. So thank *you* for doing something so unusual." And the thought began percolating in my troubled brain, that just maybe I could get myself out of this mess without going to prison.

"And your friendship with Pat and Sherry O'Shea?" I asked. "Both Utah senators showing up for dinner just doesn't happen."

"No it doesn't. Ever," he said, warming up to my incredulity. "You got to sit in Friday, before your encounter with the tattooed felons at the parking garage, for a few hours to witness the spectacle of Patrick's show-cause marathons. Bob and I had a couple of nephews who decided they had enough political pull to do just about any damn thing they wanted. They ended up in front of Judge O'Shea, cockiness and all. The high-paid defense attorneys representing each of them planned on a walk in the park. And it looked like one, too, as they got released to their parents. But on the way out the door, O'Shea overheard the boys' sniggering remarks to each other and called everyone back into court. This is second hand, of course, although I listened to the tape-recorded session and can re-enact it almost verbatim.

"O'Shea asked the boys to repeat what they'd said to each other. Their attorneys told the boys not to answer on the grounds of self-incrimination. Patrick would have none of it, instructing the attorneys to shut up and the boys to answer. The attorneys protested and immediately found themselves in contempt of court. The bailiff cuffed them and frog-marched them to the empty jury box, to wait until the conversation with the boys ran its course. After some coaxing, as well as getting caught in a lie about what the judge had plainly heard, the boys recounted their words, whereupon the judge declared both the boys and their attorneys in contempt of court and ordered them to spend the weekend in county lock-up. Remember, show-cause hearings are held on Fridays."

"That's Patrick for you," I said.

"That's not all if it," continued Kimball. "On Monday afternoon, not first thing in the morning but in the afternoon, Patrick had the four of them again brought before him. Neither the boys nor the attorneys had been permitted a change of clothes. The judge thoroughly dressed down the not-so-proud legal eagles in the presence of not only the boys but of the boys' extremely irritated parents. Then he told the boys that they might reconsider their not-guilty pleas from Friday, plead guilty, and then he then would put them on probation until their eighteenth birthdays, the first thirty days of which they would wear T-shirts twenty-four/seven on which would be written *I am a privileged snob who stole a car because I thought my parents could buy my way out of the consequences* on front and back. He gave the attorneys five minutes to consider his offer, but warned them that sticking to their not-guilty plea would find their clients remanded to the county jail until trial. On their way to confer with the attorneys, Patrick also postulated that they might stay out of showering with the prison population for a weekend, but they doggone well couldn't do it for the month it would take him to work them into his trial schedule."

"They took the deal," I commented.

"They certainly did," said Kimball. "And talk about a complete turn around. Their parents came to Bob and me, separately of course, raging on about civil liberties violations and improper judicial conduct. We independently laughed in their faces and suggested their enabling parental practices had embarrassed the both of us. A little over a year later, after both boys had left on missions for the LDS Church, interestingly one to Kiev and the other to Taiwan, Bob and I took Pat and Sherry to the dinner that began our friendship."

"The attorneys have any hard feelings toward the judge?" I asked.

"Not after they heard of Bob's and my interest in the outcome," he said.

"No, I imagine they wouldn't," I said. "And *Daddy's little felons* didn't get any new members. The boys do okay?"

"You might say so. They're both in law school now."

19
Temperature Rising

enry Davidson got to the Salt Lake County Sheriff's Office ahead of me, and waited until I arrived shortly after midnight. He used his card key to get us in the main doors and greeted the night-shift duty officer through the bulletproof glass. He turned on the upstairs lights as we rounded the corner into the detectives' area.

"How's the senator?" he asked.

"Senator Kimball is quite a guy." I sat down and hit the space bar on my laptop to activate the screen and see how the reconstruction progressed. Surprisingly, the job completed a mere five minutes before we got there.

"Why'd he want you to hear the president's speech?"

"Evidently, some of the ideas I shared with the senator made it straight to the president," I said. Then something on the download caught my attention. "That's odd."

"I'll say," said Davidson. "How often does something make it to the president so fast?"

"No, that's not the odd part. According to the restore log at the Internet backup site, two simultaneous file restores have been taking place, both with the same username/password but to different IP addresses."

"Two?" said Davidson.

"Yeah. Mine and one other that's only about half-way complete."

"Any way to find out where the other system is located?"

"We'll see," I said, bringing up my own special set of packet tracing and sniffing tools. "The IP address is in…Japan? What the hell is going on from Japan?"

I didn't want to bring the Japanese system down, so I launched just the automated probe part of my viral toolkit to test for vulnerabilities. Again, odd. The system had plugged all the obvious hacker entry points, and didn't offer any Web services. Time to escalate to level two, invade but do not destroy. More quickly than I would have predicted, the IP address went completely offline, hanging the progressing download. I could no longer ping the address, so some on-the-ball systems administrator must have quite literally pulled the plug.

"Two can play this game, buddy!"

"Morgan?" said Davidson.

"Whoever tried to grab Olive's files just went off the air," I said. "Certainly an above-average response to my little tickle. I'm going to make sure they don't get another chance at Olive's files."

In just a few minutes, I hacked the Internet backup service, changed Olive's username/password, and renamed all her files. I then erased the system logs so nobody, not even myself, could find who did what to whom and when. And nobody would ever locate those files unless I personally gave them a road map.

"Why would anybody else want those files?" asked Davidson.

"Good question. Whoever killed Olive and stole her computer would already have them," I said.

"Maybe the killer wanted to see just how much data she'd backed up?" offered the detective.

"Not bad, detective."

"I am a professional," he said. "And I only use this power for good."

"Japan, though…" I muttered mostly to myself. At that moment, the faintest smell of rotten eggs registered. That natural gas leak smell suddenly alarmed me. "Henry, we've got to get out of here, now."

"What?"

"Gas leak," I said, grabbing my laptop and leaving the Internet cable and my battery charger. "With all the electronics around here, this place is going to go any second."

I didn't need to explain any further. We both raced down the stairs. Davidson yelled at the first-floor duty officer to run, and we almost made it out the door before a deafening fireball seemed to lift the roof right off the building. Davidson and I found ourselves lying half way across the parking lot, the building a raging inferno behind us.

"The other guy make it out?" I asked, shaking my groggy head and crawling five feet to my computer which didn't seem the worse for wear.

Davidson didn't answer. I staggered to my feet, one hand clutching the computer and the other trying to staunch the flow of blood into my eye from the cut in my forehead. Davidson lay unmoving a few feet away, breathing but unconscious. I didn't see anyone else in or near the doorway. The duty officer hadn't escaped the conflagration. I went back to Henry and rolled him onto his back. His face had taken a worse beating in the fall than mine.

Firefighters from the station, just 135 feet away, arrived almost immediately, sirens blaring and sleepy firefighters still shrugging on their gear. But even with that response, the building and whatever occupants who couldn't get out in time just didn't stand a chance.

"Over here," I yelled to a blond kid who couldn't be past twenty.

"What happened, mister?" said the kid.

"Gas leak," I said. "This man needs an ambulance. One other man in there may not have gotten out. Right in the front door, bullet-proof glass cage. Ya gotta' get somebody in there to see if he's still there."

The next five minutes seemed like an hour. Davidson regained consciousness, but about the tenth time he asked me what had happened, I figured he had a good concussion. The firemen went in with oxygen and heavy gear just briefly enough to find and drag out the charred corpse of the duty officer. No one else dared go into the blaze as ceilings and melting girders came crashing down. I rode to the hospital in the ambulance with Detective Davidson and one uniformed officer who didn't take his eyes off me or his hand off his holstered sidearm. Sheriff Running met us in the emergency room of the new IHC hospital on State Street and 5600 South.

Running let the anxious uniformed policeman who'd accompanied us stand down, and the two of us sat in the triage room with Henry Davidson while the on-call ER doc examined him.

"What the hell happened?" asked the sheriff.

"As you know, Judge O'Shea signed a court order authorizing us to download the information Olive had backed up to her computer. We left the computer in his office to build the files, and then met there at midnight to check the process. Obviously, Olive's killer didn't want either us or the computer to survive."

"You mean someone blew up my building on purpose!"

"Sheriff Running, you can take that one to the bank," I answered.

"But who even knew about the computer backup?" asked the sheriff.

"Clearly the killer knew," I said. "Once he turned on Olive's stolen computer and checked the installed software, he'd see the automatically scheduled backups. In fact, as we finished our own reconstruction of Olive's files, I noticed someone else about half-way done rebuilding Olive's files from an IP address in Japan. When I launched a probe to figure out his identity, he pulled the plug."

"Japan?" replied the sheriff.

"What happened? Why am I here?" asked Henry for the fifth time, from the bed beside us. Sheriff Running turned and gave the detective's shoulder a gentle squeeze.

"There was an explosion at the county office," he answered, for the fifth time. "You got a bad bump on the head."

"A concussion," said the man in the white coat. "I'm your doctor, Isaac Bingham. We're going to wheel you down the hall for an MRI."

"Should we come with him?" I asked.

"Not necessary," said Dr. Bingham. "I know the answer to all his questions, by now. Besides, I'll send in a nurse to look at your injuries. That eye may need stitches."

After Henry had been wheeled away, Sheriff Running got back on track with the investigation. "How could the murderer have been in Japan, yet blow up my building?"

"Oh, the killer just found a few proxy servers between himself and Japan. Then he watched the error logs for anything coming from my IP address and crashed the system when I got curious. But he only rebuilt half of Olive's files when I crashed him."

"Can't he just go in again?"

"Nope. I changed Olive's account and password, then renamed the files on the backup. Nobody will ever find them unless I tell them where to look."

"And if you'd been blown up, tonight, our investigation would be dead in the water," said the sheriff.

"That, I think, was the general idea." And a good one, too. I took out my business card and wrote the username, password, and filename for the Web file backup vendor. "Sheriff, if anything happens to me, this will let your computer forensics guys get Olive's files. Something's there that the killer *definitely* does not want us to see."

The sheriff pointed to the computer still clutched under my left arm. "And you have it right there?"

"I hope so, as long as I didn't crash the hard drive. Come to think of it…" Without completing my sentence, I gently put the computer on the wheeled tray table beneath the hospital's monitoring electronics and lifted the display away from the keyboard. Closing it had put the computer into sleep mode just before we dashed out of the building. We waited until the screen came to life and asked for my password. I typed it and *voila*! "Looks like God loves Olive and wants us to catch her killer."

"And the guy who killed Sergeant Peck," said the sheriff.

"Who?" I asked.

"My duty officer at the station," he answered. "He left a wife and four children."

"I'm sorry."

"Where's Dad?" Harley whisked through the drawn curtain just as I'd said I was sorry, and her hands went to her mouth.

"He'll be fine, Harley," I said. "They just took him to take some MRI images. A precaution. A concussion and a few stitches."

She threw herself into my arms, her sobs of relief muffling into my chest.

"Your dad's going to be okay," said the sheriff.

After a moment, she stepped back and looked up at me, wiping away the tears with the back of her hands. "The news scrolled across the movie, about the explosion and one known fatality. I knew you and Dad planned to meet around midnight…." She then turned to the sheriff. "Who died in the explosion?"

"I've got to go and notify the family right now," he said. "Joe Peck had the night desk."

"Oh dear," said Harley. "I go to school with his daughter."

A somber looking woman peeked around the curtain at the sheriff, and he motioned her to wait.

"Morgan," said the sheriff. "Can I get someone up here to copy Olive's files. Right now, I really must get over to the Peck house."

"You bet," I said. "I'm not going anywhere.

The sheriff left with the woman, and I sat with Harley while we waited for Henry to get back from the MRI. I shared my assumptions about the explosion. Our close call getting out of the building made her a little nervous, especially since I didn't candy coat it. I wanted her to be nervous, because the Olive's murderer seemed brazen enough to go after every loose end, including the investigating officer and his family. Just then, my phone rang. The caller ID pulled Senator Kimball's name from my Android address book.

"Senator," I answered. I motioned for Harley to have a seat in one of the two chairs in the room.

"What in blazes is going on?" he asked. "No pun intended."

"We're fine. Henry got a bit of a concussion and is getting an MRI as we speak."

"The news said one man died in the explosion," said Kimball.

"I'm afraid so. Sheriff Running is on his way to notify the family."

"Any idea what caused the explosion?" he asked.

"Nothing definitive, but since someone besides us seemed to be downloading Olive's backup computer data, I'll give you short odds that the murderer tried to take us out along with our computer."

"Holy Moses," he said. "He's got two murders on his hands."

"Two *more* murders, from the looks of it."

"Right, Morgan. A serial killer who really doesn't want you looking at Olive's computer data. This might be a real break."

"We'll see," I said.

I let the senator get to bed, since he had church and a close flight departure. Then, just be safe, I fished the chief-of-staff-to-a-no-longer-functioning-ambassador'a card out of my pocket. Best to let the poor fellow and his wife know that her grand aunt had stumbled across a serial killer's trail and had paid for it with her life. I dialed his cell phone number, which he picked up on the second ring.

"Mister King, this is Morgan Rapier."

"Morgan Rapier?" he sounded confused.

"We met at the funeral, today."

"Oh, yes of course," he said. "Sorry, your call woke me up."

"Forgive me for calling so late, Mister King. If you haven't heard, the Salt Lake County Sheriff's Office blew up tonight, nearly killing me and Detective

Davidson. We think Olive's murderer tried to eliminate not only the reconstruction of her computer files but the two investigators, too. I figured you'd want to notify your employer and his wife before they hear about it on the morning news. One man died in the explosion and fire, by the way."

"I'm glad you and the detective are safe. Did you manage to recover the computer files?"

"Barely," I said. "Now we'll see what information they contain."

"I'll let the ambassador know," he said. "Thanks for your call."

We disconnected, and I felt actually proud of myself for *not* conjuring up the image of an orangutan to go along with his voice. Poor guy couldn't control the genes he was born with. Then, as a courtesy to my hosts and to the other Utah senator, I called the O'Sheas and then Senator Hyde to let them know of the evening's events. Senator Hyde slept very soundly, and it took me longer to connect all the dots than it did with Patrick O'Shea. He snapped awake instantly. Even Sherry got on the line for my update.

O'Shea rued the fact I hadn't "gotten off a shot at the murdering son of a bitch," and I didn't have the heart to tell him I hadn't been carrying a gun. Yet. As soon as I got to the trunk of my Mercedes I intended to rectify that situation.

"Mister Rapier," said the disheveled man who entered. The badge hanging from the pocket of his sports jacket identified him. "I'm Ed Zander. Sheriff Running asked me to drop by and copy Olive's disk files."

"Right this way, Ed."

He unzipped a laptop case and I helped him plug a direct-connect cable into my computer. Even at near-disk speed, it took forty-five minutes for him to grab all the files. He thanked me and departed just as they wheeled Henry back into the area.

"Father," said Harley softly to her dad.

"And don't you forget it, either!" said Henry in a not-so-fierce growl.

"You must be Harley." Doctor Bingham extended his hand. "Your dad's going to be just fine. We couldn't see anything on the MRI, so the worst he'll have is a headache and some road rash where his face hit the pavement."

"Road rash," I commented. "You must ride a bicycle, Doctor."

"When I can," he smiled. "Being the new guy around here, working the night shift at least lets me ride during daylight."

"Harley Davidson, eh?" said Dr. Bingham. "Great name."

"You bet your ass," said Harley, Henry and I in unison. Henry shouldn't have laughed, as his headache reminded him.

The nurse finally cleaned up the cut above my eye. Three butterfly bandages and some superglue worked as well as stitches. I left Harley with her dad. The uniformed officer who rode with Henry and me to the hospital arranged to get me a ride back to my car. Luckily, Henry's Crown Vic took the brunt of the blast, completely protecting my S550 from a flame paint job. I rolled into bed, exhausted, just past four o'clock Sunday morning.

20

Free Breakfast at Snowbird

y cell phone awakened me just after ten o'clock in the morning. I should have blown up the cell phone towers that the Snowbird ski area so conveniently located on the mountain to keep guests connected to their offices.

"Speak," I said into the infernal device.

"Sheriff Running calling for Morgan Rapier?" he hesitated as if maybe he'd misdialed.

"Sorry Sheriff. Long day yesterday, short night." And a painful one, judging from the stiffness in my hips, back, neck and shoulders.

"Fire marshal just confirmed arson. Somebody used a key card to get into the basement furnace room. They turned off the natural gas outside from the emergency shut-off, and then went inside to disconnect the furnace fitting, after which they exited and turned the gas back on. Inside, we found the remains of a Christmas light timer switch connected to a lamp in the basement. Pieces of a broken light bulb in the parking lot indicates the unprotected filament triggered the natural gas explosion when the light went on."

"Thank you sir," I said, reverting back to military discipline. Nobody kills someone on *my* watch. "Any report on Detective Davidson?"

"He quit asking 'What happened?' over and over. His daughter spent the rest of the night in the hospital with him. He wanted to release himself, but she said she'd baseball bat his knees if he tried." I think Running snorted, but I'd have to have seen his face to be sure.

"Sounds like Harley." I looked at the clock and the time surprised me. "We'll, I'd better get to work on Olive's computer files, Sheriff."

"Thanks, Morgan. Call me if you find anything."

"Likewise, sir," I responded.

After a hot shower and with computer in hand, I took a brisk walk beneath the tunnel separating my condo from Snowbird's Cliff Lodge. Skiers still lined up to take the tram past the base camp to schuss over the six-hundred-plus-inches deep snow, while diners took advantage of the wonderful Sunday brunch menu in the lodge. Surprisingly, even after my two Harley burgers and Kimball-supplied Ben and Jerry's of the night before, my stomach demanded a substantial breakfast. I found a corner booth that had an electrical outlet, and plugged in my spare computer power adaptor. The hostess brought me a menu along with a Sunday *New York Times*, and I scanned the news while I waited for my steak and eggs. Heck with the brunch buffet. I needed *meat*, protein. Vegetables and fruit are what food eats.

The president's speech made headlines, and the *Times* officially declared *The Medina Doctrine* historically as important as *The Monroe Doctrine*. They conveniently ignored the *Gulf of Tonkin* resolution, in favor of accentuating the positives of their new hero. They even poured some praise on Senator Kimball's bipartisan contribution to the plan, although not enough praise to warrant calling it *The Kimball Doctrine*.

The other front-page story talked about the furor in the Islamic world over Mohammed bin Faisal Al Saud, my friend Benny. Rumors had him surfacing first at JFK, and then in San Francisco. A little something gnawed at me, if he did indeed go to San Francisco. Maybe he had more competence as a hacker than I'd given him credit for.

I didn't hit the trifecta; otherwise Lavar Kendrick would have also made the front page of the *Times*. Well, I *almost* did, judging from the page three headline: *SEAL Pulls Punches When Jumped By Bullies*. The story actually mentioned my video link. Checking my Android browser, almost two million viewers had watched Lavar's embarrassing show of machismo. My simple prayer: Please God; don't let him take it out on his family.

But Lavar, Benny, the Russians, and the Chinese had to take a back seat to my main goal, finding out who killed Olive, widowed Sergeant Peck's wife, injured Henry, and tried to kill me. This had become personal.

I also loved that Snowbird and the Cliff Lodge offered free Wi-Fi Internet access to the guests. Rotating steak, eggs and keyboard clicks, I carefully looked through Olive's email mailboxes, both incoming and outgoing, and looked at her most-recently updated files. Lots of correspondence on genealogy and particular file with .paf as the file extension. I'd never heard of it, but hey, my Google-makes-everyone-a-genius mantra accurately described life today as well as it did yesterday. I googled ".paf" and quickly learned it stood for Personal Ancestral File, for which I could download a free program from the LDS Church site. Three minutes later, I opened Olive's .paf file and traced her family tree back into 1500 England, Ireland and Scotland. Interesting but not too relevant to a Twenty-first Century murder investigation. Once I resolved the directory in which she'd stored photographs of all the dead people, herself now included in that group, each photograph appeared next to the name as I navigated the family tree. Again cool, but so what.

She'd most recently accessed this file, but I really couldn't tell which names in the family tree had the most recent hits. Dead end. So I went back to her email, keeping the genealogy program open in another window. Her most recent email contained several references in a subject line to "the murderer George Wood." She evidently spent a lot of time navigating a bureaucracy intent on keeping the details of his trial, conviction, and eventual pardon secret. The outgoing folder contained 2nd, 3rd and even 6th requests for information as part of her subject line. Those she signed with her maiden name, Olive Curtis Fretwell, instead of Olive Jenkins. I sorted the outgoing requests alphabetically by recipient, and then switched to the mail inbox to see if any of her requests had been answered. Not a one, as it turned out. Interesting.

I went back to Olive's most recent outgoing email, and saw several references to her repeated telephone calls. Telephone calls! Had we grabbed all of Olive's telephone traffic from the phone company, both land lines and cell phone, if she had one?

"Boy aren't we hungry," said the Cliff hostess. I looked down and saw that I'd managed to scour the plate clean, sopping up egg yolk and steak juice with my toast.

"Look at the bright side," I replied. "The plate's so clean you won't have to wash it."

"I know that voice," she said. "Aren't you that Internet guy who slugged Lavar in the throat?"

"Oh dear me," I sputtered. "Do I look like a violent man?"

She gently touched the butterfly bandages over my right eye and said, "Yes, darling, you do."

"Right. Could we kind of keep this between us?" I tried to plead with my eyes as well as with my voice. "Get me the check and I'll make it worth your while."

"With pleasure," she smiled and disappeared. Before I forgot, I dialed Henry's cell phone number. Hopefully, the hospital hadn't taken it from him.

"That you, Morgan?" he answered.

"Caller ID gets me every time. How's the head, Henry?"

"Will you please come and get me out of this place," he said. "And my head hurts, screw you very much."

"If I spring you, Harley might take a baseball bat to my kneecaps."

"The sheriff has a really big mouth. Seriously, Morgan. Get me outta here. I have to walk around behind Harley, apologizing for her brisk treatment of the poor nurses who don't jump every time I press the request button. And *Heaven help* the poor nurse who couldn't find a vein from which to draw blood. Harley ran her out of the room and demanded that the supervisor get someone in here who'd had some medical training."

"Sounds like she'll make a good orthopedic surgeon," I said. "Hey, I'm on my way in there, but did you have somebody run Olive's phone records."

"Come to think of it, no we didn't," he said after a pause. "You got something?"

"Maybe," I said. "Olive's outgoing email had numerous requests, the latest suggesting unreturned phone calls. We should find out who she'd been trying to call."

"I'll get right on it. Now *please* come and get me. The nurses flinch every time Harley smoothes her hair."

My hostess approached me with several waiters and someone else who looked like he had some authority. "Got to go, Henry. See you in a few."

"I see you brought back-up, in case I won't pay my tab," I gibed.

"It *is* him," said the older guy. "Pleasure to have you, sir. Your breakfast is on the house."

"Beg pardon?" So this is how it feels to be a celebrity.

"I'm Michael Harvey, manager of guest services for Snowbird," he said. "We've just been in the back office, watching your video. It's an honor to have a courageous U. S. Navy SEAL with us. Please accept our thanks for your combat service." His entourage displayed more teeth than the Jackson Five in their prime.

"I'm humbled by your graciousness." I smiled. They smiled. Somebody at a table across the room started clapping. Then everyone in the lodge joined in. Clapping. Then standing and clapping. A moment we'd all remember, especially when the evening news carried pictures of me being handcuffed and whisked away in a train of black Suburbans.

I gathered up my computer and power adapter as smoothly as I could, and slipped two twenty dollar bills into the hostess's hand on my way out, whispering, "Please put this into your communal tip jar."

She gave me a big hug. So did the manager. So did a lady with purple hair, just before I escaped through the door onto the tram deck. Morgan The Beloved has left the building. Selah.

21
More Auditions for Lavar's Got Talent

 arrived in Henry's private hospital room about noon. The nurses on the floor actually took faster steps whenever they walked by his door, making sure to avoid another encounter with Florence Nightingale's evil twin.

"Hi ya, Harley," I said. "I've come to spring your old man."

"Oh Faaaaather," she called toward a closed door. "You can come out of the bathroom now."

The door opened. Out stepped the fully although somewhat raggedly dressed detective. He quickly sat down in a wheelchair and said, "Home, Morgan."

"Yes, home, where he'll get a lot more competent care than in this slaughterhouse," she said loudly enough for patients two floors above and below could hear. Harley held the door and I wheeled Henry down the hallway to the elevator. Nobody tried to stop us. She stayed with her dad in the lobby while I jogged to my car and pulled it under the patient-pickup canopy. Harley then followed us home…on her Harley.

"They don't have helmet laws in Utah?" I asked.

"Nope," muttered Henry, somewhat sheepishly.

I didn't say anything else. I didn't have to. Like razzing a teammate for missing an easy fly ball, he'd be saying far worse things to himself that I ever could. Following us, Harley could sense my care in missing potholes and not taking corners fast enough to aggravate Henry's headache. She stayed well behind us as if to keep some tailgating Sunday driver from rear-ending us.

Bad news blocked the Davidson garage. Three monkeys—see no evil, hear no evil, and speak no evil—named Lavar, Lamar and Laverl. I stopped short of the driveway, and Harley pulled even with my window.

"I blew it, Morgan," she said. "That picture I had Dad take of you and me in his office."

"You shared it with a couple of friends, who shared it with a few more friends?"

"Forgive me. I'll call 9-1-1." No more the terror of incompetent nurses, Harley reverted back to Henry's little girl.

"No 9-1-1 quite yet," I said, and handed her the videophone I'd gotten from Dave Turner at Channel 2. We'd come close enough to the house for the phone to link up to my online video service using Davidson's Wi-Fi router. I pointed the camera at her and said, "This is Harley Davidson, who will be recording the next episode of *Life With Lavar*. Harley, park your bike and then come back and take the camera."

Her crooked-mouth smirk was patented Elvis, and she gunned the big motorcycle into the driveway. Laverl and Lamar each had to jump to the side or get run over. Harley keyed the automatic garage door opener in time to whisk into the garage, kill the engine, and come strutting past the three stooges to take the camera phone. I didn't have to tell Henry to stay in the car. His headache did that for me.

"Ya might want to put this one on the Internet, too, big man," said Lavar. No doubt, his friends and family *had* seen our pilot episode of *Dancing with Lavar*.

"We're already filming, Lavar," I said, and pointed to Harley. "We're upping the cinematography budget on our sequel, if that's okay with you.

"Be my guest," he gave his trademark smirk, first to his brother Lamar and then to his cousin Laverl. At least he had someone to smirk to, unlike our first encounter in the courtroom. Indeed he saw himself playing to an audience, either of his equally intelligence-challenged sidekicks in a barroom, or now to several hundred thousand, thanks to the miracle of viral networks. Not taking my eyes off the three, all now smirking for the camera, I stepped clear of the car.

"Lavar, I just have one question," I said.

"Go ahead SEAL-man, ask your question," he sneered in his best imitation of cool. "You got me with a cheap shot to the throat, last time. Ain't gonna happen *this* time. What's your question?"

"Do your kids flinch every time you raise your hand to scratch your head?" I'd have to remember to give Henry credit for the script line, straight from *Harley*

Versus The Nurses.

"What does that mean?" He looked from side to side, first at Lamar and then at Laverl for the answer. Not a MENSA candidate in the bunch, each of them seemed more interested in playing it buff and tough for their encore performance. Especially cousin Laverl, who only got a voice part in the original made-for-Web movie.

"I did a court records check on you and your wife-beating, child-stealing brother." Now, not only did I play to the scene in our non-pay-per-view Internet movie, but also I wanted to make sure our audience could figure out who wore the white hat in this flick. "The police have made frequent visits at your house, responding to domestic disturbance complaints. Your wife never pressed charges, but the reports say you pretty routinely use the misses and the kids as punching bags. That's why I wondered whether or not your kids flinch every time you run your fingers through your hair."

While Lavar considered his answer, and the size of the audience that might hear that answer, I took off my wristwatch and put it into my left-hand pants pocket. Neither Lamar nor Laverl spoke, appearing to maybe reconsider their co-staring roles. Lavar decided on an answer, since my silence didn't give him an easy out.

"That's a lie!" He blinked, tensing to get going with the move before I painted a worse picture of his character.

"Easy enough to check, isn't it?" I clapped my hands together once, loudly. It startled all three, just as I'd hoped. "Let me tell you what's about to happen here, Lavar. Listen up too, Lamar and Laverl, because there's going to be a quiz later.

"Lavar, I'm going to break some bones just like you broke in your wife. They'll also help you remember the times you sent your kids to emergency. See, the first time we had our little situation; I tried to apologize and make it right. Your brother got thrown in the slammer, and I pulled your pants down in public. That's why I took it easy on you. I felt bad for needlessly embarrassing you and even offered to buy you a beer. But now, after checking out your history of abuse, I'm going to give your family a gift. Actually a gift wrapped, in plaster casts and loaded with pain killers."

I paused. "Oh, and here's a denouement. That's a big word you'll have time to look up while you're in the hospital. If you *ever* lay hands on your wife or children again, I promise you that a group of much bigger, far meaner, and profoundly less charitable United States Navy SEALs will come for you, and make sure your hands or feet never *ever* again get a signal from your brain. Thanks to RSS feeds, the SEALs will see every time the police get a domestic disturbance call from your neighborhood."

Laverl actually shivered as he correctly visualized the outcome, and Lamar looked at his brother with a what-the-hell-have-you-gotten-me-into stare.

"Mighty big talk," shouted Lavar as he drew a .45 automatic he'd stuffed down his belt in the small of his back. I slapped the back of his hand and it went skittering across the cement. His two companions simultaneously produced switchblades that snicked open as I used the momentum of my gun-slap to pivot on my right leg and lash the side of my left foot squarely into Lavar's rib cage. The satisfying crack of at least three ribs marked part of my promise paid. Rather than rush me with their knives, Lamar and Laverl stepped backward to stay even with Lavar, who now lay flat on his back.

"The forty-five needs to be cocked, Lavar. My camerawoman Harley could have disarmed you."

While Lavar struggled to his feet, Lamar and Laverl circled around to either side of me. Their move might have looked good on television, but in reality they split the assault and gave me individual targets to take down. Plus, their choice of weapons made better drama than practical sense. I'm a big guy with a fairly thick layer of muscle, and the odds that they could take me out before I'd come within lethal range of them approached zero. Now a Somali pirate with a machete, *he* would have been a formidable foe, as I remembered my previous SEAL experience rescuing the captain of a hijacked freighter. But these yokels? They might be scary in a biker bar, but …

I took out Laverl with a spin kick to the side of his head. At six-five, I had the reach, and his knife came nowhere near my groin. Figuring Lamar just *had* to take the opportunity to close on me from behind, I used the momentum of my spin to side step. Just in time, too. Lamar's blade slashed just past my jugular, followed by him. Since my arms had been extended for balance, I retracted them, thereby increasing my rate of spin in time to send my right elbow slashing down to meet his collar bone. Another satisfying crack told me Lamar would be sleeping on his back for a few weeks, as broken collarbones make rolling onto your side an excruciatingly painful mistake. Two down, one to go. I hoped Harley had captured the scene.

Sirens blared in the distance. Good old Henry probably made the 9-1-1 call when he saw the gun. I'd better hurry. I now faced Lavar, who'd staggered to his feet. His left hand pressed against his rib cage, and his right hand pointed a derringer at me.

"Harley!" I called out. "Step to the side. Do *not* get behind me."

"This one's cocked, SEAL man," yelled Lavar.

Lavar with his a derringer, especially in his adrenalin-rushed state and holding his broken ribs, stood a better chance of winning the lottery than hitting me. And even if he did, a small-caliber/low-velocity slug couldn't stop me. Even a lucky shot to the head might not make it through my skull. Eye socket, yes. But as long as I kept my fist between the gun barrel and my eye, Lavar took far more dangerous risks than I did.

"Harley," I said without taking my eyes off Lavar. "Remember those little EKGT exercises I showed you?"

Lavar seemed to wait for her answer. I didn't. With all the speed I could muster, I closed on him and gave the knee on which he'd placed most of his weight the hardest kick I could muster. Simultaneously keeping my left fist between his gun and my head, I swept upward with my right hand against the heel of his gun hand. Lavar must have been looking at Harley, because he didn't pull the trigger until the gun was very nearly vertical. And, of course, his knee bent backward in a way God had never intended. Well, maybe God had intended Lavar's knee to end up that way, but only from a divinely perverse sense of justice.

Lavar went down, too stunned yet to begin howling. I continued my forward momentum with him and landed with his bicep between my knee and the pavement. The satisfying snap of his humerus marked my promise to his wife and kids *paid in full.*

After assuring myself that Lamar and Laverl stayed put, I walked toward my still-recording cameraperson. "Harley, as I told you last night, U. S. Navy SEALS do *not* fight for sport, and we do *not* pull our punches. Heaven help an enemy who misunderstands that." I then made a throat-cutting gesture for Harley to turn off the videophone.

The police arrived, along with an ambulance. Good thing, too, because my knee kick had severed a major artery. Rapid EMT action saved Lavar from bleeding to death.

22
LoJack No Jack

o sooner had the police and ambulance left than the borrowed phone rang. He blocked the caller ID, but only one person had this number.

"Hi, Dave," I said.

I couldn't understand a single word he said, as he both roared and laughed his first sentence. Naturally, I hung up without another word and turned off the phone.

"Turner at KUTV?" asked Henry as Harley helped him from my car into the house.

"The one and only."

"Think he's going to figure out not only that you about got blown up but also architected the president's cyber war doctrine?"

"He won't find out from me," I said.

Harley gently eased him onto the living room couch and handed him the TV remote. I took Henry's easy chair and rested the laptop on my thighs. The Android rang just as I leaned over to plug in the power adapter.

"Speak," I said.

"You're a one-man wrecking crew," shouted the familiar voice of Patrick O'Shea. "You get the Salt Lake County Sheriff's office burned to the ground and then put three of my little felons in the hospital."

"And managed to get one of the good guys killed, too."

"*You* don't own that one, Morgan. Understand?" I waited too long to answer him, so he continued with both barrels. "Hey, listen up sailor! Some murdering scurvy coward kills a defenseless old lady, and then goes after the people trying to find him, and kills one of them. This is on *his* head, not yours. And when you find him, if you don't end his mortal stay on earth, then I sure as hell will! No plea bargain. No possibility of parole. I'll get that boy a fair trial, everything by the book, with no possibility of reversal or appeal. Then he's going to get the death sentence, fair and square. We're still good at that in Utah.

"In fact, I'm going to the target range this afternoon. So I can be ready in case he tries to jump my bailiff during the trial. Then I can just plug him and save the system some money. What are you *laughing* at?"

"Sorry, Your Honor," I said. "You are one piece of work. And I needed that laugh."

"That's the spirit! Cowboy up and get that maggot-infested scum. He's dead and doesn't even know it."

Judge Roy Bean has been perfectly reincarnated. I hung up on the judge, O'Shea not Bean, just as Harley brought Henry and me BLT sandwiches.

"Okay, what do we know?" asked Henry between bites. Harley sat at his feet on the end of the couch. She didn't have a sandwich, and I suspected the Lavar episode had badly startled her. If her dad noticed, he didn't say anything.

"First, the killer didn't start his own download of Olive's computer files for at least five hours after we did. Why the delay? Certainly not an airline flight, since he still had to be in town to try and kill us last night." As if on cue, my Android dinged me with a text message that the Wolfram Alpha Grid had finished processing Salt Lake City Airport long-term parking entries and exits, looking for quick-turnaround customers. I logged into the grid and not one but two cars fit the criteria. Of course! I'd bet money that one would be a rental used as a placeholder for the *borrowed* vehicle.

"Henry, this is pretty weird," I said. "One car had entered long-term parking around eight o'clock AM, had exited barely twenty minutes later, and then re-entered the lot about three in the afternoon. The second car had entered five minutes before the first, and exited at three-ten in the afternoon, just ten minutes after the first car had returned. What do you want to bet that one is a rental?"

I took the law-enforcement back door into the Utah DMV computer system—anybody with VICAP/NCIC credentials knows how to do this—and ran the two plates. "Ta-dah! One 2009 Chevy Malibu, jointly registered to a man and wife in Holiday, Francois and Kathy Lambert, and the other a Hertz rental."

"What do you want to bet…?" Henry let the question hang. He also quit eating.

I brought up the license-plate spreadsheet the other detectives had compiled from the funeral and did a search on the Malibu plate number.

"Got'cha!" I stood and carried my laptop the two feet to Henry, so he could see the match. "Here it is, McGruff. And the location column says he parked on the street."

"For a quick getaway, Deputy Dawg." Henry reached for his own cell phone and dialed from memory. "Hello, Watson? … Yeah, it's me. Hey, that spreadsheet you did of the license plates, we got a hit on a possible seven-hour theft of a Chevy Malibu from airport long-term parking. Along with the Hertz rental that kept the parking place warm. Call Hertz and find out who rented this tag number. This is urgent, because the guy in the Hertz probably blew up the station and killed Peck!"

Henry gave his detective co-worker the Hertz license number. To Harley's credit, she hadn't said a word, yet seemed to deduce the train of thought just from our conversation. After he hung up on Watson, he restated his conclusion, as if testing it for errors. "If the killer has the rental car, then he still might be in town. Or at least returned the car this morning to catch his flight. Right?"

"He's here to do a job. The job's not done. Ergo, he's still here. That is unless he's decided things are too hot, in which case he's on the lam big time." A suspicion gnawed at me. What could Olive possibly have on her computer that put a serial killer at risk? "Time to look at the serial killer's other victims, Henry."

"Uh, my printouts got burned up with my office." The way Henry said it seemed like his first realization of officelessness. I didn't remind him that his photos of Harley went up in smoke, too.

"Not to worry. I downloaded them on my computer." I tried to quickly put him at ease. Soon enough, someone would hand him the melted ball of steel that used to be his service revolver. "If you've got a laser printer connected to this wireless router, I'll blast out hardcopies of the crime reports."

Harley again displayed initiative and ran back to Henry's den to make sure the printer was turned on and fully stocked with paper. Just after I'd queued up the reports to print, Henry's cell phone rang.

"You called Hertz and…" Henry paused for the other detective's answer. "Put out an APB on that car, now! Driver considered to be armed and extremely dangerous. And get us the ID on the driver, any security footage, the drivers license picture…Good…Thanks. Keep me posted."

"Driver's license will be a fake, and the credit card stolen," I speculated. "Also, I'll bet you a buck that we don't get any security footage, nor an eye witness to the guy. His fake ID probably belonged to the Hertz Gold Club, so he just walked off the plane and into the pickup lot. Any photo at the exit will show a guy in a hat."

"But he still has the car," said Henry, hopefully.

"He may have outsmarted himself at the airport, Henry. If he doesn't think we're looking for him, then he may not have disabled the Hertz LoJack transmitter."

"Hertz uses LoJack?" Henry said it too loud, and put his hand on his head in a futile attempt to stop the throbbing.

"Not widely known. Call Detective Watson back and ask him to get the Hertz LoJack number for the car. Then, I guess since your building burned down, you can get the Salt Lake City Police Department to send the signal and track that car for us." My voice got louder as I realized how close we just might be to nabbing our murderer. VICAP printouts could wait. We had a bad guy to catch!

The Davidson household buzzed with activity for the next thirty minutes. Henry called Sheriff Running and gave him the news. I called Judge O'Shea and told him to get ready for a breakthrough. Harley retrieved a spare portable police flasher I could magnetically mount on top of my car, since Henry's Crown Vic still sat in front of his burned-out police station. I even grabbed some duct tape to mount Dave Turner's phone/camera on the dashboard of my car. And Henry took some Anacin and Coca Cola to deal with his headache, since no way in hell would he *not* be a part of this chase.

Almost thirty minutes on the nose, we got the call. The LoJack transmitter had been activated, and we had the coordinates of a stationary car. Harley really wanted to come with us, but when her dad saw me retrieve the guns and ammo from the trunk of my car, she knew she didn't stand a chance of auditing *this* graduate level class.

"Is all that stuff legal?" said an amazed Henry Davidson as Harley looked on in some amazement herself. "Actually Morgan, is *any* of that stuff legal?"

"Why Henry! I am a duly deputized officer of the law." I tried to sound shocked that he could ask such a question, but the UZI and the Mac10 deserved a more serious answer to this officer of the law. Wouldn't want him to have such an obvious conflict of interest. "But actually, these have been properly registered with the ATF and in Utah, and I'd be glad to show you the documentation now or later. I suggest later, for obvious reasons of expediency."

I put on a double shoulder holster into which I put two nine-millimeter semi-automatic handguns. I left the fully automatic weapons in the trunk, but handed Henry a 12-gauge riot gun and box of double-ought steel shot cartridges. Finally, I loaded a laser-sighting Smith & Wesson .357 magnum revolver with armor-piercing shells.

"Put this on the floor by your feet, Henry. Worse comes to worst, this'll go clear through his car and nicely dissect the engine block. You know we've got to stop this guy, right?" But Henry wouldn't take his eyes from my open trunk.

"Get buckled into the passenger seat and let's go hunting," I said.

I mounted the KUTV camera phone to my dashboard with duct tape. Not that I intended to suck up to Big Dave and his television station, but my gut told me I needed a continuous record of my adventure. Worst case, it wouldn't be my word against the guy I intended to take down, and take down hard. We bid Harley farewell after giving her instructions to lock the doors, Henry established cell phone contact with the Salt Lake City Police Department who relayed the LoJack coordinates to us, and we set out on the big game hunt. Embarrassing as it is to say, when we caught up with the guy who murdered Olive Jenkins and nailed her severed little fingers to her ceiling, I wanted to make sure he urinated blood for a week after the encounter. If he lived even *that* long.

23

Two Corpses Take
One Last Joy Ride

hile I *married* Henry's cell phone to my second
Bluetooth port, he softly sung Willie Nelson's *On
The Road Again.* "On the road again, just can't
wait to get on the road again…."

"Hold your horses, cowboy. And buckle up. I don't want to get a ticket."

"I'd give you one, too, Morgan."

"Even though you're the passenger violating the law?"

"Law says the driver gets the ticket. Now let's go hunting."

As we pulled away, he made sure Harley went into the house as he'd asked
her to. Then, he dialed Salt Lake Dispatch and got a dedicated LoJack operator
on the speakerphone.

"That you, Marilee?" he asked when the operator came on the line.
"What're you doing down there?"

"Well, Henry," said the woman's voice on the car speaker. "Since my office
got burned down *along with your Christmas present*, I needed a place to ply my
trade."

"Let's talk Christmas presents later," he said. "You got a twenty for me on
the LoJack signal?"

"Since we locked onto it, the car hasn't moved from about 100 North
Temple and State Street," she said.

"Look," said Henry. "We don't want to spook our guy. If the car is parked,
then he might be nearby. Please tell all units to stay away from the car."

"Roger," said Marilee. "What's *your* twenty?"

"We're in Sandy headed north. It'll take us about fifteen minutes." Henry
muted his phone and then turned to me. I'd just pulled onto Seventh East
heading toward the freeway at 10600 South.

At about 3300 South, Marilee's voice interrupted our silence. "Henry, your car is on the move."

"Give me the numbers, Marilee."

"Henry, you there?" she asked.

"Sorry, I had it on mute," I said as I hit the unmute switch on my steering wheel.

"I'm here," said Henry. "Give me the location numbers. We'll intercept and do a visual on the guy."

"He's headed south on 200 West."

"Roger that," said Henry. "We're 35 or 36 blocks and closing."

Just as we hit the 600 South off ramp, our tracker announced, "He's now westbound on 500 South. Looks like he's headed for the freeway. I can't tell which direction, yet."

"Roger. Morgan, blast off this baby and take your first left. We're a block away from his freeway entrance. Marilee, let us know as soon as you can where he's headed."

"South. He's going southbound on I-15."

"We're just a block away. Notify all units that a white Mercedes S550 is in pursuit and to stay off I-15 south."

"Goodness Henry, you're moving up in the world," she replied. "How can you afford an S550 on a detective's salary?"

"It's not *mine* for crying out loud. It's Morgan Rapier's, and he's driving me."

"The SEAL man!" she exclaimed. "We just watched today's *Lavar's Not Talent* show. The Salt Lake chief of police actually wanted to call it *Idiot Apprentice*, but…"

"I hate to interrupt this chatter for official law enforcement business, but I'm just turning up the southbound I-15 onramp," I said. "Where's our guy?"

"He's maybe a mile ahead of you around 1300 South, still on I-15 and doing the speed limit," she said. "I *know* that voice. Pleased to meet you Morgan Rapier."

"Marilee is it?" I asked

"Marilee Stenovitch. And I'm not married."

"Marilee!" said Henry. "Pay attention to the task."

"Henry, I keep throwing myself at you and what do I get? A burned down

Christmas present."

I gave Marilee my Utah license plate number and then said: "Please get the word out to UHP that I'm a Salt Lake County deputy sheriff in hot pursuit. Wouldn't want to get pulled over at the wrong time."

"Yes sir," she said, this time all business. We overheard her talking with the dispatcher and getting the message out to both the city and county police. In the meantime, we rounded the I-15 onramp doing almost eighty, and I thanked both Misters Dalmar and Benz for all-wheel drive and such a magnificent power plant. Sunday traffic didn't give us much trouble, and I pulled a PostIt note from my shirt pocket.

"Henry, here's the tag number of the blue Hertz Malibu." Then, moments later, "Marilee, we're just passing the 1300 South off ramp. I think I see our guy nearing 2100 South."

I'd turned on the KUTV cell phone and activated the video recording. Time to start creating an evidence audit trail. We pulled even with the Malibu near 4500 South.

"Crap," said Henry. Barely tall enough to look over the steering wheel, the Latino driver couldn't be older than sixteen. "Marilee, why don't you get some official police cars at the 7200 South onramp. Our perp must have left the keys in the car, intending for it to be stolen."

I discretely backed off and assumed a position about one hundred yards behind the now-jacked LoJacked Malibu.

"Virtually no traffic here," I said. "Let's let the cops do the rest."

"Marilee," said Henry. "Tell the units at 7200 that the driver is a kid on a joy ride. We'll back off and let them take him down."

"Roger, Henry."

Just as we passed the I-215 interchange, three UHP cars with lights flashing neatly sandwiched the Mustang—left, right and front positions—and simultaneously blasted one startled kid with their sirens. The kid immediately slowed the Mustang and allowed himself to be herded onto the right-hand shoulder.

To his credit, the Hispanic driver didn't do something stupid. He let the car coast to a stop, keeping both hands on the steering wheel. I put Henry's magnetic flashing light on my own roof, turning on my hazard blinkers and pulling off the highway right behind them. A surprisingly on-the-ball UHP trooper pulled about five car lengths behind me, lights flashing, and laid orange cones from my car to the stopped Mustang. I left my engine running and we both got out and approached the stolen Mustang and the officers surrounding it, their guns drawn. Poor kid probably thought his current plight ranked in the top-ten list of over reactions.

The car thief just shook his head as the officers pulled him from the car, cuffed and Mirandized him in both English and Spanish. Detective Davidson stopped the arresting officers and addressed the boy: "This isn't your car, is it son?"

The cuffed and cowed young man just looked at the ground.

"We really need to find the man who had this car," Henry continued. "You help us, we can maybe make this go away for you."

The boy's eyes met the detective's, flickering between suspicion and hope. Anybody who offered to make an army of gun-wielding policemen go away stood one step below deity, especially to a streetwise fourteen-going-on-fifty gang banger. The kid bet on the cop.

"Found the keys in it," came the five most succinct words he could muster.

"You didn't see they guy who left the keys?" asked Davidson. "We're really after him." The detective *didn't* say he wanted a description in the worst way, because the kid might just make one up.

"Nah, mister. I di'nt look for no people. Jus' keys in cars."

"Here's my card, kid." Davidson handed the boy his card and then addressed the arresting officers. "Can't tell you how to do your job, but I recommend you keep this at a joy ride by a juvie. If he or his buddies can ID the driver, I'll go to bat for him with the judge."

"You might want to wait on that," said an officer who'd just popped open the Mustang's trunk. Henry and I stepped closer to witness the grotesque final contortion of an older couple crammed together.

"That would be…" started Henry.

I completed his identification: "…likely Francois and Kathy Lambert of Holiday and owners of a Chevy Malibu currently parked at the airport."

"And missing the little fingers on each of their hands," said the officer.

One street-wise joy-riding juvenile fell over in a dead faint.

24
Andover Class Reunion

lad I didn't pump a round through the Mustang's trunk," said Henry. "Might be a problem explaining the post-mortem slug in the bodies." We sat in an unused interview room at the Salt Lake City Police Department. They'd done their best to accommodate the needs of a burned-out Salt Lake County law enforcement organization. The Lambert double murder iced the cake created by the county officer who'd been burned to death the preceding night along with the ongoing search for Olive Jenkins' murderer. And my two-gun shoulder-holster rig raised some eyebrows at the station until Henry vouched for me. I still got to show everybody my deputy badge along with carry permits.

"Just one more thing I'd be explaining," I muttered. I usually didn't feel so worn out on a Sunday night, and the prospect of starting a new week with my plate this full filled me with dread.

"What do you mean 'just one more thing' you'll be explaining?"

Lack of sleep makes you sloppy, especially around people with finely tuned antennae for nuance and general clues that would elude most any ordinary citizen. Time for Morgan to pay attention and do some damage control. The list of things I'd likely be explaining to various local and federal authorities just about exceeded my ability to remember them. I decided to share the least of my worries with Henry.

"I was just thinking that my license plate hack into the Salt Lake City Airport parking facility might be illegal. Which means that our finding the Lambert bodies and any evidence obtained might be thrown out of court as fruit of the poison tree. After all, I *am* a deputy sheriff and theoretically an arm of law enforcement. We also throw out our knowledge of the killer's attendance at Olive's funeral. Illegal search and all that."

Henry sat silently, and then brightened with a solution.

"Relax, Morgan. The Salt Lake City Airport is a municipal property and therefore freely accessible to other agencies, like us."

"Good point," I said, doing my best to look relieved. Heaven forbid I should blurt out something about Russia, China, a billion or so Muslims going into cardiac arrest, and the ensuing destruction of at least two prominent political careers, maybe three if the former ambassador to China gets caught in the jet wash. Oh yes, and one district court judge. Some heptathlon. Maybe I could suck President Medina into the swirl and make it a what? An octofecta? Right now, though, my life would be complete if I could nail Olive's murderer. A few hours ago it seemed close.

"Something else is bothering you." What a bulldog!

"Yeah, *Detective* Davidson," I said. "In case you haven't been keeping up with current events, we're back to zero looking for Olive's murderer."

"Not really, *Deputy* Rapier," he shot back, reciprocating the emphasis on our respective job functions. "We've now got a bunch of people scouring airport and car rental security footage, looking for our guy. And our forensics team is looking for hair and skin that don't belong to the Lamberts. Something will break."

"Maybe you're right. At this moment, it seems the best use of my time would be to look carefully at Olive's computer files and see what the hell she has that caught the attention of a serial killer." I looked at my watch and confirmed that the clock in the station kept pretty good time. "Eight o'clock. Think I'll call it a day. You look like death warmed over, yourself."

"My headache went away."

"No it didn't. And you need a lift home."

"Right-o, Morgan. I need a lift home, don't I?" He stood slowly, and I could tell his headache really hadn't gone anywhere at all. "In case you're wondering at some of the looks you're about to get, you are now famous down here for the way you isolated the car rental switch."

"Good," I said and closed my laptop, hastily wrapping my power adapter cable around the whole unit. "At least they won't be buzzing about poor Lavar."

I followed Henry down the hallway and across the detectives' bullpen. My optimism about Lavar had been premature.

"Lavar has left the building!" came one voice.

"Lavar can't dance," said another.

"Glad Lavar got kicked off the island," snorted a third, a female voice.

Laughter escalated with each comment.

"Like I said, Morgan," mumbled Henry. "You're famous around here."

Twenty minutes later, I handed Henry the NCIS/VICAP printouts in front of his house. "See if you can find some common patterns in these serial killings. I'll go home and see what I can mine out of Olive's computer files."

"Now I can tell Harley my headache went away."

"Sure, Henry. As soon as I'm down the street you can tell Harley your headache has left the building." Then I did the Schwarznegger trademark line: "But *I'll be back.*"

"Let's see what we come up with tonight. I won't need a lift to my new office in the morning," he said. "They've got to line me up with a car, and there's the paperwork hassle. How about noon downtown?"

"Noon it is, unless either of us comes up with something."

On my drive up to Snowbird, I called Patrick O'Shea and gave him an update on the Lamberts and my close-but-no-cigar identification of the killer's transportation. He confirmed Henry's assessment that no search warrant had been needed to rifle through the airport license plate numbers. He then reminded me that Sylvester Stallone and Judge Roy Bean had a shooting contest, and demanded a Monday morning showdown. I agreed to pick him up and drive to the gravel pit just over Point of the Mountain. To hell with a gun club.

I slid into my underground garage about 9:00 PM. My rear-view mirror caught just the flash of a shadow stepping into the garage as the automatic door descended. Whoever had entered the garage behind me disappeared behind my rear bumper, crouching. My first impression—to slam the car into reverse and crush the intruder between the now-closed garage door and my bumper—gave way to a little mercy. Having put my fair share of people into the hospital today, I opted to pretend I hadn't seen the man. So I started whistling a tune from, of all things, *Camelot*, to cover the sound of cocking the nine-millimeter semi-automatic I'd drawn from my left holster. Before I'd fully extracted myself from the car, a loud laugh filled the now-enclosed garage.

"*What do the simple folk do?*" sang the slightly foreign-accented voice. Two hands appeared from behind my trunk. "I'm unarmed Morgan; don't shoot me." Slowly and now humming the rest of my song from *Camelot*, Mohammed bin Faisal Al Saud arose from his crouch.

"Benny?" I said in disbelief.

"You could pull that trigger and get several thousand imams to sign over half their afterlife virgins to you," said my old Andover buddy.

"Not to mention collecting the bounty on your head," I said, quickly pointing the weapon toward the ceiling, lowering the hammer and then holstering my gun. Of course, *he* could have plugged *me* quite handily, but his smile seemed just too genuine. No doubt at all why he sought me out, though. Nuh-uh Mohammad!

"You're a better hacker than I initially gave you credit for," I shrugged.

"That's my line, Morgan. But I didn't find *you* by hacking your system."

"Well then, Benny. If you've come to blow me up, push the pin. Otherwise, let's go upstairs and let me start apologizing to you for ruining your life," I said. "And you can tell me how you deduced my treachery if *not* by hacking me."

His loud laugh again filled the garage. "I'm hungry. In exchange for some food I'll tell you a *really good* story."

"Deal," I said. "That is, if my management service stocked the pantry when they opened it back up for me Thursday night."

"Thursday night? Which would be the day you sent that letter to my email list and then left your apartment in San Francisco."

I punched the security code, and Benny followed me up the cedar-lined staircase. Since I didn't feel a knife slice between my ribs, he clearly didn't intend me any harm. Either that, or he really wanted me to suffer on grander scale. After putting my laptop on my living room coffee table, I turned and offered Benny my hand.

"You owe me more than a handshake," he said as he embraced me.

"Yeah, I suppose I do." As men go, Mohammed bin Faisal Al Saud definitely qualified as handsome. Clearly a late bloomer, the gawky six-foot Arab had filled out into the spitting image of a young Omar Sharif. Brown eyes and a smile that could light up a gymnasium. Tall for his part of the world, he cut a rather imposing figure in his black turtleneck sweater, gray slacks and penny loafers. Probably calfskin penny loafers hand made in Paris, if I correctly remember Benny's clothing preferences.

"Hey, we're in luck," I said to the open refrigerator. "Coke, Diet Coke, bottled water, pomegranate juice, and cold cuts on Grandma Sycamore white bread." After a quick peek into the freezer compartment I added, "Or I can nuke a pizza, some Black Angus cheeseburgers or some burritos."

He didn't take long to decide. "How about Coke and a ham sandwich."

"Whoa!" I gave him a look normally reserved for drug dealers and transvestites. "You really are off the reservation. A *ham* sandwich, my Islamic friend?"

"Like my letter said, Mohammed couldn't have been a legitimate prophet and very likely got his revelations from Satan. Or better yet, as you yourself said way back at Andover."

"Ahaaaaa. Help yourself, Benny. I think I need to sit down." I *did* need to sit down. As I remembered Mohammed bin Faisal Al Saud from our Upper Middle and Senior years at Andover, he tried hard to obey Islamic law, even at the risk of co-ed ridicule in the formerly all-boys school. At some point, I peeled a large carrot from the fruit drawer while Benny created a sandwich that would have made Dagwood Bumstead proud. Several kinds of meat, including ham, pickles, olives, Walla Walla sweet onion, Dijon mustard, tomato, all washed down with liberal sips of Coke Classic.

He unselfconsciously watched me watching him eat. I guess a lot of people watch royalty eat. I chomped on my carrot like an amnesiac Bugs Bunny who got banged in the head and forgot his "What's up, Doc?" line. Besides, I didn't want to interrupt the ravenously hungry Mohammed, my Andover friend Mohammed, not the ancient prophet of Islam. So I waited until he daubed his mouth with a paper napkin, probably the first time in years he'd not held cloth napkins in his perfectly manicured fingers.

"What's up, Doc?" I finally asked.

"Well, you rascally rabbit who left the face of a pig on my screen after sending your little missive to my entire email list," said Benny.

"Kind of high-risk behavior, hacking somebody's server from your personal laptop," I said. "So if you didn't infer my identity from your intrusion, how *did* you figure it out?"

"Think about it, Morgan. You started my apostasy from Islam back at Andover. When I saw the content of the letter I supposedly sent to all my associates, relatives, friends and mere acquaintances who found themselves blessed enough to be in my computer address book, I *knew for sure* who'd written the letter."

"Something in my *letter* tipped you off?" I asked. "What could I have possibly…?"

Again the laugh. What a jolly fellow, Benny. I'd just burned down his life and he could still laugh. He calmed down enough to take another sip of his Coke and then said, "Remember that comparative religion class at Andover? The one where the guest imam rent his garment and stormed out of the room, and then the rabbi actually took a swing at you? And you made the Reverend Mr. Coffin of the Episcopal Church and dean of the Yale divinity school actually cry?"

"Vaguely," I said.

"Vaguely? You single-handedly insult all of Islam, destroy the intellectual demeanor of a Rabbi, obliterate the theological basis of Episcopalian Christianity, and you *vaguely* remember the incident?"

"The Jesuit kept his mouth shut. I remember that," I said.

"No he didn't," Benny said. "The Jesuit just sat there and laughed at the circus."

"I always thought of the Jesuits as God's Own storm troopers," I said.

"But you don't remember what you did to set off the imam?" Benny cocked his head and bore into me with his laser-like gaze.

"Not really. I'd been reading the Koran to learn Arabic, so it probably shocked him I'd actually memorized some of Súrah number seven in Arabic. I think seven is the number."

"No, I don't think your memorization in Arabic got on the imam's nerves," Benny said. "Maybe it's because you used one verse in particular to imply that the Prophet Mohammed likely received revelation not from Allah but from Satan."

"Aha! And I must have used that same verse in the letter I wrote and sent under your name."

He pointed at me and clicked his thumb like a gun hammer. "Verses number one-hundred-fifty-seven and one-fifty-eight, …*the Prophet who can neither read nor write…* you said that never in the history of God's dealings with mankind did He have an illiterate prophet, and that He quickly educated His holy prophets to embrace and record His words. And…"

"…and that only Satan promoted illiteracy and would actually prompt someone to brag about it." It came back to me quickly. I must have been composing Benny's fake letter since prep school. "That sure did set the imam's turban on fire, didn't it?"

"Then came the rabbi," Benny said.

"After the imam went storming out, screaming about blasphemy, that pompous rabbi should have kept his mouth shut," I said.

"He just affirmed your literacy argument," Benny said. "Although your treatment of the imam had caused a small nuclear explosion in my own brain. That thing about the treatment of captive women in Súrah number four also got the imam's goat."

"Well come on! When in the history of mankind has God commanded His troops to have sex with captive women?"

"I know. Verse twenty-four," said Benny. "Morgan, I seriously thought about garroting you on the spot and claiming the diplomatic immunity of my father, that is until you turned the rabbi's literacy argument against him."

"I just told him he obviously didn't understand what he had read in the *Torah*, otherwise he'd be a Christian," I said. "Either that, or that he'd completely ignored Isaiah."

"No, I quote your exact words: *Either that, or completely ignore Isaiah you dumbass.*"

"I was on a roll, huh?"

"And then the Reverend Mister Coffin tried to take the high ground and you swatted him like a fly," Benny said. "That whole experience is permanently etched into my memory. You told him to shut up. That his whole religion was based on Henry VIII's desire to get a divorce."

"Actually, I just asked him if he wanted to bear his solemn Christian testimony on the efficacy of divorce," I said. "And the big boob started to cry."

"Weren't you affiliated with *his* church? Or have you since changed?" asked Benny.

"Yes and yes," I said. "When the Episcopal Church started ordaining practicing sodomites as legitimate ministers, I decided that a church founded on sexual misconduct probably didn't represent the God I worshiped."

"After that classroom debacle, you seemed pretty chummy with the Jesuit," Benny said. "Are you now Catholic?"

"Nope," I confessed. "Since my wife died, God and I have been having a bit of a tiff."

"I'm sorry about your wife."

"Me, too." Kind of a conversation stopper, but Benny deserved an honest answer. He recovered quickly, though, befitting the son of a high-ranking ambassador.

"What *did* the Jesuit priest say to you after class that day?"

"He just slapped me on the back and said he couldn't have done a better job himself," I said. "Yep, Jesuits are formally trained as God's storm troopers. And you, Benny? What are *your* religious leanings?"

"All I know is what I'm *not*," he answered. "Your forging my signature on that letter couldn't have come at a better time. And you see why I knew who wrote my own explanatory letter now, don't you?"

"Which still doesn't explain how you tracked me down so quickly," I said.

"I got your San Francisco address from the Andover Alumni Directory. After that, I found you with just one word."

"One word?" I couldn't come with a one-word anything. I must have been really fatigued, because Benny's answer couldn't have been simpler.

"Lavar," Benny said.

Dang! And Benny knew he had me, too. But curiosity quickly prevailed, and I asked, "Okay, you knew I played *Survivor Lavar* in Utah. You still managed to find my condo, and more importantly, you managed to get here without making national headlines. Nice trick."

"Finding you proved easier. Public real estate records, since you didn't take any great pains to make your Snowbird condo purchase a secret," he said. "But getting here without attracting attention didn't just happen. News picked me up in New York and then in San Francisco, because I flew a royal family 727. I got here, however, in a repossessed G2. Some builder in Arizona couldn't afford the checks his ego kept writing. A taxi to a downtown hotel, $200 to a hooker in a bar for giving me a lift to the quarry trail head, and UTA to Snowbird."

"Nobody recognized you?" I asked.

"Not when I wore this." Benny pulled a U.S. Navy SEAL baseball cap from his inside jacket pocket. "Ironic isn't it?"

Irony squared if you knew the whole truth, I reminded myself. *Now for the big question.*

"You indeed found me, Benny. Out of curiosity, with a request for my help, or maybe even to put my head on a stick. What's *your* pleasure?"

"How very Arab of you. Feed me first, show me hospitality. All before we get down to business." Mohammed bin Faisal Al Saud, aka Benny, had probably been waiting four days to affix me with his half-amused/half-purposeful stare. He'd maybe even practiced it in front of the lavatory mirror at 35,000 feet on his family 727.

"And?" I said, not wanting to deflect my question.

"Since you're carrying not one but two semi-automatic 9mms in shoulder holsters, you might have been expecting someone besides myself to pay you a visit?" He gave me that practiced look, again. "Someone maybe devoid of benign intent?"

Come to think of it, I *did* pull a gun on him in my garage. One of two currently nestled snugly. Again, the man whose life I'd turned upside down deserved the exact truth.

"I came to Utah at the request of a dear friend, to help track down a murderer. Things seem to have heated up, and we might have been getting close. In your travels, did you hear of the explosion last night that destroyed the Salt Lake County Sheriff's office?"

"One man died last night," he said.

"A detective and I almost bought the farm in that one, too," I said.

"Oh. Then you're in law enforcement and hence the need for weapons?"

"Not exactly," I said. Why do people keep asking me if I'm in law enforcement? "I had some skills to help in the forensic analysis of the victim's computer, so they deputized me at the request of my friend, who also happens to be a district court judge here in Utah."

"They're certainly right about your computer skills," he mused. Little did he know.

"Back to my question to you," I said. "Why are you here? Curiosity? Help? Or even payback?"

"Besides tracking you down, since you have for all practical purposes nullified my entire life, there seem to be a disproportionate number of, what do you call them, oh yes: *life coaches* in the western United States and Utah in particular. I need a new life, so I might need a life coach."

"Awh Benny, don't get me started on life coaches. You think I was tough on the imam and the rabbi, life coaches are several steps down the food chain even from those charlatans."

"Morgan, you really *are* in a tiff with God!"

"No, actually He and I are on the same page here. Imams and rabbis are at least selling the party line and trying to convince people to obey God and the scriptures. Life coaches are an altogether different breed. You pay them money, and they tell you what you want to hear. Whatever goal you have, they'll teach you how to attain it. They'll share with you *The Secret*, if you give them money all along the way. Call it Scientology without the rattlesnakes in your mailbox."

"Don't *ever* let me introduce you to a life coach. He'd take a swing at you and end up on YouTube."

"Anyhow, that's the extent of my spiritual advice, Benny. I suggest you read the Bible and make your own decisions from there."

"Let me see one of those," he said, pointing to the .45 under my right arm.

I didn't hesitate, and handed the weapon across my table to him. He seemed pleased, even surprised, that I didn't take too long to calculate his request, although I figured I could slam the table toward him at the first sign his thumb itched to cock the hammer. Before my eyes, he ejected the clip, then the chambered shell, and proceeded to break down the gun as expertly as I'd ever seen it done.

"Nicely maintained, Morgan," he said, examining the pieces lying in front of him. "A lot of custom machining, too."

He then reversed the process and reassembled my .45, all except for chambering the lone round. That, he handed to me while radiating his best Omar Sharif grin.

"You want me to write my name on this bullet?" I took it from him.

"Not necessary my old friend," he said. "I just wanted to take one of your three options off the table. If it had had your name on it, the bullet would have been part of your brain by now."

"Which leaves us with curiosity or help." I chambered a round from the clip, and then ejected it to insert the lone bullet and reinsert the clip. He didn't answer until after the gun again rested in my right-hand holster.

"Curiosity or help," he said. "Could be a little of both, I suppose. Suddenly not having to spend my days studying the Koran or looking for ways to insert myself into tasks befitting a member of the Royal Family, I wanted to see what gives other people's life meaning. Since you not only started me on this journey, way back at Andover, but also pushed me over the edge last week, I thought *we* might reconnect face to face. What gives *your* life meaning, my religious terrorist friend?"

"Crikey!" I said in my best imitation of the late crocodile hunter Steve Irwin. "With a Hajj to Mecca now out of the question for you, you made your journey to me!"

"In some cultures, you'd now be responsible for my soul."

"Crikey!" I said, again. *How do I keep myself from becoming the religious mastermind behind The Great Muslim Apostasy? Or the great Lightning Rod of Islam?* "How about I just let you focus on stuff that's interesting?"

"Interesting." He didn't state it as a question, but more as if he wanted to roll the word around in his brain. "I'd like to find something interesting?"

"Interesting like the way you hacked into my San Francisco server," I said. "I *know* you found that interesting, because you did the most gifted job I've seen come out of your part of the world."

"Interesting," he said, again.

25

Since Benny Doesn't Have Anything Better To Do...

or the next hour, Benny and I had an *interesting* conversation. I filled him in completely on our search for Olive Jenkins' murderer, including the Salt Lake Airport parking lot license plate exercise that located the Hertz car as well as the late Francois and Kathy Lambert in its trunk. He expressed particular interest in how the contents of Olive's computer could possibly have motivated a serial killer to not only end her life, but to attempt to destroy my reconstruction of her data files, along with Detective Davidson and myself.

At some point during our conversation, I retrieved the laptop from my car and set about copying Olive's destroyed data to a desktop computer in my study. After the wear and tear my laptop had been through, I wanted to make sure my copy of the data didn't suddenly disappear into a black hole, or what one of my engineer friends calls *write-only memory*. I also wanted to set Benny up with his own computer, so he might focus his considerable intellect on helping me solve the murder. Besides, it might also serve to keep him out of sight. While the Utah population of Muslims didn't tip any scale of critical mass I could imagine, I didn't want to risk getting my house firebombed by someone who'd just spotted the famous heretic and had a rush of pus infect their brain with homicidal ideas.

"That's your third yawn, Benny," I observed. "How about I show you the guest bedroom?"

"I don't understand how I could be so hammered." He shook his head as if trying to dislodge his fatigue.

"You're a sea level kind of guy. We're over six thousand feet here at the house. And you have a headache coming on?"

"As a matter of fact," he said.

"I've got just the ticket." I went to the pantry and retrieved a bottle of water. "Put this by your bedside tonight and try to stay hydrated."

"Good idea. I haven't felt like this since I stayed at the L'Alp d'Huez hotel in France."

"Excellent comparison, except our base here *starts* where L'Alp d'Huez summits." I motioned him to follow me upstairs to the guest room.

Luckily, the maid service had prepared the bed with clean linens. Even then, Benny didn't hit the sack until eleven-thirty. I went back to my own room and sat in bed with my laptop. My own preferred problem-solving style is single-threaded, and I'd have liked to spend the rest of my consciousness focusing on Olive Jenkins. Unfortunately, world events demanded attention, too. Lavar's encore performance rapidly approached his initial reality debut in Web viewers. Russia and China now focused on the new Medina cyber war doctrine, both condemning it as over reaction and denying their culpability in promoting digital attacks against the United States. And both the Taliban and al-Qaeda had placed bounties on Benny's severed head. My command and control notification system was now swamping my Android device with notifications, so I changed my cyber control dashboard to focus only on my ability to stand down and to monitor my "dead-man's switch" life insurance policy, designed to make the bad guys think twice before icing me. I also made sure my backup command and control mechanisms were functional, just in case someone took my Twitter CCS out of the picture and I had to let the whole furball run from alternative systems.

I checked the videophone Dave Turner had given me and which I'd put in silent mode. He'd tried to call me a dozen times, but calling some media whore, even a likeable one like Dave, could serve no useful purpose. Right how, his only job was to be my video alibi.

Olive's computer files snatched the last fifteen minutes of my day. What the heck got her killed? Excluding her email, she'd most recently spent time in her genealogy file. But I couldn't tell where, and with over thirty thousand names to choose from, I might as well spent my time in a phone book. So I decided on another thread of thought and examined the email she'd sent over the last week of her life. Again, the only even *remotely* smoking gun dealt with "the murderer George Woods" as Olive called him.

A lady sending email about a murderer, and who subsequently gets murdered herself is quite a coincidence, even if the original murder did take place in 1863. According to Olive's email to the state archivist, the prosecutor in the murder of her ancestor, James D. Doty, later became governor of the Utah Territory and granted George Wood a pardon. Also curious. And that he died on June 13, 1865 just after granting the pardon. Really really really curious. But what could this possibly have to do with Olive Jenkins' murder?

Sleep overtook me as I pondered those long-ago events. About seven the next morning, I awoke to the sound of someone rummaging around in my kitchen. I padded out of my main floor bedroom barefoot and in my camo boxer shorts and saw Benny back in his black slacks and turtleneck.

"You didn't convert to Mormonism, did you?" he asked.

"Nope. Why?"

"Where in blazes is your coffee maker?"

"Ah!" I said. "Under the sink. Here, let me get it set up for you."

"Under the sink! You don't use it daily?"

"Alas my Arabian coffee fanatic, I'm afraid I'm a natural born addict," I said, connecting the unit into a counter-top plug. "So this is just for honored guests. But for me, one cup turns into a continuous all-day-long affair. Wastes a lot of time. Makes me a little crazy."

"You realize of course that coffee is called *The Wine of Arabia?*"

"And *you* realize I'd probably have picked up some special imported coffee beans had I known you'd be my guest?" I plopped a pre-packed strainer into the machine and poured water from the somewhat dusty coffee pot into the top. "At least I rinsed the dust out of it for you."

"Allah be praised," he said.

"Wrong direction. But we should probably eliminate references to deity until you sort things out."

"Old habits, Morgan."

"Speaking of habits," I said, "You always struck me as being fastidious. How about some brand new, never been unwrapped, underwear and a shirt? Your pants will have to suffice until we can get you to a store."

"Thanks, of course," he shrugged. "But I'm still thinking about the coffee situation. How's the coffee at the ski resort?"

"Benny, please *do not* show your face outside this door until I return. There's a million dollar price on your head."

"I saw that online this morning. A lot of money for this old noggin, so it's a good idea for me to stay invisible for a while."

"Tell you what," I said. "I'm going shooting with Judge O'Shea a little later. Then I'll check in with the detective I almost got killed Saturday night. You stay here to see if you can draw any conclusions why someone would murder Olive Jenkins because of data on her computer. When I get back, we'll pick up some clothes for you and then go to my favorite restaurant. Here's a cell phone. Don't answer it unless you see my caller ID."

I gave him the videophone from Channel 2.

"I took the battery out of my own cell phone," he said.

"Good thinking."

"Why should I not answer if I don't see your caller ID?" he asked.

"Because the guy who gave me this phone manages a CBS-affiliate television station, and he'd fall all over himself to get your story," I said, emphatically. "It would be a career maker for him."

26
Muscle Memory and a
Shootout with "The Boys"

 showed up at Judge O'Shea's door promptly at eight AM. I managed to shower, get Benny working on Olive's computer files and committed to laying low in my Snowbird aerie early enough to arrive at Judge O'Shea's as promised. Sherry answered the door and ushered me into a study, where Hizonor so forcefully hit the *return* key to print something I suspected might be one of his *Judge Roy Bean Moment* rulings.

"Morgan!" he bellowed. Yep, a memorable sentencing would emerge from that stentorian tone. "Sounds like you're smoking the bastard out."

"Language, Pat!" scolded Sherry.

"No pun intended, Your Honor," I said. "But *he* just about smoked *us*, Saturday night."

"He did indeed." O'Shea motioned me to a leather seat opposite him. "And when Lavar gets out of the hospital, he's going right back to jail. Parole violation his having any kind of firearms. Lamar and Laverl, too. Wait until you hear *those* sentencings!"

"Cut him *some* slack, Your Honor. After all I *did* pull his pants down in your courtroom, and then slugged him in the throat before a million-plus audience."

"Don't know about that," he said and leaned back in his reclining leather chair. I sat strictly at attention in my non-recliner, something I'm sure he had calculated when he furnished his room. "Sherry thinks all *Daddy's Little Felons* should be sent to Morgan Rapier for a little reality check."

If she only knew how broad an audience Daddy's Little Felons *might include*, I thought. "At least Lavar is out of the picture for the foreseeable future. He kept popping up at the most inconvenient moments."

"Any more progress finding the son of a bitch who murdered Olive?"

Sherry didn't interrupt him this time. Profanity or not, she wanted this answer badly.

"Detective Davidson and I are getting together later this morning," I said. "And I've got another pair of eyes analyzing Olive's computer files to determine what they contained that got her killed."

Fortunately, O'Shea's preoccupation with his upcoming sentencing kept him from asking questions I didn't want to answer about my "other pair of eyes." Sherry stared at the butterfly bandages on my forehead with enough intensity that I couldn't resist giving her a little more hope concerning our investigation.

"It's turning into a real 'guy' movie, Sherry. Our side is a little behind on the body count, but we've got the bad guys on the run."

"Good," she said softly but with a bitter growl. "I'm glad it's not a 'chick flick' with just one death at the end of the movie."

I didn't feel right about promising at least one more death at the end of the movie, but maybe my clenched jaw told her things had become personal for me. At any rate, Sherry seemed satisfied enough the progress Pat had previously shared with her to let us go off in a car loaded with enough guns and ammo to start a small revolution. Patrick quickly folded the paper from his laser printer and stuffed it into his jacket pocket as we said our goodbyes to Sherry. On the way out the door to the car, Hizonor picked up a sealed plastic garbage bag full of clinking cans. The garbage bag rode in style, in the back seat, since my trunk served as our well-stocked armory.

"Where to?" I asked as we pulled away from the front of the O'Shea home.

"Know the frontage road on the west side of the Point?"

"Sure." Heck, I'd ridden my bike over it hundreds of times.

"There ya go," he said, pulling the sheet of paper from his jacket.

"But where precisely on that road?"

"Don't worry," he said. "You'll know."

His quirky smirk stopped me from any more queries. He had something up his sleeve, so I drove on and let him make a big production of unfolding his papers.

"Want to hear how I'm going to sentence a child-molester this morning?"

Oh boy. Another Judge Roy Bean special. I couldn't remember exactly how many of his sentencing orations I'd sat through over the years, but they all started with the same pattern.

"What's the question you're going to ask the defendant?" I asked. Every one of O'Shea's sentence declarations always started with the judge asking the miserable devil a question.

Hizonor gave a gritty chuckle. "I'm going to ask him if he sings in the shower."

"Okay," I said, drawing out the first syllable of the word. I could immediately predict something about prison showers and molesters, but why spoil the judge's fun? "So after your give and take about singing in the shower, lay it on. But as I recall, even sexual abuse of children is not a capital offense, so Judge Roy Bean can't hang him."

The judge growled in reluctant agreement, and then began reading. I drove. He read.

"Spring showers have been blessing this little valley, almost like Camelot, raining only at night so we could enjoy comfortable, cloudless days. Our blossoming landscape coexists peacefully with the rivers flowing from snowcapped mountains. Birds are singing *their* shower medleys, David Leeland VanDeventer. But you will not hear *those* songs. Families will cycle on dedicated trails from Utah Lake all the way to the Great Salt Lake. But you will not hear their laughter. The mellifluous scent of our flowers will attract the buzzing song of honeybees, but you will not hear that song, either. Sprinklers will put a beautiful sheen on newly mowed lawns, and neighborhood barbecues will invite friends to renew conversations halted with the first snows, and small dogs will be on extra good behavior for those delicious scraps of meat. But you will not hear those little yelps of joy. All of humanity will hum in perfect harmony and contentment. But you, David Leeland VanDeventer, will not be here to partake of that song.

"Because I herewith command the sheriff of the county to drag your sorry carcass to the state prison in Draper, where you will serve out what will probably be the remainder of your life for the twenty-five separate counts of sodomy, aggravated sexual assault, premeditated predatory behavior, creation and solicitation for sale on the Internet the documented perversions with which you caused the wholesale destruction of innocence and ruin of so many little lives. The maximum sentence for each offence will *not* run concurrently but sequentially for no less than one-hundred-twenty-five years.

"And if there is a God in heaven, may He grant that the only song you hear for the rest of your miserable life will be a chorus in the prison shower of other kinds of predators singing *I Wish I Were a Little Bar of Soap* as they slippy and they slidey all over your wretched hidey. It is my heartfelt prayer that this happen every single day of what I hope will be a very long stay in prison, and that the first lyrics you hear on passing from this life to the next will be 'Light him up!' To all of which I say amen and amen and *amen*! Bailiff, get this worthless scum out of my courtroom, and then call maintenance to hose the place down!"

The imaginary gavel in his hand slammed down on the dash in front of him. I'm glad he didn't set off the airbags. I whistled. He took a deep breath.

"Interesting, isn't it Morgan, how an innocent song from one generation could suddenly describe a plague in ours?"

"It *is* the end of innocence, isn't it?" Singing *I Wish I Were a Little Bar of Soap* to a kindergarten class could get the teacher or even a grandmother arrested today.

"The end?" he finally looked at me. "Hell, Morgan. It never got started."

"But we're not giving up, are we?"

"No dammit, we're not giving up."

And neither did the judge appear to be giving up on his plotting and scheming. I crested the Point of the Mountain frontage road and immediately knew where Hizonor had planned to do a little shooting. About a mile into Utah Valley, half-a-dozen blue and red flashing lights illuminated a gravel pit on the east side of the road. A smattering of city, county and UHP patrol cars greeted us. Surrounded by men already wearing their ear protectors, the scene bespoke a modern-day contest of OK Corral alpha males who wanted to take on the top gun, which would apparently be one slightly famous U.S. Navy SEAL named Morgan Rapier.

"I trust you have your carry permit," smirked the judge.

"And my federal automatic weapons license, too. In case they want to look in my trunk."

Judge O'Shea jumped out of the car before I'd come to a complete stop. His high-fives told me that at least *this* cadre of law enforcement professionals held Hizonor in some esteem. But of course, any jurist who claimed Judge Roy

Bean as his alter ego would naturally be highly regarded by guys who put their lives on the line every time they slapped on a badge and kissed their wives goodbye. I hit the OFF button, since the actual ignition key never had to leave my pocket, and exited my side of the S550. Eight guys at least as tall as me, and one about half my height, waited for the judge to make introductions.

"Morgan Rapier, meet the best of the best," said O'Shea.

The way they shook hands, I didn't know if my hand would be able to pull the trigger. Of course, that could have been their motive. Disable me to level the playing field so Hizonor might stand a chance. I went down the line, acknowledging more than a few fellow or former comrades in arms.

"Semper fi," I said to Stan Pavish, noticing a Marine tattoo on his right forearm. "Manole and sorry about the knee" to Nafe Hauga, a sports name I knew from when the former Tongan offensive lineman for BYU blew out his knee in his last regular season game a decade earlier. Both Pavish and Hauga served with the Salt Lake City PD. County officers Larry Kratzer and Kevin Liu also tried to crush my hand. O'Shea introduced me to Utah Highway Patrol officers John Chyzik, an older Huey evacuation medic from Viet Nam and Milton Appelbaum, the only short guy in the group. Appelbaum had one prosthesis below the left knee, courtesy of his stint in the Israel Defense Forces as a platoon commander. Lehi police chief Constantin Delvanis, a Greek immigrant then introduced me to M. R. Rangaswami. The name, Rangaswami, and the three gold stars tattooed on his forearm clued me in: "India Defense Forces, Captain Rangaswami then?" I commented. O'Shea saved the most prominent introduction for last.

"And this is my dear friend Pete Boni, who won the medal of honor in Viet Nam."

I saluted Boni. "I think you served with my dad, Morgan Rapier, Sr. in Viet Nam. He used to tell me of your medal citation over Sunday dinners. Pleasure to finally meet you, sir."

"No sir's anymore. Call me Pete," he said, returning my salute and then shaking my hand as vigorously as his compatriots. I tried not to wince. "Your dad still own The Fist in San Francisco?"

"Yes sir, er, Pete. I'll tell him I ran into you out here."

The judge interrupted and put us all into perspective: "Morgan, you and me, along with my bailiff Stan Faucett, round out a kind of *Dirty Dozen*."

Ah, I thought. *Now, Hizonor is playing the Lee Marvin part.* "Gentlemen,"
I nodded.

"No gentlemen around here," sniggered O'Shea.

For the next hour, we took turns shooting cans off a plank about fifty yards
toward the gravel pit. Mountains of dirt and gravel to either side of us guaranteed
that none of our rounds left the area. It took a while before my well-gripped
hand shook off the cumulative effect of their hearty greetings. A stopwatch
determined our pecking order shooting the beer and soda cans, since nobody
except Judge O'Shea ever actually missed the target. Eventually, he took over the
stopwatch, leaving the contest to the pros. The shorter the time, the higher the
ranking. Our competition finally got down to me and Milt Appelbaum, Uncle
Miltie as the others called the one-legged Israeli platoon commander. We both
used heavily modified Glocks, and virtually tied for a best time of four seconds
in dispatching ten cans.

"Looks like we have a draw," said the judge, who looked at his wristwatch
more anxiously as 9:30 AM rolled around. He may have been thinking about
his child molester sentencing that morning.

"How about a tie breaker?" shouted the short Israeli. "Full fifteen round
clips, fifteen cans, fast draw starts the clock."

Appelbaum looked the spitting image of Bob Costas, and shared the call-
me-short-and-I'll-punch-you-in-the-nose attitude of the sportscaster, too.
Knowing the judge was getting antsy to be in court, I decided my shooting
hand—and my muscle memory—could handle raising "Uncle Miltie's" bet.

"Since bad guys don't often oblige by standing quietly on a shooting
board," I said as I pulled the yet unused bag of cans from the back seat of my
car, "How about we stick to ten, but do it skeet style?"

"You want to shoot skeet with a handgun?" exclaimed O'Shea.

"How are we going to get them all airborne at the same time?" stuttered
Milt, trying to buy some time to consider the magnitude of the problem.

Of course, I had it all figured out. To our right was some orange traffic
control netting stretched between two metal posts. I calmly walked to the trunk
of my car and retrieved a Bowie knife with which I cut the netting off the anchors
and laid it on the ground. Emptying the judge's garbage bag of cans, I separated

two piles of ten cans. One pile of green ginger ale cans, and one pile of Orange Crush cans. I put the green ones onto the net and gestured to the two Salt Lake PD guys.

" Stan and Nafe, get on each side of the netting, and when I yell 'Pull!' you fling these babies into the air. We'll sort out the green cans and orange cans, and then count holes."

"Holy crap!" said UHP's Chyzik.

"No, holy cans!" corrected Appelbaum. "You go first, Morgan. Pull!"

Stan and Nafe must have gotten some kind of nod from Appelbaum as I explained the rules, because they jerked the ten cans into the air before I could draw my weapon. Bad news that my left-hand holster contained a Glock with an empty clip. He wasn't counting, however, that I had a second, unused Glock, in my right-hand holster, which I drew with my left hand and then changed to my right as I cocked the hammer. Also good news that one cartridge was in the chamber, as otherwise an embarrassing click followed by the landing of unventilated cans would have been the only sound.

Ten cans. Thirteen shots total. A lot of cans changed direction in mid flight. The group quickly scattered to retrieve my green cans. Since all our other targets had been beer, Coke and Pepsi cans, the green ones stood out. Well, *almost* all the group went on retrieval duty. Appelbaum and Hizonor just stood there gaping first toward me and then downrange, and then back toward me. Medal of honor recipient Boni stayed back with us, too. Sometimes you get too old to just run after a bunch of cans.

"Your dad told me about that Republican Guard business in Iraq," whispered Boni after he stepped close enough that neither the judge nor the Israeli could hear. "Bad guys didn't just stand in a row for you then, either."

I shushed him, as the incident to which he referred had been classified. He rolled his eyes, as if to say, *That's why I whispered.*

Later, on the way downtown, the judge barely in time for court and me headed for the Salt Lake City building so kindly lent to the now headquarterless Salt Lake County Sheriff, Hizonor seemed to have forgotten all about his sentencing dialogue. He just wanted to talk about our shootout.

"Ten cans, thirteen shots, twelve holes!" he shouted. "I've never seen anything like it. Damn Morgan, I couldn't have done that with a shotgun!"

"And you tried, too." I turned to wink at him.

"What do you mean?" he indignantly responded.

"I saw you putting birdshot loads into that elephant gun of yours. And even then, you got outshot by the rest of your crew."

His silence lasted for several heartbeats. Finally, "Think anybody else knows?"

"I don't think so," I fibbed. Anyone who'd ever been around gunfire could hear the difference between a slug and birdshot, but since nobody had said anything, we could both pretend my new best friends missed the obvious. "But that stuff really ruins the rifling in your gun barrel."

"Ooh, yeah," he realized. Then back onto the morning's competition: "My boys are going to remember this day for a long time!"

"Milt pulled himself together and didn't do badly."

"What, three cans and fifteen shots?"

"Pat, that's three more than I expected him to get."

"So how did you manage to get them *all*?"

"Muscle memory and lots of practice," I answered. "A whole lot of practice."

Hizonor didn't say anything else until we neared the courthouse.

"Nice idea," he said, as if continuing a conversation we'd been having.

"What's that?"

"Nice idea setting up a Twitter account called 'daddysfelons' for them to have broadcast to their cell phones every time you have an update on the progress of Olive's murder case."

"No, Your Honor. A *brilliant* idea. Having guys who can shoot like that as close as a text message could be a big deal over the next few days, given the away team body count so far."

"Could save some innocent lives," he agreed.

27

A Graduate Course in Dealing with the FBI

enry Davidson met me in the hallway as I entered the Salt Lake County Police Department offices. He seemed quite anxious to head me off at the pass, so to speak, before I entered the temporary offices allocated to the burned-out County Sheriff's staff.

"Henry, how's the headache?"

"Okay, until I got to the office and walked into the FBI buzz saw," he sighed.

"What's the bad news? It could have been another week before they got here."

"That was before one Morgan Rapier brought the full force of two United States senators squarely on their heads," said Davidson.

"That's great. I'm glad they're here!" I said.

"No *you're* not. No, no, no *you are* not. Especially *you* are not. Not *you*. Not glad."

I followed Henry into the men's room and watched him splash cold water on his face. He looked in the mirror, likely considering the possibility of stepping into a less troublesome universe on the other side. But he saw my reflection behind him and gave up on the fantasy, rinsing his face with more cold water and then using ten or twelve paper towels from the dispenser to dry himself.

"We're getting some action on their unsolved and un-apprehended serial killer," I said over his shoulder. "That's bad?"

"Look, Morgan. You've got to cool it in there. They arrived this morning with my boss, Sheriff Running, and have just about convinced him to un-deputize you and escort you to the first airplane out of here."

"They could try," I said. A few hackles couldn't help but rise on the back of my neck.

"Joseph, Martha and Mary!" he said. "It's my job on the line here, too."

"Relax, Henry, and tell me chapter and verse what exactly is going on here."

Henry took another handful of towels and daubed at some water droplets that fell on his shirt. "Sheriff Running arrived with our Quantico guests, and I began to brief them on the current status of our case. I started with your recovery of Olive's computer files. They got all huffy about our needing a court order, and I thought I calmed them down by telling them we had such an order. But they seemed bent that you then just went in and grabbed the files without going through proper channels.

"I then went to your clever assessment that the serial killer must be from out of town, and that he must therefore have flown in and rented a car, substituting it at the airport for a just-parked long-term-parking vehicle. They went a little crazy about your hacking into the airport security camera footage, even though I assured them you had been duly deputized and that the airport was part of the local government and that we therefore had a right to that access. They seemed particularly interested in the way you farmed out the license-plate recognition job to your grid of unnamed computers. I couldn't tell them who owned the grid or what security precautions had been put in place.

"The final straw that broke the proverbial camel's back, or maybe you'd call it the harpoon that took the camel completely out of the picture, was where you logged into NCIC and VICAP to get the profiles of the other serial murders involving amputation of little fingers. They seemed certain you couldn't possibly have accessed that data without violating all kinds of laws, deputy or not."

Sheriff Running interrupted Henry's litany of the morning's meetings when he entered the restroom to relieve himself. He must have been semi desperate to accomplish the task, because even though he saw me he didn't lose his stride to the urinal. He must live clean, too, as the healthy spray against the porcelain testified to a small prostate and an A-number-one bladder.

"Glad you're finally here, Morgan," he said. "I thought we'd be getting congratulated for some damned fine police work. Instead, we're in a procedural pissing contest."

"Which you would no doubt win," I said. Mother always told me that just because you think it, you don't necessarily need to say it. Yup, should'a listened to dear old Mom. The sheriff just shook his head, finished the task and zipped up, and then exited the room without washing his hands. We followed, and I made a mental note *not* to shake hands with him ever again.

The FBI team seemed to have taken over the conference room, every inch of the large table covered with their files, laptops, briefcases, at least one jacket, and assorted coffee cups. The sheriff made introductions.

"Deputy Rapier," he began, possibly as a signal to me of my quasi-official membership of his organization. "Dr. Chip Hardman is the director of the FBI's CASMIRC, which stands for Child Abduction and Serial Murder Investigative Resources Center." Good old Chip didn't stand, preferring to stay seated, glaring at me.

Sheriff Running continued: "This is Lisa Willis, Supervisory Special Agent assigned to the National Center for the Analysis of Violent Crime. She's the profiler on this case." Lisa ignored her director's practiced rudeness and gave me a firm handshake."

"Xavier Brown is the computer specialist and Edward McCartney is a senior investigator." Again, both followed the SSA Willis's lead and shook my hand. McCartney looked the standard button-down collar FBI guy, and Xavier looked the hulking computer nerd in a jacket that didn't fit or even begin to cover his protruding belly. About my height but obviously outweighing me by a hundred pounds, his belt buckled well below his protruding stomach reminded me of many an introverted hacker who could work all night while putting away one large double-crust pizza and a six-pack of Jolt.

Dr. Chip didn't wait for us to be seated, probably hoping I'd remain standing as if in some formal oral examination. Maybe I'd fidget.

"Mister Rapier," he began. "Notwithstanding that you've made quite an international name for yourself beating up locals, why shouldn't I have Sheriff Running cuff you and take you into custody for unauthorized access of the Law Enforcement Online network?"

I should have known better than to instinctively react to his provocation, but the adrenalin still pumped from my morning shooting with The Dirty Dozen. I didn't realize how truly angry I'd become with humanity's status quo, or with people like Lavar. Rather than stand there and answer him directly, I made a point of finding the chair opposite him across the table and, after taking out my wallet, easing myself into the seat. Ever so casually, I took out my Defense

Intelligence Agency identification card and sailed it perfectly into his chest, imitating a stage magician with a deck of cards.

"Doctor Hardman, is it?" I began. "As in The Morgan P. Hardman Child Abduction and Serial Murder Investigative Resources Center?"

"Morgan Hardman is my father," he replied, put somewhat off balance by my knowledge of the organization.

"Well sonny," I said with more than enough edge in my voice. "If inbreeding didn't make you too stupid to read, I just passed you my Defense Intelligence Agency security clearance, which I assure you is a hell of a lot higher than yours. That gives me LEO access, along with legitimate privileges to look at stuff they'd cuff *you* and toss *you* into jail for viewing. Now give me back my ID, before I break the table in half and retrieve my own damn card."

Sheriff Running sat back in his own chair, the hint of a smile on his formerly troubled face. Henry Davidson stood a little taller. Chip Hardman blinked as if he'd just been dressed down by his father who shared the same name with me and, when I leaned ever so subtly toward him, slid my card back across the table. Brown, the computer specialist Xavier, and McCartney the investigator, both looked everywhere but at their boss. And if I didn't miss my guess, Supervisory Special Agent Willis almost blew her own brains out suppressing a snort.

Now red faced and pedaling backward as fast as he possibly could, Hardman tried to salvage some personal status: "We seem to have started on a sour note, for which…"

I should have let him do the mea culpa. But I didn't. Four dead people had wiped the smile right off my face.

"According to Detective Davidson, who briefed me as I entered the building just now, you have spent the morning in a pissing contest," I looked at the Sheriff, who had to pinch his lips with the same thumb and finger that had recently taken care of business at the urinal. "You've been in a procedural pissing contest, instead of getting to work solving three new murders, four counting the Salt Lake County officer burned Saturday night.

"Where I come from in the federal pecking order, my officers earned their positions based upon competence and not inheritance. I will assume, until they prove differently, that the rest of your team all earned their current posts based upon merit. You, however, will be on the next commercial flight out of here. Unless you want to see just how much damage I can do to your career, not to mention your body."

Nobody said anything. So I slapped my hands on the table and stood, never once taking my eyes off the cowering Dr. Chip. As the sound echoed around the room, the good doctor stood and exited. I pointed to the sheriff: "Make sure he gets on an airplane. We'll take this from here."

He did and we did.

Yes, I'd probably made a serious enemy out of Dr. Hardman. But he'd be a long-distance enemy. And like most cowards, he probably wouldn't go at me full tilt until after he'd had a chance to rein in his staff, making sure everybody got their stories straight, should people higher up the food chain wonder what exactly happened. At least I hoped that would be the scenario.

Xavier, the computer specialist, actually asked me for a copy of the Linux scripts I'd used to farm out the license-plate reading task to the Wolfram grid. He and senior investigator McCartney humbly agreed they'd never have made the logical deduction that led us to the rental car and timely discovery of the Lambert bodies in its trunk. Independent of Henry Davidson, Lisa Willis had profiled all the other cases involving severed little fingers and compared them to Olive's murder. With Hardman out of the room, she much more freely shared her concerns.

"I just can't believe that Olive's murderer is the same person who committed the other crimes," she said. I saw Henry Davidson nodding his head, so he'd evidently come to the same conclusion.

"If that is the case," I said, "then the whole logical framework whereby we located the rental car and the dead Lamberts is suspect. Remember, my hypothesis that the killer's victims in other states meant he lived out of town, and a wild hunch that he'd be attending the funeral in a *borrowed* car led us to Hertz and to the Lamberts."

"Let's keep an open mind for a moment," said the profiler. "I'll agree that the person who killed the Lamberts had some reason to attend Olive's funeral. And maybe even give a high degree of probability that the same person killed the previous victims in the other states. But the victimology of Olive Jenkins is too dramatically different from the others."

"If you don't mind my asking," I changed the subject slightly, "How long have you people been on the trail of our serial killer?"

Lisa's answer bespoke some embarrassment: "Ten years."

"Ten stinking years! The three of you, ten years?"

"He's been one step ahead of us the whole time," mumbled the computer guru. He scratched at a mustard stain on his amply protruding stomach. I felt almost embarrassed for them; sorry I'd even brought it up. Sorry also that I'd been so emphatic when I found out how long the serial killer had eluded them. Ten years, and it took me a mere two days to start piling up bodies. Victimology, though.

"If Olive didn't fit the profile, why then would your serial killer…?" I actually answered my own question before the words left my mouth. "Copycat!"

"Give the man a cigar!" said Henry.

"Interesting theory," I granted them. "I won't throw it out quite yet. Could you run us through the victimology."

At the end of an hour, they'd convinced me. We had a copycat killer trying to throw us off the scent by imitating a serial killer. The other victims had been, to put it rather bluntly, abusive trailer trash women with long records of complaints and social service interventions in their lives. Olive Jenkins, on the other hand, had never so much as received a speeding ticket. While one hundred percent of the other victims had been habitual welfare scammers, Olive had donated a substantial portion of her income toward helping others. And where the other victims earned little more community standing than a few fellow abettors attending their city-paid funerals, Olive drew hundreds of prominent and sincere mourners.

"In short," said Lisa Willis, "The other victims barely qualified to be classified in the same *species* as Olive Jenkins."

The curious analogy ricocheted around my brain and threatened to shake something lose, but senior investigator Ed McCartney displaced the pending brainstorm with another question: "Why would a serial killer come to the funeral of a copycat victim? And why would he kill two innocent people just to get an untraceable car?"

Henry wiggled his fingers like a schoolboy trying to get his teacher's attention. He and profiler Lisa seemed to be on the same wavelength. She smiled at him and nodded for his thoughts.

"First," said Henry, "If I happened to be a serial killer with a well-thought-out justification for turning my psychosis into reality, and if someone up and copied me, I just might come looking for him, myself. How *dare* anyone else come uninvited into my world?"

"Very good, Detective Davidson," said Lisa. "And the Lamberts?"

"The Lamberts just might not be so innocent," Henry continued. "The M.E. reported that their little fingers, all four of them, had been severed and stapled inside the glove box of the car they left at the airport. A little checking indicates the Lamberts were no strangers to the Child Protective Services system in Utah."

"Somebody gets a star on their forehead," I said, winking at Henry.

"A gold one," said the profiler, who genuinely beamed at Henry. The gold would stand out nicely on his now-red face.

"Which would mean that not only are we looking for Olive's killer," said Davidson, trying to look casual and unblushed, "But so is the original serial killer."

"Which gives us," I conceded, "Two killers, one of whom tried to cover his tracks with imitation, and a second out to find and probably kill the imitator." And words from Patrick O'Shea's child molester sentencing he'd read to me on the drive to the gravel pit: *If there is a God in heaven, may He grant...* Yes, may He grant that we bag them both.

Again, senior investigator Ed McCartney weighed in: "How could the real serial killer have any hope of finding our guy? All we have to go on is the possible motive Olive's killer hoped to suppress by stealing her computer."

"Then that's our key," said the until-now silent FBI computer guru Xavier Brown.

"He's got a point," I agreed.

"Could I then suggest two tracks in our investigation?" said Henry. When nobody objected, he continued: "We'll get our guys seeing how the *real* serial killer lured the Lamberts to the airport and their deaths, including any Hertz and airport security footage of his arrival. Morgan and Xavier will focus on the other track, trying to find what Olive's computer had that might be a motive for her murder."

"One tweak," said Lisa Willis. "I'd like to see all Olive's phone records for the month before her death. That will help me build a full profile of her last activities, in addition to her email files."

I really didn't want to bring my friend Benny into the team equation, since it might lead to a whole new set of questions from the FBI. In fact, having left him alone in my Snowbird condo made me plenty nervous all by itself. As we hunted a killer, himself being hunted by another killer, a whole bunch of killers hunted my apostate Muslim friend. And, not to beat the hunting thing to death, but the full force and power of at least three major world governments probably had operations in place to find and have a serious conversation with the scoundrel who brought down two of those governments' ability to conduct any kind of Internet intercourse. Yep, time for me to go baby-sit Benny.

"Ms. Willis…" I began. She gently interrupted me.

"Please call me Lisa. Or if you must use an honorific, it's Miss Willis."

"Of course. Lisa," I said, sneaking a look at the obviously pleased Henry Davidson. "Might I assume that, in the absence of Dr. Hardman, you are riding point for the FBI?

Both Xavier Brown and Ed McCartney nodded in quick agreement.

"Yes," she said. "And we are at the complete disposal of Sheriff Running and the Salt Lake County Sheriff's Department."

"Thanks," I said. "If you and your team can work with Henry and a now vitally interested police department out to find a cop killer, I have another associate with whom I'll focus on Olive's computer, too. Henry has a copy of the same data I recovered late Saturday night. Between us, we might be able to come up with a motive."

"Why don't your bring your associate here to work with us?" she said.

Good question. Maybe a piece of the truth would satisfy her.

"With due respect, my associate is seriously incognito," I said. "I will let *him* choose whether or not he wants to make himself known to you. But in the meantime, I intend to respect his desire for anonymity. So if you'll excuse me."

"Just one more thing," she said. "I wanted to let you know, Chip Hardman has had that coming for a long time. You made all our hearts leap for joy the way you dismissed him."

"I've been wading through guys like that my entire life. About three years ago, I promised myself I'd turn each encounter with men like Chip into a him-or-me encounter."

"We all warned him off," she said. "When Xavier showed him the two streaming videos of you and Lavar, I exactly predicted your response to his assertion of authority."

"He's not a good listener, is he?"

"Better than you'd think," she said. "But he wanted to impress me. I don't work directly for him, but am here under assignment."

"At his request, eh?" I said, rhetorically. Henry's jaw tightened. Clearly he and Lisa had some chemistry, and Henry's protective instincts—maybe even a tinge of jealousy—kicked in. I repressed the urge to wink at him.

On my way down the hallway toward the elevator, Xavier Brown clopped along beside me in his big size-sixteen rubber soled shoes. He fumbled for change in his jacket pocket. "Buy you a soda, Mister Rapier?"

"Please, call me Morgan." I almost declined his request, but his shyness and perpetual lack of eye contact with me deserved more courtesy. Besides, my body screamed for a little hydration. "Actually, I really could use a Coke. Thanks Xavier."

We found the soda vending spot in the foyer by the elevator. It took Xavier three tries with a well-worn dollar bill before the machine took his money. One dollar bought not one but two Cokes, testimony to some good vending machine bargaining in behalf of the men in blue.

"Inspired job tracking down Olive's backup files," he said between long gulps from his can.

"We got lucky." I sipped my own Coke and we took the elevator down one level. He fumbled with his cell phone in one hand while holding his drink in the other. Then one more baffling piece of data occurred to me. "But somebody else also figured out about the backup, too."

"You don't think it was Olive's murderer?"

"Why would he want to do a restore? He has the computer?"

"Perhaps he wanted to see exactly what information the police had in their possession."

"Only if he's an idiot," I said as we exited the elevator and walked out the front door, toward my car. "All he had to do was check Olive's backup logs to determine if any files had not been copied to her online archive. Besides, whoever logged on and tried to restore the file didn't strike me as an idiot."

"How so?"

"I backtracked his proxy address to a server in Japan. The moment I tried to hack that server, our mystery man immediately took down the whole server. This guy was no idiot." I didn't go on to say that our skulker had a lot more brains than the Russians or Chinese, whose computers I easily overcame with the same set of electronic lock picks.

"Hum," he mumbled. Then he shocked me beyond belief, almost as if he'd read my mind. "That's probably the kind of stuff that the Russians and Chinese are using on each other's computers."

Mary, Martha and Barabbas! I thought to myself. He's FBI. An FBI computer wizard. Questions to self: Is the FBI working on tracking down my virus and do they have a copy of the initial insertion code, which even at the machine-code level has an awfully lot of identical code to my shot at the Japanese server? But I relaxed, since there is no way the FBI could put two and two together, since there was a statistically insignificant chance they'd have the code I used to attack the Japanese server. *Whew, for a minute there…*

"Who knows? The world is full of hackers," I answered a question with a question, hopefully with a calm voice. And since I didn't want to go anywhere near mention of Russia and China, I dished out an oversize serving of humility: "There's probably a lot better guys out there than me."

He didn't answer, but he didn't nod in agreement either. I pulled my car door open, the key in my pocket triggering the automatic unlocking. He finally quit fiddling with the cell phone, which he put into his pocket.

"You really think this copycat killer can be found from data on Olive's computer?" Xavier made eye contact for the first time since we'd met. For a split second I didn't see the shy, introverted overweight loner in those eyes, but a driven and extremely intelligent focus that looked more like a laser beam. I made another note to myself not to underestimate him. And I gave him my unambiguous answer.

"My friend, you can take that one to the bank."

28

"Mister President, where is Jack Bauer when you really need him?"

 exchanged BAU team cell phone numbers with Xavier before bidding him farewell and starting my drive. Listening to the local news station on my way back to Snowbird, I immediately felt like a circus performer juggling a chainsaw, a lit torch and a sword, all while balancing on a tightrope 300 feet above the crowd. No net. Oh, and I offended the lion tamer, who has turned his beasts loose below, just in case I survive the fall. "But to thine own self be true," said that silly wonk Shakespeare. That's what my tombstone should say.

Chainsaw, torch and sword. The Russian chainsaw, the Chinese torch, and about a billion Muslim swords. And the FBI lion tamer whose father and I share the same first name. Both the Russians and the Chinese seemed to be focusing on the economic reality of no electronic infrastructure. No air traffic control. No mass transit scheduling. No railroad food deliveries. Their plight far exceeded my expectations. Ordinary people suffered, rather than the outlaws and government-sponsored espionage rings that deserved everything I could throw at them. While the international hackers probably thought it expedient, even cute, to hijack a few cycles from servers dedicated toward infrastructure services, my virus couldn't tell the difference. If you hosted an attack, you went down. So did all your friends. Period.

The Muslim world also appeared to be polarizing with rather strident rhetoric. Interestingly though, one Iranian cleric seemed to equivocate in favor of opening a public dialogue led by my friend Benny. If said cleric hadn't lost his head by morning, then some good might be salvaged by my rash reprisal. The car accelerated a little more, as I anticipating a more positive conversation with my houseguest.

I'd had my Android on vibrate and hadn't really paid attention. Now, sneaking a peek at my incoming missed-call log, the number of Gordon Kimball and D.C. area calls surprised me. Somebody wanted help faster than my timetable allowed. Before I could call the senator, the car's integrated Bluetooth display signaled an incoming call from Judge O'Shea. I thumbed the answer button on the steering wheel.

"Your Honor," I said.

"Morgan, did you hear the news?" He sounded excited. Unfortunately, I had heard lots of news, most of which I sincerely hoped he didn't associate with me.

"What news?" I replied.

"Navy recruiting offices all over the country are swamped with applicants who want to try out for SEAL Team Three," he yelled. Then he laughed. Then he yelled again: "Everybody wants to be a soft spoken Lavar-kicking SEAL just like you. You're famous Morgan, famous!"

Oh, *that* news. Great. "No Patrick, I hadn't heard. We've been in a meeting with the FBI team."

For a minute, I thought my Bose speakers had blown out, that is until the graphic equalizers could deal with more yelling from the judge. My ears just caught the last part of a sentence: "… Sheriff Running filled me in on your meeting. He wished he'd sold tickets to the way you handled Director Blowhard."

"That would be Director *Hardman*," I corrected him. "By the way, you ought to tell Sheriff Running he should wash his hands after he takes a leak."

More laughter. "I did, once. In the men's room at the courthouse, I said I must be mistaken about his going to Harvard, and he said 'But I did indeed go to Harvard.' I said I thought Harvard men washed their hands *before* they urinated, but he did neither. Running winked at me and said, 'That's because us Harvard men don't pee on our hands.'"

I didn't want to spoil the fun by telling Hizonor I'd heard that joke way back at Andover. So I made sure Hardman had indeed left Utah: "Hopefully the sheriff got Hardman on a flight out of town."

"Boy did he. That FBI Learjet had wheels up before Running's county Suburban made it off the airport property."

"Good," I said.

"Any developments on Olive's case?" he asked. "The ambassador's wife wanted to be kept up to date."

"One major development," I said. The guy sure hung onto his boss's former title. "We're pretty sure there are two murderers. Olive Jenkins appears to be a copycat crime designed to point us toward a well-known serial killer."

"Whoa! Then we're only after one here in Utah? Olive's, right?"

"Au contraire my little cabbage head," I said. "It appears that the *real* serial killer has evidently come to Utah looking for his imitator. He lured the Lamberts—who, by the way fit his victim profile—to the airport, killed them, and stuffed their bodies into the trunk of a rental car. Complete with his calling-card mutilation."

"Then we're back to Olive's computer," said the judge.

"That's where I'm headed now," I said. "A computer-whiz friend of mine and I are spending the afternoon on it, in parallel with the FBI computer guy. Hopefully we can come up with something, soon."

My speakers beeped, indicating another incoming call. The Caller ID simply said *White House*, and I couldn't think of a single good reason to take the call. So I hit the IGNORE button and continued with O'Shea.

"Anyhow Patrick, we seem to be making progress on a couple of fronts. Please thank Senators Kimball and Hyde for lighting a fire under the FBI."

"You could show your gratitude to Senator Kimball by taking my call," said a new and *very* familiar voice, albeit one with whom I'd never had a personal conversation.

"Mister President?" I stuttered.

"Yes Mister Rapier, it's the president. My people have been trying to call you all morning. I decided to take the initiative myself. I need your help."

"Sir, I had no idea you could break into a cell phone conversation…"

"…That's small potatoes," he interrupted. "What I *can't* do is diffuse the rapidly deteriorating conflict between Russia and China. And a senator who I know and trust thinks *you* can help us."

"With due respect, Mister President, the Russians and the Chinese will have to wait until I meet a commitment to dear friends to solve one murder that has become four murders. I believe, through Senator Kimball, I shared with you the reality of the Russian-Chinese breakdown and the likelihood that they wouldn't be ordering fast-food deliveries, let along launching ICBMs at each other."

"Yes you did, and for that bit of insight I am grateful," he said. "Unfortunately, my intelligence people tell me that we're twenty-four hours away from food riots in major Russian cities. Doesn't the potential for loss of life trump your puny murder investigation?"

The president had a good point. Smart guy. Certainly smart enough to bitch slap the some well-established liberal dynasties and become president.

"Food riots in twenty-four hours," I said. "Where the heck is Jack Bauer when you really need him?"

"Jack who?" asked the president.

"The guy on FOX's television series *24*. Jack Bauer can save the world from any given meltdown in just twenty-four hours."

"Well, we don't have Jack Bauer. For better or worse, all I've got is Morgan Rapier. Now if you were just shooting off your mouth about being able to help us properly communicate to the creator of the virus and get an anti-virus solution, let me know and we'll do our best to solve the problem through other channels. But if you actually can help us, I implore you to consider the human cost of your refusal to do so."

Why do I keep backing myself against these walls? *Mister President, let's consider for a moment the human cost of my being fully forthright with you right now. I go to jail. You are an accessory after the fact to my crime, which means you must either have me immediately arrested or risk your own political career.* In truth, the body count of people who seemed hell bent on going down with me threatened to outnumber the fingers on my right hand. He definitely hit the nail on the head by suggesting that the human cost of my failure to help Russia and China bordered on staggering. No matter what else I did with my life, I absolutely could *not* take that to the grave with me. While I might have been somewhat estranged from God since my wife died, I had enough faith in the balance scales of justice and mercy in the hereafter to suggest my chances for ever again reuniting with Annie would definitely be in peril. But I had to buy some time to consider my options, and had to do so convincingly.

"Mister President," I began, swallowing in advance of the bitter pill headed my way. "Senator Kimball did *not* overstate my ability to help you. However, this is not a secure line as you must be well aware. If you could have someone in Salt Lake City deliver a DSA-level-1 encrypted cell phone to my home in Snowbird in the next couple of hours, we can continue this conversation."

"Consider it done, assuming I can get out of my rotating crisis meetings by then," said the president. "Between the Middle East and this little problem, we're burning a lot of brain power. By the way, thank you Morgan. May I call you Morgan?"

"Of course, Mister President," I said, resisting the urge to reciprocate and invite myself to call him Oscar. I also resisted offering any advice at all on his other crisis, which of course I'd also caused. "And sir, my solution may surprise you. For your own political protection, as well as my physical protection, I strongly suggest you invite Senator Kimball to join the call and that *no one else* be in our initial conversation."

Now, we'd see how smart the president was. Could he read between the lines and not ask a question the answer to which would put him in political jeopardy? He didn't disappoint me. We agreed to chat again as soon as a secure phone showed up at my condo. During the rest of my trip up Little Cottonwood Canyon, I listened to the voice mail messages I'd ignored all morning. Man, that Secretary of Defense and his counterpart Secretary of State pushed the envelope for civility, not to mention downright extortion if I didn't return their calls. Each seemed to be in a mad rush to speak with me first, before the other one. They'd have a long wait.

My Snowbird condo stood undisturbed, with no sign of firebombing or sword-wielding Middle-Easterners to disturb my beautiful mountain home. After two passes down the street I felt confident enough to remotely open the garage door and slip into what could be my last non-maximum-security-federal-lock-up home. I didn't see any way at all to keep Benny out of the equation much longer, either. Yeah, my upcoming call with the president would be a barnburner.

29

Book of the Dead & a Dead Man's Switch

enny, you staying out of trouble?" I yelled up the stairs.

"Probably not," came his voice from my family room computer area. "At least your house is still standing. Which must have concerned you, given the multiple passes I noticed in your reconnaissance."

Mohammed bin Faisal Al Saud—aka Benny—relaxed in front of the computer. I didn't recognize the rest of my family room, as the furniture had been moved aside and the floor now resembled a mosaic of laser printed sheets anchored to my hardwood floor by Scotch tape and connected by red, black and blue lines drawn on them with laundry markers.

"Made yourself right at home, I see." I waved my hand at the floor behind him.

"Since you kind of cleared out my social calendar for me, along with my daily prayer cycle, the best use of my time seemed to be focusing on Olive's computer files," he said. Benny tossed the Channel 2-supplied cell phone to me: "This cell phone you gave me has rung constantly. Same caller ID, some guy named Turner."

"Glad you didn't answer it." I snatched the phone from him and slipped it into my pocket. Again, pointing to the floor, "Nice decorating job. Your artwork makes it look kind of Egyptian."

"Right out of *The Book of the Dead*, so to speak," he nodded. "Very perceptive of you, too."

"I get that sometimes. And?"

"And I think I know why Olive Jenkins was murdered," he said as casually as if commenting on the weather. He finally looked up from his computer screen at my open mouth and statue-like posture. "That's a start, right?"

Mohammed bin Faisal Al Saud slid back his chair as he stood and walked in his stocking feet across part of the floor decoration, until he stood over a family tree printout. "This genealogy program is really quite fascinating. Quite literally, this is a book of the dead. "

"I'm holding my breath, Benny!"

"Net result, then. Without question, Olive Jenkins' killer is a descendant of George Wood, the man who killed Olive's namesake ancestor Olive Olivia Coombs in September of 1863." Benny folded his arms as if challenging me to argue with him.

"Wait one stinking minute," I said. "You're telling me that Olive got murdered because she pried into a one-hundred-fifty year old crime? Who cares!"

"Morgan, Morgan, Morgan," he said, his voice dripping with condescension. "I come from a world where we've been killing each other over injustices that happened four-thousand years ago. One-and-a-half centuries is a mere blip. Besides, Olive didn't get killed because of her investigation into the original murder. She had to be eliminated because of her subsequent research into events *after* the murder. In fact, she traced the descendants of George Wood and built a convincing case for opportunistic killings that reach into this decade.

"It's all right here, chapter and verse. Starting with the Territorial Governor's untimely death just days after granting a pardon to the man he prosecuted for Olive Coombs murder. The key is in Olive's recorded sources and notes I found on the death of her ancestor and Olive. On a whim, I did a name search on the genealogy program and found a completely unlinked set of genealogies on George Wood and his descendants. They had no blood or even adopted relationship to Olive's family, and I'd never have found them by just searching Olive's family tree. Kind of like a free-floating strand of DNA that could never be associated with anything at all."

Benny pointed to a separate tree structure by his right foot. He'd also printed out the notes associated with several of those individuals, including copies of newspaper articles and court records.

He continued: "Here's a story of the rather surprising death of the Wood's former prosecutor James Doty, who'd been appointed territorial governor of Utah by none other than Abraham Lincoln. Olive speculates that Doty's cook, actually a step-child of George Wood, poisoned him and promised an antidote on the condition that he pardon the murderer. Clearly, no antidote existed and the governor died on June 13, 1865."

"Does she offer any proof of this assertion?" I asked.

"Oh yes indeed. She also has proof of a back-up plan for the pardon. Are you familiar with an event called *The Mountain Meadows Massacre*?"

"Vaguely," I said.

"On September 11, 1857, a wagon train of settlers was massacred in Southern Utah. The mob tried to disguise the crime to be the work of Indians, but subsequent investigation uncovered the plot. One man, a Mormon, was even executed for his participation in the crime. Olive Olivia Coombs murder came about because some of the other Mountain Meadows killers feared she planned to name all the participants. They saw Olive taking notes around Cedar City and figured she must be compiling evidence against them. In fact, Olive's curiosity had to do with her missing husband, who preceded her from California to Utah. He disappeared, and when Olive arrived she noticed that some of the women around town wore clothes taken from Olive's trunk, which her husband had in the wagon with him. She'd already located his prize cattle, frozen to death in a remote arroyo, secreted there by whoever had killed her husband and then stolen the cattle. Had someone just stumbled upon a dead man, the law of the plains entitled them to the contents of the wagon and any nearby livestock. Hiding the cattle meant he'd been murdered for them.

"One afternoon in 1857, after he got liquored up, George Wood left a bar and set out to silence Olive Coombs once and for all. He killed her and shot a little girl in the head. The little girl didn't die, but spent the rest of her life in a relative state of dementia. Olive's other children were farmed out to Cedar City residents to bring up as their own. One of those children was Olive Jenkins' grandfather, who tells the story of a pioneer parade in Cedar City. An old woman tapped him on the shoulder and pointed to the parade master in the lead wagon and said, 'See that man? He killed your mother and then got pardoned.' It turns out that after the pardon, George Wood somehow rehabilitated his reputation and became one of the respected founding fathers of Cedar City, Utah.

"In fact, here's a photo of his tombstone, the largest monument in today's

Cedar City Cemetery. And here's a photo of the house his family donated to the attached museum, showing the workmanship of this illustrious Cedar City pioneer."

"That's some good job of rewriting history," I agreed.

"Oh, this family seems to have done more than rewrite history. But hold that thought about *writing history* for a moment. According to Olive's notes on George Wood's progeny, they eliminated the occasional business or political competitor. One of George Wood's sons, Brigham, killed an Achibald Bennett over a real estate deal in Cedar City. And Brigham's grandson, Brigham Wood III appears to have lucked out when a political opponent in a close race disappeared while hunting deer and whose bullet-riddled remains turned up in the spring thaw."

"And that takes us where?" I asked.

"Right now, to Brigham Wood III, currently a member of the Utah State Senate. Olive has proof he snuffed his political rival about ten years ago. And if he didn't kill *Olive*, then someone protecting him did."

"What proof?" I whispered.

"You're going to love the irony," beamed Benny. "In his seventies, about five years ago Brigham III divorced his wife of forty years, Bathsheba Hill Wood, and married a lobbyist thirty years his junior. Olive had befriended the ex-wife who found the Wood family *Book of the Dead*. The diary outlines a kind of insurance policy started by George Wood, in which he named all the original participants in the *Mountain Meadows Massacre*. He used the existence of the book to hold Cedar City politicians to their commitment to get him pardoned. Subsequent members of the family have actually added their own crimes to the book, in their own handwriting, in some kind of twisted secret society. Bathsheba made a copy of the book, had it notarized and sealed, to be mailed to Olive by the ex-wife's attorneys upon Bathsheba's death. You want to guess when Bathsheba died?"

"Maybe a week before Olive's murder?" I suggested.

"Ten days, my little lamb pelt!" shouted the triumphant Benny.

"But we don't have her copy of the ironically named *Book of the Dead*, do we?"

"We have the next-best thing." Benny grabbed a sheaf of pages that had been slowly printing from the laser printer. "Olive scanned the book and then password protected the PDF file on her system. It took me a while to find the file and crack the password. Here's the printout."

I reverently took the sheaf of papers from Benny and scanned the first few pages. Boy oh boy! A bunch of prominent Utah families would probably chip in for Brigham Wood The Third's legal defense fund, just to suppress this document from the public record.

"Holy Moses," I said. "What's the name of the password-protected PDF file?"

"It's called GWBOTD.pdf, which stands for George Wood's Book of the Dead. Olive had squirreled it away in a hidden directory."

I scrolled up Lisa Willis' number on my Android address book and tapped it to connect via my auto-recording call forwarding service. She must have seen my caller ID and answered on the first ring. I told her to hold while I linked Henry into the call."

"Henry, Lisa. We all here?" I said.

"I guess," said Henry. "Two of the three of us are in the same room. So why the conference?"

"Because one of you is going to put your phone on speaker, in front of a tape recorder," I said. "In case something happens to either of us. My own copy of this conversation is being auto-recorded on a remote Web site with a dead-man's switch. I winked at Benny, who rolled his eyes. If I don't log in and reset the switch, the link to this conversation will stream to my Twitter account in 24 hours. Tell me when you have the recorder activated."

It took some fumbling around, during which FBI computer specialist Xavier asked me about my "dead-man's switch" idea, which he said had surprisingly never occurred to him. Finally, Henry got back on the line and announced the date and time of our conversation for the recording.

"Xavier," I began. "Before I tell you what we found, so as not to cover anything obvious, have you come up with anything?"

The silence on the other end of the call had to be a nervous one. I continued.

"Okay, then. Let's cut to the chase. In case an exploding volcano at Snowbird cuts us off, do two things. First, open Olive's genealogy program and do a search on George Wood, born in 1822 and died in 1908. Read *all* the notes and sources Olive appended to those files. And read all the notes associated with George Wood's descendants.

"Second, find an invisible directory containing the PDF file named GWBOTD dot PDF. It's password protected. The password is…" I turned to Benny who had written it on a piece of laser printer paper and held it up. "The password is, all lower case, b00k0fthedead where all the letter *ohs* are really zeroes. Got that?"

"We got it, Morgan," said Henry and Lisa simultaneously.

For the next twenty minutes, I told them what they'd find in those files. Occasionally, Benny prompted me to add a detail or make clear a train of logic. I then summarized possible next actions.

"I suggest that Olive's *Book of the Dead* scan ought to be enough to get a search warrant for Brigham Wood The Third's home, safe deposit boxes, and recreational property. Also, you need to chat with Olive Jenkins' probate attorney. Third, since Olive received the file just ten days before her death, all her incoming and outgoing telephone calls should be closely analyzed. Fourth, I wouldn't jump the gun on sequestering a grand jury to consider the case against Brigham Wood The Third until you get a political consensus on the explosive effects of releasing names of the *Mountain Meadows Massacre* participants. I'm personally curious if the Mormon Church has enough integrity to let the truth go out without editing."

My catch-a-killer cookbook recitation stopped with a knock on my condo door. I stepped to the foyer and observed two big guys in dark suits, one of whom carried a briefcase, which probably contained an encrypted cell phone. I motioned to Benny to get out of sight, abruptly concluding my call with Henry and the gang, disconnecting before I opened the door. Whoever gave these guys their instructions must have lit a serious fire under them to do their job, make sure I was who I said I was, and then leave me to do whatever The Powers That Be wanted me to do with the encrypted phone. They passed me a note with a phone number I should call in exactly 23 minutes. I memorized the number and returned their note. If they recognized my face or name from the Lavar videos, neither showed any sign.

30

Even Partial Disclosure
Brings Full Accountability

ecision time. Actually, I'd already made the decision. But I could take it back, now, if some sudden inspiration convinced me to withhold a revelation that might cause Mohammed bin Faisal Al Saud serious brain damage. When I re-entered the family room, Benny slipped the 9mm automatic back into his waste band. Both of us had a healthy respect for knocks on doors.

"Ya did good Benny," I said. "I owe you. The O'Sheas owe you. The FBI owes you. The Salt Lake City and County police owe you. Have a seat, because I have about twenty minutes to place my life completely in your hands."

"But you already have, Morgan. Giving me a loaded gun, leaving me alone in your home with time enough to plan and execute something nefarious and terminal."

"Just death? No problem. I'm ready to join Annie any time," I said. "I'm talking about placing the rest of what could be a long and very unhappy life in your hands, should you choose to use the information in a way harmful to me. Anybody can be a hero for a split second before finding out first-hand the true nature of eternity. But it takes real courage to look ahead to years of misery in mortality."

He pursed his lips and gestured agreement. He sat again in front of the computer and cupped his hands in front of him. "Here are my hands, ready and waiting for your life."

Not wanting the gesture to go unrewarded, I placed the encrypted cell phone into those waiting hands. "Benny, in about nineteen minutes I'm going to talk privately with the President of the United States and one senator from Utah."

Benny's left eyebrow raised about an inch higher than his right, and he pointed to himself.

"Nothing to do directly with you, unless you want me to add your situation to the agenda, of course. No, the reason for the call is the virus that has virtually crippled both the Russian and the Chinese. Friday night, after dinner with both Utah senators and my hosts, the O'Sheas, I suggested a plan for dealing with Russian and Chinese attacks on U. S. computers. Less than twenty-four hours later, the president announced the implementation of my plan. Evidently, Senator Kimball has a close relationship to the president and made a compelling case for a new kind of Monroe Doctrine."

"Okay, you are going to speak with the president about the new Medina Doctrine of deputized privateers. How does that put your life into my humble hands?" he asked.

"That's not going to be the conversation, Benny. The president asked for my help diffusing the escalating situation over there, and because of the human cost of potential food riots due to the complete breakdown of their communications infrastructure, I agreed to talk to him about the problem. Unfortunately, they can't wait for us all to solve the Jenkins murder. And after the phone call, I may not be available to continue on the case."

"Your life still isn't in my hands, Morgan."

Time for me to stop pussyfooting.

"Benny," I cleared my throat before continuing. "I got a call from the O'Sheas asking for my help solving Olive's murder. Just after their call, I unleashed the virus that precipitated the ill-fated email to everyone in your address book, a crime by the way which could land me in jail for a good many years, then I agreed to come right out. But before leaving town, I also launched the viral attack on the Russian and Chinese servers that had been attacking me for the last few years."

Mohammed bin Faisal Al Saud looked down at the encrypted cell phone in his hands and nodded several times. Then he pretended to pull the pin from a grenade, tossed the phone to me and intoned, "Allah Akbar!" We simultaneously expelled air from our mouths in a simulated explosion.

"My life in your hands yet?"

"Oh yes," he laughed loudly. A James Earl Jones kind of laugh.

He then stood and paced around the room, stopping periodically to look and me and laugh again.

"Glad you think it's funny."

"Morgan, in less than a week you brought two superpowers to their knees, turned the Islamic world on its end, and became the most famous recruiter in history for the U. S. Navy SEALs." Benny surfed in his stocking feet across my hardwood floor, tearing or scattering his carefully placed printouts as he slid. "You're a god! Maybe I should be worshiping *you*."

"No godhood for me. Alas, I'm just about to become what Sherry O'Shea calls one of *Daddy's Little Felons*. Maybe one of his *Big* ones. And the reason the president couldn't talk with me the minute this phone arrived has to do with another series of critical meetings he's having on the Middle East and Islam."

Again, Benny paced around the room making explosion sounds and laughing. And inventing new ways of addressing me: "Morgan Akbar…Morgan the beneficent…Morgan the magnificent…Rapier the raper, or is it rapist?… Morgan damn it!…Morgan H. Rapier!, that's a curse, by the way…Be careful or I'll unleash a Morgan on you…Morgan, Martha and Mary!…Holy Morgan!…"

"I got it, I got it!" Clearly, I had to channel his thinking. "Any advice for me before I call the president and confess my sins."

"Sounds like a religious rite to me," he said. "Seriously, though, can you solve the Russia/China meltdown?"

"Piece of cake." I said. "I enter one of two passwords. Password *A* permanently cleans up the world in about twelve hours. Password *B* does the same thing, but must be re-entered every forty-eight hours or things will come crashing down, again."

"You really love those dead-man switches, don't you?" he said. Then in realization of my candid answer, "Hey, why did you burden me with the *A* and the *B* scenarios? By telling me this, you not only give me power but, under the wrong circumstances, you cost me my life."

Suddenly, as an afterthought, he asked: "Uh, where do you enter the passwords."

"On Twitter, of course. Then I told him why I burdened him with the knowledge. "My attitude is that *partial* disclosure still brings *full* accountability. You deserve total forthrightness on my part after what I've done to your life."

"You didn't do anything to my life that I didn't want done," he said, seriously and without his previous levity. "I could easily have blamed the email on a hacker, and all my Muslim friends would have believed it because the alternative would have been unthinkable."

"Thanks for getting me off the hook, guilt wise," I said. "As nearly as I can see it, in about ten minutes the amount of free choice left to me will dramatically decrease."

"Twitter, huh?" He seemed stunned.

"Why not?" I answered. "Simple. Elegant. And untraceable, if you do it right. Again, any advice?"

"Sure. Enter the dead-man's-switch password and then tell the President to wait twelve hours because you've solved the problem. If he asks for more of an explanation, you tell him he doesn't want to know."

Benny had a point. This is exactly the approach I took with Senator Kimball when he pressed me for information I didn't want to share.

"And if he presses me?" I asked.

"Tell him about the dead-man's switch," Benny quickly responded. "That by not re-entering it regularly will re-activate the virus and send the world into permanent darkness. Tell him it's his bargaining chip to hold over the Russian and Chinese hackers, public and private, who might again be tempted to conduct business as usual."

"You've got a knack for horse trading," I said.

"Camel trading," he snickered. "Haven't you ever heard the term *Arab rug merchant*? We *love* to barter."

I thought for a moment about all the negative scenarios that might derail me. And one emerged: "What if something bad happens to the person with his foot on the dead-man's switch? How can we guarantee some freak accident won't throw the world into darkness?"

Now the ball bounced into Benny's court. He didn't take long to answer.

"Send the *B* password to the president and let him do with it what he will. Further, tell him there is an *A* password in someone's possession that will permanently disable the virus."

"And if he asks who has the *A* password?" I asked.

"Morgan, I'm really going to have to take you to a Saudi bazaar for a week.

The answer is obvious."

"Not to me." I looked at my watch. Almost time for my call.

"Under-promise, over-deliver," he said, Socrates reasoning with an idiot.

"Huh?"

"Surprise him with new data," he finally said, exasperation in his voice. "Tell him that I'm sitting here with you and that I have the *A* password."

"Holy Moses!"

"No," he smiled. "Holy Morgan. You're a god, remember? I'm not worthy to be in your presence."

"I can't predict what will happen when the president finds out about you," I said as forcefully as I knew how.

"Only God knows," he immediately responded. "Maybe that's the way we should leave it. You're not a god after all."

One last look at my watch, then I dialed the president. Unfortunately, Benny's presence made it impossible for me to build on the scenario he'd so graciously provided me. I had to fess up *immediately* of his presence in the conversation. And besides, maybe I couldn't predict every aspect of the future. We were *both* in God's hands, for good or ill.

31

Forgive me POTUS, For I Have Sinned

"Mister President," I said upon being connected. "Morgan Rapier here."

"Morgan," responded the familiar voice. "I'm in my private study with Senator Kimball, per your recommendation."

Now for the hard part, I thought, bracing myself for the disclosure that had better come now, rather than one second later. Clinton advisor Dick Morris had made the cover of *Time Magazine* two consecutive weeks in a row in 1996—on September 2nd and then again on September 9th—first as the architect behind Clinton's victory and the very next week as the man who had to resign in disgrace for letting a prostitute listen to his conversations with the president from a hotel extension.

"Mister President, I have someone here with me, too. I think both you and the senator will be vitally interested in hearing his story." I paused to let the revelation sink in, as well as to brace myself for the 'who' of it. Nobody said anything on his end, so I continued: "With me is Mohammed bin Faisal Al Saud, son of the former ambassador to the United States and later to Great Britain, Turki bin Faisal Al Saud, which makes him the grand nephew of King Abdullah of Saudi Arabia."

"How on earth…?" gasped Senator Kimball.

"Senator, Mister President, I went to Andover with Mohammed. With your permission, I'll activate the speaker phone."

"I would very much like to chat with your guest," the president instantly replied. "His motivation, his insights, and even his recommendations would be much appreciated, especially in light of the meeting I just finished in the White House Situation Room."

I obliged and pressed the speaker button. "Mister President, my friend, who I call Benny from Andover days, is now on the line."

"Mister President," said Benny. "And please feel free to address me as 'Benny,' since 'bin Faisal' sounds way to close to 'bin Laden.'"

"Morgan," said the president. "My head is swimming with questions. You're driving at something here, so I think I'll wait to vent on you until after you tell me what on *or under* earth is going on. But please be advised, after this conversation you may be speaking in a much higher voice."

Okay. Time for the elevator-to-hell pitch. "Mister President, Senator Kimball. Last Wednesday night, I received a call from Patrick O'Shea asking for my help in solving the murder of Olive Jenkins. I agreed and, before leaving town, it seemed as good a time as any for me to launch a little payback on people who'd been trying to hack my computers from abroad.

"I launched my first attack at an anonymous Middle East hacker who'd been nosing around my systems. I planted an email bomb in his system that sent a scathingly anti-Islamic/anti-Mohammed letter to everyone in his address book. Unknown to me, that hacker happened to be my old friend from Andover. Again, unbeknownst to me, Mohammed bin Faisal Al Saud, also known as Benny, had been nursing a crisis of faith that started with a joint encounter we had at Andover almost twenty-five years ago. The vivid memory of that encounter left him no doubt who had written the letter attributed to him, and he set out to find me. He showed up here, renewing our acquaintance last night. We had not spoken for twenty-five years."

"You realize your retaliatory email is a violation of the current Cyber Crime law?" interrupted Senator Kimball. "Your admission to us doesn't give the president or myself much wiggle room. And for us to ignore it makes us accessories after the fact to your crime."

"I am well aware of that, Senator," I answered. Whereupon I winked at Benny, who must have thought I might be about to execute his strategy for the Russia-China debacle. I intended the wink as a thank you to him for his gracious offer. "However, the story did *not* stop there."

Both politicians *had* to suspect what the other dropping shoe contained. Their combined silence hung like a giant anvil about to drop on all our heads. Time to cut the last thread.

"Also, Mister President and Senator Kimball, before I left San Francisco to come help the O'Sheas," I began, ignoring Benny's frantic gesturing and his mouthing of the word 'No!' as he shook his head. *Sorry, Benny. I appreciate your offer, but I prefer to live the life of a warrior to that of a politician.* "I also launched the viral attack on Russia and China. Senator Kimball, I could speak with great confidence about my ability to help you and the president and our country, because I created the virus. And, by the way, I can also stop it."

I could almost hear the human waste splattering on the White House windows, as well as the rush of pus hitting the brains of two *very* smart, *very* savvy politicians, possibly contemplating the end of their respective political careers. Benny busied himself mouthing the words 'You're crazy!' over and over again.

All I *could* hear over the speakerphone was a loud sigh, and wondered who did it. Heck, maybe both of them sighed. Benny appeared now to be holding his breath, frozen in anticipation of what might be coming toward me. I couldn't help but speculate that the approaching animal had serious teeth and a humongous appetite for human flesh.

"How fast can you stop it?" asked the President.

To his credit, he didn't ask how many other people knew of my exploit. Which meant he hadn't gone into CYA politician mode and that his country and the world situation came first. I found myself almost as surprised as Rush Limbaugh might have been, given the radio commentator's animosity toward the current Pennsylvania Avenue resident.

"I can have it eradicated from Russia and China in twelve hours," I answered.

More silence. This time, two distinct sighs came from the speakerphone.

"Will you eradicate the virus?" asked the president.

"That's your choice, Mister President. Given the unanticipated human cost, transportation, food disruption and such, just give me the word and I'll make it so. If you'd like to present some ultimatums to the Russians and the Chinese, I can delay the process. But at this point, I am at your complete and total disposal."

The word *disposal* took several meanings, a fact which couldn't possibly have escaped my listeners, even Benny, for whom English couldn't be his primary language.

"What other end game did you imagine?" Senator Kimball piped in for the first time.

"Frankly, Senator, I didn't think my victims would be so completely incompetent tracking me down. In fact, I thought our own government would have tracked down the source of the virus and be hot on my trail by now.

"But be that as it may, I knew I'd have to inoculate the infected computers at some point in time, and created a method to make that happen."

"Morgan," said the president. "You've put the senator and myself into a very difficult position."

Benny's head nodded up and down like a dashboard goo-goo doll in the Baja 500 off-road race.

"Mister President, I think the senator can attest to my sensitivity to that issue," I began. "He asked some hard questions when we talked, and I told him he didn't want to know the answers. Now, I think, he understands. Let me give you some more data on which you can make an informed decision.

"First, right now there are only four people in the entire world who know the details of this virus, and all of them are on this conversation.

"Secondly, you cannot let another individual into this circle without becoming an accessory to my crime. Realizing that, I am certainly ready and willing to hold a press conference tomorrow morning and take complete responsibility for my actions. During that press conference, I will tell them of this conversation, and that you allowed me the courtesy of coming forward myself. But had I not done so, you and the senator had no choice but to contact the authorities and bring the full resources of United States law enforcement into the picture. To do less would make Watergate look like a speeding ticket in comparison.

"Thirdly, because of the position I have put you in, I promise right here and right now that I will *not* avail myself of my Fifth Amendment right against self incrimination. To be sure, I'll get the best legal representation available to try for an acquittal based upon justifiable self defense, but I will *not* lie, nor will I mount a stonewall defense.

"Fourth and last," I said, pausing for my most risky and least-likely scenario. "If this series of recommendations is unacceptable for national security reasons, and if you can talk Senator Kimball into being a part of it, I'll stand on the street corner of your choosing at the time of your choosing and let your black ops team simply take me out. My wife is dead and I don't have another living soul who cares one way or another whether I live or not. Mister President, it's your call.

"And by the way," I said as an afterthought. "Your first question of me had to do with saving lives and not with political considerations. For that you have my thanks and my confidence that you'll make the right decision."

Silence. Thirty seconds passed. And I could hear breathing on their end of the line, so nobody had muted the phone to consider myriad frantic scenarios.

"First, Morgan," said the president. "Door number four is a non starter. Not only would I have to have you shot, but there'd be bullets with Senator Kimball's and Mohammed bin Faisal Al Saud's names on them too. I'm never going to play that game."

I wondered if Senator Kimball's eyes opened as wide as Benny's.

The president continued: "There are legal as well as national security issues that make it absolutely necessary for me to involve other people. Contrary to both the belief of my supporters and the vilification leveled at me from my opposition, I am *not* an emperor with unilateral authority. And I do *not* want to behave like one, now. I am therefore going to invite the senator, my personal White House legal counsel, and the Joint Chiefs of Staff to meet with me immediately in the Situation Room. Since they're still in the building, the meeting will take place immediately. I will call you back on this line in about an hour. Is that acceptable?"

"Yes sir, it is."

After we'd disconnected, Benny and I sat in silence, staring at each other.

"Got any plans for the next hour?" Benny finally asked.

"I'd kind of like to catch Olive's killer while I'm still a free man."

"Sure, take the full hour," said Benny. "You might have time left over to make a sandwich."

"Speaking about sandwiches," I said, "I'm hungry. How about we treat ourselves to a last meal over at the Cliff Lodge?"

"They might even offer a decent cup of coffee," Benny said with new enthusiasm.

32
Photo Op
With a Viral Superstar

aving donned his U.S. Navy SEAL baseball cap, Benny accompanied me down the walkway and through the tunnel to the Snowbird lodge. I also wore the SEAL cap from the back window of my car, figuring a few too many people might otherwise recognize the famous Lavar basher. If the staff recognized me, they didn't let on. Well, *maybe* they didn't let on. Benny and I *did* get the best place in the house, a corner table with a spectacular view of the mountain from floor-to-ceiling windows. And our server appeared instantly with ice water, warm rolls, a description of the daily specials, and a coffee blend that made Benny's eyes roll back in his head.

I ordered a well-done buffalo burger, an off-menu specialty named after gunfighter-turned Salt Lake Sheriff and Brigham Young bodyguard Orrin Porter Rockwell.

"That's Buffalo, New York?" asked Benny.

"Nope. That's buffalo as in Buffalo Bill Cody feed-the-railroad-workers, snorting, stampeding dinner-on-the-hoof buffalo."

"Make that two," Benny said to our server, a striking blond who must have been into old movies and recognized his likeness to Omar Sharif. "I'd like mine on the rare side, please."

"Of course you would." She smiled just a heartbeat longer than necessary, and then sashayed away like a runway model at a Paris fashion show.

"That could get her beaten by the religious police in Arabia," he muttered. Through sheer force of will he turned and gazed at me a suddenly serious demeanor. "What do you think is happening in Washington, DC right now?"

"Let's see, now. The secretary of defense has a phone in each ear, one conversation with the Lieutenant General in charge of CyberComm and the other with my last commanding officer. The secretary of state wants me in prison and is winking flirtatiously at the attorney general to back her up on my public prosecution, which the attorney general would love to spearhead. The department of commerce probably just wants me to quickly fix the machinery of international trade. Senator Kimball is whispering to the president how vulnerable they both are to public discussion about what they knew and how long they've known it. And the president is thinking of his new cyber marshal program and how quickly it will go up in smoke, along with his political effectiveness, if the good senator should go public with the genesis of that program. Oh, and the secretary of state is also bending the president's ear about my role in precipitating your apostasy from Islam and the current turmoil it's causing in the Middle East."

"Shouldn't they get you to fix the virus problem and then have us both quietly killed?" Benny asked in all seriousness.

"I suppose that's one option. But I think too many people know who did what to whom. These guys can't keep a lid on it."

"What's your prediction, then?" Benny sipped his coffee, newly filled by our enamored server. I waited for her to sashay away again, before answering.

"The solution to the Russia-China virus issue is pretty straight forward. Fix it with some serious quid pro quos from the thieving swine and wait for their next shenanigans. The real conundrum is you, the Middle East, and what half-a-billion-or-so of them might do when they find out you're here with me. They wouldn't have trouble letting me off the hook without you as a complicating factor."

"You shouldn't have told the president about me, huh?"

"Unavoidable. I couldn't have had you in on the conversation without notifying him immediately."

"Why did we do that, then?" Of course, Benny knew the answer and provided it immediately. "Oh yes. You could not only help him solve the Russia-China problem, but you could help him solve the Islam problem, too. But wait! You told him you sent the virus that sent email to all my contacts. If you hadn't said that, then I could have worked with him to turn, as you Americans say, lemons into lemonade."

"Sorry Benny, but in for a penny in for a pound, as the Brits say. Not to have been fully forthcoming about my involvement with you would have backfired eventually. Besides, I refuse to lie."

"Schmuck, as my Israeli friends would say."

Two buffalo burgers with all the fixings interrupted our conversation. Half way through the burgers, our lives got significantly more complicated. I should have extrapolated the unintended consequences of Harley you-bet-your-ass Davidson's posting her photo with me on social networks to Lamar, Lavar and Laverl showing up at her house to even the score. Viral videos and my being a celebrity guest at Snowbird's Cliff Lodge dining room—their previous offer of a free meal being a tip off—should have made me a little cautious about letting the staff shoot camera phone photos with me. Alas, what do you do when a humble waitress shyly approaches and asks if one of her associates can capture her posing behind me. This time, however, it didn't even cross my mind that Benny might be in some of the photos, even peripherally. Heck, given my chance meeting Sylvester Stallone or Harrison Ford, I'd predetermined that if the occasion seemed appropriate—like maybe I'd saved one of their friends from certain death under the wheels of a speeding train—that I'd humbly ask the superstar to record my cell phone voice mail message. "Hi, this is Sylvester Stallone answering the phone for my good friend Morgan Rapier. He's out helping me save the world, but wait for the beep and leave your message. If he lives through the adventure, he'll call you back." You get the drift, right?

Not long after we left the restaurant, this lapse in my judgment nearly killed not only Benny and me, but it put everyone in the restaurant at risk. I let them take the obligatory photos with me, again insisted on paying for what would have been another meal on the house, and then killed some time before my next call with the president.

33
"Tag 'em and bag 'em!" or "Where are my 72 virgins?"

 s soon as we got back to the house and closed the door behind us, Benny immediately went online with news queries about Middle Eastern developments. The encrypted cell phone rang a split second after I reached for it.

"Morgan Rapier and our mutual friend here," I answered.

"Oscar Medina and Senator Kimball here," said the president. "The senator and I have just stepped out of a knock-down/drag-out shouting match in the Situation Room."

"Let me guess, Mister President." I said. "The attorney general and the secretary of state are ganging up on the secretary of defense and the joint chiefs?"

"Morgan, if I didn't know better, I'd say you'd been eavesdropping on my meeting."

"I don't have to eavesdrop to know that the CIA, the NSA, and the FBI want my technology worse than they want my head. Defense, too, given my previous clandestine accomplishments on their behalf." I paused a few seconds to let them validate my accuracy with their silence. "In the meantime, the secretary of state has her panties in a knot over everything, but is using the Middle East as the proverbial straw, and the AG is siding with her for those stated reasons, hiding real reasons having to do with public image. Did I miss anything?"

"Commerce and the Treasury just want the good old days back, so their electronic funds transfers and treasury auctions can proceed merrily along," said Senator Kimball. I could almost see the smile on his face as he spoke.

"Mister President, I will do exactly what you ask me to do," I said. The laser printer hummed to life and Benny waved for me to look at the computer screen. Late-breaking Twitter news aggregation appeared to validate Samir Attar's story that the first critical discussion of Islamic legitimacy in the last two hundred years had split the Arab world nearly in half. "Even if it means making good on a G. Gordon Liddy-type offer to stand on a street corner waiting for a bullet."

"I don't think the secretary of state's husband lets her anywhere near loaded weapons," said the president. Muffled laughter in the background betrayed Senator Kimball's amusement. It also signaled that the president probably landed on the side of defense, at the apoplectic consternation of his State and Justice Department heads. Otherwise, the senator would be considerably more taciturn.

"Then the bullet isn't an option, Mister President?"

"Effective *last* Wednesday, you are officially recalled to active duty, with a rank bump from Lieutenant Commander to Commander in the United States Navy SEALs," the president said rather formally, as if reading from a prepared statement. "Commander Morgan Rapier, you are now tasked as liaison with Cyber Command under Lieutenant General Steve Daly, but you will report directly to me. Do you understand your orders?"

"Yes sir, Mister President," I answered. Benny just sat there saluting me.

"Could you explain to me the necessary steps in order to disable the Russia-China computer virus?"

Piece of cake. I quickly filled the president in on the permanent password, as well as the one that had to be renewed every forty-eight hours.

"Twitter!" exclaimed the president.

"I use one-hundred characters," I answered. "I'll text the passwords to you at the end of our conversation. Cyber Command can use them as you direct them."

"Thank you. Now, Commander Rapier, I'd like a few words with your guest."

"Mister President," answered Benny.

"Your situation Benny, actually causes me much more consternation than Morgan's declaration of war on Russia and China. The secretary of state is all over the map on implications to our Mid-East relationships. She seems to think every Arab government will regard your exile to our country as a tacit act of war by the United States on Islam."

"With due respect," began Benny, "are you aware that the Muslim world is divided nearly in half, those who want me dead and those who welcome the long-overdue dialogue?"

"I have received no such assessment," came the president's stunned reply.

"Then you are being, and I believe this is the correct idiom," Benny winked at me as he held up the laser printer sheets. "You are being sandbagged by your secretary of state. According to the news-feed aggregation I'm getting, fully half of the Islamic world is leaning toward my desire to open a self-examination. The news stories should be hitting the major wire services momentarily."

"Then you're saying…" began the president. But his sentence ended with a muffled thump from the mountain behind us.

"Sir?" I said. "Mister President?"

No signal displayed on the encrypted cell phone LCD display. A much larger explosion sounded down the valley, followed immediately by the Snowbird avalanche alarm. I quickly shoved the useless cell phone into one of the pockets of my cargo pants.

"I know those sounds!" exclaimed Benny. "Shaped demolition charges."

I hurried to my balcony, snatching my astronomer's telescope along the way. Positioning it for a perfect view down into the Salt Lake Valley, I saw three Hummers barrel into view. The lead vehicle had a machine gun mounted on the roof, and a bearded man standing through the vehicle's skylight, sweeping his weapon from side to side.

"Quick, the garage downstairs!" I shouted to Benny. Before leaving the room, I ripped a thumb drive off its chain around my neck and plugged it into the USB slot on the computer Benny had been using.

"What's happening?" he said as we took three steps at a time getting to my garage.

"My guess, your buddies tracked you to Salt Lake City through the jet you repossessed, and waited for information on your specific location. They got it and have come here to solve a significant religious problem."

"The president's staff leaked it?" he gasped.

"Not a chance. More likely that one of the photos taken over lunch made it to FaceBook or YouTube and then to Twitter. Your friends knew you'd landed in Salt Lake City, and poised themselves to act immediately once you'd been located. The first thump we heard took out the cell phone tower at the top of the tram. The second bigger explosion sealed off the only road out of here. They cut the landlines, too. Any guesses on their plan?"

"Kill me and then helicopter out?"

"Almost," I said as I rummaged through the cabinet in front of my car and flung a Kevlar vest at him. "First, they film you recanting your criticism of Mohammed and Islam. *Then* they'll cut your head off on camera."

"I don't see how they could force me to…" he began, but completed his own thought mid-sentence. "Hostages. The Cliff Lodge. I recant or they do some pretty bad things to a lot of very nice people."

"That would be my guess, too." I tossed him one of my 9mms in a shoulder holster, and slung the other holster over my own body armor. I then divided six clips between us and grabbed two rifles. I gave him the loaded twelve gauge and kept the AR-15 for myself. "Put this box of shells in your pocket and remember that the shotgun is best used within eight feet. Now let's get to the Cliff Lodge before they do."

Benny followed me out the side door as I stuffed six more AR-15 clips into the webbing on my vest. Encrypted cell phone in my cargo pants, Android in my shirt pocket and a couple of ammo clips in my other cargo pants pocket. Benny still had the Channel 2 phone in one of his pockets. We hit the tunnel on a dead run and rounded the deck to the Cliff Lodge entrance just as two hooded men reached the stairs. Both brandished AK-47s. Definitely not your typical hunters. Not hunting season. Not hunting weapons, notwithstanding the NRA reluctance to limit their distribution.

Mohammed bin Faisal Al Saud didn't think twice. His nearly point-blank shotgun blast cut the first man in half and then took off the head of the companion unlucky enough to be just behind him and two steps below. As he racked another shot into the chamber, I flipped my AR-15 onto three-shot auto and started firing before I could clearly see who might be behind them. I call it *actuarial firefighting*, reasoning that no innocents could possibly be standing on the stairs between members of any hit squad. The numbers worked in my favor. Three, three-burst shots took out three more assassins.

While the shooting couldn't have taken more than fifteen seconds, the terrified faces of restaurant patrons, my new best friends on the Cliff staff included, sat in stunned silence. I motioned for them to hit the floor, which everyone did. Even the staff.

"Three Hummers. Three teams," I said. "One up the stairs. The other coming up in the elevator, and the third flanking us from the bridge toward the ski area. You get inside and cover the elevator. I'll take the bridge to the ski area."

I grabbed the only visible AK-47 from the first assassin and then held the restaurant door open for Benny while I covered his back, and told the serving staff, "Terrorists are going to try to take you hostage. Push your tables over and keep your heads down. My friend is going to cover the elevator and I'm going to go find the rest. If anybody has a satellite phone, now is the time to call the authorities. Cell phones and landlines are probably down. Dave," I said to the manager. "Take this AK-47 and protect your staff and guests. Don't let anyone come into this room."

Everyone seemed to accept my advice at face value. Dave took the weapon and went back to the first group of guests, now crouching behind an overturned table. Benny rushed through the restaurant and out the elevator landing doors, securing himself in a corner with full view of both the elevators and the interior stairs. I then raced the opposite direction, toward the wooden bridge that connected the ski area with the upper deck. Along the way I replaced the half-used AR-15 clip with a new one and vaulted the railing at the end of the bridge, taking cover behind a brick post. From there I could see anyone coming around from the parking lot as well as gunman who might try the same stairs as their dead comrades.

Time to think. The other teams *had* to have heard the shooting. Perhaps they expected the first team to have taken the restaurant, assigning themselves to guard the other entrances. Turns out to have been a bad idea, given the totally unexpected firepower awaiting their A-team, the members of which, just now realizing they had left mortality, might be inquiring about their promised virgins. My question, here and now, concerned whether or not these yahoos knew the difference in sound between their own AK-47s and my AR-15.

Thankfully, I resisted the urge to look toward the restaurant as Benny's shotgun blasts echoed from the cement elevator enclosure, because five more attackers simultaneously sprinted around the corner, heading toward the bridge. Clearly, this team hadn't been well trained in urban tactics, nor did they know the sound of an AR-15, because they ran in a cluster rather than using a point-recon/trailing-lookout formation. I flipped to full auto and put them all down, changing clips before the last man hit the ground. I then used five rounds from my 9mm to make sure they stayed down. It took me a few more seconds to approach the Cliff Lodge deck door. I waved my hand in front of the glass before opening it a crack and calling out.

"Dave, it's Morgan. Are you all okay in here?"

"Yes, Morgan, you're clear to enter." Dave peeked over his table, the AK-47 aimed toward the elevator entrance.

"Benny, you clear?" I called once inside.

"Five down out here," he answered. "Two in the elevator and three on the stairwell."

"Five more down on the deck," I said. "We've got to get these people to a safe place, because whoever took out the cellular towers will be coming soon to see about their buddies."

The chef stuck his head out the kitchen door and held out a portable ham radio. "I called the police using Snowbird ham radio. They have helicopters en route. Unfortunately, so do the television news stations."

"Please let them know we *think* we've taken down all three teams of bad buys, but may have one more team who took out the cell tower."

"We got the guy who blew the cell tower," chortled the chef. "Just heard on the walkie-talkie from the top. Some idiot took the tram up and actually asked the operator where he could find the cell tower. A bunch of mountain bikers are sitting on his chest as we speak."

"Nobody hurt?" I asked.

"Not yet," he said. "But they have good cell phone service up there, and the bikers are taking turns posing with the bearded chap all wrapped up in bicycle inner tubes and then transmitting the photos and even videos to YouTube. Every time he yells something about Allah, they smack him good and then take more pictures."

Amazing. Nobody hurt but bad guys! "Good job, then. Please tell the police to be on the lookout for their escape helicopter. I don't think these guys are martyr types."

"Will do," he said. "And by the way, *you're* the ones who did a good job."

I walked back across the restaurant to some shell-shocked patrons, and relieved the manager of his AK-47. "It wouldn't be good for someone to mistake you for one of the shooters, eh Dave?"

"Uh, Mister Rapier?" asked one of the guests.

"Yes?"

"Could Snowbird maybe give you certificates to eat at one of our sister restaurants in the valley?" he said, the faintest hint of amusement gleaming in his eyes. "I'm not sure my heart can take entertaining you here ever again."

I noticed Benny at the window, his arm around our sobbing waitress. He tousled her hair and sauntered toward me, carrying the shotgun barrel up. He whispered, "You were right about the photo going to FaceBook. She's distraught, but I told her not to sweat it."

Over the next hour, the sky around Snowbird had more helicopter traffic than the L'Alp d' Huez finish in the Tour de France. News choppers stayed airborne under threat of death from Salt Lake, Summit and Wasatch county law enforcement dispatchers. One hospital life flight unit received landing clearance for paramedics, and the Snowbird clinic treated several guests who'd been pistol whipped as the attackers converged on the Cliff Lodge. Luckily, none of the injuries proved serious.

Sheriff Running as well as Wasatch County Sheriff Todd Bonner and Summit County Sheriff Dave Barricks each managed to get to Snowbird. Running took the Salt Lake City helicopter. Bonner and Barricks had to take dirt bikes over Guardsman Pass from Park City and then across the Wasatch crest and down into Alta. I resisted the urge to ask Sheriff Bonner if he had a son named Junior to commemorate the Steve McQueen movie role. It's not every day you drop one probably castrated-on-YouTube Arab and the corpses of his fifteen companions on three smallsville sheriffs. Benny and I had to turn our weapons over to deputies, even though I qualified as a deputy myself. Something told me I'd never see them again.

"You mean to tell me, *Deputy* Rapier," said Sheriff Running, "that in addition to working on *my* murder case and becoming the United States Navy SEAL Internet poster boy for your treatment of one Lavar Kendrick, that you just happen to be school chums with the man who has single handedly set the Arab world on fire?"

Don't forget declaring war on China and Russia, too. "It's a very small planet, Sheriff," I said. Pointing to Benny, "This man needed a friend and tracked me down. He had killers on his trail, and they found him here. Had I not been here with modest firepower, who knows how many innocent people might have died today?"

Sheriff Running's next question had to wait a military-green Blackhawk helicopter to land just a hundred feet beyond the footbridge. The hotshot pilot demonstrated considerably more competence than anyone else trying to get to the crime scene. The man in black strutted across the bridge, flanked by two MPs carrying submachine guns. As he got closer, the single star on his collar identified him as a Brigadier General. The rotors on his ride spooled down just as he got to us, and just as Sheriff Running turned back to me.

"Yes, Deputy Rapier," continued Running, a likeable bulldog even if he didn't wash his hands after he urinated. "Let's talk about your firepower. Specifically, one fully automatic AR-15."

"Let's not!" said our new visitor.

"Wait a doggone minute," said Sheriff Running. "We are in the middle of…"

"Sheriff," interrupted the general. "This is now a national security matter." He then turned to his MP escorts and gestured toward the dead bodies now lined up on the patio. "Tag 'em and bag 'em, then wait for your ride. And don't forget their eunuch buddy."

"Yes sir!" came the crisp response.

"Hold on," said Sheriff Running.

"As a direct order from the President of the United States, these men need to come with me. Immediately," snapped Brigadier General Harrison. And we did. Without further discussion.

34
Smile, You're On Television

e lifted off as crisply as the Blackhawk had landed. I couldn't contain my amusement. Below the star pinned onto his collar, his unit insignia looked like it had been stapled above his left shirt pocket.

"Since when do they issue Air National Guard uniforms in black?" I shouted to our host over the noise inside the cargo bay. All Brigadier Generals are evidently not created equal.

He rolled his eyes and leaned toward me. "I borrowed the shirt from my son-in-law at the house, and pinned on my star and unit designation during the chopper ride up here. Unfortunately, I'm the highest ranking officer that could make the trip on five minutes notice."

"And I'll bet you always wanted to say 'Tag 'em and bag em!' didn't you?"

Benny couldn't hear our conversation, but quickly ascertained from our body language that something moderately entertaining just happened. Five minutes later the Blackhawk dropped us on the roof of the federal building where, after we bid National Guard Brigadier General Harrison our best wishes for a quick return to his family barbecue, four seriously armed agents ushered us to a video conference room on the top floor. The large screen had already been linked to the White House Situation Room at the head of which stood the president, Senator Kimball, most of the cabinet, military men I assumed must be the Joint Chiefs, and lastly, unobtrusively standing in the background, the president's cyber czar Harold Smith, who had served both Republican and Democratic administrations. I'd once heard Smith speak at a Black Hat security conference, and figured he'd been giving the president some excellent non-partisan technical advice.

As one of the MIBs showed us to our seats, Benny slipped the Channel 2 phone out of his pocket and whispered, "Think you could find a WEP key for me somewhere, so I can check the news out of Saudi?"

I nodded and tried to be unobtrusive about pulling the Android from my pocket and invoking a security cracker. We sat down and I made sure Benny could see the Android screen from beneath the table. I quickly ascertained that the conference room had active cell phone jamming in progress, but they'd overlooked network jamming. Probably figured nobody could crack government-level encryption, anyhow. I didn't have to crack theirs. I cracked one in the building next door. Benny smiled.

"Mister President, Senator Kimball," I said. "And ladies and gentlemen, I'd like to introduce my old friend Mohammed bin Faisal Al Saud."

"Please call me Benny." Mohammed bin Faisal Al Saud nodded toward the camera in front of us, nestled below the screen.

"Am I correct," began the president, "That the only man who might help us quickly undo the virus attack infecting Russia and China went into a firefight with fifteen well-armed killers?"

"Sixteen, counting the eunuch," mumbled Benny. Our microphones must have been really good, because the military men barely suppressed snickers while the secretary of state looked as if her head might explode. I decided to quickly move the conversation forward.

"Yes, Mister President. It seemed like the right thing to do, saving those civilian lives."

"Outgunned fifteen to one with a world meltdown on the line." The president gave a long sigh.

"Sir, with due respect, our attackers drew the short straw, going up against a U.S. Navy SEAL." Then I looked at my compadre and added, "Make it fifteen to two. Benny here took out almost half the attackers all by himself."

I noticed Navy Admiral Mike Hall, JCS chairman, fake a cough as he covered his mouth. I'd served with the admiral and thought him to be a wise selection. Several of the other military men at the table didn't dare look at each other, lest one of them break into laughter. The secretary of state, on the other hand, absolutely couldn't contain herself.

"I for one have had enough of this male machismo measuring contest," she growled. "In the last week you've…"

"Madam Secretary," said the president loudly and forcefully enough to stifle a litany I could probably have repeated better than she could.

I'm sure you have *had enough of male machismo measurement, Madam*

Secretary, thanks to your husband, I thought to myself and luckily remembered mother's advice that just because you think it doesn't mean you have to say it. I'd failed the test with the FBI's Chip Hardman, but getting it right the second time showed some small but satisfying personal progress.

Unfortunately, the Secretary of State couldn't take her cue from POTUS, and she looked at Benny. My own thoughts ran along the lines of complimenting whoever had set up the video cameras to give the appearance of the face onscreen actually appearing to look at person to whom she spoke. Feigning much more control, even a friendly smile, she began again: "Mister bin Faisal, you've managed to put the entire Middle East on the brink of civil war. We've worked awfully hard in this administration to encourage more moderate dialogue, and all that work seems to have evaporated in the last week."

My wireless security cracker must have locked onto a strong signal and provided Benny with a WEP key, because he held up his Channel 2 Web phone, pretending to look at a Google feed when, in fact, he wanted to get a good video of the Secretary of State and said: "Mister President, according to my news feeds, the Middle East is leaning strongly toward bringing the discussion I forced into the public arena. Have you not been informed of this development?"

"We have no such information," she quickly responded. The secretary looked as if she'd been spit on. An aide quickly whispered in her ear, but she never took her eyes off Benny.

The president turned to look at her as he spoke. "Uh Benny, what is the source of your information?"

"Sir, I'm looking at both Twitter and Google news aggregation services which, I'm sure, are available to your team. If you'd like, I can text you both the URL and the query that gave me my results."

Someone who I assume must be the president's chief of staff pointed to a monitor positioned above the conference screen that showed Benny and me. The president's eyes scanned from our right to left, apparently reading several lines. Eventually his eyebrows raised half way up his forehead.

"That won't be necessary Benny," said the president. "I'm looking at the data as we speak."

Now, I *knew* the query and could see no way Benny could have linked onto a wireless system, entered the query and already retrieved the data he said he had. So I made a quick give-me-a-peek motion with my head and gazed toward his cell phone. He obliged. We were *seriously* hosed, because I did *not* see a Web page data feed. Instead, I saw a video image of the president's team— every one of them perfectly framed on the conference feed—being transmitted online to my video service. I could almost feel the ground vibrate beneath us as KUTV2's Dave Turner must have been jumping up and down to make sure his news department captured every single high-resolution frame and sound from his newest embedded reporter. Okay, this had become a very bad idea on so many levels. What in blazes did Benny have in mind? I don't rightly recall the look I shot at Benny, but his beaming grin spoke one word: "Gotcha!"

The secretary of state must have thought the "Gotcha!" referred to her lack of critical information, and she did a magnificent job of pedaling backwards. "We need time to analyze this data."

To the left of my screen, someone urgently passed a note to Admiral Hall, and the JCS head quickly passed the note to the president. The president read the note, smiled for the first time in the meeting and quickly held up his hand in a don't-do-anything gesture to someone off screen. His next words told me exactly what the note contained, when he said, "Madam Secretary, this is my meeting. Please be quiet or leave the room. That goes for everyone else. With the exception of Harold Smith, all non-cabinet, non-JCS personnel will leave immediately."

I could see guards briskly ushering a group of people, mostly people off camera, through a door to the right. Translated, the president's message to us— and I have no doubt Benny read it loud and clear—was that he knew this feed was on the Internet, that he wanted to make sure no one besides himself, especially the secretary of state, knew about the broadcast, and that he would be performing in this little one-act play for the world.

Benny decided to give the president some time to collect his thoughts and finish clearing the room of non-players. "In answer to Madam Secretary's desire to further analyze the data, I reiterate that I don't particularly care what she thinks. As a member of the Saudi Royal Family, albeit without current diplomatic portfolio, I am here as a private citizen who has been asked to help Mister Rapier and the local authorities solve a murder. True, I came into this situation with the help of my old friend, but my personal religious views and whatever effect they might be having in my homeland are internal to my faith and not remotely subject to discussion with you."

The secretary of state *would not* be stopped. "Nobody in your part of the world will believe that we were not behind your defection from Islam!"

The president didn't try to shut her up, this time. Whatever the conservative right might think of his politics, nobody could accuse him of being stupid. Nothing in his arsenal of rhetoric could do better to get America off the hook as an agent provocateur than letting this discussion play out.

"Madam Secretary," Benny said, shining his million-watt smile toward the screen, "I made my religious convictions known while still in Saudi Arabia. I left that hallowed ground of my own accord in order to spare my family physical danger, and to begin a private and personal search. I enlisted my friend of twenty-five years to help me in that quest, and found myself in the company of a man on his own adventure. I am *not* a defector of any kind. I do *not* renounce my homeland, and I am *not* requesting any kind of asylum. Not only are you uninvolved in my quest, but frankly you're irrelevant."

Had this been the Olympics, we would have seen Benny literally pass the relay race baton to the president. Before the secretary of state could form her next words, the president said: "Enough, please."

Then to both of us, he said: "Mister Mohammed bin Faisal Al Saud will be treated as an honored guest for as long as he desires to continue his visit. And we are most appreciative to U. S. Navy SEAL Commander Morgan Rapier for thwarting your assassination today by killing fifteen of sixteen attackers at the Snowbird Ski Resort in Alta, Utah, and his doing so without a single casualty."

Neither Benny nor I wanted to correct the numbers and attribute seven of the kills to Benny. Then nodding to Smith, the president in an apparent aside to the others in the room but really playing for a *much* larger audience, said: "For those of the Joint Chiefs and my cabinet who are not aware of it, Mister Rapier is also the architect of my Monroe Doctrine-like Cyber Marshall line in the sand and a key player in helping us be of assistance to our Russian and Chinese friends."

Turning his attention back to me, the president concluded the meeting before the secretary of state could *really* muck things up. "Morgan, Commander Rapier, thank you for your service today. I'm going to adjourn this meeting. You, myself, and the secretary of defense can continue this call when I get back to the Oval Office."

"Yes sir," I said. The secretary of state still appeared not to be in the same playbook, since any aides who might have clued her in to her public performance had been ushered from the room. Before the president signaled a disconnect, he took one final shot at framing the Islamic discussion with my impish and super sly companion.

"Benny, we have some Islamic scholars on my team that I think could use the benefit of your insights. I would consider it a great personal favor if you could spare them some of your time."

"I'd be delighted, Mister President."

After the president terminated the conversation and before I could snatch the phone from him, Benny aimed it at me. Behind him, I could see the door open a crack, but the eyeball on the other side of the crack was not going to come bursting into the room until Benny terminated the video streaming session. Smart.

"Morgan, you saved my life today. Thank you."

"Maybe I shouldn't have," I said as matter of factly as I could. "You just recorded a private meeting with the president, his cabinet and the joint chiefs of staff. This was a serious violation of trust. Now give me that thing!"

No sooner had I snatched the camera from him and turned it off than it rang, the caller ID being none other than Big Dave from Channel 2. I clicked the connect button, but held the phone away from my ear. Both Benny and I could easily hear what appeared to be the blare of a roaring elephant, interspersed with words like "…scoop of the century…" and "…broadcast quality!" I hung up just as the two MIBs came into the room. One of them had his hand out. I gently placed the offending cell phone in a hand that probably could have crushed it.

Instead of crushing it, the MIB deftly thumbed through several menus until, satisfied with the result, said, "It's not our wireless link, because we don't have one. Somehow, these guys got into a secure wireless router in the next building."

"Gentlemen, please wait here for a call from the president," said the other MIB, who took the phone from his companion and pocketed it.

35
The Best Place To Hide Stuff

he call from the president started almost immediately. He and Senator Kimball linked up with us from the Oval Office, voice only, just the two of them. After arranging the connection on a secure phone, the two MIBs exited the room, leaving Benny and me alone for the call.

"Whether you two realize it or not," said the president, "you may have just ended the Secretary of State's career."

I jumped on it immediately. "Mister President, I was absolutely not aware Benny had initiated a streaming broadcast of our video conference. I cannot begin to imagine the problems this may have caused you and your administration."

"Who said anything about problems?" I could hear the smile in my commander-in-chief's voice. "Thankfully, Madam Secretary didn't complete her sentence about your involvement creating the virus that hit Russia and China. Otherwise, we'd have a whole new set of problems to face."

"Yes, sir," I stupidly replied.

"By the way, Commander Rapier, your old friend and my JCS chairman Admiral Mike Hall made some notes on your one-man demolition derby over the last week. Just for the record, your actions have pretty well monopolized my office and include inciting a cyber war between Russia and China, nearly starting a civil war in the Islamic world, getting the Salt Lake County Sheriff's office blown up, achieving national fame as the U. S. Navy SEAL that beat up the Kendrick boys, inspiring the creation of a major cyber-crime policy with your influence on my friend Senator Kimball, killing fifteen terrorists who sealed off Snowbird with a landslide, and, oh yes, abetting in the covert broadcast of my situation room meeting with the JCS and some of my cabinet, said broadcast causing terminal embarrassment to my secretary of state."

The president paused, waiting for some contrition on my part. With his prior who-said-anything-about-problems comment, it occurred to me I didn't owe him any contrition.

"Mister President, Admiral Hall misstated the timeframe, since it has not technically been a whole week. I still have two days to go."

This time, Senator Kimball's voice broke in: "The Lord God Almighty took six days to create the world. Are you figuring to destroy all of creation tomorrow, *before* taking a day of rest?"

"Senator, you might not be that far off if you consider what is about to happen to your power base here in Utah," I said. "My original motivation for setting in motion the events of this week involved helping Judge O'Shea solve a murder. I just turned over to the local authorities a copy of a diary created as an insurance policy by one of the Mountain Meadows Massacre culprits that lists all the other participants. Quite a few Utah families have direct ancestors who participated in those murders."

I could only imagine what might be taking place on the other end of the phone line. The president figuring that now he *really* wouldn't have much competition for re-election from Utah. Senator Kimball wondering about his or his wife's revered ancestors, not to mention the reputation of his church.

When he *did* speak, the senator's point of view quite surprised me.

"Morgan, we're going to let those chips fall where they may. And I predict you will *not* get a different directive from anyone in Mormon Church authority, either. Whatever you do, wherever it leads you, I personally want you to find Olive Jenkins' murderer, and it is my preference that he survive his encounter with you so he can stand public trial."

"Senator," interrupted the president. "With due respect, can we afford to leave Commander Rapier in Utah to complete that investigation, when global events of such import demand his attention?"

"Morgan?" said the senator.

"Give me one second to check on something," I said. Luckily, the MIBs hadn't confiscated my Android. I quickly connected with the wireless network Benny had used to transmit his earlier video, and pinged the static IP address of the computer I'd left in Snowbird. It responded immediately.

"Senator. Mister President. Before Benny and I set out to neutralize the terrorists, I plugged a USB device into my computer at Snowbird. The minute they restored landline phone service, my computer launched a command to disable the Russian and Chinese viruses. That process has been going on for…"

and I paused to look at a special peer-to-peer clock on a cloud server I'd actually secreted in the Pentagon, "…the virus disabling process has been going for eighty-seven minutes. I predict the process will complete in slightly over ten hours. As long as I keep entering computer-generated passwords every forty-eight hours, Russian and Chinese computers will stay healthy."

"It's called a dead man's switch," added Benny.

"You promised to text me those passwords just before the terrorists interrupted our conversation," said the president. "We should take care of that now."

"Might I ask you a question about that, sir?" I said.

"I'm your commander in chief. I *could* make that a direct order."

I didn't rise to the level of insubordination I felt bubbling up within me.

"Yes, sir, you could. But I'd consider it a personal favor if you answered one question."

"Let me hear the question, first," said the president. "Then I'll let you know if I can answer it."

"Thank you, Mister President. Have you, or have we, the United States of America, secured any quid pro quo should we succeed in neutralizing the virus attacks?"

"What would you suggest?"

"You're asking me?" I asked.

"That's *two* questions."

"Yes, sir, it is two questions." Man, these politicians sure are sticklers for precision. Then I shut up. Time to check this president's true IQ, and time to see how much rope he'd really give me. His answer both surprised me and raised some serious questions I couldn't begin to pose, let alone answer.

"Commander Rapier, as the architect of my new cyber doctrine, if you can stand the heat of a senate confirmation hearing as this administration's Cyber Marshall, then the quid pro quo commitments from China and Russia are your domain. If these or any other entities, be they government or private, violate a well-articulated set of conditions, then *we*—that's the royal *we*, but more precisely *you*—unleash the hounds of hell on them."

Okay, my problem should be obvious. How could POTUS place so much trust in a man whom he'd not only *never* met, but about whom he hadn't even heard until the last week? Senator Kimball couldn't have that kind of sway, since even the senator didn't know me. Maybe the O'Sheas had expressed unlimited faith in me, and maybe even my service record could vouch for me somewhat, but damn it, governments and bureaucracies aren't meant to function with such resolve and such unprecedented efficiency. This didn't happen when the founding fathers put together our constitutional framework, and it hadn't happened anytime since. Well, maybe with the possible exception of Ronald Reagan's off-the-cuff demand of Soviet President Mikhail Gorbachev to "…Tear. Down. This. Wall…."

But Reagan was a conservative ideologue. This president? Maybe a liberal ideologue? A liberal ideologue in cahoots with a conservative Utah senator? I couldn't come up with a topological framework to classify this situation. Which meant I might not have to, because such an alignment of planets simply couldn't happen. But what other hypothesis fit this outrageous set of circumstances? Well, only one that I could think of on such short notice. Time to test that hypothesis.

"Mister President. Senator Kimball. Something about our entire dialogue does not pass the test of reasonableness. You both know that I could *not* pass any kind of senate confirmation process. Somebody, on one or both sides of the aisle, would have to ask if I knew the source of the virus. And I'd answer truthfully that I had created it. Under those circumstances, you would be ill advised to nominate me, because felons don't normally get confirmed."

"Ah, but Commander," the president quickly replied. "You acted as a representative of the United States, under my authority and direction. And as for your confirmation, due to the sensitive nature of the intelligence you possess, it would have to be a closed session of the Senate Intelligence Committee."

Suddenly I got it! "Excuse me for being so dense," I began. "I've been having a dickens of a time figuring out how you could act so decisively in such a short time. Clearly, my virus landed in the middle of another *situation* and saved somebody's bacon big time. Somebody, somewhere, had precipitated a melt down, only I melted *them* down first."

"Benny," said the senator. "Could you excuse us for a minute?" And with that, one of the MIBs came into the room and gestured for Benny to follow him. Moments later, alone in the room, a lot became much more clear.

The president quickly cut through all my remaining questions. "Morgan, everything I'm about to tell you is beyond Ultra Top Secret. If word of this gets out, it could cause us incalculable damage. Simply put, your virus inadvertently saved the world banking system from a doomsday attack orchestrated by a person or persons unknown but most likely a joint-government sponsored effort by Russia and China. We'd been given several ultimatums that I won't go into right now, but which by their nature could never have been made public. Simply, they would have effectively ceded tacit control of the world financial system to Moscow and Beijing, yet given them plausible deniability as the perpetuators of the change. We'd come within twenty-four hours of *someone* pulling the trigger if we didn't capitulate.

"Morgan. Commander. Your virus stopped them cold. We've got quid pro squared. Suddenly, both governments have come to the fore and flat guaranteed the culprits would not only be prevented from ever again resorting to this unprecedented international extortion, but that they'd be semi-publicly executed—that's shorthand for we've got 'em and we'll send you the film—the minute we take the vise grips off their testicles. We've also received other unspecified concessions that are, well, let's say above your pay grade to discuss."

"Putting the puzzle together," I couldn't help but inject, "That would include their United Nations and/or World Court endorsement of your recently stated cybercrime doctrine?"

"You've a pretty good tactical sense for a non-politician," said the president. "I hope you'll trust me with those passwords, now?"

"Yes, sir, Mister President," I said. And after inviting him to have Cyber Command's Lt. General Steve Daly and Cyber Czar Harold Smith join the conversation, I spent a few minutes going over the mutating password protocols for both the dead-man's switch and for the permanent-stand down password.

After some behind the scenes muttering I couldn't quite understand, Smith came on the line. "Using Twitter is certainly an elegant and remarkably foolproof command-and-control approach, Commander."

"It is, sir, if you don't let it get out that Twitter is our communication vehicle," I said. "I wouldn't put it past an uninvolved third party to launch a denial-of-service attack on Twitter and bring them down for seventy-two hours."

"Speaking of a third party with motive," said the president, "Does our Middle-Eastern friend know these protocols?"

"Yes, Mister President, he does," I answered.

Again, more mumbling on the other end of the line. After a moment, the president pointed out the elephant in the room. "Morgan, Lt. General Daly makes a very good case for putting Benny into protective custody and eliminating any possibility that he could contact anyone in the Islamic world."

"Sir, you're my Commander in Chief, and Lt. General Daly is my line officer. So I am duty bound to obey your orders. Might I point out, though, an alternative course of action?"

"By all means," said the president.

"First, I've built in several back doors to enable and disable the virus at will. So the unavailability of Twitter might be inconvenient, but not catastrophic. Secondly, and this is your area of expertise so I'll only raise the issue for your consideration, Benny is now rather famous in the Islamic world. He essentially stood up to the President of the United States in a high-level meeting that's now being broadcast *everywhere*. If you give him respect and trust, you essentially give that same respect to Muslims worldwide. A byproduct, too, tests Benny to see if he can be trusted. He doesn't know I have other ways to manage the virus."

"Very good points, Commander." The president paused, possibly waiting for a thumbs-up signal from others in the room with him. The sound of rustling paper preceded his next comment. "Ah yes. Uh, before a plane slams into your building, could you share with us those alternative methods? Just in case."

I complied, telling them of my surreptitious server located in the Pentagon, the one-time username and password that would get them into a burn-after-reading file.

"Where the heck did you say that server is?" asked an incredulous Daly.

I told him the exact floor and room number of one of the inner-ring Pentagon server farms. And its backup sitting in the Camp Williams, Utah NSA Cyber Security Center.

"You have *got* to be kidding me!" he replied.

"Can you think of safer places, sir?" I said.

"If I *could* think of them, I wouldn't tell you about it," said Daly. To the others in his room as much as to me, he added: "Mister President, I don't know whether to recommend Commander Rapier for a medal of some kind or to make his activation and promotion one of the shortest in the disciplinary history of the United States military."

"He has that effect on people," chuckled the familiar voice of an old friend.

"Admiral Hall, I presume. Sir," I added.

"Couldn't let the head of the JCS miss out on the fun," said the president. "Mike has just confirmed to me that your de-lousing of the Chinese and Russian cyber-structure is starting to take effect. Which means I'd better get back on the old analog phone with my two new best friends and make sure they understand their obligations to deliver on their promises to the United States of America."

"Before we end this conversation, a request?" said Senator Kimball.

"Senator?" replied the president.

"Since Morgan has delivered on his commitment to defuse the virus, and since it might make a great deal of sense to keep our Islamic celebrity at arms length for a while, I would very much like to leave those two in Salt Lake City to wind up the murder investigation that originally brought them together out there."

Of course, his request exactly duplicated my own wishes. I couldn't very well abandon the O'Sheas. But I couldn't refuse a direct order from my commander in chief, either. So I weighed in: "With due respect, sirs, that would be my preference, too. I consider it a matter of personal integrity to see this murderer brought to justice, and a great personal favor to be allowed to do so."

"Mister President," said Admiral Hall somewhat emphatically. "I'd like the Cyber Command to start drilling into Commander Rapier's brain *yesterday* and find out how *he* and *his* virus work. Any delay would be a dangerous dereliction of my duty to the country."

Okay. Care And Feeding Of The Command Chain 101. Do *not* contradict your boss's boss in front of his boss. Not unless you truly want to be scooping out latrines with your bare hands. I'd made my case. The senator had made his request. Time to shut up. I strained to hear any background discussion, but the president must have raised his hand for silence as he considered his decision. Yep. Discussion over. The boss now expected his current audience to have a little more deference to his prerogatives than did his secretary of state earlier in the discussion.

"Morgan, can you get Benny back in there?" asked the president.

I didn't even have to stand, because the door opened and one of the MIBs gestured for Benny to come back in. He managed a cup of coffee in one hand and a cinnamon roll in the other. From the expression on his face, both appeared to hit the spot. Leave it up to Benny to find a good cup of coffee. I pointed to his steaming beverage and rolled my eyes. His shrug came across more like a challenge.

"Hi, Benny," I said. "Found some coffee?

"Benny," said the president. "Would you be willing to assist Commander Rapier in wrapping up his law enforcement obligation to the great state of Utah?"

Benny looked at me with raised eyebrows, and answered his query with an affirmative nod. I also took out my Android and went into the Unix command mode to link with one of my more diabolical secret cloud servers. I figured I'd do a reconnaissance after the president finished with Benny and hung up with us. If the senator had his Android with him, I'd hot mike it and just make sure no one had any hidden agendas.

"Mister President, I'd very much like to stay out here and do just that," Benny answered. "In my opinion, we're pretty close to apprehending the culprit."

"Very well, then. But at some point in the very near future, a few of us would like the benefit of your wisdom concerning Islam and Saudi Arabia." The president paused at a comment from someone in the room with him, then continued. "Normally, I'd turn such a conversation over to the state department, but after your little stunt in our earlier conversation, I think my secretary of state may be out on Pennsylvania Avenue chasing cars."

"It's tough to keep secrets in this information age," said Benny. "A *glass house* information philosophy, where the world can see deliberations at the highest levels, would seem to be the best approach to defusing all the conspiracy theorists. And believe me, quite a few Islamitards have probably joined your secretary of state in their frothing and snapping antics. They are *very* suspicious of western involvement in my apparent defection from the faith."

I mouthed "*Islamitards?*" to him, which evoked a wry smile.

"Should I need either of you, may I confirm your contact information?" said the president. "And Morgan, I assume you left the encrypted phone at Snowbird in your hurry to take down the jihadists?"

"No sir. I have it with me right here." I patted the lower of my two right-hand zippered pockets to make sure I hadn't misspoken. "And if you would permit me, Mister President, I'd like to get the video phone your people confiscated from Benny. He shouldn't be using his own cell phone."

Minutes later, the MIB returned Benny's phone as he and his clone ushered us down the stairs and into the Humvee waiting just outside the back door of the Federal Building. Good thing, too, as the lobby of the building teemed with reporters and camera crews. KUTV2's Dave Turner obviously hadn't wasted any time capitalizing on his news scoop. Now *everyone* wanted a piece of the *Morgan and Benny* show.

36
Trust But Verify

hat in the name of Mohammed are you doing?" said Benny as we sat on the balcony of my Snowbird condo. It had taken UDOT crews several hours to clear the canyon landslide so traffic up and down Little Cottonwood Canyon could resume.

"Quiet, Grasshopper. Eat your Five Guys burger," I said. We'd talked our driver into stopping at a burger joint in Sandy prior to taking us home. "It's nearly midnight, I haven't taken you clothes shopping yet, tomorrow will be a long day, and we need to find out if there are any political undertows that could drown us."

All the cell phones sat inside the house, in their respective chargers. We relaxed in the open air, the total darkness only interrupted by the light from my laptop screen. It seemed a good idea not to turn on any lights, since we didn't want any reporters knocking on my door. Having hot miked the senator's Android from a cloud server hosted in San Francisco at Grand Central Computing, I'd recorded whatever his microphone picked up in the time following our conversation with the president. Of course, the surreptitious activation of his cell phone would terminate the minute he tried to use it or when an incoming call shut it down, but from the size of the audio file about to play back, it appeared I had a good deal of their discussion. In answer to Benny's question, I Bluetoothed the sound from my laptop to two small speakers sitting on the glass-topped table between us. The president's voice came through loud and clear, which meant Senator Kimball carried the phone in his suit jacket's inner pocket.

"You know, senator, that the wheels of government will never again turn as smoothly as they did today?"

"That's because we ran a battle and not a bureaucracy. No congress. No competing agendas. No special interests jockeying to protect cash cows. No overseers trying to justify their existence. Too bad we can't keep the hounds of hell off our backs forever." The senator paused to sip something with ice in it.

Benny reached over and positioned the mouse over the PAUSE button, hitting it with a decisive tap of his finger. "By the prophet's beard, what did you just do?"

"That's a rhetorical question, so why don't you answer it?"

"You *hot miked* the senator's cell phone? You eavesdropped on a conversation between the President of the United States and the senator from Utah?" Benny seemed like he wanted to say more, but couldn't think of what it might be.

"I can see you're not, what did you call it? You're not an *Islamatard.*"

"But I thought that hot mike stuff was nothing more than an urban myth."

"You're right, Benny. It's an urban myth. Nobody can do it." I took the mouse from under his hand and clicked on PLAY. He grabbed it right back and hit PAUSE.

"*You have bugged the President. The Commander in Chief.*"

"Yeah, Benny. And you publicly bugged the secretary of state, today."

Benny just stared at me. Several times, his mouth tried for form words, but gave up in frustration. I couldn't tell if I'd hit home with his own complicity or whether the double-meaning of the word "bugged" simply inspired his speechless awe. Shock and awe, that's it. Shock and awe. So I snatched the mouse and clicked on PLAY. The conversation picked up right where it had left off, and the president responded to Senator Kimball.

"Gordon, your stumbling onto Morgan Rapier when you did defies all logic, even if it *did* cost me my secretary of state."

"Divine providence, Mister President. I don't believe in accidents."

"And you don't believe Rapier could possibly be involved in a larger disinformation conspiracy designed to bring the country down?"

"No, I don't. And neither do you, especially after seeing his service record and listening to Admiral Hall's first-hand endorsement of the man. However this happened, Morgan Rapier is a bona fide hero on multiple fronts who has done one more thing the historians will probably never get right."

"Which is?" asked the president.

"Which is getting you and me on the same page, at least this once. Up until last week, I doubt we'd have agreed on the color of the sky."

"Given your right-wing environmental position, we still might not agree on that."

"Okay, maybe I should have said 'day of the week' instead," said the senator. "But you had an ultimatum from some characters to whom you would have had to acquiesce had not Rapier gotten a phone call asking for his help solving a murder and which, before he left for Utah, made him therefore decide to lower the boom on said characters. Call it divine intervention or simply a highly unlikely convergence of events."

"Now that you've verbalized it, maybe there *is* some divine providence operating around here. What are the odds that Rapier would have launched his attack had your friend *not* called him?"

"Incalculable," said the senator without a pause. "Especially since you didn't fully explain the Chinese blackmail scheme to Morgan."

Suddenly, Benny's hand no longer hovered over the mouse. Snatching it and hitting PAUSE took last place to finding out *what* Chinese blackmail scheme sneaked out of the senator's mouth.

"Hard to believe that, without Morgan's shenanigans," continued the president, "By this time next week, the Chinese Yuan Renminbi would have replaced the U.S. dollar as the new worldwide reserve currency."

"I certainly wouldn't want that to happen on *my* watch as pres..." the senator's voice cut off mid-sentence.

"What happened? What happened!" said Benny.

I pointed out the blinking icon on my hot-mike server. "The senator had an incoming call that automatically terminated my peek-a-boo session."

"I don't see how you got into that server, wherever it was."

"It's not a named server. I have a large number of non-named servers at various IP addresses. I'm going to have to burn down this one, so to speak, because we do *not* want copies of that conversation to exist anywhere on the planet."

"By Mohammed's camel's rancid scrotum, I should say we don't want copies of this floating around!" Benny looked about to hyperventilate. "What *did* you guys talk about when I had to leave the room?"

"Birds, bees, flowers and trees," I answered.

"Yeah, and the moon up above," he sang the 1966 Herb Newman lyrics.

"And the thing called love."

I then proceeded to burn the server from the inside out with a seven-hundred instruction assembly language program that rewrote every sector on all the hard drives, zeroed out all EPROMs in both the main processor and all peripherals, and then notified the Grand Central co-hosting SysAdmin to personally oversee incinerating the entire rack of equipment, on camera. He'd do exactly as I'd asked, in order to guarantee himself a nice bonus. I then threw the IP address back into a different server pool in Chicago, explaining every step of the operation to Benny.

"Now that *that's* done, I can get some sleep," I said. "After listening to that last conversation, I have a lot less heartburn over how quickly the president acted on the senator's recommendation from me. Now, notwithstanding Mohammed's camel's rancid scrotum, let's lock this place down and hit the sack. We *really* have to go clothes shopping for you tomorrow."

37

Test Driving The YAK-43

o sooner did it seem that my head hit the pillow than several phones rang simultaneously. Benny's KUTV2-supplied phone hummed from the next room, my Android rang, and the encrypted phone supplied by the Feds rang. I heard Benny punch his phone to off, which I did with my Android after looking at the clock. Eight o'clock AM. I can't remember *ever* sleeping so long, so soundly. I judged it best *not* to punch the encrypted phone to transfer the call, since I hadn't even experimented with setting up a voice-mail account. No CallerID showed up on either the Android or the *special* phone, but it could only be two people.

"Speak," I said. No reason to identify myself.

"Mike Hall here for Morgan Rapier."

"Admiral, Sir!" I found myself standing at attention, old habits and all. And the JCS chairman must have heard my bare feet hit the floor.

"At ease, soldier. I can hear you standing at attention in your stocking feet."

"Bare feet."

"Come again?"

"I'm not in my stocking feet, sir," I said. "I'm standing in my bare feet."

"Well, judging from the front page of the *New York Times*, *The Wall Street Journal*, and every other newspaper, blogger, TV news anchor, and radio talk show host in the country, you sleep in combat boots, eat nails for breakfast and regularly crap lightning," said the admiral. "Every assignment editor in the country has been hounding the president for access to you, not to mention every self-important politician and bureaucrat who would kill for a photo opportunity."

"That pretty well covers it, doesn't it sir?"

"Not by a long shot, Death Eater."

"Death what?"

"That's your new call sign. Death Eater." For the first time, I detected an almost-smile in his voice. "The president must have been reading *Harry Potter* to his daughters, and came up with the name all by himself."

"I'm not familiar with *Harry Potter*," I said. "But Death Eaters sound like bad guys."

"They *are* bad guys, which by the way won't get you any argument from the secretary of state or her husband, who are quite busy doing damage control after Benny's little stunt."

"Speak of the devil," I said as Benny padded in from the other room. He put his thumb to his ear with his little finger over his mouth and mouthed "Who?"

"Speak of...oh...Benny is with you?"

"In the flesh, Admiral. Should I put it on speaker phone?"

"Please," he said with uncharacteristic politeness.

I clicked on the speakerphone and set the unit on the coffee table to amplify the sound. "Benny, please say hi to Admiral Mike Hall, chairman of the JCS and an old comrade in arms."

"Good morning," said Benny.

"Aasalaamu Aleikum, Mr. bin Faisal," said the Admiral.

"Sabah il Kheer, Admiral," said Benny. "And please call me Benny."

"Good morning to you too, Benny." The admiral paused, maybe to see if Benny picked up on his English translation of the Arabic greeting. Benny seemed pleased, giving me his who-is-this-guy? look. I owed the admiral reinforcement.

"Admiral," I said. "Benny is impressed with your Arabic.

"Yeah, well, *I am impressed* that Benny is getting almost as much press in the U.S. as you are," said Hall. "More press around the world, as a matter of fact. At least in the Middle East, since China and Russia don't have their presses up and running, yet."

"Come to think of it, there probably isn't an insurance underwriter in the world who would sell Benny a policy," I said.

"You either, Death Eater," the admiral immediately replied.

"Snowbird and the Muslims painted a bull's eye on my forehead, too."

"Islamic shooters are the least of your problems, son. You haven't seen the news about the Church of Scientology in San Francisco?"

"Damn!" I said, snatching my Android and looking for messages from my monitoring station across the street in San Francisco. No messages. Which meant they'd hit my place *before* doing something to my supposedly anonymous server farm in the basement of the church.

"Damn right, damn!" The Admiral continued. "Sometime before four o'clock this morning, two unrelated teams swept into the Scientology compound, discovered each other, and started shooting. A lot of Chinese and Russian bodies show they mixed it up pretty good. With body armor and high-tech weapons on each side. How long do you think it'll take them to find your apartment and make some well-educated guesses as to your involvement?"

"At least one team already knew of my involvement even *before* their dust-up." I sat down, swamped by the mental arithmetic of travel between San Francisco and Utah.

"What do you mean they already knew?"

"Admiral, I had a mini-cam overlooking the site, with a special sound/video AI programmed to send me a text message whenever the activity below me exceeded a rather high threshold. I never got the message and…" I paused as I tried to bring up my remote feed on the Android. No feed. No acknowledgement to my ping for the DNS address. "…and my whole system is offline. Yes, they could have tracked down my server farm. But there's no way they could have hit my apartment first without having been tipped of by somebody who knew of my involvement. And that would have to be somebody in the administration."

"We'll look into that. But Morgan, you and Bennie need to get down the mountain and into protective custody, and you need to get down that mountain *now!*"

"Any survivors on either attacking team?" I asked.

"Probably not," said Admiral Hall. "Seems the Scientology crowd didn't take kindly to an armed assault on their premises. They appear to have finished off the victors before the police arrived."

"So maybe I have some time, then."

"Doubt it. You're not dealing with the B-team from some third-world country."

"Better listen to this guy," said Benny.

"Morgan, these were elite shock troops every bit as good as our own Delta Force fast-response teams. And they've got government-level resources behind them, quite capable of fielding multiple teams on simultaneous missions. It's more important than ever. Get out of there!"

"We're on our way, Admiral." I didn't wait for him to acknowledge me before hanging up. No shaves. No showers. Just a mad dash to dress and slam together a few self-preservation essentials before….

The sound of shattering glass followed by flash-bang detonations in the room from which Benny and I had just fled shook the whole house. More crashing glass as commandos rappelled down rope lines and swung into my now gutted living room. *Holy howling hell!* No time for subtleties, I instinctively dove for the closet and my *snatch bag*, a backpack I hoped I'd never have to use but kept around in case I had to go from naked to killing machine in less than 10 seconds. And I might as well have been naked, given the boxers and T-shirt covering me. Another "thud" announced a second flash-bang had been tossed into the room with me, to which I responded by jumping all the way into the closet and closing the door behind me. Three, two, boom! I had one bare foot into a running shoe and the other almost into one when a second and third explosion shook the house. My room and Benny's. Okay, so someone on the outside had thermal imaging equipment and knew exactly where we'd gone. No shots, though. Good sign for both of us, since they must have wanted at least one of us—me, to be precise—alive.

Stay down, Benny, I thought as I hefted the snatch bag over one shoulder and chambered a round into my Desert Eagle. I opened the door a crack just as a black-clad figure in full body armor sailed into the room. A big guy with a tuft of blond hair poking from under his helmet and around his earpiece. Ergo, Russians. My Desert Eagle boomed, or at least I think it did. The Russian flash-bang must have nailed my hearing, as the only sign my gun worked was the Russian's head exploding in a mist of red. Full body armor meant I had no choice but to go for a headshot. As a nationally ranked SOCOM player, headshots got me extra points. Today, the headshot meant the bad guy wouldn't be getting off a return shot and thanking whatever deity he worshiped for first-class body armor. About now, this bad guy would be answering all kinds of metaphysical questions about which the rest of us could still only speculate.

Another tennis-ball-sized shadow sailed into the room. I pulled the door shut again and tried to equalize the coming change in atmospheric pressure by opening my mouth wide and exhaling. Another boom. Only one this time.

Benny must not have found a closet.

I waited for the inevitable rush of a well-trained team. Nothing happened. Yep, they wanted me alive. Russians wanted me alive. Which meant dart guns and a hostage. I swallowed, trying to clear my ears. Somebody in the living room yelled something, but the ringing drowned out the sound. Again, I swallowed and peeked through a crack in the closet door. No movement, but more clearly enunciating voices.

"Rapier," yelled a deep voice in perfectly unaccented English. "Your friend lives if you give yourself up within ten seconds."

Holy howling hell! whistled through my soggy brain, again. *Benny, what have I gotten you into?* Fact, whether or not I gave myself up, Benny and the Russian with the exploding head would be facing eternity and getting some answers from a God who, in my humble opinion, should be yea verily pissed of over the actions of at least one of them.

"Nine – eight – seven …" continued the same voice.

"Enough with the countdown, morons. I'm coming out," I yelled.

Forget everything in the snatch bag. Well, *almost* everything. If they wanted me alive, then I needed just two items, which I fished out of a side pocket. I slipped the pre-printed medical ID necklace over my head and prepped the other package. And Heaven help me if they didn't nail me with a dart gun, because there would be three of us—me, the headless Russian, and Benny—jockeying to put a proper spin our lifetime achievements in front of Our Father, who, if He went by the name Allah, would take a special interest in my activities of late. So before stepping out of my hiding place wearing nothing but running shoes, boxer shorts, a T-shirt, and hiding my trusty Desert Eagle behind my right leg, I injected myself with a drug cocktail brewed up by a veterinarian I'd befriended on a bicycle ride. If I didn't get shot with one of three commonly used tranquilizer mixtures— ketamine hydrochloride, an opiate, or succinlycholine— I'd act really crazy before dropping dead. And since most tranquilizer darts are designed for large animals, I injected myself with an equally large dose of diprenorphine, chased by a smidge of naloxone and topped off with dantrolene.

"…six – five – four …"

"Man, your macho tough-guy act is really getting on my nerves," I said, staggering out of my closet and stopped in the living room doorway. I raised my left hand and used my finger to dig into my ear, acting about as disoriented as I truly felt. Those drugs I'd given myself *did* act fast. The tallest Russian stood with his left arm locked around Benny's throat and his right-hand holding a Makarov PM 9mm to Benny's temple. Three others spread out, mistakenly assuming I believed they'd shoot me with their U.S.-made MP5s. I wanted to say, *Hey, that's my gun you idiots! Where's your national pride? Why aren't you using suppressed OTs-14 Grozas?* Of course, my mouth wouldn't work anymore, damned drugs from the damned vet, and everything suddenly ran in slow motion. I could see—thank Mary, Martha, and Snoopy—three air pistols coming up in the non-MP5-carrying hands of my black-clad visitors. Slowly, but nevertheless drawing a bead on me. Benny's eyes looked quite large, either from recognition of my own Desert Eagle coming into play a little faster than my opponents', or possibly due to oxygen deprivation from the chokehold around his neck. Only one thing stood between him and summary execution after I'd been sedated with not one but three darts, and that thing took the head off the tall Russian holding him. My Desert Eagle boomed just as "thufft – thufft – thufft" three darts nailed my torso.

I quickly dropped my gun, not wanting to tempt retaliation from any of the MP5s and with my mission accomplished as far as Benny went, and did my Sarah Bernhardt dying-swan act, rolling my eyes back and teetering forward. I didn't hit the ground, as three sets of very strong arms caught me. Benny took advantage of his de-captorization—okay, my drug euphoria had me making up new but terribly interesting words—and sailed through the shattered patio windows and off the balcony. He'd somehow managed to slip into guestroom slippers, because that's all I saw as he went head first toward the trees behind my house: the bottoms of those slippers. Hopefully he grabbed a trunk or a branch fast, because those suckers stood sixty feet tall. My three abductors, and it took all three of them, manhandled me out the front door and into some kind of shrieking hurricane.

I sneaked a peek as a jet-black stealth fighter settled into the road in front of my condo. Where the heck did the Russians get a two-seat VTOL aircraft? It kind of looked like a Yakovlev 41, but the YAK-41 only came with one seat. The UB two-seat model supposedly never got off the drawing board. And the YAK-43, much more advanced on paper, never did either. So surprised as to nearly forget my feigned unconsciousness, I almost asked them how they got this plane built without NATO knowing, and how they got it financed after the fall of the USSR. But I didn't break out of character, letting my head loll instead and doing my best imitation of a bag of wheat. A very big bag of wheat.

With help from their pilot, the three commandos lifted me into the right-side seat, buckled me in, and flex-cuffed my hands. The next thing I knew, the pilot sat back in his seat and the canopy lowered over my head. The twin turbines spooled up and I felt the plane shudder, beginning to lift. My life continued to lumber along in slow motion, although the tranquilizers from the Russian darts had started to neutralize the effects of my wake-up-the-horse-and-send-him-off-to-the-races appetizer.

I *knew* I wanted this plane intact. The president did. Admiral Hall did. One minor problem, though: other than an air combat simulator in a prototype Zipper Interactive game for the Playstation IV, I did *not* know how to fly this sucker. I *did* know, however, that unlike the American F-16 and the Joint Strike Fighter planned but never deployed, both of which required the ejection seats to be armed manually before firing them, that the Zvedzda K-36 ejection seats used by the Russians had to be armed as part of the pre-flight checklist. Further, while the side-pull ejection mechanism in U.S. plans would have been impossible to activate with my flex-cuffed hands, that the Russian ejection mechanism happened to be center pull, and that my legs straddled the activation handle, putting it within easy reach of my bound hands. But my own escape would still allow the pilot to escape with this great, top-secret prize. Only one choice.

I bumped the pilot's shoulder with my head. When he turned to see my wide-awake eyes staring at him, I said, "Hey, is this really a YAK-43?" I think he nodded in the affirmative, but before he could fully register my intent, I leaned across and with both of my restrained hands reached between his knees and pulled his ejection mechanism, recoiling not a second too soon.

The canopy blasted off the plane, followed by a rocket-propelled pilot in his seat, probably articulating something to the effect, "Why yes sir, this is a YAK-43. You surely do know your airplanes."

My next choice was rather binary. Either I could try to handle the stick and steady the now climbing plane, or I could reach for the throttles on my left and power this baby down. Since my own simulated flying experience involved custom settings on my Playstation controller, called *inverted mode* for aircraft, I couldn't be certain of the real-life effect any given stick movement would have on airplane performance. So I reached to my left and completely throttled down the craft, after which I engaged my own between-the-legs ejection mechanism and blew into the sky.

No more slow-motion adventures for me. I'd seen videos of Zvedzda ejection from ground level and marveled that anyone could live through such an experience. Designed for high-altitude ejections at Mach speeds, the K-series seats boasted more non-fatal deployments than any other technology, anywhere else in the world. In fact, after the fall of the USSR, our own government even talked with NPP Zvedzda about adapting the technology to U.S. warplanes.

Gazoom! Woosh! What a ride into the sky, followed by a perfect chute deployment and detachment of the seat-rocket mechanism. Most pilots can navigate their descent using guide handles that hung from each side. My bound hands just held onto the ejection handle for dear life as I floated down, right onto the Cliff Lodge patio where I'd had shooting practice the day before. Across and up the canyon a ways, a rented Suburban full of three Russian commandos and their support crew cushioned the hard landing of their VTOL YAK plane. The plane looked pretty well intact. The commandos on the other hand, had been downsized rather dramatically beneath the twenty-ton behemoth. The pilot hadn't fared nearly as well in his descent as I had, and currently hung from a quad chair lift anchoring pole about a hundred yards from me.

"Morgan Rapier?" asked a out-of-breath man wearing a Snowbird Polo shirt.

"Sorry to drop in like this," I said. "And you're…?"

"Michael Harvey," said the Snowbird event manager."

"Michael, you wouldn't happen to have a pocket knife with you?" I held up my flex-cuffed hands. "Those Russians tried to kidnap me and things got a little out of hand."

"Uh, yes." Harvey fumbled a Swiss Army knife from one of the pockets in his cargo shorts—have we all managed to start dressing like Charlie Harper in *Two-and-a-half Men?*—and made short work of my restraints. With his help, we released the parachute harness and I staggered to my feet, only to drop to one knee from dizziness. "Whoa, Mr. Rapier, you okay?"

"Guess not, Michael. They drugged me up," I said, plopping into a sitting position. "You'd better call the police. *And* keep people away from that guy hanging from the quad pole. He's probably armed and not that all-fired anxious to talk to the authorities."

Sirens coming up the valley meant Michael wouldn't have to make the 911 call, so he helped me into one of the restaurant chairs that had been moved outside while maintenance crews repaired bullet holes and broken glass from yesterday's dust up Benny and I had with the Iranians. *Benny!*

As if on cue, Benny staggered up the stairs and sank into a chair beside me. The scratches on his arms, legs and face proved he had indeed snagged a tree after his stunt dive off my deck. He handed me my Desert Eagle, which meant he'd stopped at the house.

"Thanks, Benny. I needed that." The gun dangled from my hand, which hung limply from the arm rest of my chair.

"Good shot, back there in the house," said Benny.

"No it wasn't," I said. "I aimed for your head. So they couldn't torture you."

I couldn't keep a straight face, however, as his briefly horrified look sent me into convulsions of laughter. He started laughing, too. I vaguely noticed the gathering crowd, one of whom held a KUTV2 camera. And I was so loopy that I didn't register the real significance of a black-clad Chinese man waiving his team back down the stairs and onto the back of waiting motorcycles. In retrospect, the live news broadcast from Dave Turner's crew saved our lives.

38
"That's no rain drop!"

enny busied himself surfing the television news channels while I sat propped up in my bed in the Alta View Hospital ICU, blood gas display finally rising over ninety percent, heart rate finally below one hundred, and blood pressure finally above that of a recent cadaver. Armed guards every twenty feet, both inside and outside the hospital didn't leave much to the imagination of any commando team searching the Salt Lake Valley as to which hospital I'd been admitted. I'd been taken by helicopter to the hospital and had just finished a stint on the kidney dialysis unit, along with a serious tongue lashing by an incredulous doctor who took exception to my pre-tranquilization drug injection.

"Those drugs are used on large farm animals or elephants on safaris," the doctor had shouted. "At least the medical ID necklace gave us a running chance to keep you alive."

"Guess I shouldn't have asked a veterinarian for advice, eh Doc?"

"If I find out the name of that flipping vet, I'll have him sweeping stables in Moscow!" shouted the doctor. Then he shouted at me: "The good news is, Russians did *not* use ketamine. Bad news, your diprenorphine dose would certainly have killed you. *But,* good news again, your opiate neutralizer naloxone also neutralized the diprenorphine. Do you have any idea how lucky you are?"

"If you only knew, Doc."

He stormed out and left me with my OCD news junkie Benny, who sipped apple juice and kept yelling for a decent cup of coffee. Then he yelled for the nurse to be quiet: "Hey, hey, here it is, Channel 2. Quiet everybody."

The cameraman, probably at the Cliff Lodge doing a follow-up story on yesterday's events, heard the noise and turned his focus toward the Russian jet just as it lifted off, tracking both ejections and my subsequent landing on his very deck. And there we sat, Benny and me on the Cliff Lodge deck, me with my Desert Eagle hanging from my right hand and both of us laughing like school girls. At least we calmed down, once we saw the camera.

"Awh nuts, they got a raindrop on the camera lens," I said.

"That's *not* a raindrop," snorted Benny. "Your boxer shorts gaped open when you uncrossed your legs. They're blotting out a shot of your manhood."

And sure enough, when the camera went in for a close up, the blurred spot disappeared. I wondered how long it would take the *National Enquirer* to get the undoctored footage. Given that Channel 2 had been on top of the story from the beginning, they pretty well had all the facts, which the news anchor perfectly articulated. In his most sincere, Emmy-toned voice:

> **"This is Shawn Bezzant with an exclusive KUTV2 update.**
>
> **"Earlier today, you saw this exclusive breaking news from Snowbird's Cliff Lodge, where major violence erupted for the second day in a row. Yesterday, Islamic assassins out to collect a bounty on the head of the apparently apostate Mohammed bin Faisal Al Saud, had their murderous plan thwarted by the now-famous United States Navy SEAL Commander Morgan Rapier and his close friend bin Faisal, affectionately known as Benny.**
>
> **"Just this morning, Commander Rapier repelled a second attack by Russian commandos, again at Snowbird. This footage aired live this morning, mere minutes after the attempted kidnapping of Rapier aboard a top-secret vertical take-off and landing, or VTOL, stealth jet. The commander successfully ejected the craft's pilot, after which he managed his own ejection. The story is still unfolding at the time of this interview."**

Benny and my laughter immediately died with the appearance of the camera, although I *thought* myself to be far more coherent during the filming than I now appeared to be on television.

"Morgan? Morgan Rapier? We're broadcasting live from the very site of yesterday's shootout. Could you tell us what just happened?"

The camera close-up showed me looking a bit loopy, blinking and trying to shake off my drug haze.

"A bunch of Russians drugged me and then tried to kidnap me in that big black plane sitting on top of a crushed Escalade over there."

I raised my right hand, the one carrying my Desert Eagle, and pointed toward the road behind the camera, which panned around to take in the scene.

"That's a plane that NATO and everyone else didn't think got built. Unless I miss my guess, it's a Yak 43. A two-seat Yak 43, fully stealthed. Its predecessor, the Yak 41, didn't even have two seats. So much for good intelligence."

The camera swung back around to me, and the interviewer asked,

"Is this related to yesterday's attack on Mister bin Faisal?"

"Benny," interrupted my friend. "Just call me Benny."

I jumped in. "No, the kidnapping involved entirely something else." The close-up camera missed Benny gently tapping my left arm, but I didn't miss his telling me to shut up about the reason for our rude awakening. I did nod in recognition of his signal and rotated the big Desert Eagle in a circle pointing skyward and then behind me. "The Russian pilot is hanging on the lift pole up the hill. You're going to want some police up here when you get him down."

My head kept rolling from side to side, during the interview. And the sound of police sirens intruded more loudly, echoing off the mountains around us. The camera swept to my left as someone in the crowd shouted something about "What pilot on what lift pole?" The next person in the picture wore all black and waived a Makarov PM 9mm pistol identical to the one his teammate had pointed at Benny's head.

"Sveenya!" shouted the Russian pilot as he raised the gun in my direction. It sounded a lot like the English word *swine*.

I must have replied with an expletive, subsequently beeped from the soundtrack by the same guardian of public morals that blurred the gap in my boxer shorts, and by the time the cameraman had the presence of mind to zoom back into a wide-angle shot of both the pilot and me, the sound of my Desert Eagle already echoed in harmony with the police sirens. The pilot lay on the deck, clutching the shoulder only partially attached to the arm connected to his now-empty gun hand.

"Good thinking, winging him so the authorities can interrogate him," said Benny.

"Damn, Benny," I slurred, "I missed another head shot."

I then watched myself slump into unconsciousness, my own gun dropping to the deck. At least I'd crossed my legs, closing the gap in my shorts and thereby eliminating the need for the optical raindrop.

"This man's been drugged and needs immediate medical attention," yelled Benny over the ensuing pandemonium.

In his studio now, the reporter concluded his money-in-the-bank audition for a national news anchor spot.

"Our own KUTV2 helicopter evacuated Commander Rapier and his friend Benny to an emergency facility, where we understand doctors are working to purge his system of whatever drugs his kidnappers used to immobilize him. At the request of both local and national law enforcement, as well as military authorities, we have agreed *not* to disclose that location, for reasons of national security and, naturally, for the safety of Commander Rapier in what appears to be an important and ongoing international news story."

A close-up of the Russian plane filled the screen.

"As for the top-secret Russian aircraft, a source at Hill Air Force Base who wishes not to be named has confirmed Commander Rapier's speculation that the VTOL craft does indeed resemble the Yakovlev 43 drawing-board design of a craft that was thought to be abandoned with the fall of the Soviet Union. That it should appear now, fully stealthed, seems to have the entire U.S. intelligence community reeling.

Join me at seven o'clock tonight on KUTV2 for a special one-hour prime-time look at exclusive footage of Commander Rapier's last few days here in the state of Utah. Until then, this is Shawn Bezzant signing off.

"Oh golly Miss Molly," I sighed.

"You weren't really aiming for the pilot's head, Morgan?"

"Benny, I don't even remember taking the shot," I said. "And when we go buy clothes, I want to get a new style of underwear. How about those almost-knee-length Haynes jobs that Michael Jordan used to advertise?"

My lingerie musings ceased as a commotion in the hallway notched up several decibels with one familiar voice demanding immediate entrance and at least one guard chambering a round into his semi-automatic. I nodded to Benny.

"Don't let them shoot the judge."

Benny jumped from his bed beside me and pulled his saline drip stand toward the door with one hand while holding his hospital gown closed behind him with the other. Before he could reach the door, two very large Marines appeared. Sandwiched between them stood a sputtering Patrick O'Shea. His feet didn't touch the ground. My eyes immediately focused on a weapon held gingerly in one of the soldier's free hand.

"My what a big gun Your Honor brought with him," I said. The Marine sergeant held a .357 Magnum Colt Python Silhouette from the Leupold scope mounted atop its eight-inch barrel.

"You know this guy?" said the man holding the weapon.

"Oh yes I do, sergeant. That's Judge Patrick O'Shea, the man responsible for bringing me out to Utah in the first place."

"See, I told you," said the judge. "Now put me down and give me back my gun!"

"Sorry Sir, but no guns allowed in the hospital," said the sergeant.

"What …!" snapped Hizonor.

I jumped in. "Technically, Sergeant, the judge is an officer of the court and allowed to carry personal protection at all times. I'll vouch for him."

With great reluctance, the guard detail released O'Shea and watched warily as the judge put the gun in the biggest shoulder holster I'd ever seen. Without so much as a "thank you" Hizonor stalked past Benny and plopped into the one visitor's chair in our room. Once seated, he glared at the Marines until they disappeared back down the hallway. He didn't wait long to affix me with his full wrath.

"Jumpin' Jehoshaphat, Morgan!" he followed with a very long sigh. "I ask you out here to help with a murder, and in less than a week you've practically started World War Three. Then comes an Arab hit squad—no offense Benny—Russian commandos in a top-secret aircraft, not to mention crafting the president's cyber marshal program, getting the sheriff's office blown up, and oh yes, beating the hell out of the Kendrick family on a national Web feed. Have I missed anything?"

"Yeah," I said drolly. "How about getting one law officer and two civilians killed as I homed in on your murderer?"

Suddenly the judge calmed down. "Those murders weren't your fault. Crap happens when you go after bad guys. I'm proud of you, son. You're making a difference. One hell of a difference, actually."

"I think my house keeper would agree with you, Patrick." I thought how much damage a couple of flash-bang grenades can do to the inside of a condo. Not to mention brains from two Russian commandos splattered all over the walls. I made a note to call Utah Disaster Clean Up as soon as the forensics guys finished their police work at my place. And I fully expected the Snowbird homeowners' association to have a note nailed to my front door offering to buy me out at double the appraised value. *Yes, Mister Rapier. The Cliff Lodge wanted to do a* booming *business—honestly, no pun intended—but enough is quite enough.*

"And speaking about homing in on the murderer," said the judge, remembering the reason for his visit, "I just issued Detective Davidson and those BAU folks a search warrant for Brigham Wood The Third's home, offices, out houses, and the rear ends of his farm animals. Pretty compelling evidence you uncovered. The former ambassador is impressed, too, not to mention being yea verily humbled by several of his and his wife's families' ancestors' participation in the *Mountain Meadows Massacre.*"

"Hold on a minute, Your Honor. You told the ambassador?" Pictures of astronomical political fallout played out in HD.

"Not directly, but you know I've been keeping him up to date through his chief of staff Heber King. And I made sure Senators Kimball and Hyde know too, although their families appear to be unscathed." The judge's eyes probed me for the cause of my concern.

"And nobody sounded nervous about these disclosures?" I asked.

"Not at all. In fact, the last thing anyone suggests is cover up. What's done is done."

"Gotta' hand it to them," I said. "These guys have guts. How's Sherry taking all this?"

O'Shea winked at the mention of his wife. "She's excited to see this unfolding. In fact, I have her dropping off a copy of the search warrant to the former ambassador's residence. He wanted to see it. And his wife is also vitally interested, although for her it's a double-edged sword. On the one hand, she's delighted with your progress. On the bad-news front, it appears she has ancestors with at least *some* peripheral involvement in the *Mountain Meadows Massacre.*"

"Not to tell you your job, Patrick," I said, using the familiar address to underscore my personal concern and friendship. "But isn't it ill advised to share the progress of an ongoing investigation with *anybody?*"

"Normally, yes," he said. "In this case, however, with such high-profile figures both from the 1800s and their descendants today, everyone has made it abundantly clear they *do not* want any appearance of defensive obfuscation. Better to let the truth out at any price."

"Your Honor," I said, smiling. "Quoting one of my favorite lines from the movie *Top Gun,* 'Maverick, that's the gutsiest move I've ever seen.'"

"Speaking of which, that's my line, Morgan!" The judge cocked his thumb and pointed his finger at me. "How did you learn how to fly a top-secret Russian fighter?"

"Playstation," I answered.

"Come again?"

"The closest thing I've had to formal training on Russian military aircraft came with my Sony Playstation. Patrick, if I could fly one of those things I'd have tried to land it intact for U.S. intelligence."

"The last time I checked," said the surprised judge, "Sony joysticks didn't come with a seat ejection lever. How did you even know to do that?"

"Awh heck. NPP Zvedzda ejection technology is world famous. It's far superior to anything available in U.S. warplanes, but politics made it impossible to equip our jets with anything Russian. Right, Benny?"

"Ibn himar!" shouted Benny, who seemed to be having trouble properly covering his privates with the hospital gown as he tried for the third time to climb back into his hospital bed without knocking over his IV stand. The judge looked at me for translation.

"Son of a donkey, eh?" I laughed. Then to the judge: "I think it's about time we get Benny some decent clothes. He's been making do with my stuff since yesterday. I promised him we'd go shopping. And we owe it to him, given he's the one who made the breakthrough on Olive's murder."

And I looked at Benny. What a rock! In the week over which I'd unleashed hell on earth, not to mention ending life as he knew it in Saudi Arabia, he hadn't complained once. By all rights, he should have held me down so the Russians could get in a couple of good groin kicks, after what I had done to their economy. Two deadly attacks in as many days, and still he behaved like the best friend I had in the world. On reflection, he might truly be *my* best friend. Sure, the O'Sheas and I had some history. We might legitimately count each other as friends. But *best friend* isn't a term I'd ever considered relevant. Too mushy. Fellow soldiers in arms would lay down their lives for each other, but the term *friend* somehow missed that equation. *Best friend.* I let the thought roll around in a now less-drug-addled brain. My wife had been my true best friend. And we'd shared other friendships. Not that I particularly cared one way or another for those friends, but I *did* love my wife, so I cared about them because *she* cared about them. Because I loved *her*.

Concerning the term *best friend*, I can only relate to the probably embellished tale of a Skye terrier named Greyfriars Bobby. His owner, an Edinburgh City Police night watchman, died in 1858. Bobby spent the remaining decade of his life by the grave, until he died at the age of fourteen. To me, *that* says best friend. Which means I couldn't be counted on as Annie's best friend, since I'd run like hell after she died. Forget rationalizing that I had to, oh, "get on with my life" or some such drivel. Had I sat around her grave for the last three years, somebody would probably have had me institutionalized. They might have tried. Just like the Saudi hit team. Or the Russians. Could be that's what the Kendrick boys did for a living.

Benny, though. He didn't have a life. So he came toward me in his search for meaning. All motivated by my smart aleck days as a prep school kid who used the same words twenty years later to tag a hacker. Bottom line for this week? He'd been a far better friend to me than I'd been to him. Now or ever. And there he sat, trying to keep his privates private with one hand while navigating a continually tangling tube from the IV-bag-on-wheels with his other hand. Yet even in this slapstick comedy setting—W. C. Fields simply *must* have had such a scene in one of his early black-and-white movies—to me Benny radiated nobility. I decided to test my equilibrium before popping my next idea on Benny and the judge.

Slowly, I slipped my legs over the side of the bed and used my own IV stand to balance as I slid my feet to the floor. A little queasiness, but all in all, manageable. Even when I turned my head toward the judge, no pain and no dizziness.

"Patrick, could you do us a favor?" I asked.

"Name it," he said.

"Neither Benny nor I managed to get out of the house this morning with our wallets. You know, identification, money or credit cards. Could you take us to the nearest shopping mall and put the purchase of some clothes on your American Express card. I'm good for it."

"No problem with the AmEx," he said. Then he chuckled and pointed at my gaping gown. "Might be a public outcry, however, if you two walked into a store bare assed."

"The man's right," said Benny. "Maybe we could borrow some of those green duds from a doc?"

"Swell idea," I said, removing an IV needle taped to the back of my left hand. "Your Honor, could you finagle us some scrubs and slippers from the medical staff?"

39

Graduate School: Dealing With The Media (2nd Semester)

t took quite some haggling, both to get us scrubs and slippers, as well as convincing the heavily armed Marines—who'd been given orders to guard Benny and me—to let us just walk out of the hospital. I had to finally pull rank as a full commander to order my Marine sergeant to back off. I did, however, extend the courtesy of letting him put me on the phone with his commanding officer, to whom I unambiguously passed the bull's eye. A U.S. Navy commander always trumps a Marine captain. Besides, I had one gnawing concern, but the captain nicely put that to rest.

"Captain," I said. "There may be the potential for more trouble around here that you'd better send up the chain of command. Both the Russians and the Chinese shot each other up in San Francisco just outside my apartment. But we've only seen Russians here. Is there…."

"Relax, Commander Rapier," he interrupted. "We have detained eight Chinese nationals coming down from Snowbird this morning. Evidently, the live news coverage of you and your friend on the Cliff Lodge deck made them reconsider their action. That and the sight of a stealthed top-secret Russian fighter dropping out of the sky. Apparently, their government didn't want any part of the media shit rain. I'm told the diplomats are working to do an invisible repatriation."

Minutes later, four of us—Benny, Judge O'Shea, myself and Master Gunnery Sergeant Lund, who my compromise with his captain via a direct order from POTUS saddled us with—walked out the lobby of the Alta View Hospital and toward the parking lot. Benny and I had donned green hospital scrubs, and "gunny" Lund had shed his assault rifle and wore only his side arm. I'd convinced his superiors that the military presence at Alta View blew any chance that our location could be kept secret, and that getting everyone out of there would reduce the risk of drawing the attention of any more bad guys, who might dream up some ugly hostage scenarios. As if to emphasize my prescience about our lack of secrecy, an army of reporters met us as we rounded the corner from the covered entryway. The scrubs did little to camouflage our identities. They so surprised the judge that I barely had time to grab his right hand as he reached for the elephant gun under his jacket.

"Patrick," I leaned down and whispered. "We can't have a judge plugging reporters on camera, now, can we?"

He quickly gave me his *I-don't-see-why-the-hell-not* look, but let his right hand drop back to his side. In the meantime, Gunny Lund took a position to the right of the judge and, together, we all tried to get to the parking lot and Judge O'Shea's car. And Benny, bless him forever, walked directly behind me in an obviously defensive position. We did a pretty good job ignoring them until some out-of-town reporter shouted exactly the *wrong* question.

"How many people are you going to kill today, Mister Raper?" shouted the tall woman holding a microphone with her network's logo prominently emblazoned on the camera-facing handle.

I felt Benny's hand jam into the small of my back as I stopped and turned toward cameras that quickly swarmed in for a close up. The pejorative question of how many people I planned to kill might have been ignored, but her mispronunciation of my name as 'Raper' instead of 'Rapier' pushed a very large and very red, albeit imaginary, button in my spleen. But even better yet, I recognized this woman. And I could have kissed her on the lips for giving me the chance to give Benny some well-deserved credit. Credit, I might add, at the expense of this national anchor's handlers.

The trick involved waiting until microphones other than hers thrust into my face, cameras rolling behind them. While this woman's network would edit out anything that painted their news anchor in a bad light, I felt certain that the rest wouldn't. And I intended to make sure they *couldn't*. I nodded in her direction.

"Madam, could you repeat your question?" I asked. Nobody used the word 'madam' in polite company, except when prefacing an office, as in 'madam secretary' or 'madam president' or some such title. And just as I'd hoped, the reporter took my reference as an insult and repeated her ambush tactic.

"Mister Raper, I asked how many people are you going to kill today?"

Elation threatened to destroy my poker face. Luckily, the same time-released adrenalin that allowed me to calmly go into battlefield situations prevailed, and I put on my best look-at-the-ground hangdog expression. Looking up, directly into the woman's eyes, I shrugged and gave my best injured-pride smile.

"Madam, I haven't heard someone intentionally miss-state my name since grade school. The name's 'Rapier' as in sword, not 'Raper' as in sexual predator. And as to your agenda-laden question about how many people I would kill today, the before-breakfast count so far is five. But the day is young and I'm a United States Navy SEAL Commander. Check back with me after lunch." I paused until she started to blurt out another inane question, then winked at the FOX camera and held up my finger. "Or, Madam, you can check in with me for the after-dinner body count. Between Benny and me, we got fifteen yesterday."

This time she didn't let me pause, and shouted: "So you're proud of the number of people you've killed?"

Again I did the hangdog humble before fixing her with my say-hello-to-the-devil-in-about-two-minutes look. "Madam, yesterday sixteen Islamic terrorists tried to kill my school chum Benny. We not only defended him, but probably saved the lives of many innocent bystanders at Snowbird. I did what you—all of you—pay me to do: protect the lives of Americans. Fifteen of the attackers died."

"We Americans who you say pay you have a thing called due process," she spat back. "We don't know *what* they intended, since you took it upon yourself to play judge, jury, and executioner. Ditto for the Russians you killed today, Mister *Rapier*." She pronounced my last name slowly and very correctly.

"That's *Commander* Rapier, Madam. At least you pronounced my name correctly, this time.

"So you think we should have let the terrorists kill a few hostages before we decided that fifteen Middle Eastern men with automatic weapons maybe posed a threat?" Since I'd asked a rhetorical question, I didn't feel the need to wait for her answer. "Of course, after the fact we recovered photos of Benny and me on each of the attacker's bodies. But you're right. Due process took a back seat to self defense."

"Well, *Commander* Rapier," she shrieked over the crowd's laughter. "The Posse Comitatus act of 1878 prohibits you from enforcing the law in the U.S. on non-federal property, which makes you nothing but a vigilante who, at best, over reacted, and a cold-blooded murderer at worst."

Wow, this lady really came loaded for bear! Time to take off the kid gloves.

"Madam," I began. Gosh I loved that word, 'madam' today. "I believe the United States military has the obligation to thwart an attack by a foreign power on our own soil. You might, however, find my agreement with one of your points surprising. I may indeed have over reacted. We Americans believe in fair play, and only sending sixteen assassins to contend with one U.S. Navy SEAL and one member of the Saudi Royal Family seems grossly unfair. Unfair to the assassins, that is. They should have sent a much larger force."

The reporter tried to yell another question, but I couldn't hear her over the crowd's actual applause. So I decided to cut to the chase and pound that last nail into her do-it-herself coffin.

"Today, six Russians with automatic weapons and a top-secret stealth plane attacked me in my home. Five of them died, crushed by the weight of their own aircraft I might add. Thank you and have a nice day."

Whereupon we jumped into the waiting car. O'Shea had backed into the spot, so he gunned forward and around a few scrambling reporters to make our escape out the top of the Alta View Hospital visitor parking lot and, notwithstanding a terribly illegal left turn into traffic, down the hill and into Sandy proper. The ensuing traffic jam of reporters still might have caught us, except that two Sandy Police patrol cars just happened to block the hospital exit after we'd passed them.

Appropriately, Gunny Lund rode shotgun while Judge "Roy Bean" O'Shea drove like a madman. Benny and I sat in the back seat of Hizonor's Cadillac in our green scrubs. Benny had somehow lost one of his hospital-issue slippers in our dash to the car, and he kneaded the bottom of his bare foot, scraping some sand and grit onto the plush carpet. It appeared the judge's compulsion for cleanliness took a back seat to his desire to put as much distance between us and the Media Tabernacle Choir at the hospital.

"Where to?" asked O'Shea.

"The nearest full service shopping center," I replied. "Shoe store first."

"Definitely the shoe store first," said O'Brien, meeting my gaze in his rearview mirror. "Tell your friend that carpet is tough to vacuum."

I winked back at the judge, who didn't miss much after all. Benny gave me his *Whaaaat?* look. "Not smart to make an enemy of the press."

"Me!" I backhanded his arm with the fingers on my right hand. "*Your* little covert broadcast of her patron's blunder loosed that shrieking banshee on us. Now they hate me, too."

"You know Morgan, we *could* be the two most hated men on the planet."

"Guess they'll celebrate our deaths later this afternoon, then?"

"Huh? Deaths from what cause?"

"From starvation, Benny. In case you haven't noticed, we've missed both breakfast and lunch."

"Ahhhhhh," said Benny. "*That's* why you mentioned those two meals in your interview. Judge O'Shea, do you think you might stop by that Five Guys burger place before we hit the clothing emporium? I *really* liked those burgers."

"You're not eating those things in *my* car," said the judge in his courtroom voice. Then to his shotgun-riding Marine: "You ever eat at a Five Guys?"

"No sir, I haven't," said Gunnery Sergeant Lund.

"You're in for a treat, soldier," said the judge. He looked at me in his rearview mirror. "But we're going inside. No greasing up my floor."

40
Tribute to ZZ Top's
Sharp Dressed Man

e arrived at the South Towne Mall's lower-level entrance, and O'Shea carefully backed the big Cadillac into a handicapped entrance right by the front door. He must have seen my raised eyebrows from the back seat, because he hooked a handicapped tag around the mirror before I could say something. I couldn't think of four less deserving and more fit people to be taking the slot, but improving our chances of making a quick getaway and thereby reducing possible collateral injuries to bystanders made me hold my tongue. Besides, both Benny and I felt so much better after our burgers, fries and Cokes. I'd managed to get a mustard streak down my green smock. Benny did a matching streak in catsup on his. Time for new clothes. First stop: a buy-one-pair-and-get-another-at-half-price athletic shoe store. We had to walk about a hundred yards to the shoe store, but that meant we could exit the Dillard's menswear department and be within twenty feet of a quick getaway.

"What is this place?" gasped Benny in amazement.

"It's a shoe store," I said.

"No. This *whole* place?" Benny raised his arms in a sweeping motion as he turned.

"Come on!" I said. "You've been in a shopping mall before."

Benny balanced on his one slippered foot while he wiped his bare foot on the leg of his scrubs. "I've been to Harrod's in London and Macy's in New York. But my staff brought things to me in a private fitting area. They always cited security concerns about members of the Royal Family just walking around."

"Crackie!" I said, again in my Steve Irwin voice.

"Crocodile Hunter!" We entered the athletic shoe store, and he looked around in modest confusion. "Isn't someone supposed to get stuff for us?"

"Nah," I said, dragging him toward the cross-training shoes. "I could get someone, if you want. But just find shoes that fit, and we'll pay for them and be off to a clothing store. See here on the wall? Nikes. Adidas. Pumas. Take your pick."

I grabbed some size eleven air cushioned Nikes and a bag of athletic socks, a pair of which I passed to Benny. He fussed over shoes for another few minutes before selecting some white Adidas with red shoelaces. What a sense of style. Both of us wore our purchases to the cash register where a very amused Patrick O'Shea let them run his credit card.

"Uh oh," said our Marine escort.

"What is it, Gunny?" But I followed his eyes and didn't really need an answer. Outside the store, a dozen or so people looked at us through the glass behind the store cashiers. Two teenagers busied themselves on their cell phone screens to bystanders. I didn't need three guesses, since a trio of boys saw me looking at them and hoisted their skateboards while they cheered something with the word 'Russians' in it.

"Them," said Gunny Lund, who saw the crowd as a horrendous problem. My own take relied on an ancient rock concert factoid, where the promoters approached the most disruptive elements—Hell's Angels—and hired them to provide security.

I let the judge finish paying, and then said, "Everyone, follow me. And stay close." They did.

The skateboarders quickly quieted down as I headed straight for them. Maybe they didn't realize how much larger I stood compared to their own teen-lean/close-to-the-ground physiques. I slowed down and smiled, hoping to diffuse their sudden anxiety. It worked.

"Hey, guys," I said.

"Yo Rapier," said the tallest boy, freckle-faced red head clutching his skateboard in front of him like a shield. At least he got my last name right.

"Pleased to make your acquaintance?" I held out my hand, "And you're?"

"E-Evan, sir," he said and shook my hand. His voice cracked, so I put him to be about fourteen. His dark-haired, olive-skinned companion seemed to be looking past me, and I turned to see Benny smiling at him.

"This is my buddy, Benny," I said.

"Mohammed bin Faisal Al Saud?" said the boy behind Evan.

Benny stepped around and offered his hand. "Just call me Benny."

The kid broke out the biggest smile I'd seen since Benny popped up in my garage after twenty-five years. The kid fumbled with his skateboard *and* his cell phone, putting the phone in his pocket so he could shake hands. "Taariq is my name," said the boy and shook Benny's hand.

"Nightcomer," said Benny. "Cool name, Taariq. It means Nightcomer in Arabic."

"And this is Jamal," said the red head, whose jet-black haired friend had been poking him in the back.

I shook Jamal's hand and then addressed the three of them, trying to ignore the growing crowd around us long enough to pose my question.

"You guys interested in doing Benny and me a little favor?" I asked. Evan's eyes immediately clouded, as he got set for a brush off. I quickly continued, "Our clothes kind of got blown up today, and we're out re-outfitting. You interested in coming along with us and keeping the crowds back?"

"Really?" said Evan. No more clouds. Just three kids who seemed to instantly grow a foot taller.

"Call it security," I said. "This other guy is Marine Gunnery Sergeant Lund, and he'll be leading the way. If you three could watch our backs with Judge O'Shea while we pick up some clothes, I'd sure appreciate it."

Gunny and the judge both nodded at the boys, and O'Shea couldn't resist opening his jacket so the boys could see the pistol in his shoulder holster. Gunny saw the move and looked at me with raised eyebrows. I turned back to the boys.

"Radsolutely!" said the three nearly in unison. God bless the flexibility of the English language to evolve. I bet they'd text "RADLY" or just "Ry!" to each other. The growing crowd around us seemed interested in my conversation with the new security force, which took their new assignment as seriously as I'd hoped. They kept people well behind us as we found a department store that seemed to have the rest of the clothes we needed.

Someone behind us passed a video cell phone to a friend and chuckled about "…idiot newswoman…" so I knew that at least one of the networks hadn't tried to spare the network news anchor any embarrassment. I thought to myself, *Radelicious!*

By the time we'd secured thigh-length underwear for ourselves, Benny and I had also secured our own personal shoppers, too. An army of them, mostly teenagers, scurried all over the store looking for "the perfect" items for the mysteriously handsome celebrity and his Troglodyte bodyguard. Lest there be some confusion as to who might be who, I be the Troglodyte. And as one who lives by the YouTube might die by the YouTube, I'm certain the viral advertising bonanza reaped by Dillard's had every one of their U.S. stores completely out of Lucky jeans and silk Marvel superhero shirts, as well as white pleated slacks and flowered Hawaiian shirts. Two guesses who walked out the door wearing white slacks and the garland pattern.

The metaphor didn't escape Judge O'Shea either, who reminded me of our own childhood and said, "I see you're still Rocky Balboa, while Benny gets to be Han Solo."

To which I replied in my best imitation, "Yo, Adrian. To you it's Thanksgiving, but to me it's just Thursday."

"Look at the bright side." O'Shea slapped my shoulder as we walked toward his car, followed by our *Aloha Oy* army. "As they roll the final credits on this little movie adventure of yours, the screen will be filled with kids all over the world running around in white slacks, white Adidas with red shoelaces, and really garish Hawaiian shirts."

"What about jeans and superhero shirts?" I asked.

"Nah," he laughed. "But maybe U. S. Navy SEAL ball caps."

Two ringing phones interrupted our repartee: O'Shea's and Gunny Lund's. Benny and I slid into the Caddie's back seat while our two bodyguards took their respective calls from the front seat. Henry Davidson obviously bent the judge's ear. Lund, however, handed his crypto phone to me.

"Somebody named Potus for you, Commander Rapier," said Lund.

"Thanks, Gunny," I said. "And that would be capital P-O-T-U-S for President of the United States. Your commander in chief, I might add."

The surprised Marine dropped the phone, but I caught it.

"Rapier here," I said.

"One moment for the president," said the operator. I waited. But not for long.

"Commander Rapier?" said the familiar voice.

"Mister President," I answered.

"According to my people here, this *is* a secure line," said the president.

"Yes it is, sir."

"You sure know how to embarrass a reporter!" He half chuckled, half snorted. "Death Eater, you are a one man force of nature. Nice duds, by the way."

"I beg your pardon, Mister President?"

"The Morgan and Benny show is playing on every computer, cell phone, and big screen TV in the White House. Who are those guys on your shirt? The Hulk and Silver Surfer? Cell phone resolution leaves something to be desired. And by the way, thanks for that stealth Russian fighter."

"You're welcome, sir." I didn't want to accuse my commander in chief of being on speed, but he changed subjects faster than a drugged up imam after a Baghdad bomb blast. At any rate, I didn't feel the need to answer his questions about my shirt. He had more to think about than my superheroes.

"I'm glad you weren't in uniform today, or even now," continued the president. "The Posse Comitatus act kind of does apply in the long run, and I can't have active duty soldiers running around in the continental United States blowing stuff up. That reporter you so badly embarrassed has been very kind to my administration, even though her friendship with my secretary of state and her husband will eventually become problematic."

This was absolutely *not* how I imagined a conversation with the most powerful man in the world might progress. Or *should* progress. Did I have such a thoroughly incorrect view of the way a chain-of-command dialogue ought to take place? Then again, I couldn't see much downside for the president to treat me like his long lost buddy. Other than perhaps my getting myself killed by Russians and Chinese while protecting the good old U S of A. Speaking of which: "Mister President, I understand some Chinese almost got themselves involved, today."

"We're still sorting that out." Again, the president laughed. He must really have been under some pressure that my rescue of our economic system relieved. Okay. Now that I think about it, he had every right to be giddy. "I think the existence of the Russian stealth fighter startled them as badly as it did us. Let's say they have made some serious concessions to avoid being painted with the same brush as our Moscow friends, so please keep a lid on any knowledge of Chinese involvement. At this point it would be counter productive."

"About keeping a lid on things, Mister President," I cautiously opined. "Somebody in your administration tipped off either the Russians or the Chinese about my identity."

"Impossible!" he instantly replied.

"Sir, they hit my San Francisco apartment *before* they hit my server farm across the street. Yes, they could have tracked down the IP addresses of my attack, but it would *not* have led them to my apartment."

"I'll take that under advisement. The question, now, is how soon can you put your murder investigation to bed? I'd like you out of the public eye before your self-medication tactics do you in."

"You heard about that, huh?"

"Let's just say the Surgeon General nearly had a coronary. He said that if only one of the Russian tranquilizer darts had hit you, instead of the three, that your concoction would definitely have killed you. Just one more in the long line of people in my administration who would like to debrief you when this is all over."

"About the murder investigation, sir," I said, remembering his question. "If I'm not mistaken, Judge O'Shea is on the phone with local law enforcement as we speak. Right, Your Honor?" I said to the front seat.

"We're ten minutes away from the Salt Lake City sheriff's office," replied the judge over his shoulder. "They've been quite busy while you've been playing James Bond."

I relayed his message to the president and signed off on the call. Gunny Lund acted like I'd given him a solid gold bar when I passed the crypto phone back to him.

41
The Butcher's Bill

ell if it isn't Benny and Clyde," sang out Detective Davidson as my little troop sauntered into the Salt Lake City Sheriff's office.

Evidently the president's personal involvement and concern for a rapid solution to Olive Jenkins's murder got everyone playing to an audience in their own version of the movie. Even FBI profiler Lisa Willis walked backwards in front of us, strewing invisible rose petals at our feet from an imaginary urn.

FBI senior investigator Ed McCartney endeared himself to me for life by correcting the metaphor: "No self-respecting FBI man could possibly throw rose petals at the feet of Bonnie and Clyde. I'm personally thinking of such nattily attired heroes as the personification of *Miami Vice's* Crockett and Tubbs."

"Okay, okay," said Willis. "I'm definitely seeing John McClain in *Die Hard With a Vengeance*. Remember how he brings down the helicopter with his car?"

"Yeah, but where's Benny in this?" said Davidson.

McCartney didn't miss a beat. Brown said, "He's that hacker sidekick. You know. The actor in the Macintosh commercials. After all, Benny pretty well figured out who killed Olive and why."

"Well, what about us two yokels?" said O'Shea. Not used to being left out, especially from his exalted position of godhood in the courtroom, the judge gestured toward our Marine escort Lund. The FBI trio seemed to notice our two visitors for the first time.

"Let me make some introductions," I said. "Judge Patrick O'Shea, these three folks are from the FBI's behavioral analysis unit. And his walking mountain of a companion is Marine Gunnery Sergeant Lund, whose commanding officer was personally ordered by the president to make sure nothing happens to me or Benny."

"What in the world is *that?*" gasped Lisa Willis. Judge O'Shea had leaned forward to shake hands, and his coat gapped open to reveal his not-insignificant holstered sidearm.

"And sticking with the metaphors," I said, carefully leaning in front of Lund to lift O'Shea's enormous pistol out of its holster, complete with telescopic sight. "This would be Judge *Roy Bean* O'Shea, accompanied by his chief deputy and enforcer."

The gun drew some "Oohs" before Patrick snatched it and put it back where it belonged. In my peripheral vision, I saw Gunny Lund slowly slide his hand away from his own semi-automatic sidearm, possibly wondering how it would measure up in accuracy and stopping power to the judge's, although he may have been wondering whether or not to draw his own weapon, should the judge do anything *but* reholster the telescope-sighted elephant pistol.

"One missing introduction," I said. "Where's our computer guru, Xavier?"

"The director wanted him up at ground zero to secure your computers," said Willis. "He hitched a ride on a news chopper."

My heart threatened to stop, until I realized that our justice infrastructure pretty well knew of my involvement in the cyber fracas. Yeah, it might help to have a babysitter at my place.

"Henry," said Willis in as extra-business-like tone as possible. Too business like, actually. As if to confirm a fleeting impression that something more than business had been going on between them, Henry looked extraordinarily intently at the contents of a manila folder. "Please bring everyone up to speed in the everything that's happened while *Benny and Joon* played kiss-my-what? with the Russians."

Henry almost looked like he *could* get down to business, too. But Benny surprised me once again in his long list of surprises by bursting into the *I'm Gonna Be* lyrics from the movie *Benny and Joon*. He actually did a pretty good job of mimicking The Proclaimers' soundtrack as he danced around Lisa Willis: "When I wake up, well I know I'm gonna be, I'm gonna be the man who wakes up next to you."

If I had any doubts at all that Henry had more than professional interest in the FBI agent, Benny's antics toward Willis eliminated them completely. Henry Davidson's mouth dropped ever so slightly open and the hair on the back of his neck stood straight up. Especially when Benny got to the line "...I'm gonna be the man who's growing old with you. But I would walk five-hundred miles, and I would walk five-hundred more, just to be the man who walks a thousand miles to fall down at your door." Who would have thought that Benny had such a taste for theatrics? He acted the walking in time with the melody, first away from Willis and then back toward her, falling to his knees with the last five words. He looked up at her, spread his arms, and smiled: "Not *Benny and Joon.* Make that Benny and Lisa."

Henry Davidson tried to act nonchalant and start reading from the file, but the cheers and applause drowned his words out. Mine, the judge's, the other detectives, the FBI man, even Lisa Willis. Our Marine didn't clap, not yet into the bonhomie of the situation. Henry just sat there with rapidly blushing cheeks. So far, nobody else had noticed, so I motioned to Gunny Lund to help me lift Benny back to his feet. We plopped Benny into the nearest chair.

"Henry!" I said, spreading my hands in a pleading gesture. "*Please* tell us you've arrested Olive Jenkins's killer."

Henry Davidson must have sincerely appreciated my giving him a minute to collect his emotions, and not to miss being part of the party said: "Morgan, if that reporter from this afternoon prevails with her body count outrage, your next job will be as bouncer in a Tijuana bordello."

"Whoa, Henry," I said. As badly as I wanted to get to the Olive Jenkins business, I just couldn't allow everyone in the room to keep the impression of some enormous body count. "I think you've got my *butcher's bill* mixed up with someone else's."

"Butcher's bill?" asked Lisa Willis. "I'm not familiar with the term."

"Gunny," I said to my Marine bodyguard. "Please tell our FBI profiler about *butcher's bills.*"

"Ma'am," he said, hesitating and obviously uncomfortable with any attention directed toward him. "*Butcher's bill* refers to military body count. A fellow named David Drake used it a the title for one of his military science fiction books."

"*Hammer's Slammers!*" said Benny. "Great stuff."

"Back to my point," I jumped in. "We shouldn't let the media make any gross assumptions about my own butcher's bill. Either defending Benny on Monday or squaring off with the Russians today."

"Ah, *butcher's bill.*" The FBI profiler seemed to be using her tongue to massage the inside of her cheek. She finally continued: "Morgan. We, uh, got a call from the president just after you dropped that fighter on top of the Russian special ops team. Nobody could reach you, and he ended up sharing the details of a little one-man swath of death and destruction you unleashed as you exited Iraq during Operation Desert Freedom. I'd have to agree with Henry's projection of your career path."

"I can't *believe* the president shared the details of a classified operation," I began. Then I realized I'd just confirmed the story. Damn!

"I don't know how many soldiers are in a battalion," she said. "But the president said you single-handedly took out an entire Republican Guard battalion, head on."

"The next time I talk with the President, I'll tell him not to believe everything he hears from military intelligence." That was the best I could do to backpedal and tread water without telling an outright lie. Unfortunately, my best didn't nearly throw these dogs off my scent. The FBI investigator set the hook.

"According to the president," said McCartney, "An unmanned drone captured the whole engagement with its night-vision camera. Is it true that toward the end, you actually chased the battalion?"

Okay. Enough of this! I thought. "People," I said, forced into my thousand-yard stare by the memory of that night. "Those, and I use the term loosely, *soldiers* had just ambushed a Marine supply convoy. They gang raped and then murdered a twenty-three year old supply officer. I got pissed when I came upon her horribly violated body. In fact, I get pissed off just thinking about it, so can we get down to business and talk about Olive Jenkins?"

Patrick O'Shea leaned forward as he pulled a chair next to mine and whispered, "You sure know how to wipe the smile off everyone's face."

Quite an indictment, coming from an expert in his own right. I expect all the drugs—between the Russian tranquilizers and my big-game-animal antidote concoction—had affected my emotional equilibrium. To be called out on my interpersonal skills by the judge, however, seemed rather like Attila the Hun complaining that somebody had hurt his horse's feelings. Me, I'm a friend to all and an enemy to none, unless of course that someone attacks me. Well, or they attack my computers. Or I find they've raped and murdered a twenty-three year old truck driver. Okay. Come to think of it, I'm a friend to *most* and an enemy to a rapidly growing population of end-justifies-the-means monsters. *And* their minions. No? Maybe then, I'm a friend to the meek, humble victims of the world. Some of whom get more than an occasional smile wiped off their faces.

"Guilty, Your Honor." I vocalized my last thought. Then, to diffuse my boorishness: "Everybody, I'd really truly love to wipe the smile off Olive Jenkins's murderer's face. Hopefully, he'll put up a fight."

That drew murmurs of approval. Henry cleared his throat and jumped into a status report.

"Thanks to his honor," began Henry, "Search warrants were served for Brigham Wood The Third's home, his office, a second home in Cedar City, and one safe deposit box we found at Zion's Bank."

Henry paused. Lisa Willis looked as if she'd eaten the proverbial canary, barely suppressing a smile. Everybody else seemed to be looking for a reaction from me. I didn't disappoint them.

"*And?*" I finally said.

"Jackpot," said Henry, accompanied by exhaled air from the other detectives and the three FBI agents. "Forget safety deposit boxes or a secret cache buried ten steps from the old Maple tree in his back yard. The original George Wood document sat in a wall safe behind the old murderer's picture in Brigham's office. And, as you suggested, Morgan, a sealed document, possibly the same one you downloaded from her online backup site, mysteriously disappeared from the office of Olive's probate attorney."

"Mysteriously disappeared?" I asked.

"Someone broke into his office and made a half-hearted attempt to simulate a burglary. But one file seemed to be carefully removed and then replaced, minus one envelope," said Henry.

"I don't get it," I said. "How could they be so sure just one envelope had been removed?"

"Because," said Henry with growing excitement, "Olive had made a big deal that if anything happened to her, the attorney was to distribute the contents of that envelope to the media. He remembered that she'd written instructions on the sealed envelope that a backup of its contents could be found on her computer, as well. And get this! The burglary occurred the day before Olive's murder."

"Bingo," I said.

"What's a *bingo*?" asked Benny. "It's the second time someone has used that word.

Not wanting to derail the meeting with an etymology discussion, I said: "It's kind of like yelling *Eureka!* Or *Voila!*" Then to Henry and the rest, "Do we know Brigham Wood's whereabouts on those two dates?"

"Well, that's a problem," said Henry. "Not only does he have an air-tight alibi for that two-day period, but before and during the funeral as well."

"Probably lawyered up and hasn't been the picture of cooperation, either," I opined.

"Madder than a wet hen and threatening to sue everyone in sight if his personal private papers see the light of day," said FBI investigator McCartney.

"Pure bluster," said the judge. "From what I know about the local culture, even prominent families who have ancestors involved in the Mountain Meadows Massacre would urge full disclosure. His lawsuit would get thrown out of court so fast the sonic boom would level Brigham Wood's home."

"Back to the chase, then," I said. "Who is he protecting? Because *somebody* had inside information on Olive's possession of the document, not to mention Henry's and my sniffing around her backup computer files. They've been two steps ahead of us the whole time."

Profiler Willis used this as a cue to walk across the room and flip the contents of her white board into view. She'd created a detailed time line: "Friday, Olive Jenkins receives the George Wood *Mountain Meadows Massacre* document. Ten days later, she is murdered. So some tripwire during that period alerted her murderer. Death Eater—that's you, Morgan—comes into the picture on Wednesday with Judge O'Shea's call to you in San Francisco…."

"I am going to strangle the president for coming up with that name…." I began.

"Threatening the President of the United States is a federal crime," interrupted the judge.

"Okay, okay. I'm just going to make him suffer," I said.

"Still a criminal threat in my book," said the judge.

"Politically!" I said. "I'm going to make him suffer *politically*. Please continue, Agent Willis." Which she did.

"Saturday, you attend the funeral, which the serial murderer must also have attended in a Hertz car carrying the bodies of Francois and Kathy Lambert. Saturday night, you're nearly killed in the Salt Lake County Sheriff's Office explosion. Sergeant Joe Peck *is* killed. So far, including Olive Jenkins, the killer's body count is four."

Henry jumped in. "We have two questions, then. First, what tipped the killer that Olive had the files? And second, what tipped the killer that Morgan had recovered her backup computer data?" A hand went up and Henry nodded to one of his two detectives. "Yes, Watson?"

"Carr and I have been looking at all of Olive Jenkins' outgoing telephone calls over her last ten days of life. She made several calls to the former ambassador's office, two of which lasted several minutes."

"The ambassador! The funeral!" I said. "Remember the guy who looks like an orangutan? That red-headed chief of staff for the ambassador?"

"We call him Monkey Boy," said the judge. "Heber W. King."

"King, that's his name!" I said. "During the funeral, he made a point of coming over and asking about the status of the investigation. And Senator Hyde told King that we'd located the backup!"

"So you think Heber King may have told the killer about the backup?" asked Detective Carr.

"Better than that," said Benny, who had quietly been plunking away at one of the computers at an empty desk. "Heber W. King may be our killer."

"Why would Heber give a rip about George Wood and the Mountain Meadows Massacre?" said Henry Davidson.

"Google kind of proves he does," Benny answered quickly.

"Google?" said Davidson and Willis in unison.

"Come on, detectives. Detect!" said Benny. "The 'W' in 'Heber W. King' stands for Wood. Heber is Brigham Wood's nephew on his mother's side. Heber *Wood* King. Wouldn't put it past him to protect Uncle Brigham."

"Damn," said O'Shea. "Sherry is delivering the search warrant documentation to the family via Heber King."

42
Blowing a Conviction

herry O'Shea didn't answer her cell phone. Three times, the judge's call went right to his wife's voicemail account. The judge's increasing frustration infected all of us, and only a quick reflex on my part stopped him from dialing Heber King's cell number.

"Morgan, what are you doing?" I'd never before heard quite the edge of panic I sensed in Pat O'Shea's voice. "Sherry could be with him right now."

"I know, Patrick. And we don't want him to know that we're looking for him. Because if he is the bad guy, and if he thinks we're onto him, then he'll take the battery out of his cell phone."

"I swear by all that's holy…" said the judge, reaching inside his jacket and fingering the pistol grip beneath his left shoulder.

"Time for some magic, Your Honor," I said. Then to the two FBI people, "I need a fast Internet computer connection and two cell phones, at least one of which has a Web browser on it. And a pen and some paper, preferably a small notebook."

Moments later I had what I needed. Willis had pilfered a blank investigation notebook from a nearby desk, spiral bound on the top and perfect to fit in a shirt pocket. I told Gunny to keep his crypto phone available in case we needed to ratchet a request up the command chain, and I politely declined Detective Carr's LG cell phone. He didn't ask for a reason, so I didn't have to explain I still carried a grudge over how my late wife's LG phone had seriously inconvenienced her. Profiler Willis offered her precious Android, and true to form, FBI investigator McCartney parted with his equally precious Android Platinum.

"Here we go," I said. "Patrick, give me both Sherry's and Monkey Boy's cell numbers." After he wrote those on my new notebook, I entered the numbers of the phones, along with their serial, IMEI and ICCID numbers. I also subtly motioned for Benny to join me. He instantly realized I wanted him to stand behind me, blocking my computer screen, so nobody could see me hot mike

Sherry's phone. Providentially, the person who most worried me, FBI guru Xavier Brown, couldn't observe or appreciate my tour de force hacking job. I entered my special DNS number in the command window, followed by my username and time-of-day-modified password and voila!

The computer came equipped with speakers, so everyone heard the same sound: the Doppler effect of cars passing nearby separated with silence. I superimposed Google Maps on top of a stationary red dot, blinking on the computer screen.

"What is this?" asked the judge, his voice about an octave higher than normal.

"Benny?" I replied, nodding behind me toward the sound of his ah-ha.

"Your wife's phone is sitting on the side of a road, a fairly busy one. Probably tossed out a car window. We can hear the cars."

The next thing I knew, Hizonor's six-inch Colt Python barrel became his pointer as he tapped the screen. "Where is her cell phone? Precisely."

"Up Big Cottonwood Canyon, about half way to the Brighton Ski Resort," said detective Watson.

Of course, the big question had to do with the hot miking of the phone. "Did you just do what it looks like you just did?" asked the FBI investigator. "That's more than GPS location. You just hot miked that phone!"

"I didn't know anybody could actually do that," said agent Willis.

"Urban legend," smirked Benny. "Nobody can do that."

Benny said it so seriously and without a trace of sarcasm that it took seconds before either the detectives or the FBI team recognized the put on.

"Morgan Rapier, you are one dangerous son of a bitch," said Lisa Willis. "You can just turn on and listen to any cell phone, without the owner knowing about it?"

"Not really," I said.

"But…" she began.

"Let me finish," I interrupted. "Yes, I can turn on and listen alright, but the phone *will* get warm and the battery will drain from the continuous transmission. So the owner will figure it out sooner or later."

Naturally, the judge didn't give a rip whether I'd hot miked a phone or gotten a direct revelation from the Lord God Almighty. The judge growled,

"Where the hell is monkey boy?"

"Gunny," I said as I saved the location of Sherry O'Shea's cell phone and entered the number of Heber King's mobile unit. "If Judge O'Shea tries to leave this room, please shoot him in the leg. And try not to hit a bone or an artery. Just the fatty part of the leg."

The judge gave me the same incredulous look as Wile E. Coyote does when he's chased the Roadrunner off the edge of a cliff and suddenly realizes he's standing on nothing but thin air.

"Patrick, listen carefully." I patted his gun hand. "Heber King could be involved. But he could *not* have murdered the Lamberts and stuffed them into the trunk of a rental car, because he attended the funeral with the former ambassador. That's the piece of the puzzle that mitigates against issuing a dead-or-alive order on him. So please, Patrick, let the pros track him down. Let the pros rescue Sherry, if she needs rescuing."

"Where's monkey boy?" growled the judge, clearly not used to his questions being ignored.

Another dot appeared on my screen. About two miles up Big Cottonwood Canyon from Sherry O'Shea's cell phone. Where the GPS had located her phone on an unpopulated stretch of road, this dot appeared smack dab in the middle of a residence. A big residence. With an address. And one look at the Google Earth image immediately galvanized Hizonor, who darted toward the hallway.

"Remember, Gunny. Shoot him in the fleshy part of his leg," I said.

The judge didn't make it very far, as my big Marine stood directly in his way. Gunny Lund didn't have to draw his gun or even restrain the judge, because Sherry O'Shea's voice came loud and clear from the speakers on my computer. We all turned toward the sound and listened to the unfolding drama.

"…husband will wonder where I am," said Sherry O'Shea.

"I said be quiet!" Heber King's unmistakable voice sounded louder, closer.

"You can't hold me here indefinitely," she replied.

"If you don't let me think for a minute, I'll just strangle you and cut off your little fingers just like I did Olive Jenkins'!"

The judge seemed about to jump out of his skin, but I shushed him and pointed to the blinking "Rec" light on my screen. That didn't calm him down.

"There goes a conviction," said O'Shea. "Right out the window."

"But he's confessing to the whole thing," said Benny, ever the straight man.

"Damn!" shouted the judge, pulling at his hair as he turned in a slow circle.

I cleared up privacy law and due process for my naive friend. "Benny, this is an illegal wire tap. Which means any data obtained from the wiretap is inadmissible as evidence in court, as is any subsequent data we obtain. So even if we go out there and rescue Sherry from Heber King, he can't be tried for her kidnapping, either. Fruit of the poisoned tree. That about cover it, Your Honor?"

As the legal implications slowly sunk in, the FBI team looked just as perplexed as the judge. Henry Davidson stated the obvious: "We know where Sherry O'Shea is and who she's with. Legality aside, don't we have a moral obligation to save her life?"

"I sure as hell do," said the judge, once more lunging for the hallway. Having anticipated the move, I grabbed his left wrist. Surprisingly strong for such a wiry little man, he almost broke my grip.

"Patrick," I said, rising to face him. "I will handle this. If we'd hot miked Sherry's cell phone, we could legitimately have gotten your permission to listen to the device. In my enthusiasm to track her down, I just killed any chance of convicting this guy of either murder or kidnapping. So I don't think any of you law enforcement people can be in on her rescue. When the kite goes up, you don't want the potential liabilities to yourselves or to your organizations. As it is, I'm going to have some particularly hard questions to answer when this is all over. The rest of you need to stay out of this as well. To accompany me is a career-ending decision."

"Except for me," said Gunny Lund.

"Except for you Sergeant Lund," I agreed. "*Not* accompanying me would be a career ending decision for you. I hope to hell you're MOUT certified."

"MOUT—Military Operations in Urban Terrain, Sir," smiled the Marine. "That's an old term. We now call it UO, for Urban Operations. No Marine sees action in Iraq unless they've been to Twenty-nine Palms. The Brits call it FISH, for Fighting In Someone's House. Or FISH and CHIPS, for Fighting In Someone's House and Causing Havoc In People's Streets."

"Okay, okay. Let's go FISHing," I said. I split the desktop computer's GPS screen and took a few seconds to add the FBI investigator's Android phone to the tracking GPS. No hot mike, though. Some stuff they just didn't want to know. I then linked the browser on Agent Willis's phone to the GPS locator for Heber's phone. That way, Gunny and I would know it if he hit the road. "Now, I need a ride and a gun."

Agent Willis underhanded me keys to her rental vehicle. "Black Suburban in the basement."

"Black Suburban. Naturally." Then to Henry, I said: "Might I borrow your nine millimeter?"

Luckily, he did *not* underhand it to me, choosing instead to pass it along with his shoulder holster. While I put it on and adjusted the straps, he slid two extra clips into an FBI windbreaker hanging on one of the chairs and handed it to me. Good idea to cover up the weapon, although the FBI lettering on the back of the jacket made it tough for me to pretend to be a neighbor borrowing a cup of sugar. Then again, if Heber the self-confessed kidnapper saw my back, he'd probably put a bullet in it. Which would serve me right for letting Monkey Boy get behind me.

"No offense, but what's the plan?" asked Henry Davidson.

"Simple, really. When you see my red dot enter Big Cottonwood Canyon, seal that baby off."

"*That's* the plan!" Clearly, Henry expected much more of me. Too bad I didn't have the faintest idea what other planning elements would come into play.

"Pretty much. This is a *reconnaissance in force*," I said. "While you're waiting to close the canyon, you *could* introduce Benny here to the Salt Lake Police Department's idea of coffee."

43

One Down, One To Go

I drove the big Suburban while my Marine escort kept his eye on the Android browser. The phone used by the folks back at the SLPD to track us sat safely in my windbreaker pocket. Heber King hadn't moved, nor had any hot-mike conversations prompted a call from the people I'd stranded at the police station. No accident on my part either, stranding them and going it alone. Panic-stricken husbands of kidnapped wives should never be given parts in the Urban Warfare Theater. I am a professional, so do *not* attempt this in your neighborhood.

Given a choice, I'd have dropped by my Snowbird condo and picked up some special equipment from the trunk of my car. Along with my own significantly modified Android. But any wasted time could mean the difference between life and death for my dear friend. So no flash bangs. No thermal imaging device. But maybe, just maybe, the element of surprise.

Five o'clock PM traffic coming up the canyon as people headed for home gave us plenty of background noise to cover our approach to the house. Google Maps gave us a pretty good view of the home and adjacent parking area. The late-afternoon sun came against our backs and put anyone looking for our approach at a serious disadvantage.

The Android phone rang, and I wished I'd paired it with the Suburban's Bluetooth. Because we almost got clipped by a brown UPS delivery truck coming down the mountain as it tried to avoid a bicyclist. Slow bicyclist, in my opinion, to get passed by a UPS truck. I usually passed cars in my own descents of both Little Cottonwood and Big Cottonwood Canyons. I finally managed to hit the receive key on the phone.

"Morgan here."

"While you've been in cell tower hell, it's hit the fan," said Henry Davidson. "We heard some popping sounds, like shots, then screaming. The judge's wife is screaming bloody murder. You are two-hundred feet from the driveway; get your asses in there, now!"

Davidson shouted loud enough that Sgt. Lund could hear his voice even without me putting the call on speakerphone. We'd just passed a large boulder towering over the right lane of Big Cottonwood Canyon and hit the gravel driveway in a barely controlled side skid. I kept the power on all four wheels and only just gained control as we flew across a wooden bridge and into a gravel courtyard, where we skidded to a stop in front of a flagpole. Gunny had his sidearm out and chambered a round before we'd come to a complete stop, and we both jumped out our respective doors. It didn't take any great insight to determine where we should go. We just followed the sound of a screaming woman.

"You take the door, Gunny. I'll take the window," I yelled as we sprinted across the immaculate lawn toward the single-story ranch-style house. "Let's not shoot each other."

No time to do this by the MOUT/UO/FISH book. Besides, we didn't have flash bangs, automatic weapons, or body armor. Just a screaming woman. Which meant one of us would almost certainly run into a waiting trap. Both of us, if more than one bad guy still happened to be hanging around. The only possible bright side might be that Sherry O'Shea's screams had covered the sound of our entrance. Not much of a bright side, unless our kidnapper assumed we'd approach with more caution. Then, a hasty entrance could work to our advantage. After all, who'd do a frontal assault on unknown terrain against an unknown enemy? Moi, actually. Right out of my Iraq playbook. Nobody expected a lone lunatic to rush an armored brigade, even if said lunatic wore full body armor and carried automatic weapons. Which I didn't. I had one 9mm semi-automatic pistol and whatever protection my superhero shirt offered. Maybe the kidnapper would die laughing. Or maybe I'd tear my guts out on a shard of glass as I hurled myself through the plate glass window toward which I now raced at full speed. Too late now to give Gunny the window and me the door. Oh well.

I'm sure I couldn't have been airborne for more than a second. I heard Gunny Lund hit the front door with house-shattering force. Obviously, he didn't bother to either knock or even try the doorknob. He just took out the door and probably the frame with it. As the window sailed toward me, time seemed to slow down so I could almost count the white exterior slats on the side of the house. Even though the house had to be over thirty years old, some brilliant humanitarian had made a good investment in safety glass, because the window literally exploded as I sailed through it. For a split second, I knew how NBA Sixers' pro basketball player Darryl Dawkins felt both times in 1979—once in November and again in December—when he shattered the basketball backboard during a slam dunk and created *Darryl's Diamonds*, thousands of pieces of shattered safety glass that came cascading down on his head. At least I needn't have worried about a large slice of glass coming down and chopping off my head. Instead, all these little polygons of glass rained into the room like hail from hell. I hit the hardwood floor in a roll and immediately registered an increase in the decibel level of the screaming. An increase caused as I landed behind the couch and in front of an iPod-alarm-clock-speaker combination pumping an earsplitting woman's scream. I immediately punched the power button on the speakers, and a welcome silence engulfed the room. I then turned my attention to the rest of the room where, owing to my cat-like reflexes, proceeded to pump three rounds into a strangely stationary Heber King. At the same moment, Gunny Lund did the same thing. Three rounds. Six total. Three in the front from me, and three in the back from Gunny. Six unnecessary rounds, it turned out, as Heber had likely been smoking in the infernal regions long before we arrived.

Someone had used a pneumatic nail gun to crucify him between two wooden beams in the ceiling. That must have been the popping sound they'd reported from the hot-miked phone. He was probably long past offering an opinion at that point, since several nails protruded from various angles through his scalp, eyeballs and nose. Talk about a piercing job gone bad! Heber would no doubt have been the hit of any rap party, had he been able to walk in under his own power. Alas, several nail heads made sure each hand stayed put, supporting his full weight so each of Heber's shoes hung at least three feet off the ground.

"Anybody else in the house?" I called

"Clear out here," replied Gunny from the foyer.

Gunny and I turned, both of us with our backs to the body. He surveyed the room and hallway behind him, and I did the same thing toward the bedroom wing and kitchen area to my left.

Lund backed into the room and around the late great Heber Wood King.

As I prodded recently cut ropes at the base of a load-bearing pillar and looked up, two other objects caught my eye: Heber's little fingers. No longer connected to Heber, each had been nailed into the support beams an inch or two from each hand. You might say, *just out of reach.* Then again, maybe you wouldn't. Maybe, like me, you'd be thinking *Now wait a damn minute! If Heber killed Olive and nailed her little digits to the ceiling, then who the hell…?*

"If you guys can still hear me over the hot mike link, Sherry O'Shea is *not* here. I repeat, she's *not* here. The screaming was pre-recorded and amplified with an alarm clock activated system. Someone, or someones, unknown killed Heber King with several nails driven into his skull, and then nailed his hands to crossbeams. Both little fingers were amputated and nailed to the crossbeams. If you copy me, please call me on the Android."

Within seconds, my phone vibrated, and I retrieved it from the vest of my FBI jacket.

"Heber's dead?" said Davidson.

"Deader than hell, Henry," I said.

"And his little fingers got amputated? And nailed to the beams?"

"Both of 'em." I thumbed the speaker icon so Sgt. Lund could hear the conversation.

"But he's our killer. We heard him confess to Sherry. Who killed *him*? And where's the judge's wife?"

"I've got you on speaker phone, now." I held it so Gunny could hear, too. "Whoever killed Heber has Sherry. And it can't have been too long ago, given the confession we all heard from the late King. We'll check the rest of the house. You guys had better get a forensics team up here right away."

"Keep the phone on speaker as you check the house. The canyon has been closed and we're on our way. And Judge O'Shea insists on coming, too."

Of course he'd be coming along. Maybe not a terrific idea, since the person who'd made such an example out of Heber King had probably killed a couple at the airport just so he could borrow their car and come to Olive's funeral and who wouldn't give a second thought to killing Sherry O'Shea. If he hadn't killed her already.

For the next few minutes, Gunny and I swept the entire main floor of the house, and then the basement, narrating our observations at every turn. Not a soul in around, at least none that we could see. Heber's soul could have been hanging around, wondering if there was any way he could hop back into and reanimate his worthless stiffening carcass. Because a trial and prison time *had* to beat the wailing welcome wagon that had come to pick him up for the journey to hell. I clicked off the cell phone connection as sirens and tires on gravel announced Davidson's arrival. Lund and I met the detective, the judge, a still-tagging-along Benny, and two FBI people at the crashed-in front door. The medical examiner's meat wagon pulled in behind them. And behind the meat wagon a crime-scene team.

Detective Davidson and FBI SSA Willis stepped past through the shattered front door and by me as I stood on the front porch and waited for the judge. Benny followed close behind, seeming to sense the raw emotions emanating from O'Shea. Patrick O'Shea stopped beside me and almost whispered, "Morgan?"

"Patrick, she's not here."

"Any sign of…?" He couldn't find the words to complete his question.

"No. No blood or sign of a struggle," I said. "It appears that whoever killed Heber found Sherry tied to a pillar inside the house. He cut her loose and took her with him."

"Then there's a chance…?" Again, he couldn't finish the question.

I hated what I had to do next. In my opinion, well-meaning people spread false hope and optimism in exactly the wrong situations. Sure, my dear friend could use some emotional morphine, but he verged on the ragged edge of complete meltdown. We simply could *not* let him hang around. Worrying about his emotional state would detract from a serious focus on finding Sherry's captor, Heber's murderer. While Judge Roy Bean O'Shea might be the lion king in court, he lacked the operational professionalism required for hunter-killer fieldwork. I had to take him out of the equation if any of us hoped to find Sherry and wrestle her from the hands of a considerably smarter and more ruthless murderer than Heber King could possibly have imagined. The judge, my old friend, wanted me to tell him Sherry might still be alive. I net-netted it differently.

"Not a very good chance she's still alive at all," I said. "This guy killed Francois and Kathy Lambert at the airport just so he could use their car to attend Olive's funeral."

Benny gave me the same look I'd imagine he would level on someone he found choking small children in an alley. He also demonstrated a situational analytic perspective that I hadn't considered. Before the judge could drop to his knees in grief, Benny grabbed him in a bear hug and held him up, speaking softly, a softness by the way that his eyes did *not* direct at me: "I disagree with Morgan's assessment. If the killer had simply wanted to eliminate a witness to his identity, he'd have killed your wife exactly where he found her. He had a reason for taking her with him, which means he has a reason for keeping her alive."

Then Benny set his jaw and glared at me. I had no choice but to nod back at him in agreement with his assessment. And as the judge comprehended the argument, his knees turned from rubber to iron. Benny released his grip with one hand, but still used the other to brace himself against Hizonor. He didn't realize it, but he'd just made a lifelong friend of Patrick O'Shea.

"Pat, you shouldn't be here. In fact, you can't be here. It could end your career." I stood silently, waiting for his reaction.

Finally, with steel back in his eyes, he said, "Nuts to the career. I want to help find Sherry."

Benny's raised eyebrows and shrug gave me the idea I needed.

"I'm going to need Benny on a computer, while I'm in the field. And not just any virgin-vanilla hunk of silicon, either. I need Benny in my house at Snowbird on my considerably un-vanilla systems. And *he needs* someone who knows the area. We may not have very much time to find Sherry." I paused to make sure both Benny and the judge knew exactly what I wanted. O'Shea looked at Benny for any sign that my request hadn't been designed to get them on the sidelines. Thankfully, Benny had seen my systems and knew full well I hadn't come up with a make-work assignment to keep them occupied and out of the way. If Benny had any reservations, the judge's "smoke detector" would pick up on it.

"He's got a point," said Benny. "And not only do I need some local knowledge, but it wouldn't hurt to have you and your elephant gun watching my back at Morgan's place, in case he has any more foreign visitors."

Thankfully, Benny had no guile, and the judge took my request at face value. Another presence on the porch caused me to turn. Henry Davidson stood there, hefting a small package.

"We know how he got in," said Henry. "There's a pile of UPS packages in the front hallway, none of which should have been delivered to this address. The killer got Heber to open the front door for the packages, and instead of the usual electronic clipboard for the recipient's signature, the fake UPS delivery guy had a nail gun in his other hand. The blood splatter on the slate tiles indicates Heber didn't know what hit him."

"The UPS truck!" said an excited Gunny. "We just about crashed into him coming down the canyon, as he swerved to miss that bicyclist."

"He had *Sherry* in that truck!" I said. Then to Henry, "We saw the guy coming down the switchbacks just before we got here."

Henry didn't have to be told what to do next. Within sixty seconds, every local, county and state law enforcement officer within twenty miles would be stopping UPS trucks and then calling for backup before going anywhere near it. Driver should be assumed dangerous, armed, and with a hostage.

44
Peter Drucker 101

hapter forty-four. As in .44 magnum. With both hollow-head and armor piercing rounds. Actually, amateur hour in a world full of WMDs, IEDs, and fully automatic weapons that can spit out depleted uranium slugs at three thousand rounds per minute. Never had I been more motivated to bring down a bad guy. And never before had I been so guilty of underestimating my enemy. As a result, the very reason for my trip, the very person for whom I'd been doing *a favor* now had her life on the line.

Davidson, the FBI team, my bodyguard Gunny Lund and I sat in the bullpen allotted to us by the magnanimous Salt Lake City Police Department, who also had a phalanx of uniformed officers keeping the press at bay outside the building. News of Heber King's demise and his likely involvement in the murder of Olive Jenkins had even the national news anchors in a feeding frenzy, especially with my involvement. Well hell, I *told* that morning news anchor who asked about body count that the day was young.

The mushroom-shaped speakerphone occupied the center of our conference table, surrounded by stacks of Chinese takeout. From my somewhat-the-worse-for-wear home in Snowbird, Benny and the judge shared pizza they'd picked up on their way up the canyon, courtesy of a ride from one of the policemen who'd showed up on the scene of Heber King's crucifixion. The digital clock over the water cooler read 9:00 PM on the nose. And we'd taken it on the nose all week. First, because we'd been feeding Heber Wood King every step in our progress tracking down Olive Jenkins' murderer. And second, because a much smarter serial killer had somehow stayed one step ahead of us as we closed in on King.

"Mel Brooks got it wrong," said Henry Davidson, who'd just gotten off the phone with his daughter, Harley you-bet-your-ass Davidson, after checking up on her and letting her know not to expect him home any time soon.

"And that would be?" said SSA Willis, taking the bait.

"It's not good to be King," he replied without so much as a grin.

She groaned. At that moment, the uniformed policeman I'd asked to drive Benny and O'Shea to Snowbird entered the room with shopping bag. "Mister Rapier, your friends said you wanted this?"

"Thank you, officer," I said, taking the bag. I'd asked Benny to find my encrypted satellite phone as well as my Android and send it back down the mountain. Thankfully, he'd included the battery chargers, and I immediately found power outlets and got both sets juicing up for what could be a critical duty cycle. The officer departed, and then, toward the speakerphone, I asked, "How's the place look, Benny?"

"Not bad, considering," he answered. "Very impressive home-owner services up here. They replaced all the broken glass, cut out the bloodstained carpet until the identical new stuff can be ordered in. The Saudi Royal Family couldn't get this kind of turnaround."

"Speaking about blood staining *someone's* carpet," said the judge in clipped, emphatic words, "Any good news on tracking down the guy who kidnapped Sherry?"

Henry Davidson turned from the whiteboard where we'd been summarizing the case. He spoke loudly enough to be heard by those on the other end of the speakerphone connection: "Your Honor, this is Henry. We've just been updating the timeline with all the new data. The most promising news is that we recovered the UPS truck the killer used to kidnap your wife. The driver had been tied up and gagged in the rear."

"And that's promising because he didn't kill the driver, like he did the Lamberts," said O'Shea. "Right?"

"Exactly, Your Honor," said Davidson. "Here's what else we know. First, it appears that Heber is a copycat killer. He figured to cover his true motive by making it appear Olive was the victim of a longtime serial killer. Thanks to Benny and Morgan, we pretty well know his motive. Not only covering up his family involvement in the Mountain Meadows Massacre and the murder of Olive's namesake ancestor Olive Olivia Coombs, but a subsequent pattern of murders by Heber's uncle Brigham Wood III, and his great-grandmother's extortion to get a pardon for George Wood. Suffice it to say, the local authorities are going to have a heyday with the papers given to Olive Jenkins by Brigham the Third's late ex-wife Bathsheba Hill Wood.

"Benny, what's Xavier doing up there? He's been strangely silent," I asked.

"We haven't seen him," said Benny. "Isn't he back down there with you guys?"

"How would he have gotten here? Didn't he get a ride up there on a helicopter?"

Lisa Willis's cell phone rang at that moment which she answered and, upon hearing the caller, breathed an audible sigh of relief. "Xavier, where are you?… Great!…What's your ETA?…See you then…Oh, really? I'll tell him."

She swallowed before she addressed the expectant eyes in the room: "Morgan, Xavier is on his way in, and he thought you could use your car so that's what he's using to get here. He's also bringing your laptop."

As much as I resented his not getting my permission to drive my car, he did solve a couple of logistical problems for me. So I could focus on matters more closely at hand.

Benny returned to his previous line of thought: "Okay, back to our current situation. The explosion at the Salt Lake County Sheriff's office that nearly killed Morgan and me…."

"And which *did* kill the night duty officer," I added. It seemed we all had an obligation to honor the growing body count of innocent victims.

"I'm sorry. You are indeed correct, Morgan," continued Davidson. "The circumstances of that explosion are identical to the Cedar City explosion that killed a fellow named Archibald Bennett, one of Brigham the Third's political opponents. Hence, a death originally written off as an accident is now being looked at as a homicide.

"Heber had been ostensibly keeping track of the investigation for and in behalf of his boss, the former governor and former ambassador to China. So he knew we'd found Olive's computer backup files, and he knew we were back in the station retrieving them. Another gas explosion would have gotten rid of both the evidence and the people who knew where to find the backup.

"Now things get a little murky," sighed Davidson. "How the heck did the *real* serial killer track down Heber? Morgan, can take it from here."

"Now, we're getting to what the artificial intelligence guys call *fuzzy logic*," I began. "*Fuzzy logic* allows us to draw conclusions from insufficient data. Henry, remember as I located Olive's backup file that someone else had also begun a download of the same data?"

"Yeah. You cut him off and renamed the file. Just before the gas explosion," said Davidson.

"We couldn't figure out why Olive's killer would want the backup file, since he had the original computer," I said. Then to the rest, "Henry suggested the killer might want to see how much we could infer from the backup. At the time, that seemed to be the only logical conclusion we might draw. But now, I'd like to suggest that Heber King was most likely not interested in doing his own backup recovery of the files. Heber had a much more obvious solution. He just had to blow us up, along with the evidence."

"Then who…?" began Henry. He quickly answered his own question. "The real serial killer! They guy King imitated by killing Olive Jenkins. But how did *he* find out about the backup?"

"Anybody care to make a wild guess?" I asked. FBI profiler Willis's hand shot into the air like an excited school kid wanting to be first. "Go ahead, Lisa."

"He came to the funeral, looking for his imitator! He flew into town, killed Francois and Kathy Lambert so he could use their car, and somehow identified Heber. But how did he pinpoint Heber if we couldn't?"

I replayed the funeral. My first recollection of meeting Heber King had him bulldozing his way through the crowd to get a report on the investigation for his boss. In fact, he almost knocked down one of the security guys. Senator Hyde told him we'd be able to recover the data on Olive's missing computer!

"At the funeral, Senator Hyde told King we'd be able to piece together the data Olive had on her computer. That's when Heber found out his motive could unravel. But how could the serial killer have learned this?"

Again, agent Willis opined: "Could he have been standing nearby and heard the senator?"

"I doubt it," I said. "Crowd noise would have made it impossible for anyone outside our circle to have overheard. Besides, the senators' security guy seemed to block access."

"That's twice you've mentioned a security guy. What security guy?" asked Henry Davidson.

"Some big guy with an earpiece had his back to us," I said. "Monkey Boy literally ran into him as he approached us at the funeral."

"Morgan! Uniformed county and Sandy police handled all the security. *We* take care of the senators when they come to town. And we can't afford earpieces!"

Benny interjected over the speakerphone: "Could the guy with the earpiece have been part of security for the head of the Mormon church?"

"I'd *think* he'd have stayed with the church guys, then," I mused. Big guy. Earpiece. I don't know why, but my fuzzy logic inference engine clicked to a pretty solid conclusion. "Bingo, Benny!" I liked saying 'bingo' to Benny. "That earpiece wasn't a security radio. Our big guy made sure Monkey Boy bumped into him so he could plant a bug on him. Then he could listen to the conversation from the receiver in his pocket. The receiver connected to his earpiece. This was our serial killer. He heard about the backup files. He's the one I cut off as he tried his own download. And this is the man who has Sherry O'Shea, now!"

"If he's that close to the senators, then there must be news footage of him," came O'Shea's excited voice over the speakerphone.

"Absolutely!" exclaimed Davidson. "I'll get on the horn with the TV guys and see if we can look at their footage. The copy Dave Turner gave me got burned up in my old office."

While I couldn't disagree with Henry, the reality is we simply didn't have time. In fact, the killer and Sherry O'Shea could be out of the state even by now. We needed him, and we needed him soon.

"Make the call, Henry," I said. But I didn't want the team scurrying off and misinterpreting action for productivity. "Everybody else, I have a question? At the time our serial killer planted the bug on Heber King, none of us had any idea that King killed Olive. It wasn't until we both found out about Olive's computer backup that either of us had the means to uncover King's motive. And I pulled the plug on the serial killer's download and recovery of Olive's backup file."

"Maybe the files he recovered had the data he needed," said Benny from Snowbird.

"We'll just have to see," I said, pulling my Android as far as the charger cord would reach. "Benny, I've got the IP address and passwords stored here. Let's go see if anyone found Olive's backup file. Do it from up there, using my terminal shell. It'll be anonymous."

Actually, I didn't want the FBI people nor Henry to know how many laws I'd broken by moving and renaming Olive's files at a business provider who had a reputation for security to protect. It took Benny a few minutes to follow my instructions, but the wait paid off.

"That little sand scorpion!" exclaimed Benny. "According to the access logs, Olive's renamed file has been fully restored one additional time. Wasn't you, was it?"

"Damn!" My fist slamming down on the desktop startled everyone. From their startled looks, they needed a quick explanation. And I needed to eat a gigantic piece of humble pie. "Peter Drucker would recommend you shoot me right this moment."

"Drucker, the management guru?" asked Lisa Willis, who had to be older than she looked if she recognized the name.

"That's him. He had two pieces of advice relevant to this case," I said. "First, any organization that assumes they'll be victorious because their people are smarter than the competition is deluding themselves. I have been sailing merrily along most of my life assuming that I'm basically smarter than anybody else I'm going up against. I have consistently and stupidly underestimated our serial killer. Not only did he manage to find Olive's backup files with a lot less information than was available to me, but when I tried to identify him through his proxy server in Japan he slagged the whole system. This guy is definitely *not* stupid. In fact, he may be a lot smarter than I am."

"Why should we shoot you, Morgan?" asked O'Shea. "We wouldn't be anywhere in this investigation without you."

"That's Drucker's *second* piece of advice. He said to find every so-called *indispensible* employee in your organization and fire them. And you just made my case for Drucker's second point. Without my meddling in the investigation to begin with, our serial killer likely would *not* have identified Heber King. And Heber King would *not* have felt it necessary to kidnap Sherry. Patrick, if *I* were you, *I'd* shoot *me*."

"Enough!" shouted Judge O'Shea loudly enough to cause the automatic gain control on the speakerphone pod to clip several words of his sentence. But nobody had any doubt as to his words. "By that logic, we should just fire all the police and stand down our armies. Get this into your head. We're the good guys. We get bad guys. Sometimes the bad guys are *really* bad guys who try to hold us hostage. Sometimes, hostages get killed. But it sure as hell isn't the fault of the people trying to rescue them. It's the bad guys' fault. *They* started the chain of events. *They* are solely responsible, along with anyone else who knowingly abets them or works after the fact to help them cover their maggot-infested trails. End of discussion! Got it?"

"With due respect Pat, we can continue this discussion after we rescue Sherry." I didn't use the word *if*.

"Better be wearing non-conducting shoes when we do have that discussion cowboy, because I'm going to call lightning from God Almighty Himself." I don't think anybody in the room doubted for a moment that Hizonor lacked the Moses-like authority to do exactly that. Certainly nobody doubted that the judge *himself* figured he had the authority. He continued: "So you're up against a smart guy. My money's still on you, Morgan."

And so is Sherry's life, I thought.

Henry Davidson got me off the hook with his next question. "Why did our guy kill the Lamberts just to use their car, but didn't kill the UPS driver? Couldn't he have just taken their car after they'd parked in the long-term lot?"

"Not really," said SSA Willis.

She sure got my attention. Every other head in the room turned toward her. I'll bet even Benny and the judge leaned closer to the speakerphone up in Snowbird.

"Part of what we do at the BAU is victimology. Profiling the victim is essential to profiling the criminal. The Lamberts actually fit the profile of our serial killer's other victims. Surprisingly, I might add."

She paused, but none of us dared derail *this* revelation with the obvious question. Willis seemed disappointed no comment materialized, so she forged ahead. "As I've said before, each of our serial killing victims had a longstanding criminal history of child abuse. Or more precisely, they had a long history of being *suspected* child abusers by local authorities. But so far, each had beaten the system. Some due to technicalities, some due to unreliable witnesses, and two because witnesses had mysteriously disappeared. The last two, in particular. The Lamberts."

"Which would mean they didn't just *happen* to be at the airport?" I couldn't resist asking the obvious.

"You're not as dumb as you think you are," she smiled.

Henry Davidson slid a sealed plastic bag across the desk toward me. Through the clear plastic and fingerprint dust I could read the sealed "Congratulations, you've won a trip…" header on an official Princess Cruise Lines letterhead.

"Son of a gun, he lured them to the airport." I looked from agent Willis to Henry and back to agent Willis. "Our serial killer seems to be some kind of avenging angel."

"Damn!" said judge O'Shea. "We get my wife back alive, I'll give the sumbich a medal for saving the justice system a lot of money."

Now I don't know why one thought led to another, but I started thinking how fortunate for Judge Patrick O'Shea that he wasn't holding a press conference when he commended our serial killer as a boon to the justice ecosystem. Then I remembered Benny's surreptitiously broadcasting the secretary of state getting slapped down by the president. And *then* it occurred to me that maybe I wasn't the only smart guy in the Universe who could hot mike a cell phone conversation. What if our serial killer had not only tapped into this very meeting, but what if he'd been making a recording for some later use. Heck, after what I'd done to Lavar, Lamar and Laverl—publicly humiliating them to the entire cybernation—maybe we had inspired our serial killer to up his game. My new motto: *Don't underestimate your enemy, stupid!* So far, *this one* hadn't done anything really dumb, unless you'd call falling for Heber King's imitation of his methodology and thereby getting me on his tail just slightly ill advised. Nah. But kidnapping Sherry O'Shea should be high on the list of dumb, because if anything happened to her he'd have me on his trail for the rest of his life. Or the rest of *my* life, whichever came first.

"Okay, FBI profiler Willis," I said, standing and putting a finger to my lips with one hand and thumb and little finger of the other to my ear and mouth to indicate I think we might be under surveillance. "Your turn. Give us a profile of our serial killer. Angel or Demon?"

I didn't care *what* she said. I just wanted her to keep talking while I went around the room and felt the temperature of each cell phone, beginning with the two I had on the charger. Both my Android and the fed's crypto phone felt cool to my hand. Ditto for Gunny Lund's and FBI senior investigator buddy Edward McCartney. When I got to the whiteboard I scribbled a note: *Keep talking, Lisa. I'm checking to see if someone has hot miked any of our cell phones.* Henry Davidson pointed to his cell phone, which he'd had sitting on the desk in front of him. I gently put my hand on it, so as not to cause background noise that might indicate someone had taken any interest in the device. Warm. And not just a *little* bit warmer than the other phones, either. Almost hot. Hot miked for sure!

To her credit, Lisa Willis droned on about the profile of the guy listening in. Not missing a beat, she painted a true picture that an investigator would find damning but which the killer himself would regard as a compliment to his mission: "…our UnSub, in summary, believes himself to be on a mission to cleanse the earth of truly bad people. Furthermore, this is more than a merely functioning psychopath. This individual is not only smart, but from his audacity in tracking down Heber King while staying one step ahead of us qualifies him as truly brilliant. I don't think we're going to get him, at least not until he makes a mistake. So far, he hasn't."

I mimed applause at her, and then let her take a breath as I stalled for some time to think. "I need to take a bathroom break. Getting shot full of drugs and ejected from a Russian jet, combined with pizza and beer, has me a little light-headed. Henry, while I'm in the head, maybe you can get Dave Turner at Channel 2 on the horn and see if he can expedite that funeral footage."

"Will do," said Henry. Smart as a whip, he reached for the landline phone on his desk. I snatched the Android from the charger and motioned Willis to follow me down the hall. She quickly got the intent.

"I need to visit the ladies' room myself," she said.

45

This Program Will Resume After a Short Bio Break

he officer's rest room in the Salt Lake City Police Department looked like it belonged in some third-world hellhole. The hard water deposits combined with stains created by overuse of lowest-bidder soap to make me even wonder whether the splashing that came out of tap on my face might be lethal. I'd seen better-maintained public facilities in bombed-out Baghdad. And the towels dispensed by the Waxie dispenser could also be used as sandpaper. I finished drying my face and opened my eyes. The guy looking back at me through the mirror seemed to have been through quite a lot.

"What do you see, Rapier?" asked the Lisa Willis, who'd just walked in to the men's room.

"You've probably seen the same time lapse photo of the pretty blond who metamorphoses over several years into a haggard old crone crack whore," I answered. "Well, Lisa, I'm the next-to-last-stage exhibit, except I still have all my teeth."

Just seeing my reflection reminded me how bone tired and exhausted I felt. Did I *really* look that bad?

"The teeth do give me hope for you, Morgan."

I stiffened my arms and hung my head, attempting to pop a few kinks out of my neck muscles. A number of aches and pains threatened to send me into back spasms, and an ominous growl from my lower intestine indicated a visit to the men's room might have been providential.

"Forgive me for doing this to you, agent Willis, but I need to sit in a stall while we chat for a minute."

"I didn't think superheroes ever had to stop for a nature break," she said. I must have looked like I took her levity personally, because she quickly added, "Morgan, I have three brothers. Go sit on the pot and tell me what's going on in there. The killer is hot miking Henry's phone?"

"Yep, and we do *not* want him to know that we know! I needed some time to plot a strategy, since this may be our last chance to get the guy before he kills Sherry O'Shea and leaves town." I made it to the stall and will refrain from a detailed description of my bio eruption, suffice it to say that brothers or not, Lisa Willis seemed genuinely concerned that I didn't lose something vital along the way.

"Morgan, are you sure you're okay?"

"I am now," I replied. "I'd love to get Benny and Pat in on the act, but I can't be sure that their cell phones or computer links are safe from our eavesdropper. So I need your help keeping the conversation going while I pull in some serious favors from the owner of a computer grid and backtrack our hot miker."

"What kind of grid work are you talking about?"

"There's only one hot-mike server in the world, and both me and our killer are using it. I need to sniff all the packets going into or out of that server, crack all IP addresses, back-track the receiving cell phone, then use its GPS coordinates to pay our guy a visit before he gets wise to me. Like I said, this could be our last chance, and I absolutely do *not* intend to underestimate our adversary again."

"And the grid computing you need?"

"A friend of mine invented Mathematica and has a grid set up that makes anything Google does seem like a grade school science fair project. I've got to let him know I'm taking down his Alpha grid for several minutes, so I can nail our guy."

"Wolfram, right? I've heard some negative things about some of his scientific conclusions," said Willis.

"That's an understatement. In his tour de force book *A New Kind of Science*, he categorically and unambiguously disproves Darwin. And that's just for starters. He also completely debunks modern mathematicians as buffoons who can't begin to address the so-called *really interesting* problems. In D.C. circles, he is most definitely *not* politically correct. But whether or not you agree with him, his Alpha Grid can help us tonight."

"What do you want me to do with the troops?"

"Let me call Stephen," I said. "You go back in there and tell them I'm a little ill. Hopefully Henry will have some video footage of the funeral streaming from Channel 2 by now. Ask Benny to isolate some still shots from his computer and enhance the raster images to get as good a picture of the big guy at the funeral as possible. After I call Stephen, I'll appear to stagger back into the room, somewhat under the weather. But I'm really going to be focused on tunneling into Wolfram's Alpha Grid. So I'll appear a bit incoherent and preoccupied. When I locate our guy, I'll rush back to the bathroom. When I do, suggest that Gunny Lund check on me."

"Got it," she said. On the way out the door she advised: "Make your call to Stephen Wolfram, but do *not* light a match in here or this'll be *two* police buildings that get leveled."

Fifteen minutes later—it took me a while to calm down a most agitated Stephen Wolfram, panic stricken over my co-opting his Alpha grid for even a few seconds, let alone a few minutes—I eased myself back into a *very* different meeting. Yes, I expected to watch my mouth as not to tip off the serial killer who'd been hot miking our meeting. But I did *not* expect to see Benny and Hizonor physically in the room, standing by Lisa Willis and her laptop. The only way they could have gotten from Snowbird to this room so fast would have been a helicopter, and Benny pantomimed that with flailing hands. The judge waived a sheaf of color printouts toward me.

"You going to be okay, Morgan?" said Henry Davidson, trying to make conversation as I leaned across the ashen Lisa Willis to grab the printouts from the judge.

"I'll let you know. Just don't get in my way if I make a rush back down the hall."

"You need to change vets," said Benny. He must have deduced that someone listening in on the hot mike couldn't ascertain whether he was in the meeting or not.

O'Shea didn't risk speaking, but handed me the photos, clearly frames captured from KUTV's funeral coverage. The immediate sinking feeling in my stomach almost caused me to prematurely rush back to the men's room, not to mention almost turning the air blue with self-recriminating slurs. Staring back at me was none other than Xavier Brown, albeit with his stomach sucked in. Visions of those before and after weight loss advertisements—with the *before* showing bleached white-belly bulging into the camera, and the *after* posed in color with spray-on tan accentuating perfect six-pack abs—made it pretty clear how badly we'd all been had. Especially Lisa Willis, who'd been searching ten years for a killer that had cleverly inserted himself right onto her team. No wonder he'd been one step ahead of them!

One thing required no debate. Not only did we have to terminate Henry Davidson's hot miked telephone, but also we had to get the hell out of this particular room. Given Xavier's brilliance and decade-long audacity, we couldn't take the chance of further underestimating him. Had it been me, I'd have bugged the room, too.

Think, Morgan, think! I needed three ideas. Only one-and-a-half tactics came immediately to mind.

"Henry," I said as I pointed to his cell phone and vigorously nodded my head. "You'd better call Harley and let her know you're not coming home anytime soon."

He seemed to get the message. An outgoing call on his phone would terminate the hot mike session. So far, so good. Half of my second idea needed Lisa Willis to call Xavier on his cell phone and ostensibly get his ETA. And she had to redirect him to meet us all somewhere else, which would legitimize our changing rooms without getting him suspicious. Clearly, he had Sherry O'Shea with him and did not intend on meeting with us. I certainly wouldn't chance it myself, given that the guys looking at KUTV footage of the funeral were certainly about to identify him. Which gave me my answer. I didn't need an excuse to change rooms. Given half a chance, Xavier would give it to us.

"Agent Willis, maybe you should call Xavier Brown and get an ETA from him," I said. "We could use all the computer smarts available to us."

As if on cue, the main line rang on our conference room speakerphone. *Three guesses who that is*, I thought. He had indeed bugged us, but I didn't know just how thoroughly. McCartney punched the answer button, since Lisa Willis and Henry Davidson had been busy on their respective cell phones.

"Trick or treat," came Xavier's voice. "The camera on Lisa's laptop told me everything I need to know about who's there and what's happening. Hi Benny and Your Honor. Oh and Henry, you needn't bother trying to call Harley. She's tied up at the moment. Literally actually, sharing the trunk with Sherry O'Shea."

Davidson and O'Shea simultaneously let fly some rather creative invective, cut short by Xavier's laugh. "This is a first in medical history," he finally managed to spit out. "Two cases of Tourette's presenting themselves at the same time. Relax. Harley and Sherry will come out of this just fine if you all do exactly as I say. Starting with everybody in the room moving over to stand by Lisa, Benny and Judge O'Shea."

I edged toward their end of the room but with my hand behind me in the bicycle "stop ahead" gesture, I signaled for Gunny Lund to stay where he was. My one ace in the hole was that Xavier hadn't seen him in the mix. Henry Davidson joined us in front of Lisa Willis's laptop and obviously transmitting camera. Lisa looked like she might be in need of some serious medical attention. She just glared at the computer screen, knowing that a serial killer had royally snookered her. If she hadn't looked so vulnerable, I might have asked her about the FBI's vaunted internal screening mechanism, which I understood to be annual polygraph tests and psychological evaluations. Then again, Xavier had thoroughly outsmarted me, too.

"Peek-a-boo Morgan," came the speakerphone taunt. Benny underhanded me my car keys, a rather unexpected action since Xavier had taken my car. Without my key! My face must have registered one surprise after another, because Xavier felt he needed to do some showing off. "I wondered where that key had been hiding. But it didn't matter since…"

I interrupted: "…since you followed me to my car yesterday and captured the 125kHz and 425kHz ack/nack keyless unlock signals with your incredibly non-standard smart phone." The memory of the hulking slob messing with his phone in one hand while slurping a Coke from the other flashed through my mind.

"What can I say?" he answered. "The new Droid has a seriously open architecture, both for programming and for hardware adaptation. I just Bluetoothed from my phone to a wireless key decoder/programmer in one of the pockets of my baggy jacket. Too bad we couldn't share a beer as well as some notes on creative electronic countermeasures in this brave new world."

"Xavier, there aren't many things I can guarantee in this life. But one thing is certain. You and I will never be sharing a beer."

"Oh come on, Morgan! We both kill bad guys. Me, I just concentrate on child molesters. But when I saw how you eclipsed my lifetime body count by an order of magnitude, I decided it was time to retire. Too bad we couldn't be working together, though. I'd love to show you how to find large numbers of child molesters."

Undoubtedly he could see me thinking, and thinking hard. If I could just keep him talking, or rather bragging, I just might pull victory from the jaws of certain defeat. This guy's IQ tipped the scales somewhere north of mine, if his deviousness quotient came into play. The trick would be to make him believe my thinking had to do with whatever revelations he cared to share.

"Okay, I'll bite," I said as I looked toward the still glaring and possibly comatose Lisa Willis. "I'm sure your former FBI partners would *love* to know how you find large numbers of child molesters."

I pulled up a chair and sat down beside the FBI profiler, so I could quickly swipe-type some Android text messages below the tabletop and out of Xavier's line of sight. The first thing I did was Twitter my shooting buddies at the *daddysfelons account.* It took several messages to get past the 140-character limit, and I prayed my brains out that just one the judge's *dirty dozen* had set himself up for cell phone notifications. Emails had previously confirmed that all of them had signed up to follow me, but I had no way to know whether or not they'd enabled automatic notifications. As I did this, we listened to our twisted former brother explain how he'd infiltrated the Sony Entertainment game servers both in San Diego and in Japan. Using something he called Spring Lake Technologies, he could build a complete psychological profile of violent pedophiles just from the way they played online games.

"So you kill people just from their gaming profiles?" I goaded him.

"You know better than that," he spat. "If you're trying to keep me on the phone, forget about it. I'm running a VOIP connection from around the world. But to answer your insulting question, once I find a prospective pedophile, I eavesdrop on his game-playing messages to other players. Most of these guys, and some women, find their victims by building relationships of trust over the Internet and the game servers. No matter how patient they are, sooner or later I'll intercept them trying to set up a meeting. At that point, they meet up with both me and a rather rude transition out of mortality. Now enough chit-chat. I have two people you want. You have two people I want. Get set to follow some instructions."

Heaven help me, but my biggest concern was that either Henry Davidson or Judge O'Shea would shoot me in the back of the head before I completed my next sentence. Hell, Benny or Lisa might have a bullet with my name on it, too. Benny might object to my throwing him to the wolves without asking him. And Lisa might take issue with my roll-of-the-dice profiling ploy. So using my best imitation of G. Gordon Liddy politeness—G. Gordon never *ever* raised his voice or made a personal assault, no matter how rude his caller came across to him—I laid it out hard and fast.

"Xavier, with due respect I've got to call your bluff. You know, and we know, that you have never killed an innocent person, and you're not going to start now. Clearly the two people you want in your trade for Harley and Sherry are Benny and me. My guess is that you've negotiated a price for each of us, a dead-or-alive Benny with some very unhappy imams and a very much alive me for the Chinese. You haven't thought this through, because Benny is innocent and you'd be sentencing him to certain death. As for me, you'd probably be sentencing a bunch of Chinese—innocent Chinese whose only sin would be obeying orders from their government to bring me in—you'd be sentencing those Chinese to death, too.

"So Xavier, here's the deal. I'm coming for you. If you want to live, you'd better drop Harley Davidson and Sherry O'Shea on the nearest street corner. Then you'd better use every bit of your twisted genius to get out of town, out of the country. You're smart enough to know what's coming next. This conversation is now ended."

With that, I slammed Lisa Willis's laptop shut, sending the computer into sleep mode and my audience into collective heart failure. Then, just as the murmuring started in earnest, I leaned across the conference table and switched off the mushroom-shaped speakerphone. Before Xavier could call again, I dialed my special Wolfram/Alpha number from that phone, confirmed the connection, and then let the connecting computer hang up on me.

"What have you done?" said both Henry Davidson and Patrick O'Shea almost in unison. And while she didn't say anything, Lisa Willis didn't look too all-fired enthusiastic about my pre-emptive course of action, either.

"Sit down, all of you," I calmly said. Of course, my whole intellect had entered combat mode. There'd be time for adrenalin later. That is, if neither Henry nor Patrick had decided to shoot me just for the heck of it. I did lean over and touch the cell phone in Henry's pocket, verifying to the group that it was indeed hot again, which meant Xavier was listening in on our conversation. "He's going to call back real soon now."

Lisa Willis started to emerge from the shock at having discovered a traitor on her team: "How can you be sure he'll call back? What if he truly isn't a rule-based sociopath? And what do we tell him even if he does call back?"

"When he calls, tell him Benny and I are coming for him." I didn't mention that I'd figure out a way to have Gunny Lund with us, the one piece of data I didn't want Xavier to have from listening in on us. "If he doesn't call back, then I'm wrong and may have cost us the lives of two hostages. In which case, you should call Xavier on his cell phone and work whatever deal you can to save their lives. But Benny and I won't be here to engage in those discussions."

Lisa Willis's purse hung by one strap over the back of her chair. Without so much as asking her, I unzipped the side pocket and snagged the rental car keys.

"GM Suburban, back parking lot, right?" I asked. Her faint nod verified my assumption.

FBI agent McCartney began to articulate what the frenetically pacing Davidson and O'Shea must have been thinking: "But how do you even know where…?"

The ringing speakerphone line interrupted the obvious question. I pocketed my own Android and grabbed McCartney's Droid from his inside pocket. I then answered the FBI investigator's unfinished question. "Watch and learn, Grasshopper. Watch and learn. Come on, Benny. Let's get out of here before they pick up."

Naturally they picked up before we'd left the room. Sure enough, Xavier seemed quite agitated. But we didn't hang around to get any context. Benny, Gunny and I raced down the hallway toward the back stairs.

Lucky for me, the D.C.-based hot-mike server sat behind a cleverly designed firewall and a Niksun packet sniffer. Nobody accessing the server knew the firewall existed, which had been the general idea. Fortunately for me, the Niksun scanned for terrorist-type text packets, and the hot-mike contents simply sailed by unnoticed. I grabbed the IP packets in real-time, however, and farmed them out to the ravenously hungry Wolfram Alpha Grid for which I'd promised to give Stephen Wolfram my grandchildren's grandchildren. When Xavier called back, even though he used VOIP phone services instead of a regular landline, I trapped his packets when they interfaced with the landline. Given enough computing power, I'd trace the packets to their source, no matter how many times they went around the world. If we could be on the road when the location popped up, and if my gamble paid off that Xavier hadn't traveled too far, then we had a smack down coming within the hour. From two sources: Xavier's hot-mike signal and from the VOIP packets traveling to the speakerphone. If they came from different locations, then I'd have to make a hard choice. Maybe even a live-or-die choice for the two hostages. But at least I had the computing power to give me two locations.

Grid computing first gained prominence in the Search for Extra Terrestrial Intelligence, or SETI program. Signals retrieved from radio telescopes worldwide got parsed among thousands of Internet-connected computers with cycles to spare. Using fairly rudimentary pattern-recognition algorithms, the SETI network tried to find non-naturally occurring signal patterns. If you consider the SETI system as a kind of kindergarten, then the Wolfram Alpha Grid had earned multiple doctorates. With the flexibility of Mathematica and a server armada that made Disney's Pixar animation studios server farm pale by comparison, the Niksun-fed grid now crunched all the IP packets that streamed my hot-mike data. In less than thirty seconds, I had two continually Acking-Nacking IP addresses. Both fed phone switches in Salt Lake City. Now came the hard part. I had to crack the encryption on the carrier switch to get the phone numbers. And that's what took the Wolfram Alpha Grid to its knees. Luckily, I knew one of the numbers. Namely, Henry Davidson's cell phone number formed the public key of the encryption pair. The private key happened to be the product of the public key and a very large prime number. Each computation produced a number that may or may not be a cell phone currently operating in or near Salt Lake City. In short, the fairly simple test—finding the number and testing it or both validity and current operation—got parsed to several thousand dedicated computers.

Just one problem. Microsoft had paid Wolfram a lot of money to make

Wolfram Alpha available to the Bing/Yahoo network, and their agreement carried several performance-level guarantees. In other words, if Bing users experienced certain delays in response time, Wolfram paid a significant penalty. Big-time significant. Which meant that in order to get the temperamental genius to lock down Alpha for my exclusive use, I had to disclose the full extent of my Russian/Chinese/Arabian hacking activities and promise Stephen the equivalent of a blank check written on the United States Treasury. Naturally, I qualified the promise with the disclaimer that my incarceration for numerous violations of the Official Secrets Act and direct disobedience to my Commander in Chief could negate my ability to get his check signed. Luckily, since fiscal practicality had never been high on Wolfram's list of strengths, he rolled the dice against much longer odds than I'd have done in his position. Hopefully, they wouldn't come up snake eyes for both of us. A couple of size thirteen boots clomped down the hallway behind me.

46
The Psychos-Я-Us IRA

erman field marshal Helmuth von Moltke said no battle plan survives after the first shot is fired. An equally astute street-wise philosopher named Mike Tyson said, "Everybody got a plan 'til I punch 'em in the mouth." As soon as Gunny, Benny and I emerged from the Salt Lake Police Department stairwell, we got figuratively punched in the mouth. We didn't take the elevator, because that's where the phalanx of reporters would expect some action. I figured the back stairs and police-only parking lot wouldn't be covered by those reporters. But they crowded around the single exit gate, klieg lights and all.

"Gunny, I'm going to ask you to disobey a direct order from whoever told you to stay with me."

"Commander, that's not going to happen," he said.

"Tonight, I'm just Morgan. I'm not going to pull rank, and the choice is entirely yours."

"What do you propose, Com-, er, Morgan?"

"I have a lot of computers coming up with two solutions, and hopefully one location, of our kidnapper. I had intended to get the GPS coordinates via a special phone hack, as you drove me. But if those reporters get wind I've left the building, it'll be broadcast live and we'll send the kidnapper to ground. My request is that you disrupt those reporters in a way that lets me get out of here unnoticed."

"And?"

"Gunnery Sergeant!" I gently laid a fist on his shoulder. "When you want a job done, you just get a sergeant to do it and then stand back. I would no more tell you *how* to do it than fly to the moon. Improvise soldier. Improvise."

"And afterwards?"

"Afterwards, I'll text you Benny's and my location. Unless of course you can cause the disruption and be back here as we're leaving. For sure we'll need your help."

"Promise?" his eyes pleaded, even though his voice remained strong.

"Word of honor," I said.

After making sure his cell number got programmed into both my two cell phones, I stepped into a stairwell shadow and watched him duck into the main station lobby. A minute passed. Two. I should have busied myself using my phone's secure browser to VPN into yet another server that could give me a running GPS location of the kidnappers hot-miking cell. But I just couldn't risk missing the window of opportunity through which Gunny's ingenuity would allow me to escape. That and the Wolfram grid confirming the location of the VOIP stream would guarantee me that the location on which I'd bet two lives had two verifications: the hot mike and the Wolfram tracking extrapolation.

Three minutes elapsed and then holy hell broke loose. You've got to love sergeants! Shots rang out and every klieg light on the block went dark. Amidst shouts and screams I could hear the sound of high-pressure water raining against the front of the police headquarters. My inventive sergeant must have found a fire hydrant wrench and unleashed a torrent of high-pressure water on the assembled press pool. A lot of electronics wouldn't weather the moisture at all. Nor would the designer clothes worn by news anchors. Did I say how much I love sergeants?

I shot into the back parking lot and used Agent Willis' physical key to unlock her black Suburban, fearing that the automatic unlock and blinking of parking lights might alert the news people at the gate. No need to have worried, since all the gate watchers had split for the front of the building, cameras in tow. But no sooner had I started the engine and lurched forward than a tall shadowy figure appeared at the gate, thumb extended in a hitchhiker gesture. I screeched to a stop and remotely unlocked the passenger door for Gunnery Sergeant Lund, who hopped in. Benny had the whole back seat to himself.

"Gunny, you aren't even breathing hard." I peeled down the street and around the block, before stopping. "Here, you drive. I need to lock our destination."

We both ran around the front of the vehicle, since neither one of us could easily get our long legs over the console. Both of us buckled in and back on the road, I activated my phone's browser and asked him the obvious question. "Okay, spill it Gunny. What'chu did back there?"

"Child's play, really. I threw a handful of ammo into an arc light, and then borrowed a wrench from one of the fire trucks the SLPD called in for possible trouble. Saw a lady in a Semper Fi T-shirt, who wanted $20 and a wet kiss to give me ten seconds before she finished setting off the fire hydrant. I removed the hose fitting, so all she had to do was counterclockwise the top of the hydrant. The shells didn't start cooking off until I got to the gate, waiting for you to make your move."

"Well done, Gunny. Did your job and *barely* let me out of your sight."

"All in a day's work, Commander."

"Cut the commander crap. It's Morgan."

"With due respect, Sir! From now on, it's Commander. Sir! Where we goin'?"

In just eleven minutes and twelve seconds I had two identical location confirmations. After comparing the GPS coordinates of the serial killer's phone and the VIOP origination, I disengaged the Alpha grid and hoped Microsoft Bing traffic had been virtually nonexistent for those few minutes. I then sent Wolfram a text message promising him a get-out-of-jail-free card if he ever got arrested in Salt Lake City for anything less than sodomizing a farm animal. I copied Patrick O'Shea's cell phone with the message. Hopefully the judge would ascertain that I had a location for my kidnapper. I then tweeted the location coordinates to my *dirty dozen* at the daddysfelons account.

Two sets of coordinates. One location. "Forty degrees, forty-six minutes, nineteen-point-seventy-two seconds north, one-hundred-twelve degrees, one minute, thirteen-point-ninety-eight seconds west!" It took me a second or two to paste the coordinates into Google maps. "That would be…"

"Fairfield Inn at the airport," said Gunny. "I keyed the numbers into the nav system as you read them."

"There ya go, merge onto I-80 and hit it!" By some miracle, we'd left the SLPD heading west and found ourselves on Cesar Chavez at the 500 East onramp to Interstate 80.

"Commander, what's the plan?"

"Plan? How about locked, loaded and charging?" I checked the nine-millimeter I'd borrowed from Detective Davidson, making sure I had a round chambered, and shrugged at Benny. "Sorry Benny, no more firepower for you.

Stay in the Suburban and ram into anything that needs ramming. When we got to the hotel, we'll do a quick three-sixty. Afterward, with Gunny and me planted on opposite sides of the building, I'll call Agent Willis and tell her we're here and to send the cavalry to close off the area. Then we watch for movement. If I holed up in a hotel near the airport, I'd want a ground room on a corner with an exterior exit. But that's just me."

"And your Plan B?" asked Lund.

"Ah, emergency evac if the jig is up? Good question. Thoughts?"

"Well, a terrorist would wire the hostage with explosives and have his thumb on a dead-man's switch."

"Nah, that's Plan C. Desperation time. This guy is *way* too smart for that. And besides, I seriously believe he'd rather die than kill innocents. So far, this guy only kills people he thinks deserve killing. Again, if I holed up somewhere and intended to make a clean escape when the kite went up, I'd remotely detonate a diversion, wait for the fire engines to arrive, and then walk out dressed as one of the first responders. Or as a cop."

"You're one diabolical bastard, Commander." We sailed toward the airport for a while before Gunny gave up trying to figure out how to counter my posited Plan B. "You going to tell me how to nip his escape in the bud?"

"Yeah, Gunny. Pray this guy decides to bug out the minute he hears we're onto him. You see a big guy racing out the door, or a window, to his car, let me know. Maybe we can take him down without anybody getting killed."

"Novel idea. For you, I mean, not killing any more people today."

I truly didn't want another scalp on my stick. Ever. We sailed off the 56th West exit and followed the signs to Admiral Byrd Road, although the Fairfield Inn sign stood alone on the skyline. One of the longer days of the year, the sun had just set, and about fifty parking lot lights now illuminated the landscape. I suppose there *could* have been worse news than a full parking lot, but I couldn't think of any. Once around the building and I decided which room *I'd* take, and I sent Benny in the Suburban to drop off Gunny on the adjacent corner, not the opposite end of the building which contained the lobby and dining room, and then to do a continuous sweep of the perimeter. Anything unusual should be reported with honking horn and flashing lights. I made my phone call to Lisa Willis and the rest of the team, who must have still been talking to Xavier.

"Agent Willis, please put me on speaker for the rest of the group," I began. She complied. "Morgan, we seem to be at an impasse with Xavier."

"Detective Davidson, we still warm?" I waited for him to feel his cell phone.

"We are," he replied.

"Sorry to bugger out on you guys, but Gunny and are almost to the Fairfield Inn by the airport. Address is 230 North Admiral Byrd Road. My military surveillance satellite should have our guy to within 10 feet, and I'll be there within two minutes. Call in both the SLFD and the SLPD, but explicitly forbid them to send any first responders over six feet tall into the area. If our kidnapper tries a diversion, we want to spot him if he's disguised as police or fire."

"Will do," said agent Willis.

I hung up and backed toward a grassy knoll that separated the parking lot from the street. Just after I replaced the phone in one of my jacket pockets, but before I could retrieve the Glock from my waste band, I heard the safety unclick from a weapon behind me.

"One twitch Rapier and I'll drop you where you stand," came Xavier's voice.

I slowly raised both hands and waited for an answer to mortality's ultimate question. Would Annie greet me as I passed into the next life, or do the lights just go out, forever? But no oblivion came, not that I'd know it, given the definition of oblivion. So I pivoted on the ball of my left foot and turned to face the man I'd underestimated yet again.

"I told you not even to twitch, and here you turn around."

Facing me and holding his gun far too casually stood a no longer slovenly, not-the-least-bit-pot-bellied Xavier Brown. He stood two inches taller than I did and outweighed me by at least forty pounds. And he wore my identical superhero shirt and Lucky jeans! Very clever. Look like me if he had to do his own plan-B escape.

"Amazing what poor posture and a padded jacket can do to one's appearance," I quipped.

"Showmanship, Morgan. All showmanship."

Since he hadn't pulled the trigger, I gave him my honest reaction. "Figured if you had a bullet with my name on it, I wanted to see it coming."

"If I had a bullet with your name on it, you'd never have seen it coming."

I chuckled in spite of myself. "I believe it; you've had me outfoxed from the outset. How'd you know I'd be here, right now?"

"GPS on your Android," he smirked. Of course! Smartest man in the world got played like a fine violin. Then he motioned with his gun. "I really don't want to shoot you, so please take that gun out of your belt with the thumb and little finger of the left hand and Frisbee it to your left. Then take off your FBI jacket and do the same thing with it. Please hurry, because we don't have much time."

I complied, although his next move completely shocked me. He ejected the clip from his own Glock and tossed both the clip and the gun behind him. Each landed rather neatly beside two tripods, on which sat cell phones with their cameras aimed at us. I heard footsteps clomping across the pavement behind me and spoke without turning my head. "Stand down, Gunny. This is between him and me."

Gunny stopped, and the other superhero spoke again. "Don't worry about Sherry and Harley. They're both unharmed and sitting in room 171, watching television. Actually, they're watching the Flixwagon feed on the in-room Internet. Say hi to them if you want. Or to your video audience viewing via the other video phone."

"Gunny," I called, again without taking my eyes of the UnSub. "Call Davidson and the team. Tell them *not* to take a shot, and have them get Sherry and Harley out of room 171."

"She'll be okay," said Xavier. "You were right. I've never killed innocent people and don't intend to start now."

"Present company excluded?" I asked. "Fistfight at the Okay Corral?"

"Just some pleasant conversation, between two gents, one from SEAL Team Three and the other from Air Cav. Fellow soldiers in arms, getting to know each other."

"Wait. Do you honestly think your brave Fort Hood First Team is proud of the bodies you've left across the United States?" I couldn't keep the incredulity from my voice.

"Gimme a break, Morgan. You've killed three times as many people in the last week as I've taken out in the years I cleansed the world of child rapists and pedophile murderers. And I've *never* had collateral damage. Can you say that? Especially with the food riots your little Russian/Chinese virus caused? Not to mention the bodies we'll never truly count in the Islamic world, where your buddy Benny took a page out of your play book?"

"Last time I checked the Constitution, a one man judge-jury-executioner is called a murderer." I saw him start to circle and I countered his move. "That is what this is all about? You want to prove you can beat me?"

"I know the police are going to be here momentarily, and I don't intend to increase my body count today. What I've painstakingly done over the last decade you've eclipsed in one week. I took out the bad guys one at a time. You took them down one country at a time. I infer likely pedophiles from their online gaming profiles. You wait for a hacker to attack your system, and then you blast them along with all their friends. After seeing you at work, I figure my job is done. So right here, right now, why not give Lavar and Lamar and Laverl's fans one last chance to cheer for a winner? Let's see if you can take me."

"One question first?"

"Sure, shoot!" he said, and then laughed. "Just kidding about the 'shoot' part."

"How long have you known I created the Russia/China virus?"

"The minute you tried to track me down through the Japanese server, just before the police station blew up. The FBI had the fingerprint of your original virus, and it perfectly matched the one used in your Japanese attack. At that moment, I began formulating my retirement plan."

"Which is?" I asked, suddenly quite wary I'd once again been outsmarted.

His answer came in a lightning thrust, his open hand slicing toward my throat.

One second, six feet separated us. The next, I barely had time to dodge a lethal blow to my throat. I countered with a reverse heel toward his solar plexus, but my foot just sliced through air. Reflexively, I continued my roll and raised my forearm just in time to block his kick toward my head. Clearly, this guy didn't order his martial arts manual from some mail-order outfit. I did manage to connect with a punch to his sternum, but it felt like I'd slammed my fist into an engine block. I gave that thrust everything I had, yet it didn't faze him in the least. He just kept coming at me like a diamond-tipped industrial drill bit.

Several of them.

The world around us came to a stop. Everything in it ceased to exist except for the two of us. The last time I'd experienced this level of focus, I came out of my reverie amidst the carnage I'd inflicted on a Republican Guard Battalion in Iraq. Muscle memory, years of training, and an endorphin-factory that made me immune to pain all kicked in. Somewhere in my consciousness grew the realization that I might be outmatched, but that only mattered if I cared about the outcome. Tonight, with the hostages safe and no other real obligations to keep me anchored in this veil of tears called mortality, I had nothing left to lose. Describing the scene in retrospect would be as ludicrous as stopping a Rachmaninoff piano concerto to describe each note in a particularly virtuosic arpeggio.

Minutes passed. Neither of us landed a fight-ending blow, yet neither of us escaped unscathed. Momentarily, some change in rhythm, an exterior presence triggered by our situational tripwires, caused us both to simultaneously disengage and step back. Even though I had trouble keeping the blood from a forehead gash from seeping into my right eye, and even though my opponent's left eye seemed almost swollen shut, we both knew and turned away from each other to confront some black-clad party crashers. And notwithstanding *our* gentleman's agreement not to use weapons, these guys carried guns in one hand and handcuffs in the other. Seven of them. Not as big as either of us, they nevertheless knew their way around a street fight.

"In the truck, both of you," commanded what appeared to be their leader. Out the corner of my eye I could see Gunny Lund on his knees, with his hands clasped behind his head, staring into the barrel of a submachine gun. Over his shoulder, I could see Benny with his hands splayed on the hood of the black FBI Suburban.

"I didn't *think* the Chinese would give up quite so easily," I said.

"Meet my retirement plan," whispered Xavier into my ear. The next second every muscle in my body convulsed. I'd been tasered.

47

"What do you mean I'm worth only $1 million?"

 y next conscious assessment came from inside a fast-moving panel truck. The assorted smells and storage equipment confirmed we were careening across a tarmac in an airport food service vehicle. Benny and I had honest-to-goodness handcuffs—not the flex ties any self-respecting special forces team might use to secure prisoners—threaded through eye bolts that had been screwed into the truck's metal floor. Black-clad Chinese commandos sat silently to either side of us, and Xavier seemed to have the only seat in the front of our compartment. A seatbelt and shoulder harness kept him from getting bounced out of his captain's chair, not a bad idea since a bad bump might trigger the explosive vest he now wore.

"You didn't strike me as the suicide bomber type," I said.

"Retirement account insurance," he smiled. He held up his left hand. "Dead-man's switch, in case my new pension underwriters renege on their promised funds transfers. You know what a dead-man's switch accomplishes, don't you Morgan?"

Xavier periodically squinted through his non-swollen eye at the Droid phone in his right hand. Someone must have slapped a bandage over the gash above my own right eye, since blood no longer obstructed my vision.

"Off-shore account balances, eh?" I said. He confirmed with a nod. "Might I assume that your use of the plural 'transfers' means separate organizations are contributing to your retirement?"

"Had to harvest the low-hanging fruit," he said. "Benny fetched a paltry million from the Iranians. But you, Mister SEAL Team Three, are worth a hundred times that to my Chinese friends. Seems like your virus exploit quite literally cost them the world. They seem to think your expertise can reverse that. Their money, by the way, needs to be in my account before I can excuse myself and leave you to become acquainted with your new employer."

"You mean slave master, don't you?"

"One military hierarchy to another, Commander Rapier. We're all slaves." He made only fleeting eye contact, since the contents of his phone display screen seemed to have much more interest.

Benny looked at him incredulously: "Rationalized like a true sociopath, sending me to certain torture and death. You should seriously consider converting to Islam."

"Not to mention sending these Chinese to their certain deaths." I couldn't resist extending Benny's line of thought. My comment drew intense stares from our captors, who divided their attention to securing my manacles and making furtive glances at each other. I wished one of them would have slapped me, so I could use the Bruce Willis line out of *The Last Boy Scout*: 'Do that again and I'll kill you.' But I'd already said I intended to kill them, so the line would have been foolishly redundant. Besides, for the first time in my life it occurred to me that I just might not get out of this situation at all.

Rather than address the logic of Benny's and my discussion of his moral schizophrenia, Xavier Brown used my bravado against me: "I needn't worry about Benny's death, then, because you're going to rescue him. That takes a load off my conscience. And by the way, I emailed our government a list of currently active sexual predators. Let's see if they're smart enough to do something about them." The phone screen caught his attention, after which he smiled. "And this takes a load off my mind, as well. I'm a hundred million dollars richer. A hundred-and-one million, actually, thanks to Benny. Time to say goodbye."

Xavier pocketed his cell phone and removed three others from a side pocket. My Android, McCartney's Droid, and the phone that KUTV's Big Dave had loaned us and which I'd left in the care of Benny. He casually tossed them on the metal floor of the truck.

"Oh, and I took the SIM cards out of them when we picked you up," he added. "So nobody can track you." He reached back into his pocket and retrieved three SIM cards, which he casually dropped on the floor with the phones. This seemed to greatly entertain my Chinese captors.

The vehicle slowed down and came to a stop quite near the sound of a jet engine spooling up. Xavier unbuckled himself with his free hand just as someone slid open the side-panel door from the outside. The Cessna Citation X's unmistakable wingtip split the full moon behind it. I'd have given quite a lot to get a glimpse of the Mach .92 plane's tail number, but no such luck. None of the Chinese wanted to go anywhere near Xavier as he stepped out of the enclosure, lest they somehow detonate his lethal vest. Before the door closed he turned and winked at me.

"Until we meet again, Morgan." He made a final shooting gesture with his pointer finger and then disappeared from sight as the door closed.

"Ebn el sharmoota!" shouted Benny over the jet's howling roar.

"That the best you can do," I said. "Every other *son of a bitch* in the world should be offended that you would lump that scumbag in with them."

"Profanity is not one of my strong suits." Benny shrugged. "Besides, I ought to have been worth more than a paltry million."

"The ebn el sharmoota actually winked at me," I said. A good hard jerk on the eyebolt did nothing more than peel the skin from my handcuffed wrists.

"You'll notice he didn't say he'd be seeing *me* again," said Benny. He did his own futile jerk against the floor restraints.

Our vehicle hadn't resumed travelling for more than a few hundred feet before we heard the business jet go full throttle into the clear night sky. Given our respective future outlooks, it seemed rather a shame that hail and lightning hadn't greeted Xavier's takeoff. Instead, the full moon mocked us from a beautiful cloudless sky. Son of a bitch indeed.

We continued to speed through the cool night air for a another few minutes, and I calculated that my best chance of escape would be when they released my handcuffs from the floor bolt. Rather, *if* they released me. All dressed up in a superhero shirt—albeit somewhat the worse for wear after my televised dust up with the killer—and no chance to be a superhero. My head hurt. My ribs hurt. Every major arm and leg muscle ached from blocking Xavier's pile-driver blows. Even my heel hurt in my new tennis shoes.

What the heck? I thought. Something in my shoe hurt like hell. Small consolation that my hands, cuffs bolted to the floor, could reach my foot and dig out whatever I'd picked up to chafe my heel. But I took advantage of that small consolation and snaked a finger between my heel and the inside of the shoe until I felt something metallic. About the size of…a handcuff key! Surely… my mind reeled… did Xavier actually plant my means of escape? Did he really intend some future meeting? The psycho actually winked at me. *Whatever you do, Morgan, don't drop the damned key!*

Time for a little battlefield assessment. Four black-clad commandos in the compartment with me, at least two more in the cab of the truck. Automatic weapons. Body armor. With Butch and Sundance manacled to the floor. Wrong analogy. Maybe it's Omar Sharif and Rambo manacled to the floor. And Omar is more concerned about the measly million dollars than our current dire situation. Looks like Rambo is on his own. Too bad I couldn't rationalize my plan with the "They drew first blood" line. In fact, these soldiers didn't choose to be locked in a box with their assassin. In spite of my taunt to Xavier that he'd signed their death warrants, these boys' only crime was following orders from their government. I supposed I could take one of their weapons, aim it at my own head, and paraphrase Cleavon Little's *Blazing Saddles* line: "Drop your guns or I'll pull the trigger." Trouble is, one of them would probably whip out a taser and call my bluff. Unless I didn't intend to bluff. Nah, bad idea. I couldn't leave Benny in the lurch, splattered with my brains and destined for decapitation with a dull knife on the *Mecca Today* television show.

My question about whether or not they'd be taking off the handcuffs answered itself in the negative when our truck slowed and rattled up some kind of metal ramp. The echo of our engine in an enclosed space meant we'd just driven into a large metal structure, and the slight rocking suggested a large structure on shock absorbers, likely the cargo bay of a transport aircraft.

In the corporate world, acres of low-level managers prove their worth by prevailing in the notion that no action should be taken without their considered analysis. If some adventure backfires, these so-called managers can point out that the flaws should have been as obvious to everyone else as they'd been to them. I'd never shared this point of view, recognizing the difference between *management* and *leadership*. With my captors' attention now drawn to their respective view ports, I quickly retrieved the handcuff key from my shoe and released both hands. I debated doing the same for Benny, but it made more sense for him to lay low and stay out of my way than to inadvertently jump up and get between me and one of the bad guy's weapons. He didn't seem to notice my actions, since his current preoccupations involved the embarrassingly low price he'd demanded and murmuring the Arabic version of several interspecies reproductive acts to which he'd like to introduce Xavier Brown.

"Forget the pigs and goats, Benny," I whispered as close to his ear as I could manage without taking my eyes off the back of the man nearest to me. I pocketed the key and added, "Roll into as small a ball as you can."

As he blitheringly processed my request, I leapt forward and slammed one commando's forehead into the sheet metal side of the truck. Then, before the unconscious body hit the ground, I drove a fist squarely into the face of his companion whose reflexes had been quick enough to turn his head toward the commotion. That momentum took both of us into the other two commandos, both of whose superb training had their hands going for holstered side arms. The man to my right tangled with the unconscious companion I'd hammered into him, which let me concentrate on the remaining guard. I smacked his gun hand with my left while going for another fist to the face with my right hand. Unfortunately, my luck with one-shot put downs ran out. He expertly blocked my punch and brought his knee up into my solar plexus. Good thing his gun discharged and nailed his own knee. And a good thing his weapon was silenced, as nothing would have caught the attention of the men outside more surely than a gunshot.

No longer having reason to hold onto the weapon with which he'd kneecapped himself, he obligingly dropped the gun. Three down, but then my luck really did run out. Number four had shucked his unconscious partner aside and calmly aimed his own gun at a spot between my eyes. Two seconds passed. I knew he needed me alive. So did he. Before he could make the obvious decision to nail me in my own kneecap, Benny interrupted the flow.

"I'd shoot him if I were you," said Benny.

I don't know if my assailant spoke English or not, but the unexpected comment caused him to glance toward Benny. In that instant I lashed upward with my foot and connected with the wrist holding the gun. The satisfying sound of snapping bone and the clattering gun that miraculously dropped without going off must not have been heard outside the truck, because the door didn't slam open with reinforcements. Rather than putting the last man away with another assault, I snatched up the gun his partner had dropped and motioned with it for him to sit down.

"A little help over here," said Benny. He clanked his handcuff chain against the floor-mounted bolt. Without taking my eyes off the two conscious but wounded men, I reached into my pocket and handed the key toward Benny.

"Want me to take off my shoe and grab that with my toes?"

"Right," I said and bent down until I felt his fingers take it.

While Benny uncuffed himself, I collected all the commando weapons and moved them to the front of our compartment. The men outside the cab seemed to have finished chocking the wheels and securing the truck for flight, but they hadn't opened our truck's doors.

"Keep an eye on these guys, Benny." I handed him a cocked Glock after which I retrieved the cell phones and SIM cards I'd seen Xavier drop on the floor. Since he'd clearly slipped the key into my shoe, I surmised he'd left the phones and SIM cards on purpose. Damn, maybe our little hand-to-hand combat had just been a test to see if he could bet our lives on my ability to disarm four captors. I didn't let myself get too enthusiastic about him though, since he'd put not only Benny's and my lives at risk but could have sentenced our captors to death. Not a good guy by any stretch of the imagination. We had a score to settle.

No sooner had I reinserted the SIM cards and given Benny the KUTV phone than my Android beeped with a text message notification. Shooting buddy and former Israeli commando Milt Appelbaum, Uncle Miltie, wrote "20?" repeated in messages every minute.

I answered simply, "Need U ASAP. Truck in cargo plane. Don't let take off!"

Surprisingly, our transport plane didn't sound like departure was imminent. Sure, the engines idled, but I hadn't heard the hydraulics of a retracting loading ramp. Uncle Miltie's next text explained the situation: "C130 surrdd not go anywh. You in cntrl in trk?"

Whew! Had the C-130 gotten airborne, I'd have had to shoot my way forward and hope the pilot wouldn't auger us into the Utah desert. I quickly fumbled a text answer: "In cntrl. Nd medic for bd gy."

Two bangs on the slide panel told me he'd gotten the message. "Morgan,

I'm coming in."

"It's clear," I answered. Of course, I kept my weapon at the ready, just in case part of Hizonor's *Dirty Dozen* had been captured and forced to lure us into a trap. The door cautiously slid open, confirming Uncle Miltie and I shared the same thoughts. We both breathed a collective sigh of relief.

Iraq vet Stan Pavish hopped in first and stepped past Benny to cover the two conscious commandos, followed by Viet Nam evac medic John Chyzik and his first aid kit, who immediately went to work on the man who'd shot himself in the knee. We exited the truck and followed the India Defense Forces captain Rangaswami down the ramp, tailed by the Israeli Appelbaum. Benny busied himself making some kind of video recording with the KUTV phone, although I couldn't hear his commentary. We passed half-a-dozen black-clad men lying on their stomachs with their hands flex-cuffed behind their backs. Out on the tarmac, the sight of our transport vehicle surprised me. Towering over us stood a Utah National Guard C-130. Benny panned the camera phone across the scene and up the tail section of the aircraft, continuing his unintelligible narrative.

"Bag'em and tag'em Lt. General Harrison is going to be really pissed about this," I said.

"Pretty cool, stealing a C-130 locally," said Appelbaum. "Good thing you texted me the GPS coordinates before you went offline, or you'd be long gone."

"What GPS text?" Surprises on top of surprises. "I didn't send a text between the time I left the Salt Lake PD office and when I put the SIM card back into my Android in the truck!"

"This came from your Android. Here's the whole string." Appelbaum showed me his text message chain, including the originals from me, along with his responses asking for my location. Between two of his location requests was latitude and longitude of the C-130 and its description.

"I'll be dipped! Xavier didn't really intend to sell Benny and me," I said. "He just wanted to rip off the Chinese."

"And the Iranians for a lousy million," added Benny. "He should'a got more."

"Absolutely, Adrian!" I said in my best Stallone-Rocky imitation.

48

POTUS Meets Harley
"You Bet Your Ass" Davidson

 followed Patrick and Sherry O'Shea up the gangway and onto Air Force One. Henry Davidson and his daughter preceded them. Beside me, Mohammed bin Faisal Al Saud, aka Benny, and my ever-present bodyguard Gunny Lund walked stiffly in stage-struck awe. Pulling up the rear, the FBI duo—profiler Willis and senior investigator McCartney—wondered aloud about the size of the aircraft's main cabin. And for the first time since I'd given up military transport for commercial air travel, I didn't have to duck to enter the plane. None of us had much time to gawk and wonder at the magnificent symbol of America currently parked in the Salt Lake City International Airport, as the president immediately greeted us.

"Ah, Death Eater. We finally meet," he said, warmly shaking my hand. "Thank you for putting your life on the line so many times this week."

"Mister President, about that Death Eater thing…" I sputtered.

"Forgive me, Commander Rapier. I just *had* to see how that sounded. Kind of a nice ring to it, don't you think?"

"Mister President," I said, deciding to ignore the provocation. "I'd like you to meet some people without whose contribution the world would be a much worse place today. First, Judge Patrick O'Shea and his wife Sherry, whose request for help started a rather unusual chain of events."

Flanking the president, I recognized JCS chairman Mike Hall, who rolled his eyes at the understatement. Without the O'Sheas' call a week earlier, I probably wouldn't have launched the cyber payback that inadvertently stopped the Chinese attempt to blackmail the U.S. and undercut our financial system. Nor would I have put an end to the Russian Mafia's heretofore successful banking exploits. And Benny would still be enjoying the royal life in Saudi Arabia. On the other side of the president stood Lt. General Daly, head of the U. S. Cyber Command, and his civilian counterpart Harold Smith, the president's cyber security czar.

The president warmly greeted the O'Sheas, and even hugged Sherry. "I understand you had a tough go of it at the hands of two kidnappers, Mrs. O'Shea. How are you doing?"

"Oh Mister President, I haven't been through nearly what Morgan endured," she smiled. Patrick put his arm around her and squeezed gently.

The president winked at the judge. "You're a lucky man, Your Honor. And Senator Kimball has seriously bent my ear about your reputation for creative sentencing and low recidivism. I realize that when a politician says he'd like to chat with you further, it's kind of like a southern gentleman saying 'Ya'all come back.' It's polite but they really don't want ya'all to come back. I'm serious. Would you have time next week to beat up on my attorney general? I can't promise he'll listen to you, especially considering my party's backing by the ACLU, but when he reports to me on your conversation I guarantee he won't blow you off completely. Sherry, will you make sure your husband returns the call from the attorney general?"

"I'm sure the attorney general would be *delighted* to hear about Daddy's Little Felons." She looked squarely at me as she said the last three words, as did the president. Along with a smug JCS chief and a puzzled cyber czar Harold Smith, with whom I'd debriefed earlier in the day and for whom I had the highest regard.

"Yes, Mister President, I will take the attorney general's call and do my best to share my vision of the criminal justice system."

"And who is this young lady?" The president extended his hand.

"Mister President," said Henry Davidson. "This is my daughter Harley. Harley Davidson."

"Really, now! Harley as in the motorcycle? That's your given name?"

Three of us in unison—Harley, her father, and me—said, "You bet your ass!"

I don't see how any of those four words could have ever before been uttered directly to the President of the United States. The president immediately 'grokked' that there must be some inside joke associated with the question. But before he could laugh outright, an aide couldn't resist asserting pecking order and protocol: "*Commander* Rapier! *This* **is** the president …."

Before the meeting, I'd told Henry and Harley not to hold back when the president asked Harley's name. I also told them to ignore whoever tried to insert himself into the discussion after their, our, answer. Which we all did. Actually, I could have kissed the aide on the lips for fulfilling my expectations, since my debrief with my old friend Admiral Hall. Hall and I had agreed that keeping my relationship one-on-one with the president and pointedly mowing down the myriad gatekeepers who would try to insert themselves between the president and me should be first priority. So we all ignored a now red-faced aide. The president finally laughed out loud and threw his arms around Harley. "I *can't wait* for my daughters to meet *you*!"

Then the president included Henry Davidson in a three-way bear hug. "Detective Davidson, the FBI speaks rather highly of you!"

Henry could do nothing but return the president's hug and pray that the conversation would go no further. I could almost read the words 'Who specifically in the FBI?' in his eyes. The president's exuberance gained momentum as he made his way around my small band of miscreants. To Gunny he said, "Master Gunnery Sergeant Lund, guys like you are good for one of two things. Either you're going to protect the quarterback or throw your body in front of the president. After hearing of your inventive diversion last night, my advice would be for you to consider a career in the Secret Service. I think I have some pull there, son."

Then the president saluted the Marine. Until then, I hadn't noticed the medals affixed to Lund's dress blues. One in particular solved the conundrum. All military men salute their commander in chief first. All that is, but those who wear the Congressional Medal of Honor. Those men are saluted first by the President of the United States. Lund straightened up and returned President Medina's salute. The president proceeded to shake Lund's white-gloved hand. "Seriously, Gunny. You can write your own ticket."

By this time, I thought the two FBI people would wet their pants. So did the president, evidently, because he strode over to them and addressed each by name as he shook their hands. He saved Lisa Willis for second. "I would have had your boss here, too. But a little birdie told me that Commander Rapier threatened Chip Hardman with bodily harm if they ever again came into close physical proximity."

Okay. I admit I didn't vote for the guy. But his treatment of me throughout this ordeal—his innate understanding of the unfolding situation and his willingness to give me free rein in a very fluid and dangerous series of operations—caused me serous pause. Politics aside, once again a serious international crisis let a real leader emerge from his cocoon and rise to greatness. No insulation for political protection. No plausible deniability. And not one to let a tremendous opportunity get overanalyzed into paralysis, the president saved his best for last.

"Mohammed bin Faisal Al Saud, the million-dollar man. I am very pleased to finally meet you."

"Ebn el sharmoota!" he muttered. Then more formally, "I'm now a ten-million-dollar man, Mister President. And please call me Benny."

"I'm not familiar with that Arabic expression, ebn el sharmoota?" said the president.

I jumped it: "Sir, its just an endearing nickname for you."

"Fair enough. Benny, would you do me the pleasure of flying back to Washington, D.C. with me and Commander Rapier?"

"Sir?" said a very surprised Benny.

"Some rays of sun have appeared in the Mideast through clouds I thought wouldn't clear away in my lifetime. Bicyclists like Morgan," he looked at me with a don't-speak/just-nod-when-I-tell-you expression, "Cyclists call such a break in the clouds a *sucker hole.* Anybody dumb enough to hit the road beneath a sucker hole deserves a drenching. Or worse. Right, Commander?"

The president and I nodded in unison. His attention returned to Benny. "I want to ride into the sucker hole. We can't miss an opportunity that may not appear again in a thousand years. Russia and China? Typical power politics. But to harness a momentum of sanity in the Middle East that you started? Benny. I need you. I'm begging you. And I promise not to throw you under the bus if the sucker hole closes on me."

"But after what I did to your secretary of state..." began Benny.

"If she or her surrogates get out of line, I *will* throw them under the bus. This is *my* personal initiative, not theirs."

Benny looked at me. I mouthed the word "Yes!" as emphatically as I could.

"Well sir, Mister President, I don't have much else on my calendar. And a lot of my fellow countrymen would like to catch me alone in a dark alley. Not to mention someone who wants a quick *ten* million dollars." Benny emphasized the new dollar amount.

"Good. You and your good friend President Ebn el Sharmoota will have some fun in Washington, DC," laughed the president. He didn't see my grimace. Or the Ten Million Dollar man's.

So went my last evening in the great state of Utah. We enjoyed an unimaginably delicious dinner aboard Air Force One. The president actually brought his wife and daughters with him on the trip, and they immediately became best friends with Harley you-bet-your-ass Davidson. His wife and agent Willis also struck up what appeared to be a genuine friendship. Shifting her attentions between Willis and Sherry O'Shea, Violet Medina made them both feel quite at ease. Admiral Hall and Harold Smith stayed fairly close to me throughout the evening, both brimming with questions about my virus.

In the almost forty-eight hours since Sherry O'Shea's rescue, the president had flown to Salt Lake City, held a press conference about Russia, China, the Middle East and the solution to Olive Jenkins' murder. Oh yes, and also about the *Mountain Meadows Massacre*. In all the excitement of the last few days, I'd forgotten to reset my *dead man's switch*, which meant Olive's copy of the original George Wood diary automatically went to several local news organizations and got published in their entirety by both the *Salt Lake Tribune* and even by the Mormon Church-owned *Deseret News*. George Wood, III sat in jail on murder charges, and Heber Wood King probably looked up from the infernal regions between slap-and-giggle bouts with Jeffrey Dalmer and Adolph Hitler. Neither Benny nor I could show our faces in public, and the ingenuity of the news media in their attempts to interview us and get photographs continually amused everyone. Everyone that is, except the White House press secretary, who got so bound up in quid pro quos with organizations to whom he owed favors that he didn't know whether to blow his nose or straighten his tie.

The original serial killer proved to be a continuing enigma. Former Air Cav officer Xavier Brown had weaseled his way into the FBI, somehow evaded the psychological profiles, and had passed mandatory lie detector tests flawlessly.

While he'd evaporated without a trace, the U. S. Attorney General currently had an army of legal experts trying to decide how they could communicate Xavier's worldwide database of sexual predators to proper authorities without getting into all kinds of constitutional trouble. Fifth Amendment, right to privacy, Big Brother, etc. I personally hoped that the serial killer had had the foresight to set up his own *dead man's switch* with the data. Maybe public humiliation and disclosure in the national press could leapfrog fruit-of-the-poison-tree legal constraints. I kept these thoughts to myself, since I just might have to someday nudge Xavier's data into the public domain. Not to mention nudging Xavier onto death row.

As the evening drew to an end and the guests departed, the president and his wife again hugged Patrick and Sherry O'Shea.

"Daddy's little felons," said the president to Sherry. "I like that."

With her own leprechaun sparkle, she pointed to Benny and me. "Please take good care of them."

48
Six Months Later

he two Democrats who sat on both the Senate Judiciary and Intelligence committees both looked like the *before* pictures in a laxative ad. California Senator Denise Levin and Illinois Senator Richard Kyle likely even shared a common ancestor. A slightly bloated, red-faced ancestor with Marty Feldman eyes that seemed about to launch out of their sockets at any moment. This meeting of the Judiciary Committee had *not* gone according to their apparently well-laid plans.

Right up front, I'll admit the first words out of Senator Levin's mouth doomed our relationship, both in public and certainly in any private relationship I might stumble upon in the future. If politicians have a blind spot, it might be that of projecting their own view of the world that we're all running for some election—either for political office or just in the realm of public opinion. The idea that they'd encounter another human being who had nothing left to prove and nothing left to lose might seem a total impossibility. Thus my testimony almost instantly devolved into their worst nightmare.

"Morgan Rapier," she smoothly nodded, her smile more malevolent than welcoming. "I never thought I'd be taking testimony in this committee from a stone cold killer."

This opening line clearly caught her fellow Judiciary Committee members off guard and caused several heads to snap to attention. I reached out and caught my friend and sponsor, Attorney General Elliot Hammer sitting to my right, before he could jump to his feet in righteous indignation. I patted his arm a couple of times and turned to wink at him with my right eye, thereby obscuring the gesture to anyone on the committee.

"Senator, it's Commander Rapier to you," I said, my attention back now to the rictus expression frozen on her mouth. My virtually public field promotion by none other than the President of the United States deserved acknowledgement even from this vicious crone. "If you're referring to the Utah incident where I helped intercept fifteen jihadist assassins bent on killing my friend along with anybody else who got in their way, then I'll take your characterization as a compliment."

"No, *Commander* Rapier." She no doubt expected me to aggressively parry her first salvo, which had been nothing but her ruse to tee up a bit of classified information. "I am referring to your hunting down and killing over nine-hundred Iraqi soldiers who had the bad luck of being conscripted by Saddam Hussein."

She thought she had me, since I couldn't answer her reference to a classified operation without violating some fairly stringent security prohibitions. Bad move on her part.

"A battalion of Republican Guards gang raped and murdered a female United States supply officer," I said before the committee chair could gavel me down. And before the first sound of objection to my breaking security, I completed my thought. "Yes Senator, I tracked them down and killed every last one of them. Some of them twice."

Senator Kyle turned his gavel into a machine gun of sorts. As the din of gallery and committee expletives waned from a roar to a simmering growl, he said, "That is still a classified operation which you have violated law by divulging. Notwithstanding the senator's provocation, you have placed yourself in serious jeopardy."

He tried to glare at me, but he couldn't avoid the envelope that the attorney general had removed from his inside jacket pocket and waived toward the chairman.

"Mister Chairman," said the AG when he knew he had Senator Kyle's attention. "The president reluctantly declassifies Commander Rapier's Iraqi action, which I have here in writing. The only reason for the secret classification in the first place had to do with protecting the privacy and memory of that deceased Marine and her surviving family."

The chairman's aide quickly retrieved the document from the attorney general and handed it to his boss, who read it slowly and carefully. A *Colombo* episode would have had Peter Faulk fumbling to light his half-burned stogie as he tried to buy some time. I didn't let the chairman's attention to detail buy him *any* time at all.

"Senator Levin, I have a get-out-of-jail-free card from the President of the

United States," I said. "You are *way* out of line and owe one military family a sincere apology. You owe it to them here. And you owe it to them right *now!*"

"Commander Rapier!" snapped Senator Levin, her pointed lips doing a perfect imitation of a sea turtle I'd seen on the *Discovery Channel.* "Notwithstanding your celebrity status, I felt it important that everyone here understand the kind of man you are. *We* are the representatives who have been elected by the people and charged with overseeing the intelligence activities of this country."

"Madam Senator," I began. Heaven help me, now on a roll I couldn't resist. "You seem to have forgotten which committee we're in, today. This is not the intelligence committee, on which both you and Senator Kyle also sit, but the judiciary committee. So again, are you going to apologize to the family of the dead Marine whose memory you defiled, or am I going come up there and pull the hair right out of that wart on your chin?"

"Commander Rapier," roared Senator Kyle, jumping to save his compatriot's face in front of the television cameras and several million Americans, "You seem to have forgotten you're talking to a United States Senator, and we're desperately trying to get our brains around the legalities of this hacker-for-hire doctrine you've foisted on the world."

"I insist on Senator Levin's apology to that family this very moment!" As if to punctuate my resolve, I drew all six-foot-four-inches of myself ramrod erect. My bet is that everyone in the room did some quick arithmetic, and determined a damn sight fewer than nine hundred people packed this particular chamber, none of who stood much of a chance to even slow me down as I closed the gap between myself and the senator.

"If I might," said the junior senator from Massachusetts, a former Marine. "On behalf of the entire United States Senate, I know I cannot atone for her insensitivity to the family of that poor Marine, but I would like to publicly thank you for avenging a particularly heinous act. And if you insist on carrying out your novel threat on or about the area of Senator Levin's chin, I'll block the security folk who try to intervene from my side of the room. Semper fi, Commander!"

The laugh just started somewhere deep inside me. The sight of a former Marine ready to get himself thrown out of the Senate, along with Senator Levin unconsciously feeling for the nonexistent hair on her chin, just struck me as hilarious.

"The last time I checked, *Senator*," interrupted the junior Republican senator from Massachusetts, "The cyber security doctrine to which you refer came from the president, who is also the leader of your party."

In the midst of some back-pedaling/squabbling amongst various committee members trying to get C-SPAN face time, I placed my hand over the microphone in front of me, leaned to my right, and whispered to U. S. Attorney General Hammer, "Ernie, no matter what I say, could you just chuckle and shake your head?" He owed me, big time, since the newly created U. S. Cyber Marshall program fell under his jurisdiction and not only doubled the size of his department but—as I hoped to demonstrate to him momentarily—more than paid for itself. The U.S. government *cut* of the Cyber Marshall *confiscation* fees, for which I was awaiting a confirming vibration on my cell phone, might just pay the justice department's entire budget. Thus, I could have asked the attorney general to hop up and cluck like a chicken and he'd probably have considered it. Seriously considered it.

"Would the attorney general care to share Mr. Rapier's comment with the rest of us?" Senator Levin just couldn't resist throwing her considerable weight around.

"Senator, the comment was not relevant to our discussion today," he said. Had the attorney general been really smart, he'd have lied and said I told him he had a piece of lint on his tie. After all, he hadn't been sworn in.

Of course, I *had* been sworn in, so to avoid lying I held up my microphone so I could look at the attorney general and spoke as if I were repeating my comment to him: "Attorney General Hammer, if I ever decide to commit a felony, I want to be sure and do it in California. Because a jury of people who elected Senator Levin would have to be the single stupidest population sample in the country."

A lot of unintelligible yelling followed. I amused myself by looking at the hanging light fixtures behind the senators and wondering if I could drop them on top of my questioners with just once shot each from my nine millimeter. Of course, I didn't have my nine-millimeter, security being what it is on Capitol Hill. The sound of the again-pounding gavel demanded everyone's attention, turning the din into a hum. I felt a vibration in my pocket and withdrew my cell phone. Holding it below the table, I saw the text message for which I'd been waiting, and elbowed the attorney general so he could get a view of it just below table level. He had to raise his forehead from where it had been resting on the table in front of us. He didn't look well.

I couldn't really blame him, since *his* president and *his* party and *his* senators needed to get on the same playbook. My disregard for people who errantly *thought* they had authority over me seemed to be a continuing source of embarrassment to my friends and to those who really did have line authority. Not only did the enemy of my enemy not enjoy friendship status on my cosmic Facebook page, but the friend of my friend might think twice before presuming any strong bond, too.

"Why the sad face?" I asked in my best Heath Ledger/Joker persona. I nudged the attorney general again and nodded toward the text message in my hand. He finally focused, parsed the import of my revelation, and re-energized like a man who'd just been reprieved from the gallows.

Commodore Josiah Tattnall once said "Blood is thicker than water" to justify his intervention to save British survivors after their failed land attack in June 1859 on the Peiho forts during the Second Opium War. The newly invigorated attorney general demonstrated the twenty-first century corollary: Cash trumps party friendships in Washington, DC.

Attorney General Hammer couldn't help himself. He reread my text message and laughed out loud. The already disoriented Judiciary Committee members—people who justifiably felt he owed them some deference inasmuch as they'd confirmed his own nomination—simply stared at him, their mouths slightly open. The AG quickly moved to put them out of their collective misery.

"My apologies to the members of the committee," he began. He gently took my cell phone and held it above the table. "Commander Rapier just shared with me the first fruits of his cyber marshal recovery operation. Commander, could you do the honors?"

I retrieved my phone and silently marveled at AG Hammer's political astuteness. He'd be the beneficiary if my announcement came as good news. But if the senators or the rest of the country regarded it otherwise, then anyone who wanted to kill the messenger would have me as their target.

"I have just been notified that approximately thirty-one billion dollars has been wired into the Treasury Department account by one of the authorized cyber marshal organizations," I said. "I suspect the reason for Attorney General Hammer's elation of a few moments ago is that this amount exceeds the entire Justice Department budget."

More pandemonium. More gavel pounding. And one senator shouting to get in her follow-up question.

"You said an *authorized* cyber marshal organization," shouted Senator Levin. "Who actually *authorized* this, might I ask?"

"I did, Senator." Our eyes locked in a blinking contest she couldn't possibly win. The first person to talk loses, and I had answered her question unambiguously. But she didn't want to give up, thinking perhaps that she'd still prevail with her next question.

"And by what authority did *you* act, Commander Rapier?"

"Paragraph three-b of the presidential executive order establishing the United States Cyber Marshal Service under the auspices of the Justice Department."

I could see the wheels turning in her head as she dealt with the magnitude of the number. What possible organization could confiscate that much money so quickly? Better yet, why would they share any of it with the United States? By the way her eyes darted back and forth, her analytical left brain must have been having quite a ping-pong match with her emotional right brain, a right brain already in meltdown over having its owner publicly embarrassed. Finally, curiosity overcame prudence and she asked the Big Question.

"Commander, what organization achieved a confiscation of this magnitude?"

"Senator, I determined we needed substantial resources at the outset. We therefore subcontracted with the government of Israel to work with us. Specifically their Mossad."

"You unilaterally negotiated to split thirty-one billion dollars with a foreign government!" The senator couldn't contain herself. Now, she knew not only how one organization—the Mossad—could muster the critical mass to pull off such a big job, but she also knew why they would split their take with us: Israel needed *us* to legitimize *their* action.

"No, Madam," I quickly replied, about to really enjoy myself. "We are splitting sixty-two billion with the Israelis. Thirty-one billion is our share. And by the way, most of that money came from oil-producing countries that backed a massive jihadist attempt to hack the electronics of every computer-equipped car in America and cause a one-day massacre on September 11th. The President told me I was free to announce that piece of previously classified data during today's hearing, too."

Too bad the senator waited until she got to the hallway before vomiting. I wish America could have seen it on national television. And she never did apologize to the family of the soldier whose fate the president tried to keep secret.

While unknown to me at the time, in hindsight I also wish America could have seen on national television the enormous wreckage of the alien space ship that crashed in China. It would have saved me a lot of grief.

Principle #7 of The Perfect Virus —Black Box Portability—had struck again. With a vengeance. Stay tuned.

THE END

Note: All 22 principles of The Perfect Virus are at:
http://www.themorgandoctrine.com/2010/12/perfect-virus-all-22-principles.html

Thousands of readers regularly visit my cyber privateering blog:
www.TheMorganDoctrine.com

PIONEER CABIN

This is the oldest log cabin in Southern Utah. It was built in 1851 in Parowan by George Wood, one of the founders of Iron County, who later moved it to the Old Fort in Cedar City and then to his lot on North Main Street. Through the years it was the home of many pioneers and the birth-place of 24 children. It was presented to the Daughters of Utah Pioneers by the children of George and Mary Davies Wood, then moved to the Cedar City Park May 11, 1927, where the cabin was placed on a cement base and preserved by a canopy supported with four cobblestone pillars. April 29, 1983, it was moved to the Iron Mission State Park for protection and restoration.

Iron Mission Camp
Aunt Margaret Camp

My wife, Rita, is standing by George Wood's cabin at the Cedar City, UT pioneer museum. I'm standing by his tombstone. In September 1863, George Wood murdered Rita's great-great grandmother Olive Olivia Coombs. Some intrigue came into play that effected his pardon. He returned to Cedar City to rewrite history and become a "hero" and "founding luminary." His is the one of the biggest monuments in the cemetery, even today. I've fantasized about digging up the rancid corpse and using his skull as an inkwell, but… decided instead to write about it in *Daddy's Little Felons* rather than to become one. Rita's gentle ancestors suffered greatly at the hands of George Wood and his friends as they covered up the murder and conviction, probably to protect their own involvement in the *Mountain Meadows Massacre*. All descendants of George Wood depicted in my novel are a complete fabrication. But to George himself, I say, "How in Hell are you?"

The Cyber Privateer Code

1. Any unauthorized attempt to access your computer or phish your data access privileges constitutes a crime punishable by the looting of the attacker's assets by an authorized cyber privateer. All assets. Within 6 months of the attack.

2. If it is determined that the attacker is acting under explicit instructions from a larger organization or government, the assets of that organization or government are also forfeit to the extent that an authorized cyber privateer may confiscate them within a six month period of the original motivating attack. All assets.

3. The individual whose assets were seized by a cyber privateer—or the publicly and legally designated spokesperson for the organization or government whose assets were seized by the cyber privateer—has the "right of parley" with the head of the cyber privateering organization, such meeting to take place online in a two-way video conference, such conference to be publicly recorded by one or both parties and before the disposition of the booty but no later than 10 days from the confiscation.

4. Innocent victims whose assets are directly and mistakenly confiscated by cyber privateers (and whose funds are not returned within 10-days after the parley) shall be compensated in an amount equal to four times their loss, with interest accruing on the restitution amount at the rate of twelve percent per annum. This does not include victims of the cyber criminals, since they were already victimized.

5. Notifications and requests for parley must be unambiguously left by the cyber privateer so as to allow the right of parley to be exercised in a timely fashion.

Acknowledgements

The dead guys come first. At the top of the list is my wife's late uncle John Fretwell, who spent years researching the murder of his great grandmother Olive Olivia Combs at the hand of George Wood. John was a gentle, decent guy who politely but firmly knocked down one stone-walling bureaucrat after another until he could confirm the details of George Wood's conviction, sentencing and then pardon for the murder.

Then comes my friend, the late Frank Herbert (author of *Dune*), who talked me into running for congress. He said I reminded him of his character Jorj X. McKie in his short story *The Tactful Saboteur* (a paperback copy of *The Worlds of Frank Herbert* is worth a whopping $551.73, according to Amazon; mine is autographed with the note: "For Rick—food for thought"). Frank pretty accurately forecast our present day, when a lone individual with advanced technology could bring the planet to its knees. Luckily, I lost my race for the U.S. Congress and had to go get work. Data General hired me to head up advertising and public relations, and to get tax-limitation passed in Massachusetts.

In Massachusetts, I was on the four-man steering committee that hired the late Tony Schwartz, master at guerrilla warfare and the man whose single commercial that ran one time on only one network destroyed Barry Goldwater's presidential campaign. When I knocked on Tony's New York City brownstone, I fully expected Satan himself to answer the door and slice my head right off my shoulders. After all, Tony had represented every Democratic presidential candidate since Lyndon Johnson, and I had run for Congress as a conservative Republican. I asked him if he had a problem working on a conservative political issue, and he said, "You're going to pay me $25,000; I'll be what you want me to be." That began a multi-year friendship, where he and the still-living Dick Morris taught me Guerrilla Warfare.

Dick Morris also taught me the importance of honesty in politics, a frequent topic whenever I teach a Sunday school lesson to adults. He is the only person I know who made the cover of *Time Magazine* two consecutive weeks in a row. First for being the brains behind Clinton's reelection. The very next week, he made the cover because he resigned in disgrace. But he followed his own advice and didn't try to lie his way out of "getting caught" letting a prostitute listen in on his private conversation with the president. The "not trying to lie your way out of getting caught" is the subject of my Sunday school lesson.

No acknowledgement would be complete without expressing my appreciation to Oracle's Larry Ellison, for whom I spent a couple of afternoons a week for about six years as his one-man ad agency, creating ads that took Oracle from $15 million to over $1 billion in sales. I also made Larry the captain of my Cyber Privateer Fantasy League team. I've begged Larry for years to let me introduce him at his next speech, somewhere. Alas, he hasn't taken me up on the offer (the intro would be a real barn burner).

I also add my thanks to Marc Benioff, founder of Salesforce.com, who let me do his pre-IPO guerrilla warfare attacking Siebel. I also put Marc on my Cyber Privateer Fantasy League team.

My real education in the cyberwar currently taking place came from David Appelbaum and the BIGFIX management team, the endpoint security whiz kids for whom I created ads attacking Microsoft, Symantic, Altiris, and McAfee. Of course, I attacked myself right out of a job, since BIXFIX was acquired by IBM, who had no need whatsoever for a guerrilla warrior. My first ad for BIGFIX features my first cyber privateer alter ego.

I owe the insights used to create the 22 Principles for the Perfect Virus to ex-Oracle/ex-TenFold wizard Jeff Walker. I'd worked with Jeff during his time at Oracle, and again to serve on the board of directors for publicly traded TenFold. When Jeff and I re-engaged and he explained the applications technology at TenFold, he said, "Rick, you wouldn't know a good application if it bit you in the ass." Rather than get all huffy about it—after all, I was a mathematician who had actually written a real-time operating system in an earlier incarnation, not to mention inventing the Hagoth voice stress analyzer that had gotten me on every major television news broadcast as well as on the front page of the big national newspapers—I figured I'd better shut up and learn. It turns out, Jeff was right. He created 22 principles for the perfect application. I just modified them as they would apply to *The Perfect Virus*. Thanks, Jeff.

Thanks also to my friend Joseph "Yossi" Elad, a former Israeli naval commando who not only gave me a SEAL Team Six baseball cap, but whose Quantum Leap Innovations' technology has given me "situational awareness" of currently breaking trends that shows up in my cell phone alerts long before anyone in even the tech media picks up on them, let alone the mainstream media. Full disclosure: I sit on the Quantum Leap board of directors.

I'll leave solving real-world problems to politicians like President Obama's former Ambassador to China Jon Huntsman and Obama's first director of national intelligence Dennis Blair, who *The New York Times* reported on May 21st as urging 'Counterattacks on Hackers'. Thank you two for coming up with the right solution to, as the Tony Stark character said in *Iron Man II*, "… successfully privitazing world peace."

A special thanks to copy editor extraordinaire Alan Brown. For years, Alan edited my monthly neighborhood newsletter, and his unusual intellect allowed him to spot typos, spelling and complex usage mistakes instantly and unerringly. His is an unusual intellect, and I am humbled by his copy editing generosity with *Daddy's Little Felons* as well as with my first novel, *Destroying Angel*. Alan, you're amazing.

Thanks to my mother for the title of this novel. My ninety-year-old father is still a practicing criminal defense attorney. That's what mom calls his clients: Daddy's Little Felons.

And finally, thank you Rita. During the forty-eight years of our marriage, you've kept me grounded in what's truly important. And you let me hang the pirate skull in my den. Hopefully, my setting the record straight about George Wood, the man who murdered your great-great-grandmother, doesn't offend your sensibilities.

Rick Bennett
August 5, 2013

I'd love to hear from readers who can email rick@rickbennett.com. Or you can check out my various websites and social media connections:

www.rickbennett.com—My misspent career as a guerrilla warrior
www.daddyslittlefelons.com—The official *Daddy's Little Felons* site
www.themorgandoctrine.com—My Cyber Privateering project
www.cyberprivateer.com—My articulation of the Cyber Privateering Code
www.twitter.com @rickbennett
www.facebook.com Rick Bennett
www.youtube.com daddyslittlefelons

Let me know what you think of *Daddy's Little Felons*.

www.ingramcontent.com/pod-product-compliance
Lightning Source LLC
Chambersburg PA
CBHW071403050326
40689CB00010B/1735